Sherlock Bones 3

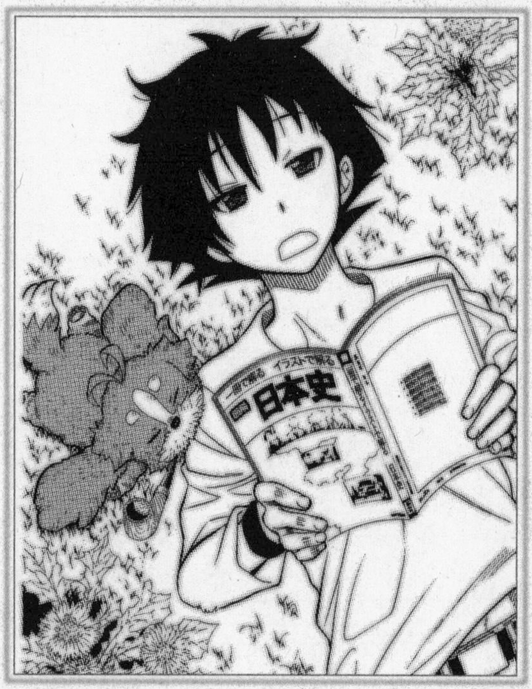
日本史

Sherdog & Takeru Wajima

Story: Yuma Ando   Art: Yuki Sato

CHARACTERS

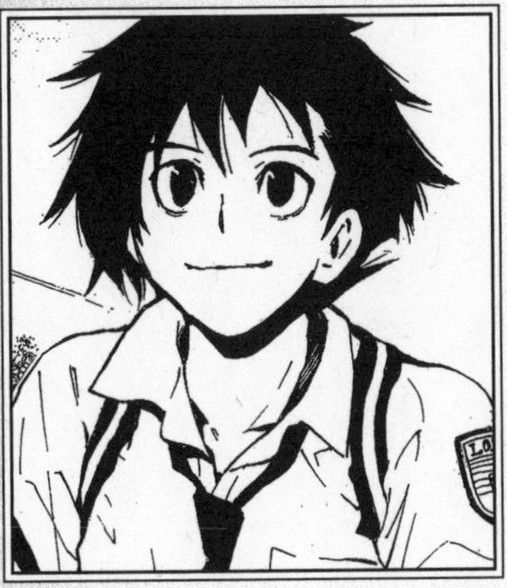

Takeru Wajima

A second-year at London Academy High School, he is an ordinary student who loves dogs. He is Sherdog's owner and the one person who can understand him. He and Sherdog must team up to solve all kinds of difficult cases. He has a crush on his childhood friend Miki.

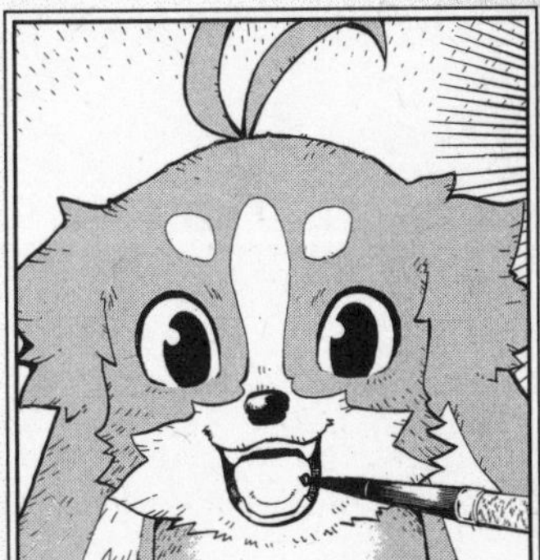

Sherdog (Sherlock Holmes)

The mixed-breed puppy that Takeru adopted. His true identity is that of the world-famous detective, Sherlock Holmes. When he has the Wajima family's heirloom pipe in his mouth, he can speak to Takeru. He solves crimes with Takeru, learning about the modern world in the process.

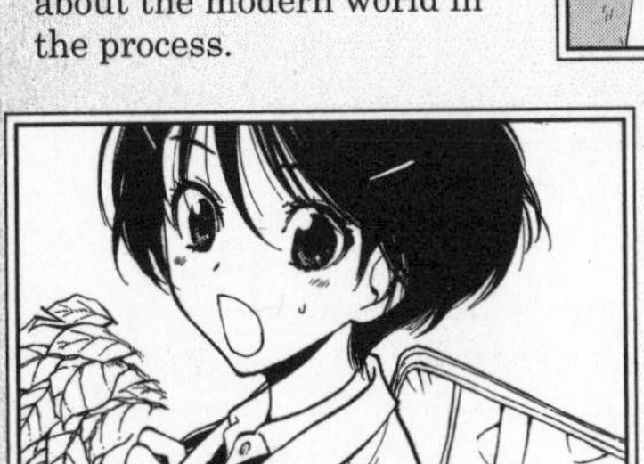

Miki Arisaka

A second-year at London Academy High School. Takeru's friend since childhood, and a member of the school newspaper staff.

Airin Wajima

Takeru's sister, an inspector in the Violent Crimes Division. She is quite an attractive woman. Sherdog calls her Irene.

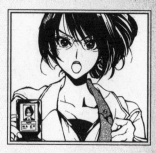

Kōsuke Wajima

Takeru's father. A sergeant in the police force.

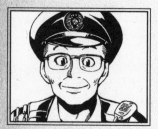

Satoko Wajima

Takeru's mother. She really hates it when Sherdog sits in her favorite rocking chair.

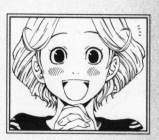

THE STORY SO FAR

"Hello, my dear Watson."
The dog spoke! Takeru took a dog home from the pound, and he turned out to be Sherlock Holmes! But apparently Takeru is the only one who can understand him speak. Named for Sherlock Holmes, but with a canine spin, Sherdog and his master Takeru find themselves surrounded by mysterious crimes in modern-day Japan!!

STORY

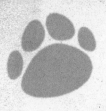

Volume.3
CONTENTS

SHERLOCK BONES

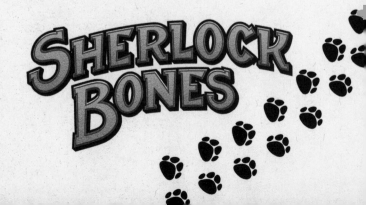

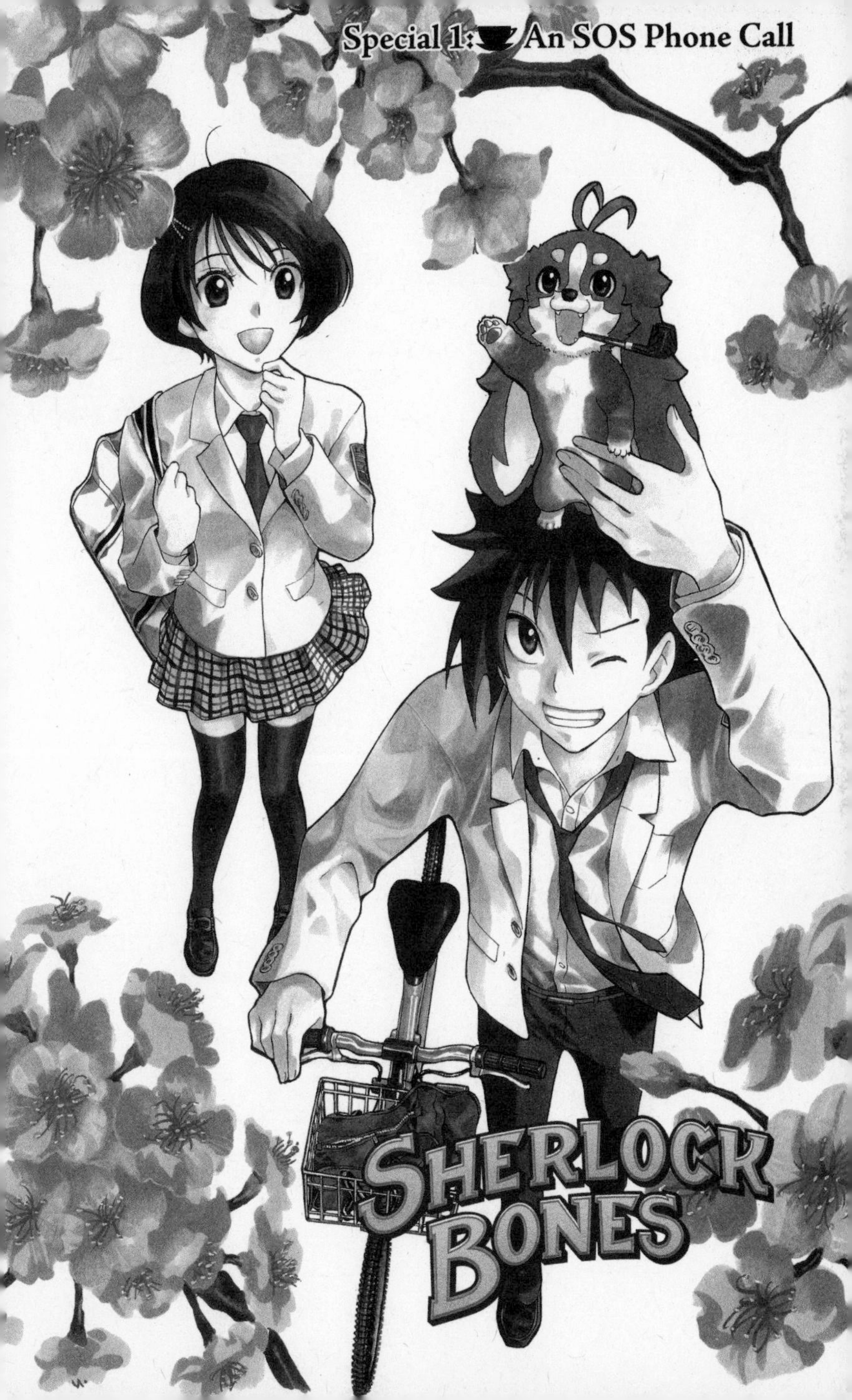
Special 1: An SOS Phone Call
SHERLOCK BONES

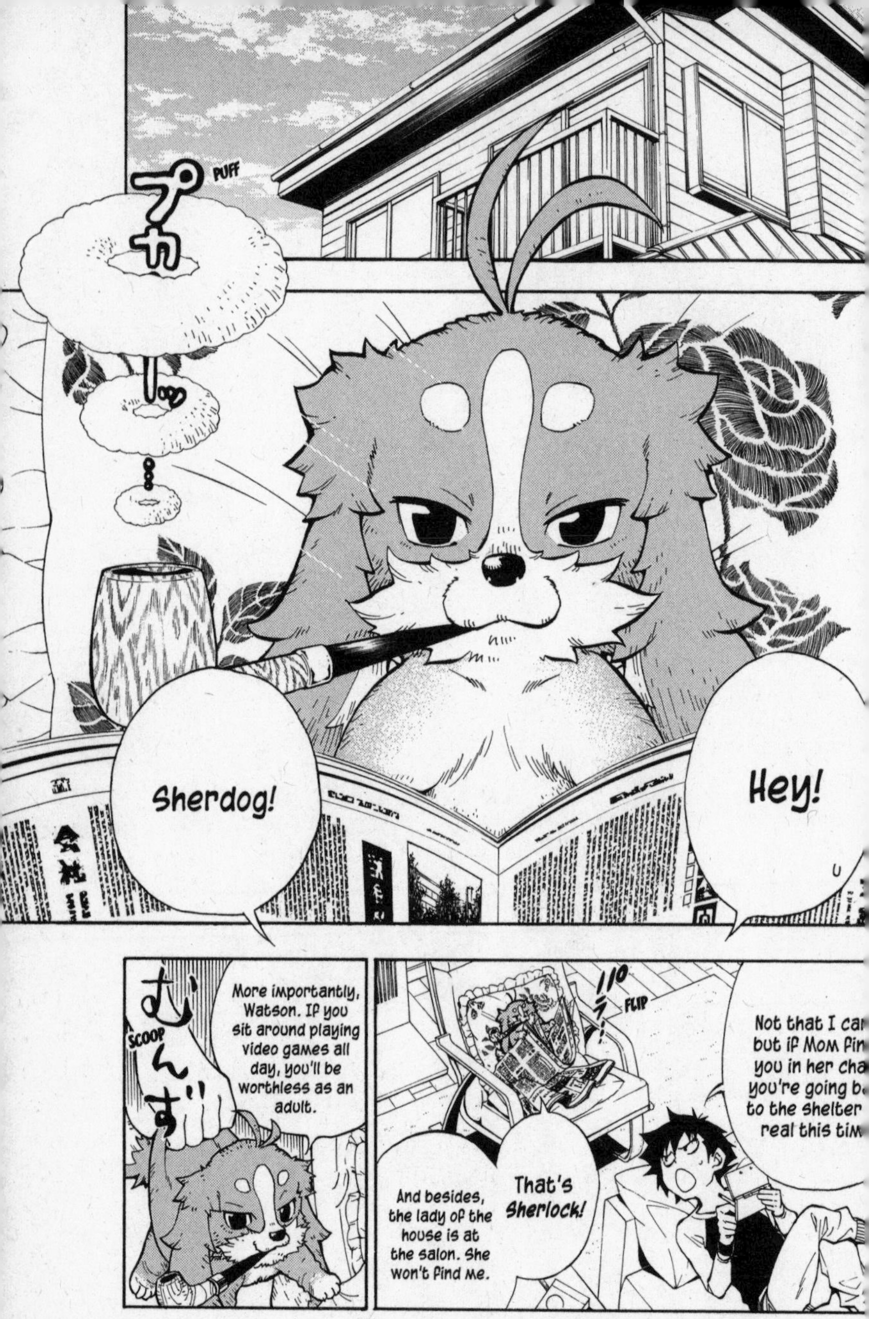
PUFF
Hey!
Sherdog!
FLIP
Not that I car but if Mom fin you in her cha you're going b to the shelter real this tim
That's Sherlock!
And besides, the lady of the house is at the salon. She won't find me.
SCOOP
More importantly, Watson. If you sit around playing video games all day, you'll be worthless as an adult.

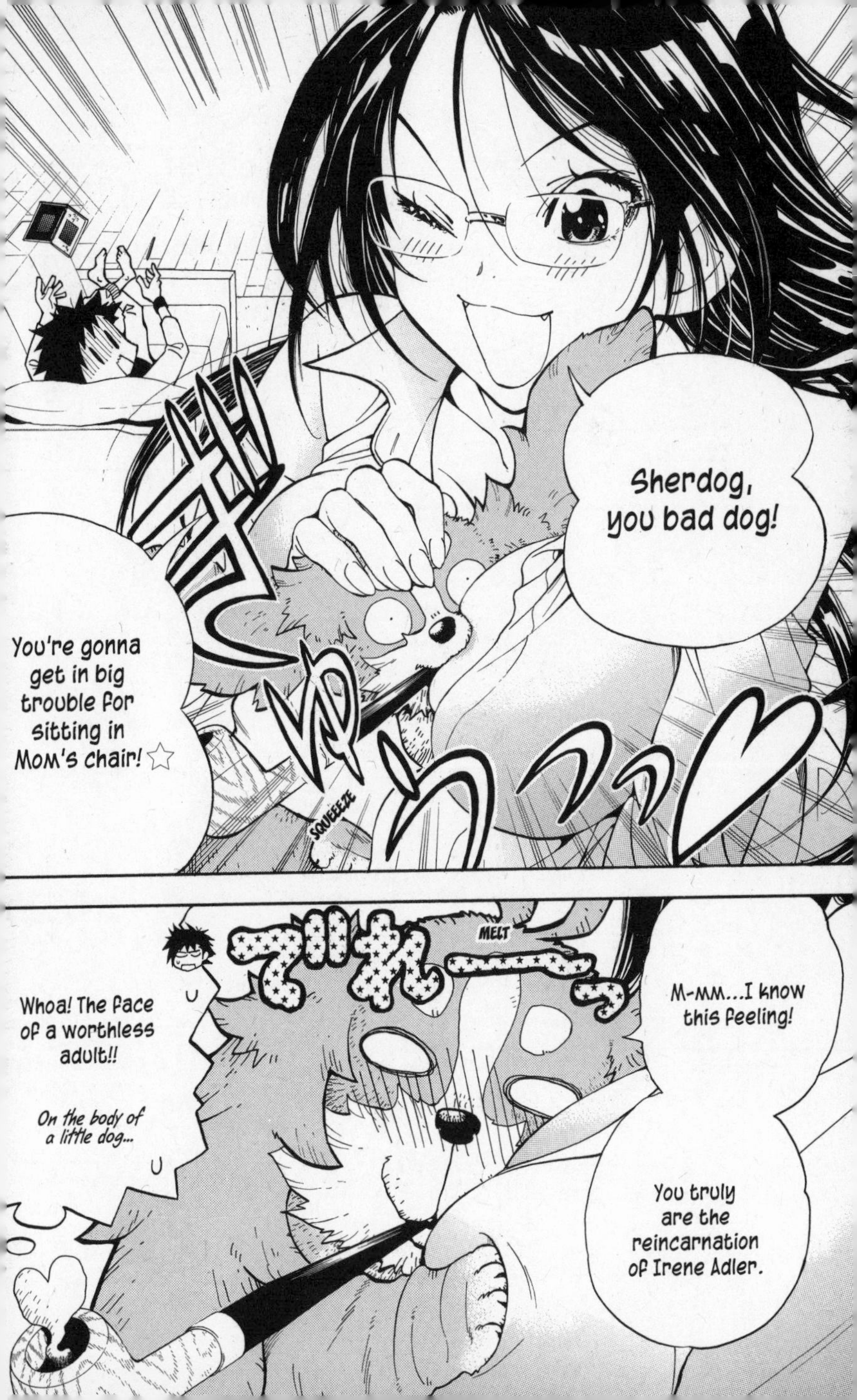
Sherdog, you bad dog!
You're gonna get in big trouble for sitting in Mom's chair! ☆
SQUEEEZE
M-mm...I know this feeling!
You truly are the reincarnation of Irene Adler.
MELT
Whoa! The face of a worthless adult!!
On the body of a little dog...

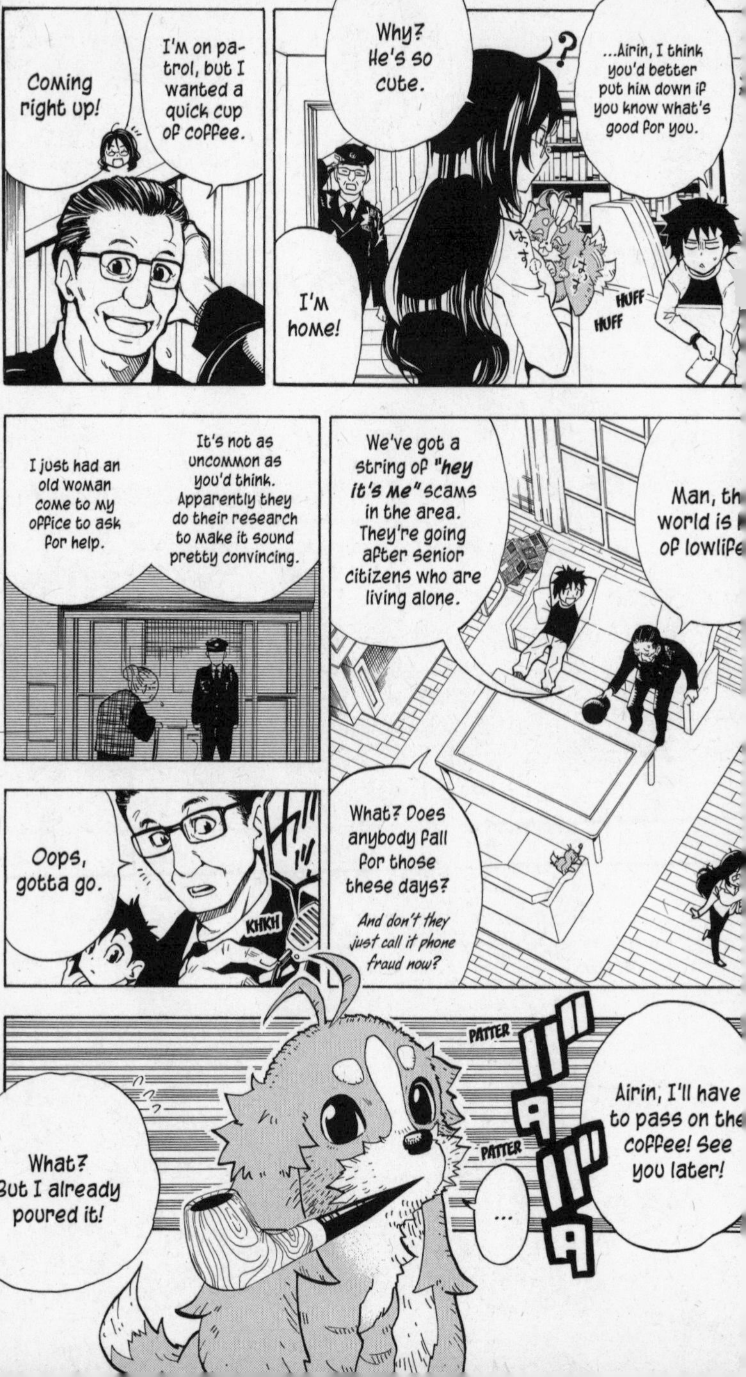
...Airin, I think you'd better put him down if you know what's good for you.
?
Why? He's so cute.
HUFF
HUFF
I'm home!
I'm on pa-trol, but I wanted a quick cup of coffee.
Coming right up!
Man, th world is of lowlife
We've got a string of ***"hey it's me"*** scams in the area. They're going after senior citizens who are living alone.
What? Does anybody fall for those these days?
And don't they just call it phone fraud now?
It's not as uncommon as you'd think. Apparently they do their research to make it sound pretty convincing.
I just had an old woman come to my office to ask for help.
Oops, gotta go.
KHKH
Airin, I'll have to pass on the coffee! See you later!
PATTER
PATTER
...
What? But I already poured it!

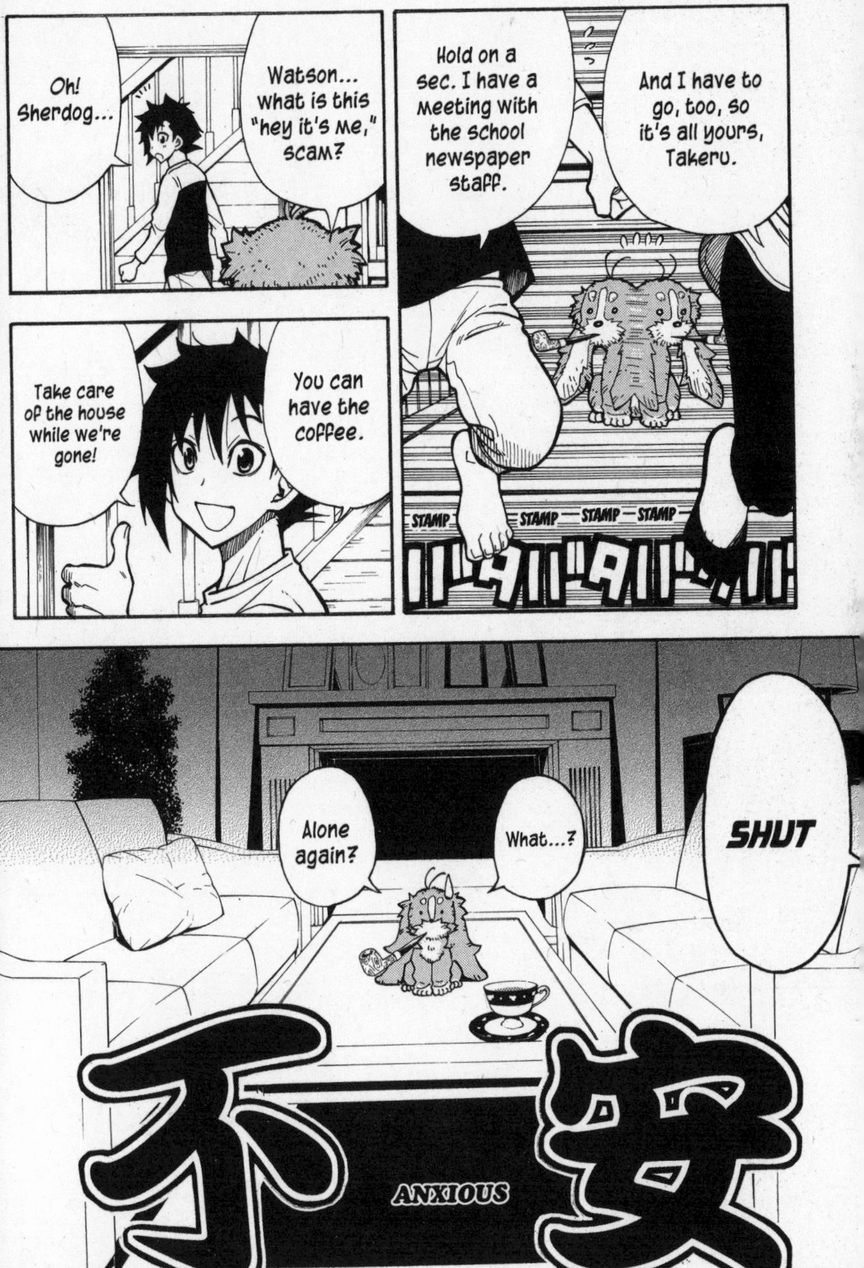
And I have to go, too, so it's all yours, Takeru.
Hold on a sec. I have a meeting with the school newspaper staff.
STAMP STAMP STAMP STAMP
Watson... what is this "hey it's me," scam?
Oh! Sherdog...
You can have the coffee.
Take care of the house while we're gone!
SHUT
What...?
Alone again?
不安
ANXIOUS

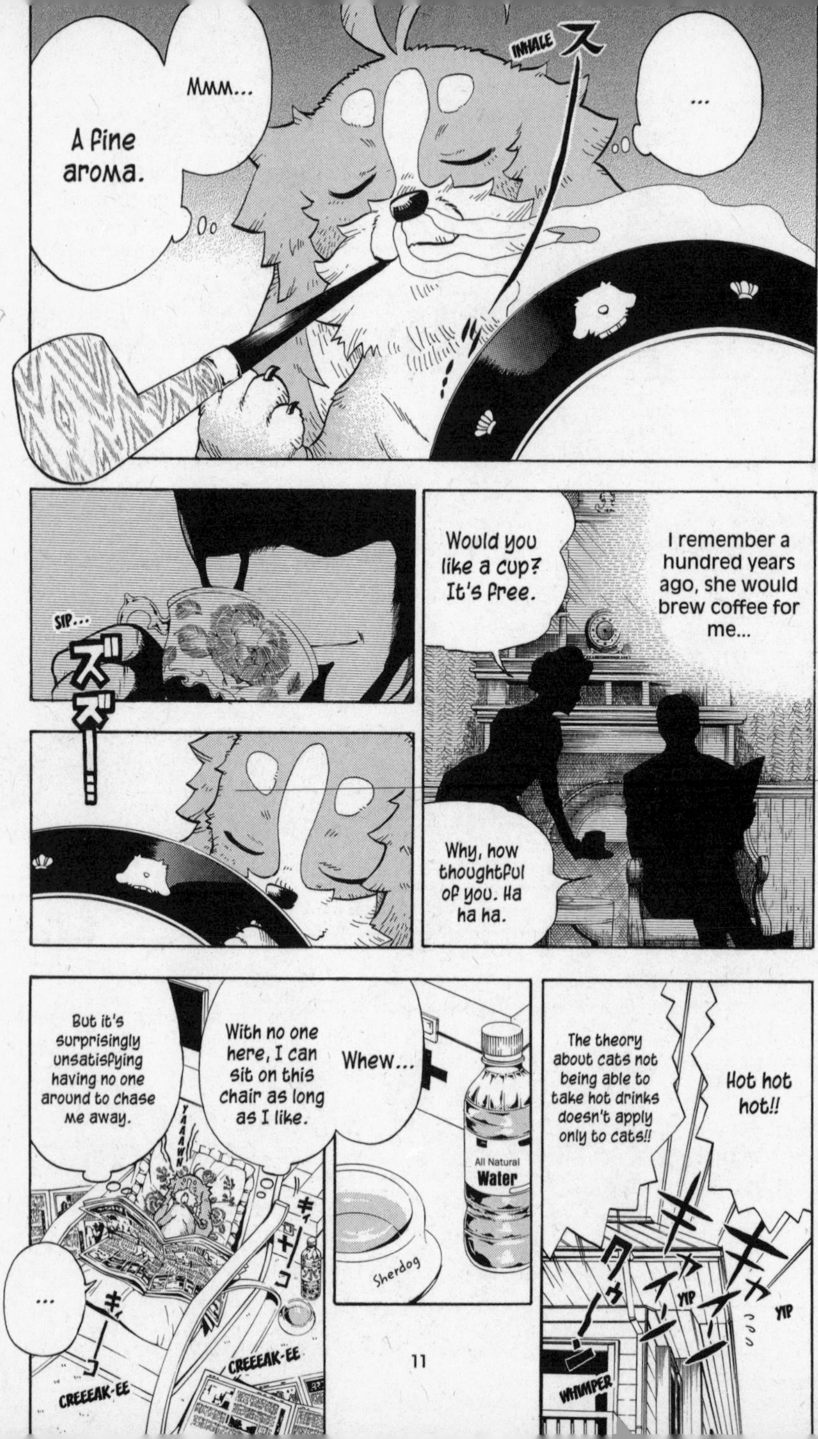
INHALE
...
Mmm...
A fine aroma.
I remember a hundred years ago, she would brew coffee for me...
Would you like a cup? It's free.
Why, how thoughtful of you. Ha ha ha.
SIP...
Hot hot hot!!
The theory about cats not being able to take hot drinks doesn't apply only to cats!!
YIP
YIP
WHIMPER
Whew...
All Natural
Water
Sherdog
With no one here, I can sit on this chair as long as I like.
But it's surprisingly unsatisfying having no one around to chase me away.
YAAAWN
...
CREEEAK-EE
CREEEAK-EE

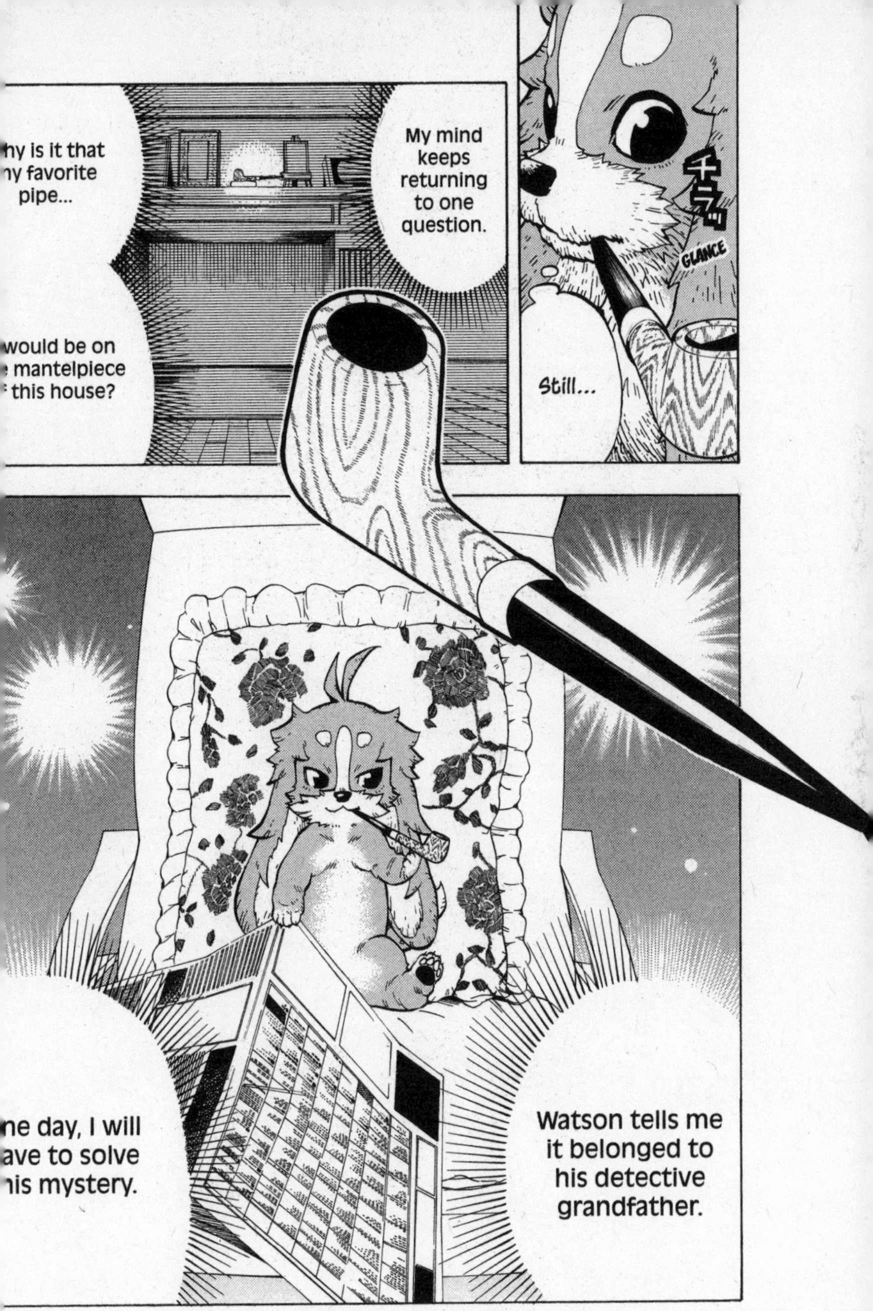
チラッ
GLANCE
Still...
My mind keeps returning to one question.
hy is it that ny favorite pipe...
would be on e mantelpiece this house?
Watson tells me it belonged to his detective grandfather.
ne day, I will ave to solve his mystery.

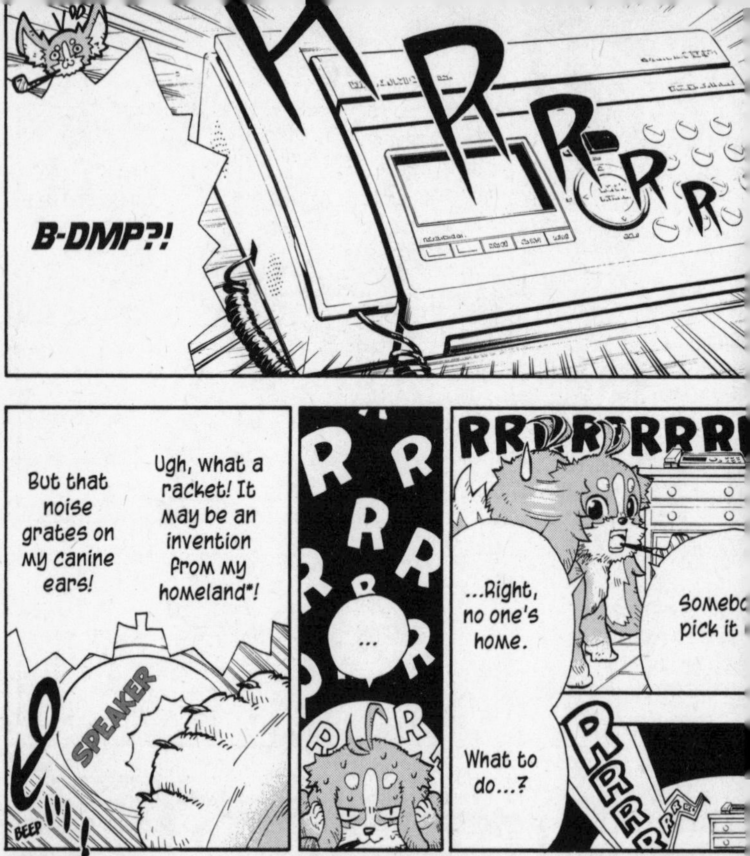
HRRRRRR
B-DMP?!
RRRRRRRR
Somebo
pick it
...Right, no one's home.
What to do...?
RRRRR
R R R R R R
...
Ugh, what a racket! It may be an invention from my homeland*!
But that noise grates on my canine ears!
SPEAKER
BEEP

*The telephone was actually invented in America by the British Alexander Graha

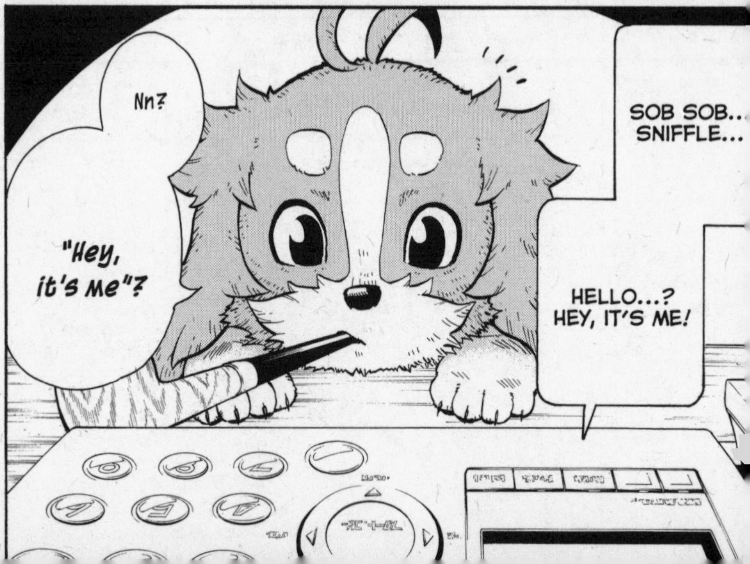
SOB SOB...
SNIFFLE...
HELLO...? HEY, IT'S ME!
Nn?
"Hey, it's me"?

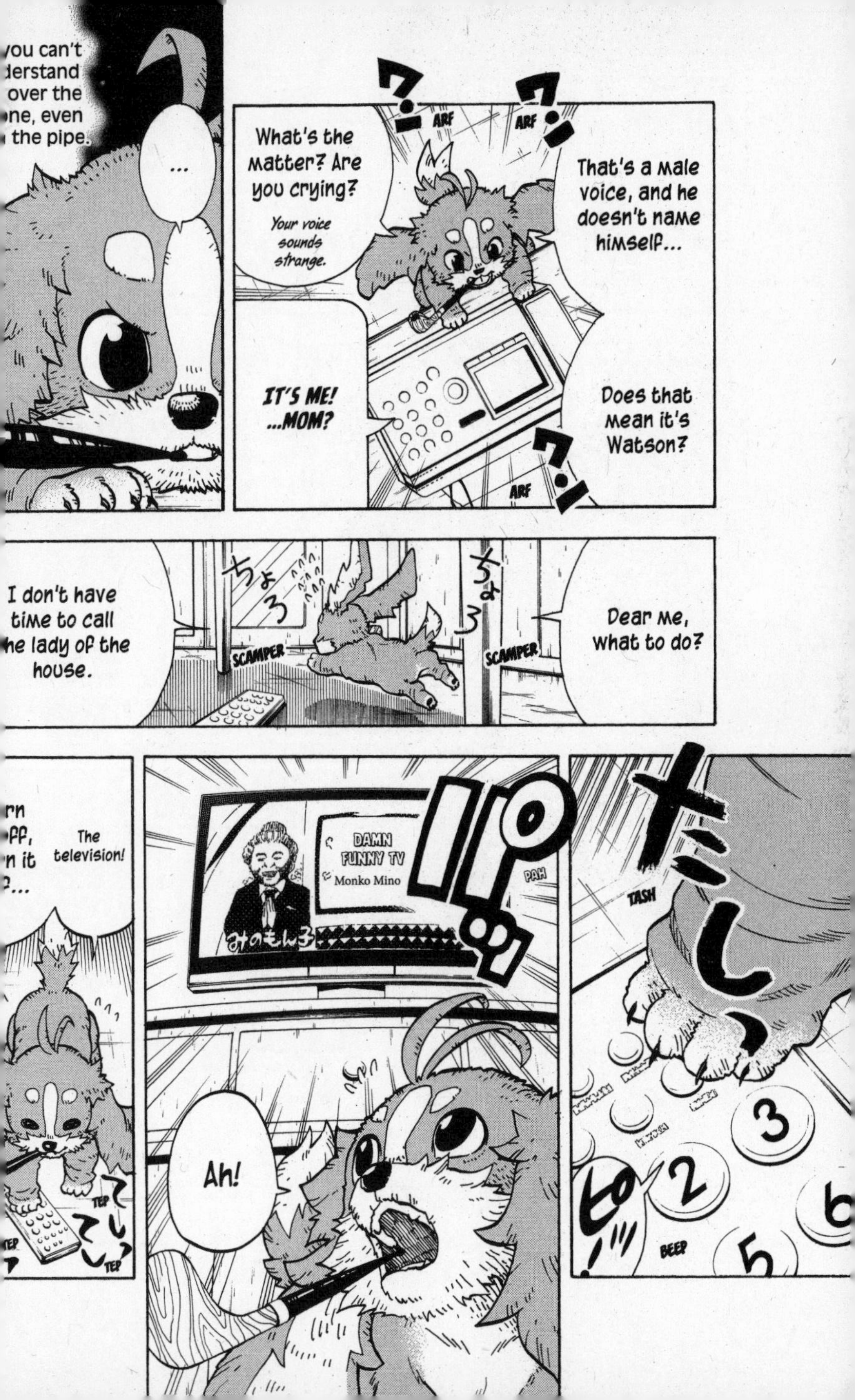
That's a male voice, and he doesn't name himself...
ARF
ARF
What's the matter? Are you crying?
Your voice sounds strange.
Does that mean it's Watson?
IT'S ME! ...MOM?
ARF
you can't
derstand
over the
ne, even
the pipe.
...
Dear me, what to do?
SCAMPER
I don't have time to call the lady of the house.
SCAMPER
TASH
BEEP
PAH
DAMN FUNNY TV
Monko Mino
みのもん子
Ah!
The television!
TEP
TEP
TEP

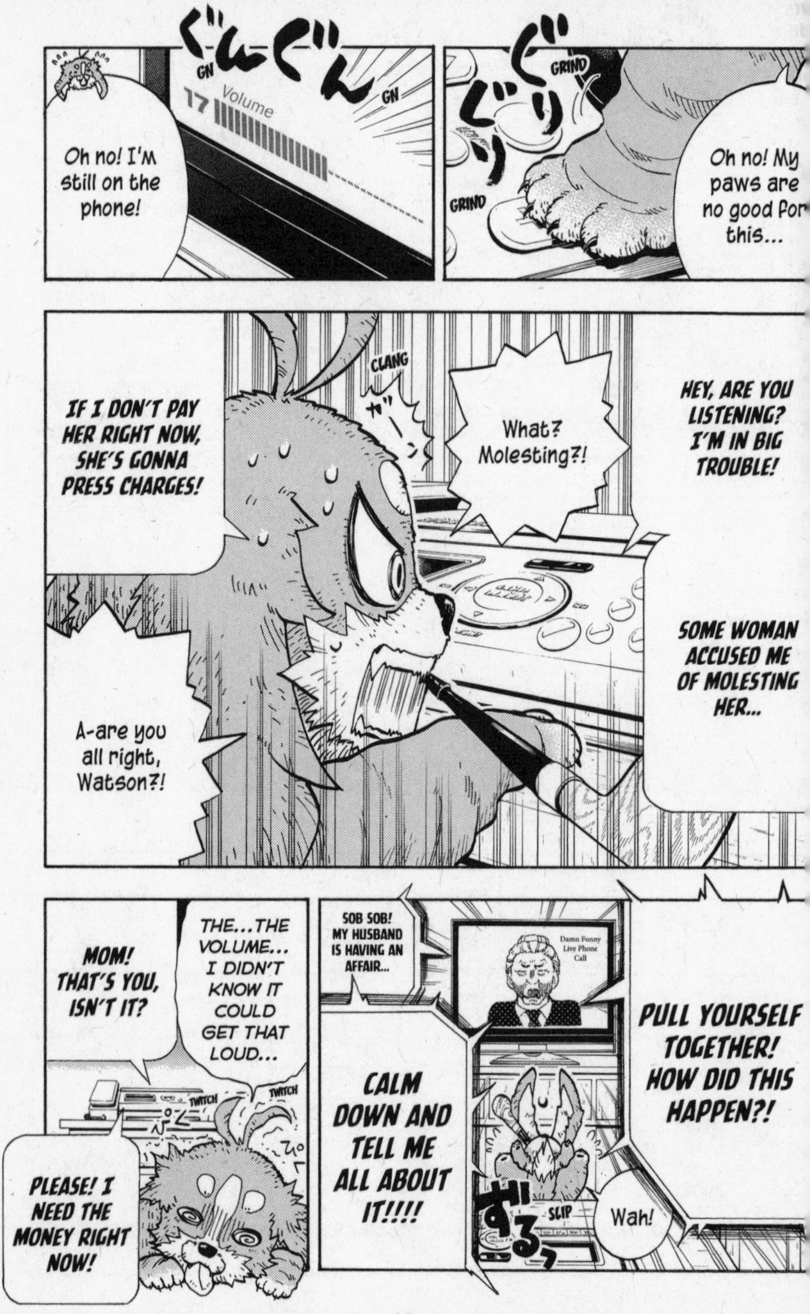
ぐりぐり
GRIND
GRIND
Oh no! My paws are no good for this...
ぐんぐん
GN
GN
17 Volume
Oh no! I'm still on the phone!
HEY, ARE YOU LISTENING? I'M IN BIG TROUBLE!
What? Molesting?!
CLANG
IF I DON'T PAY HER RIGHT NOW, SHE'S GONNA PRESS CHARGES!
SOME WOMAN ACCUSED ME OF MOLESTING HER...
A-are you all right, Watson?!
PULL YOURSELF TOGETHER! HOW DID THIS HAPPEN?!
Damn Funny Live Phone Call
SOB SOB! MY HUSBAND IS HAVING AN AFFAIR...
CALM DOWN AND TELL ME ALL ABOUT IT!!!!
ずるっ
SLIP
Wah!
THE...THE VOLUME... I DIDN'T KNOW IT COULD GET THAT LOUD...
MOM! THAT'S YOU, ISN'T IT?
TWITCH
TWITCH
PLEASE! I NEED THE MONEY RIGHT NOW!

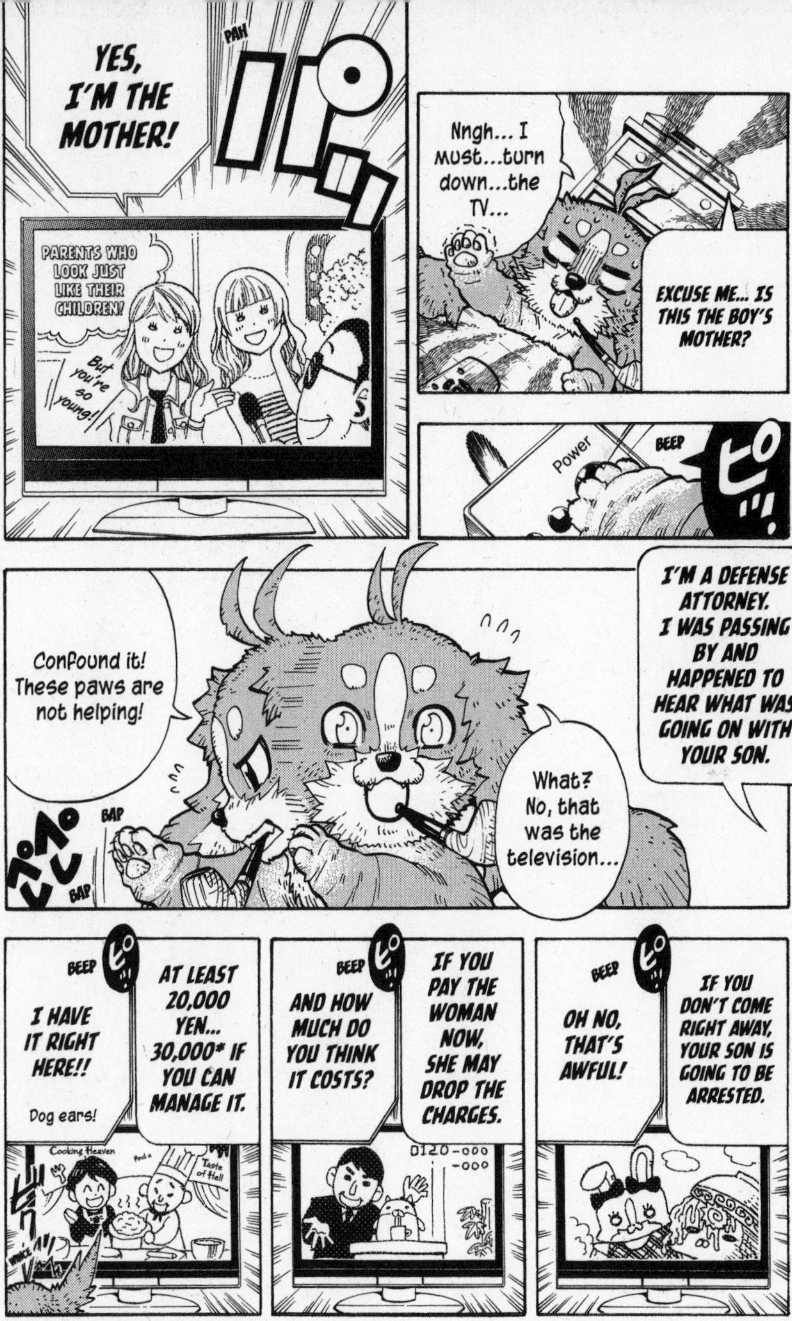
EXCUSE ME... IS THIS THE BOY'S MOTHER?
Nngh... I must...turn down...the TV...
Power
BEEP
PAH
YES, I'M THE MOTHER!
PARENTS WHO LOOK JUST LIKE THEIR CHILDREN!
But you're so young!
I'M A DEFENSE ATTORNEY. I WAS PASSING BY AND HAPPENED TO HEAR WHAT WAS GOING ON WITH YOUR SON.
What? No, that was the television...
Confound it! These paws are not helping!
BAP
BAP
IF YOU DON'T COME RIGHT AWAY, YOUR SON IS GOING TO BE ARRESTED.
BEEP
OH NO, THAT'S AWFUL!
IF YOU PAY THE WOMAN NOW, SHE MAY DROP THE CHARGES.
BEEP
AND HOW MUCH DO YOU THINK IT COSTS?
0120-000
-000
AT LEAST 20,000 YEN... 30,000* IF YOU CAN MANAGE IT.
BEEP
I HAVE IT RIGHT HERE!!
Dog ears!
Cooking Heaven
And a Taste of Hell
WHACK

*About $200 and $300, respectively.

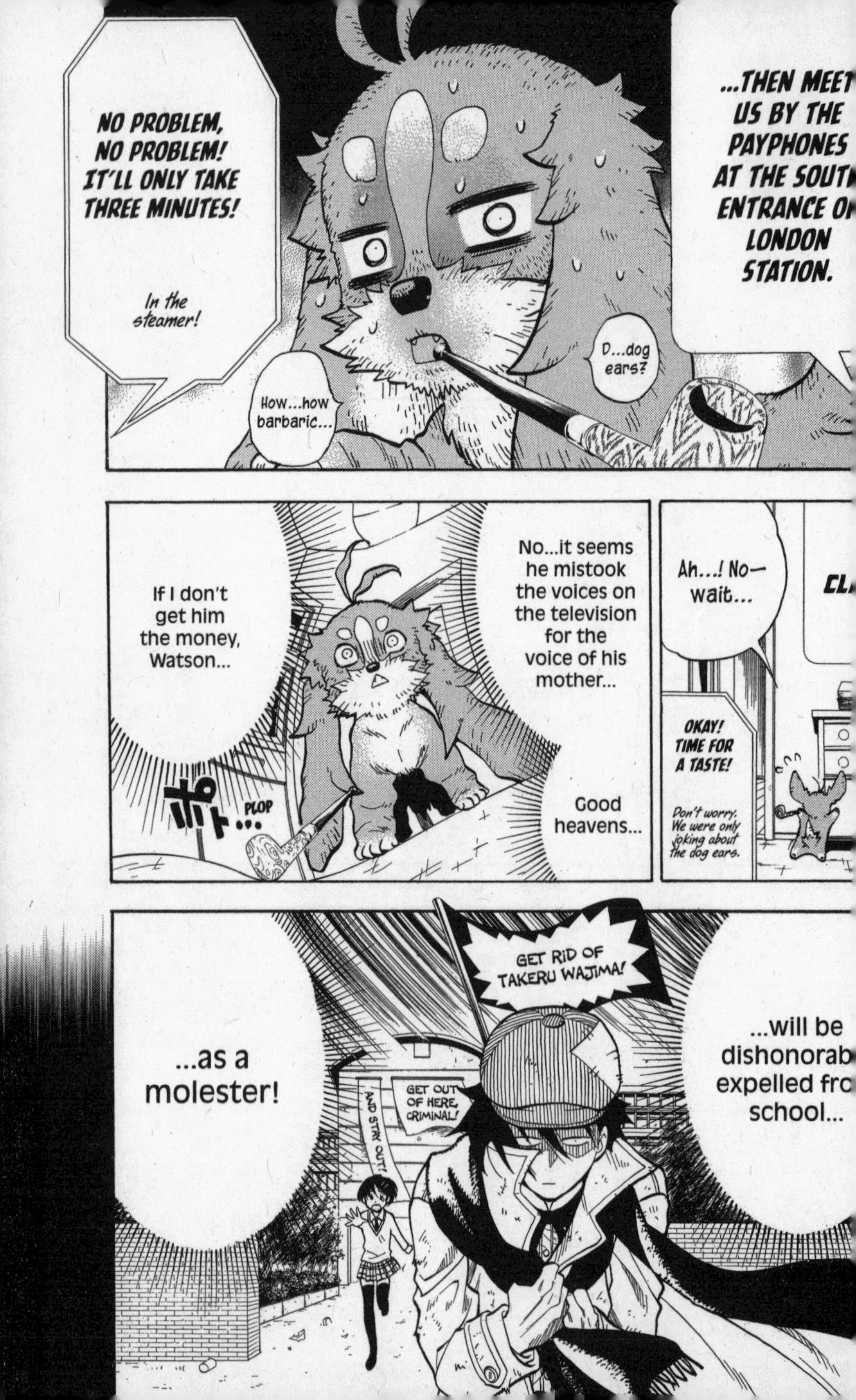
...THEN MEET US BY THE PAYPHONES AT THE SOUT ENTRANCE O LONDON STATION.
D...dog ears?
NO PROBLEM, NO PROBLEM! IT'LL ONLY TAKE THREE MINUTES!
In the steamer!
How...how barbaric...
CL
Ah...! No— wait...
OKAY! TIME FOR A TASTE!
Don't worry. We were only joking about the dog ears.
No...it seems he mistook the voices on the television for the voice of his mother...
If I don't get him the money, Watson...
Good heavens...
PLOP
...will be dishonorab expelled fr school...
GET RID OF TAKERU WAJIMA!
GET OUT OF HERE, CRIMINAL!
AND STAY OUT!
...as a molester!

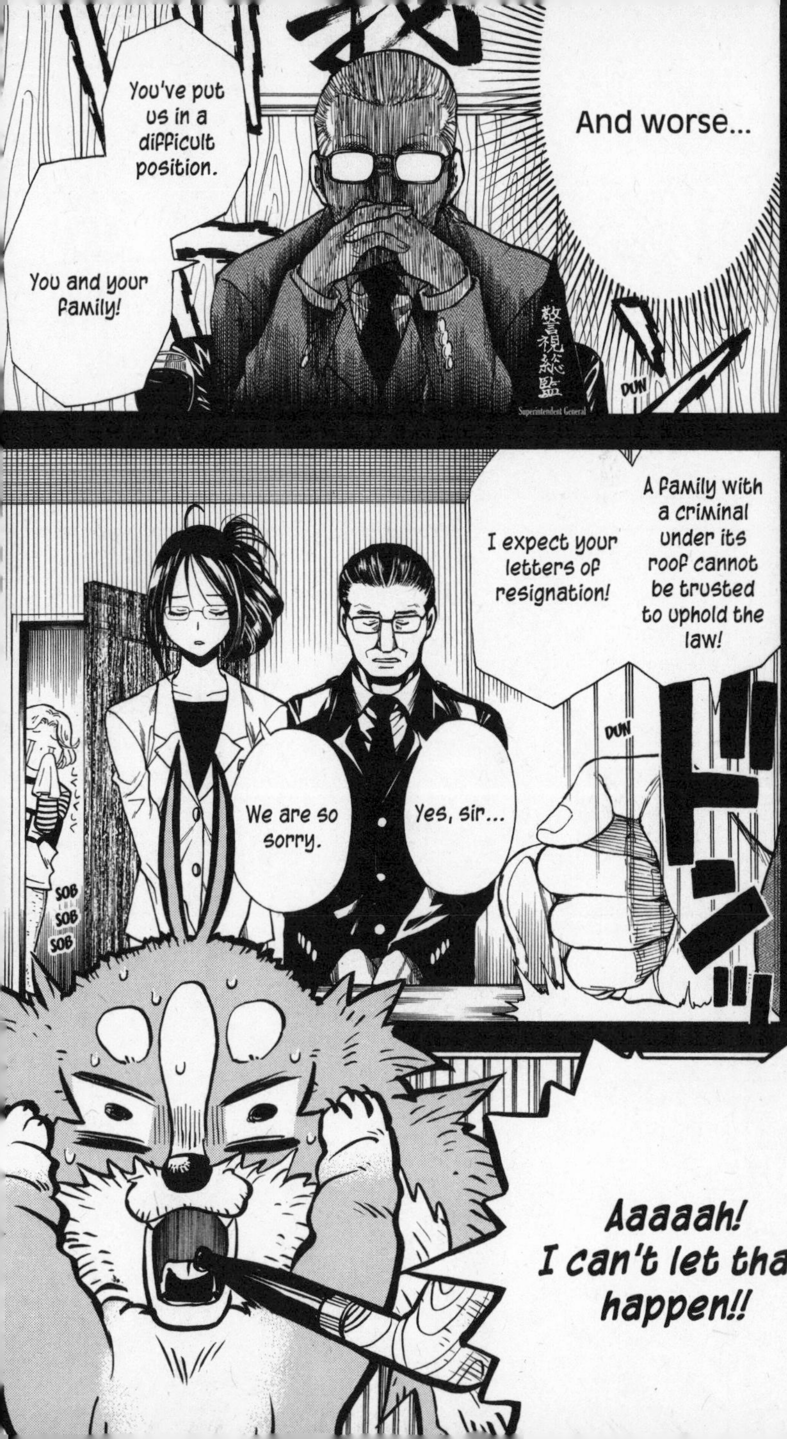
And worse...
You've put us in a difficult position.
You and your family!
警視総監
Superintendent General
DUN
A family with a criminal under its roof cannot be trusted to uphold the law!
I expect your letters of resignation!
DUN
Yes, sir...
We are so sorry.
SOB
SOB
SOB
Aaaaah!
I can't let tha
happen!!

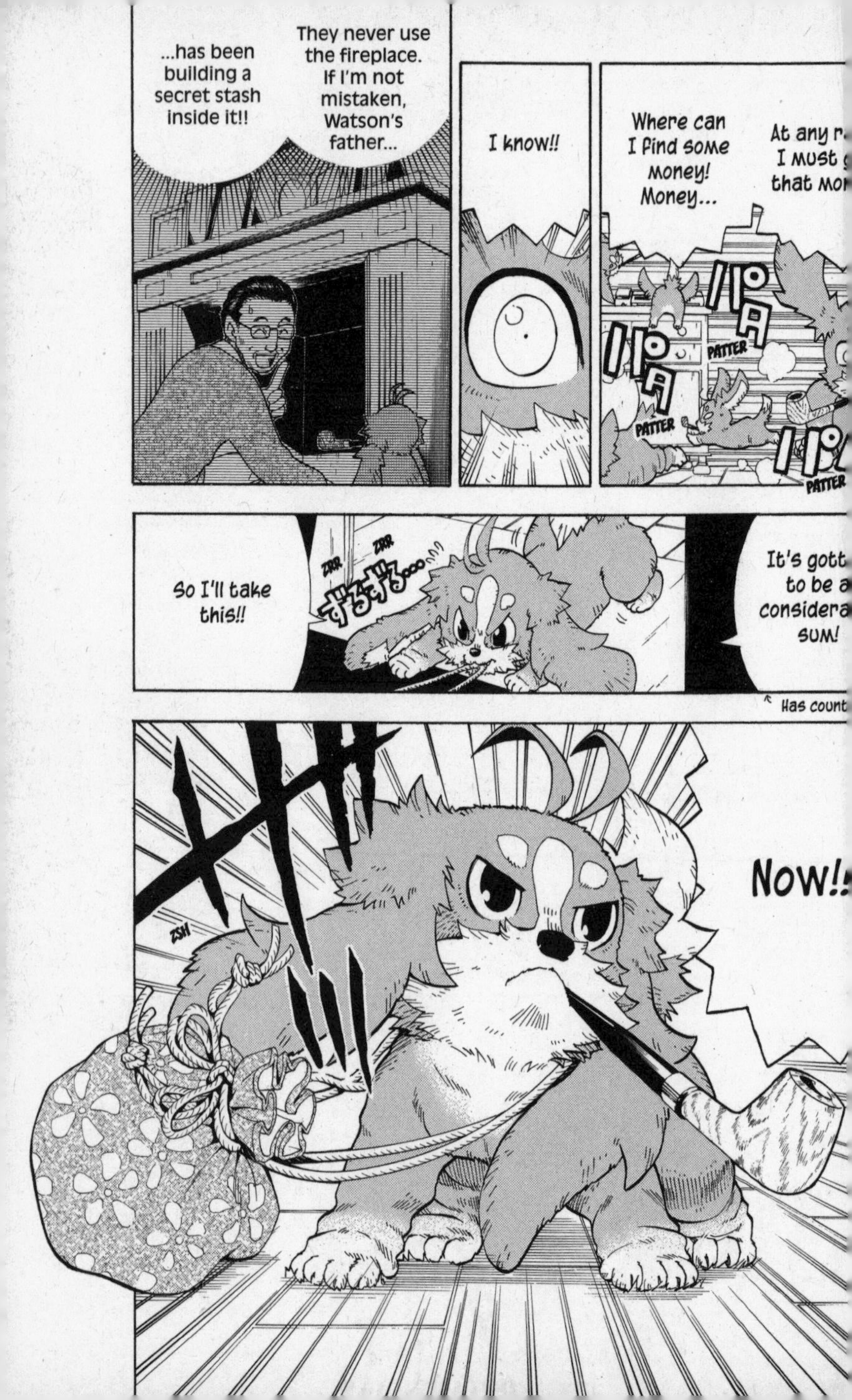

At any r
I must
that mo
Where can I find some money! Money...
パ
PATTER
パ
PATTER
パ
PATTER
I know!!
They never use the fireplace. If I'm not mistaken, Watson's father...
...has been building a secret stash inside it!!
It's gott
to be a
considera
sum!
Has count
ZRRR ZRRR
ずるずる
So I'll take this!!
NOW!!
ZSH

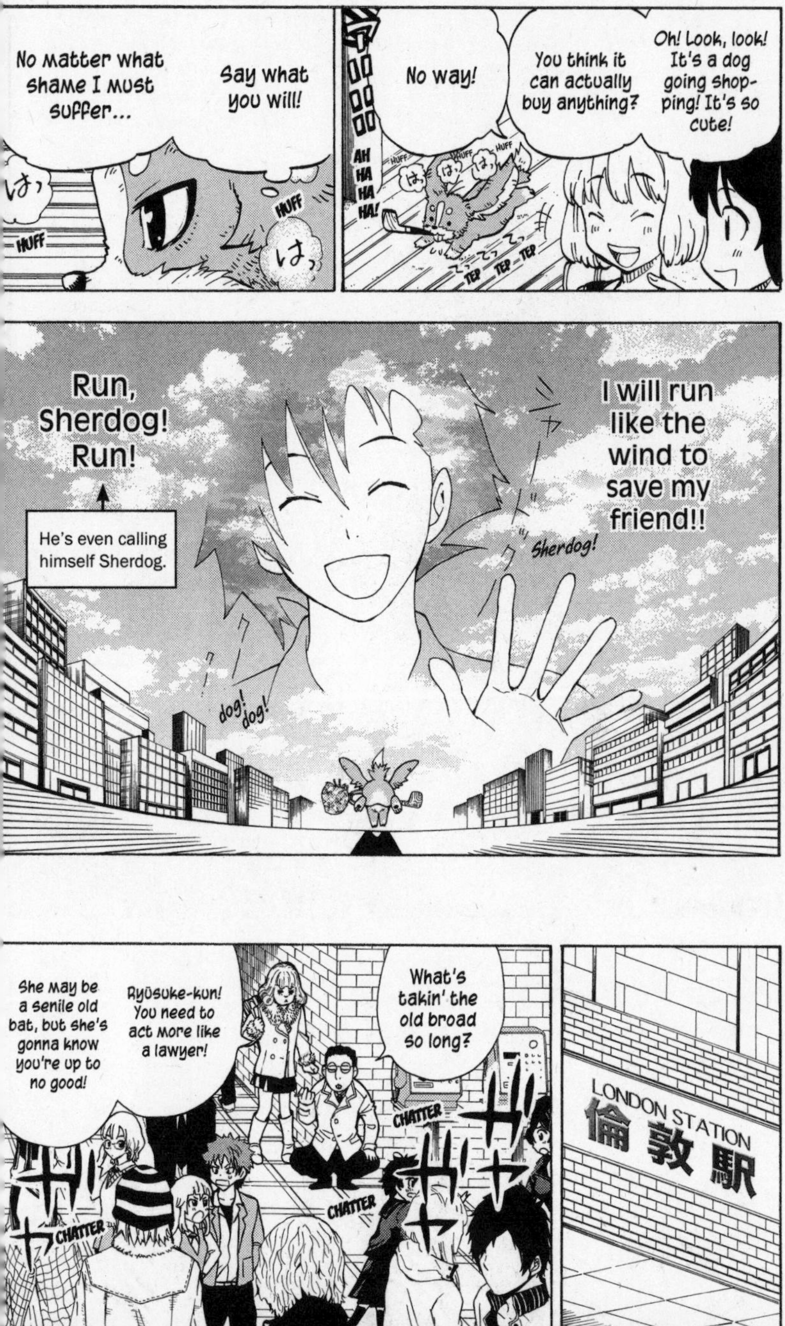
Oh! Look, look! It's a dog going shop-ping! It's so cute!
You think it can actually buy anything?
No way!
AH HA HA HA!
HUFF HUFF HUFF
TEP TEP TEP
Say what you will!
No matter what shame I must suffer...
HUFF
HUFF
I will run like the wind to save my friend!!
Sherdog!
Run, Sherdog! Run!
He's even calling himself Sherdog.
dog! dog!
LONDON STATION
倫敦駅
What's takin' the old broad so long?
CHATTER
Ryūsuke-kun! You need to act more like a lawyer!
She may be a senile old bat, but she's gonna know you're up to no good!
CHATTER
CHATTER

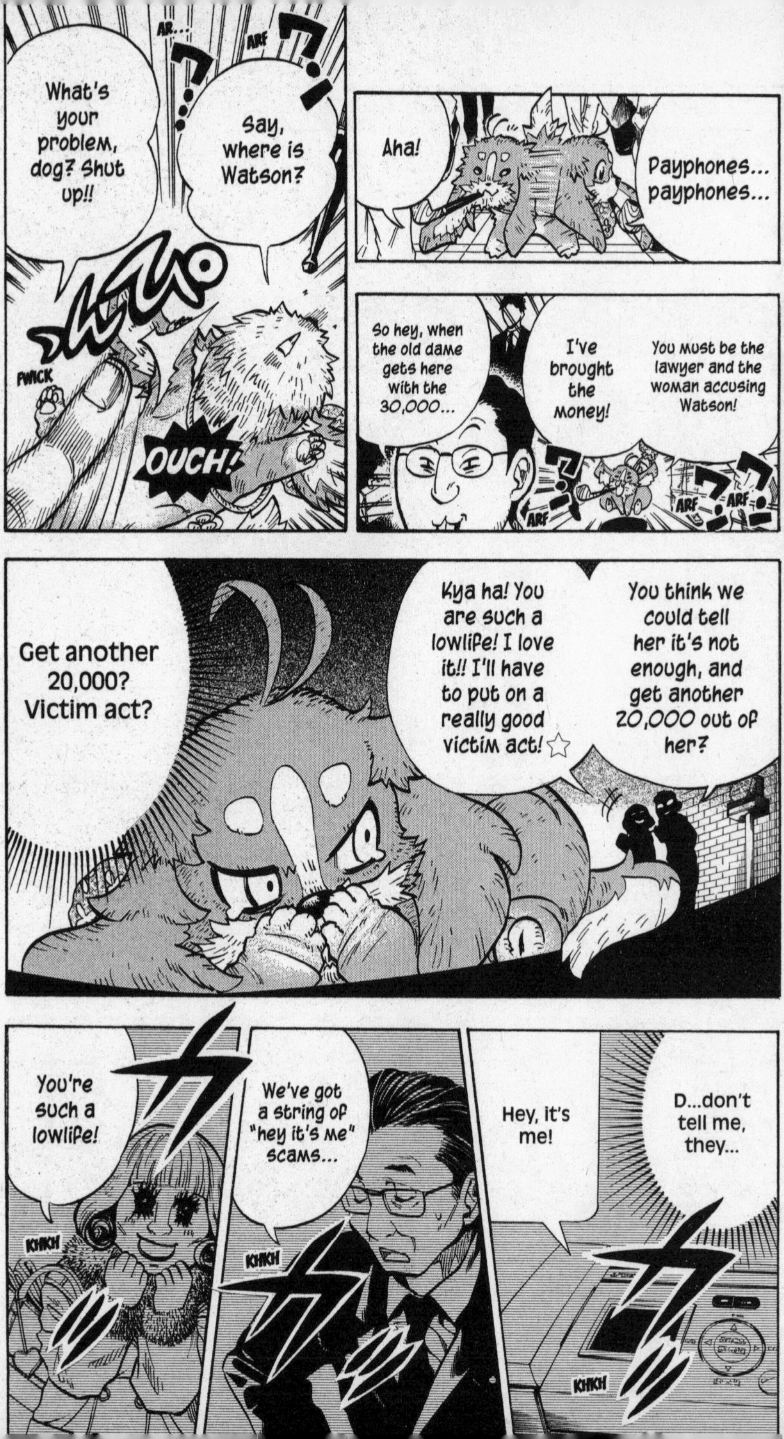
Payphones... payphones...
Aha!
You must be the lawyer and the woman accusing Watson!
I've brought the money!
So hey, when the old dame gets here with the 30,000...
ARF
ARF
ARF
ARF
Say, where is Watson?
AR...
What's your problem, dog? Shut up!!
OUCH!
PWICK
You think we could tell her it's not enough, and get another 20,000 out of her?
Kya ha! You are such a lowlife! I love it!! I'll have to put on a really good victim act! ☆
Get another 20,000? Victim act?
D...don't tell me, they...
KHKH
Hey, it's me!
We've got a string of "hey it's me" scams...
KHKH
You're such a lowlife!
KHKH

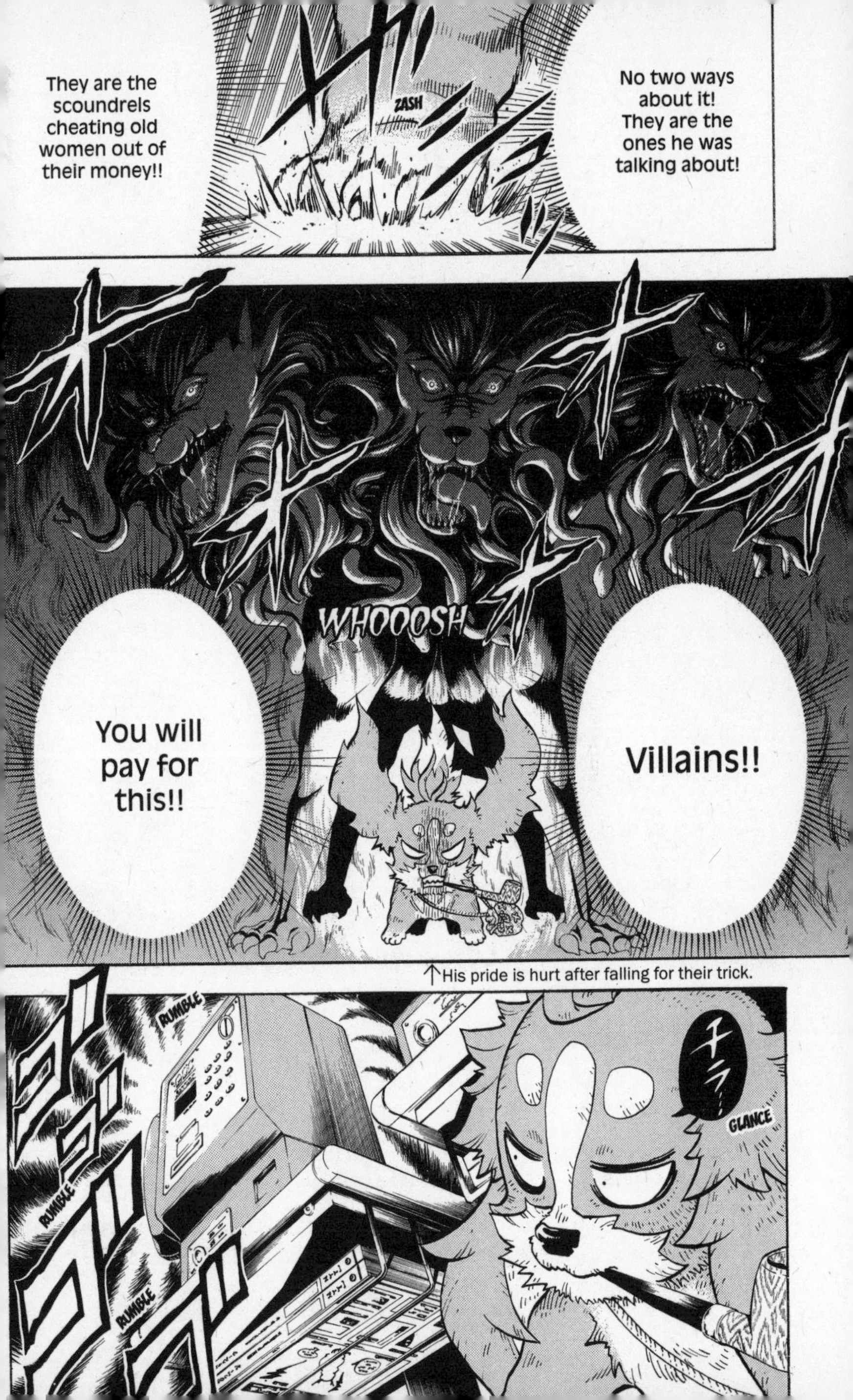
No two ways about it! They are the ones he was talking about!
They are the scoundrels cheating old women out of their money!!
ZASH
Villains!!
You will pay for this!!
WHOOOSH
↑His pride is hurt after falling for their trick.
GLANCE
RUMBLE
RUMBLE
RUMBLE

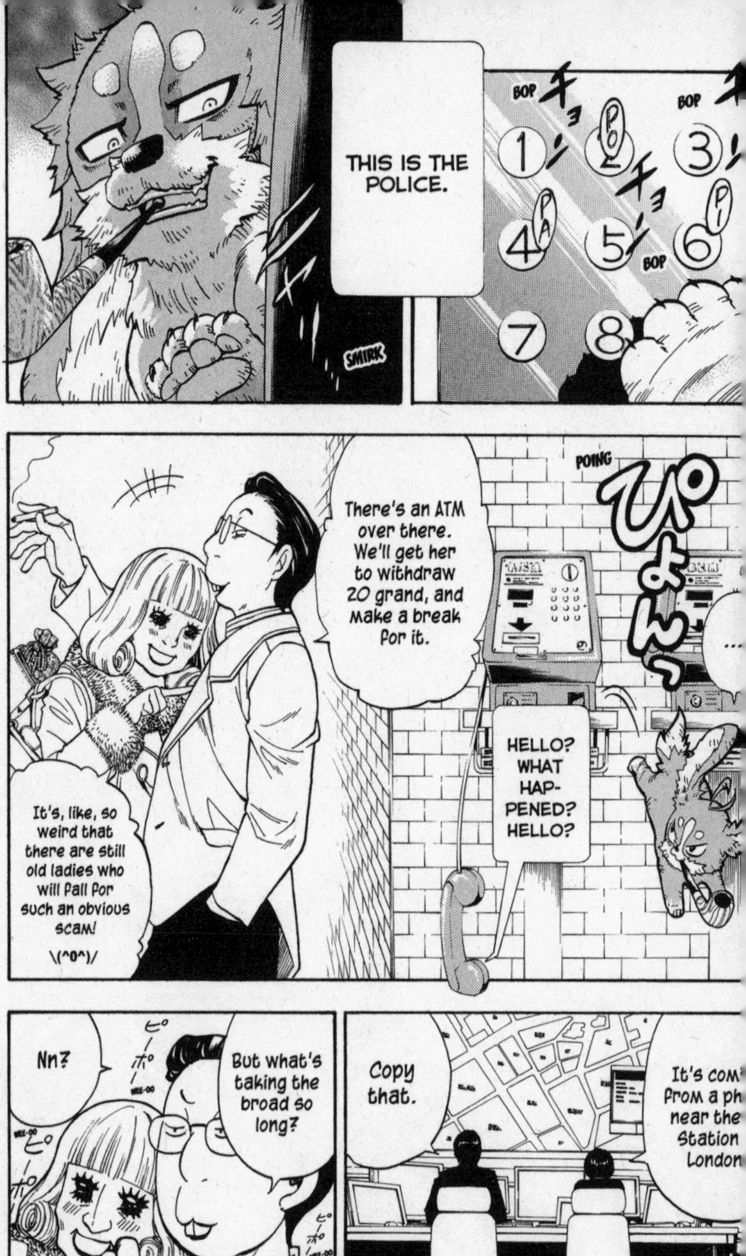
BOP
BOP
THIS IS THE POLICE.
BOP
SMIRK
POING
ぴょんっ
...
HELLO? WHAT HAP-PENED? HELLO?
There's an ATM over there. We'll get her to withdraw 20 grand, and make a break for it.
It's, like, so weird that there are still old ladies who will fall for such an obvious scam!
\(^0^)/
It's com
from a ph
near the
Station
London
Copy that.
But what's taking the broad so long?
Nn?

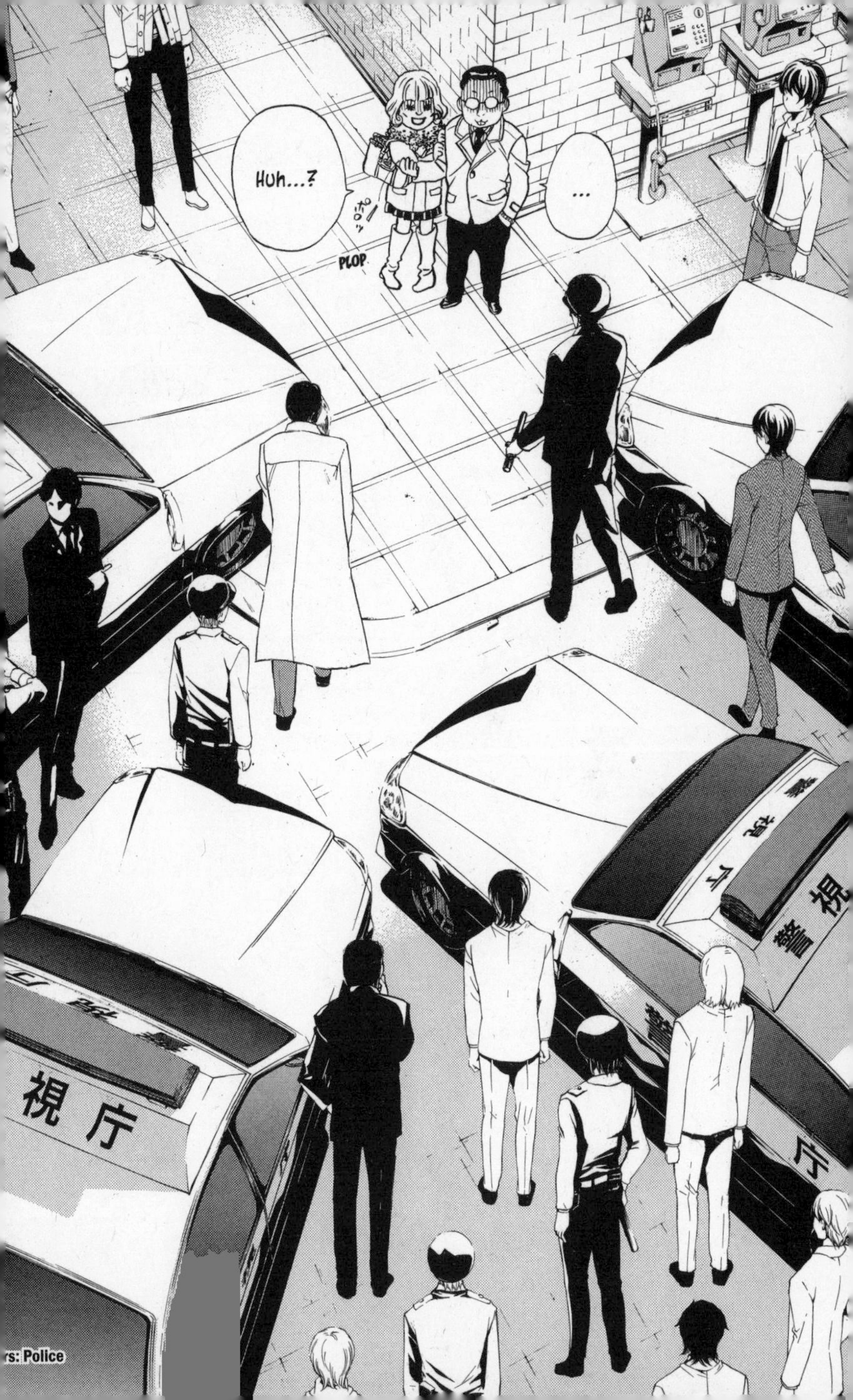
...
Huh...?
ポロッ
PLOP
rs: Police

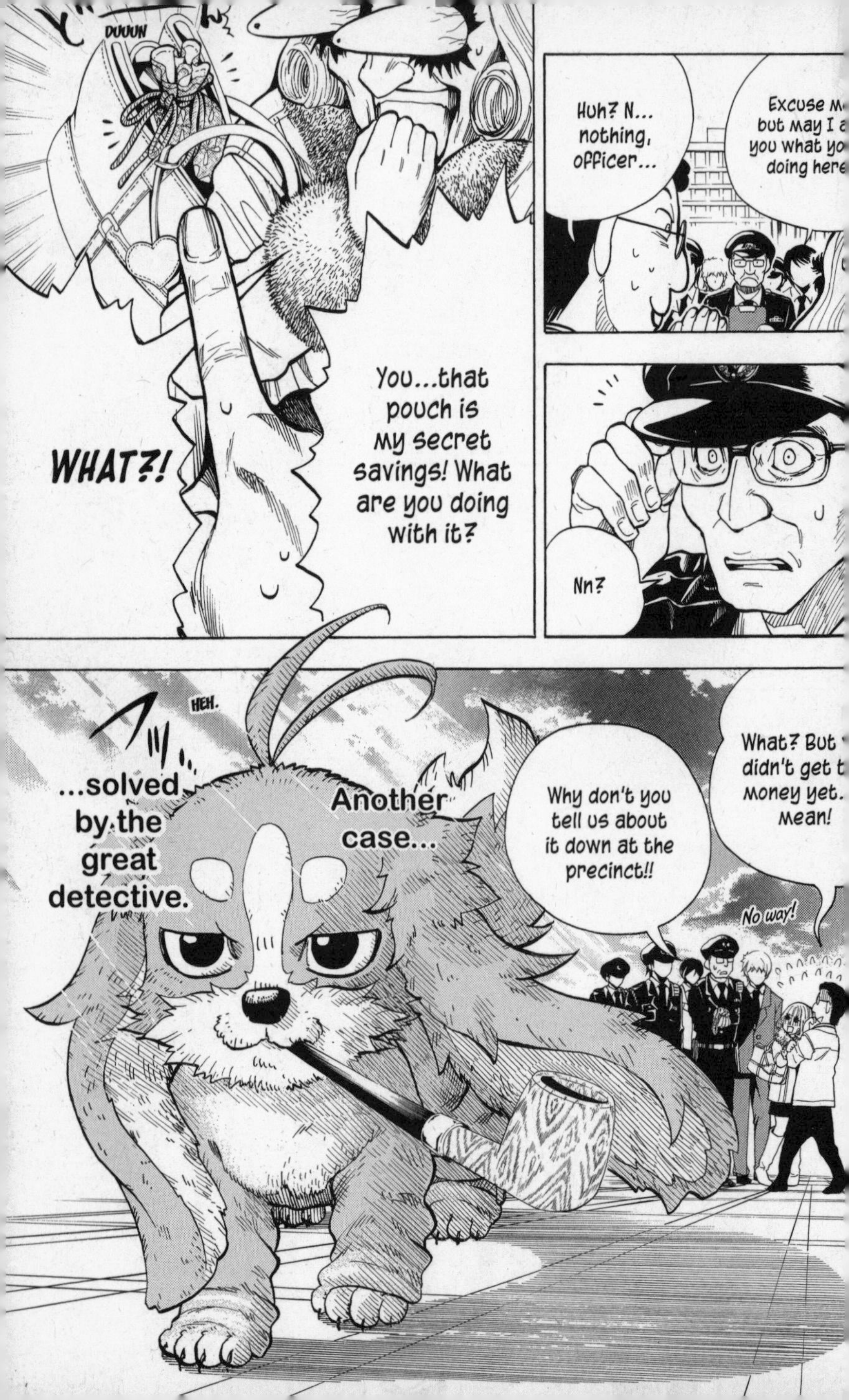

Excuse m
but may I a
you what yo
doing here
Huh? N... nothing, officer...
Nn?
DUUUN
You...that pouch is my secret savings! What are you doing with it?
WHAT?!
What? But
didn't get t
money yet...
Mean!
No way!
Why don't you tell us about it down at the precinct!!
Another case...
...solved by the great detective.
HEH.

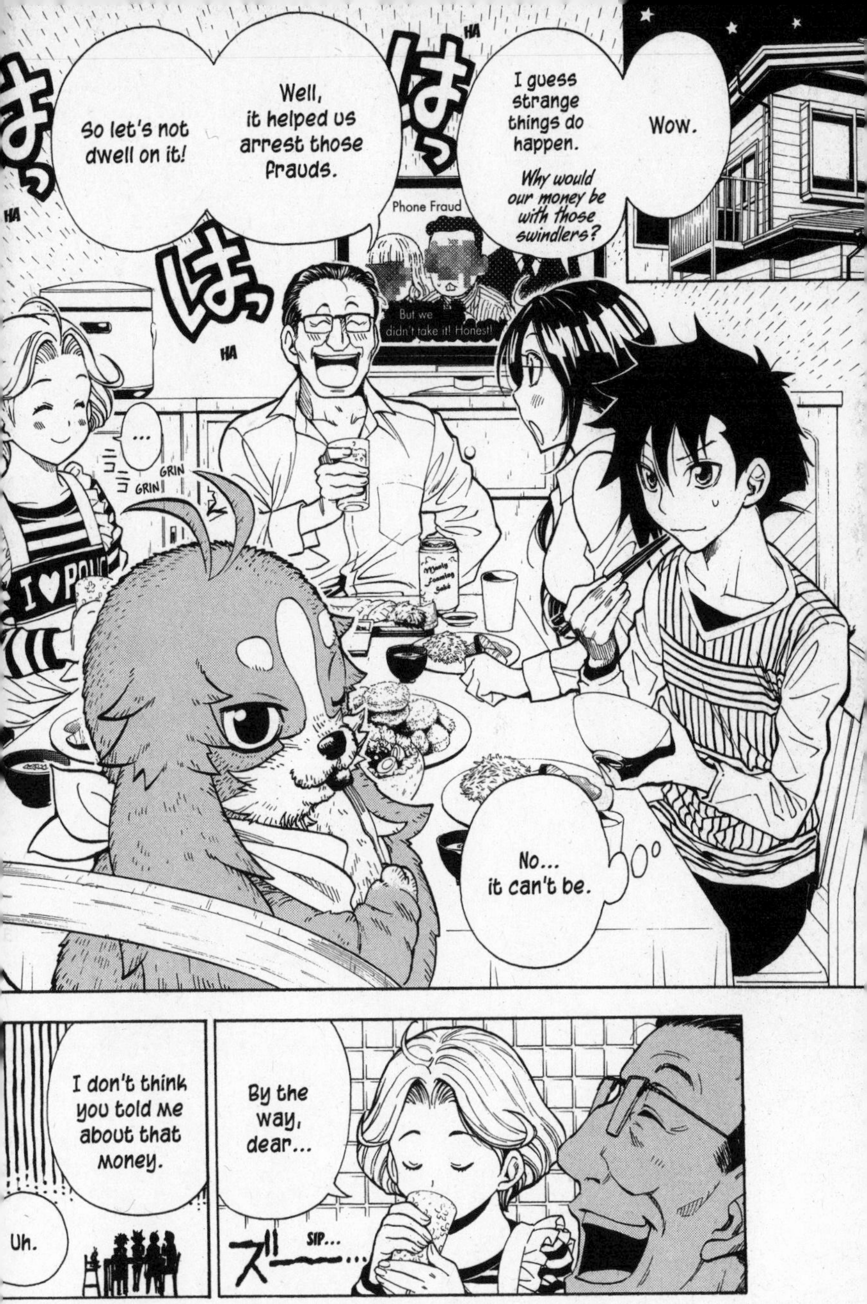
Wow.
I guess strange things do happen.
Why would our money be with those swindlers?
Phone Fraud
But we didn't take it! Honest!
HA
Well, it helped us arrest those frauds.
So let's not dwell on it!
HA
HA
...
GRIN
GRIN
No... it can't be.
By the way, dear...
SIP...
I don't think you told me about that money.
Uh.

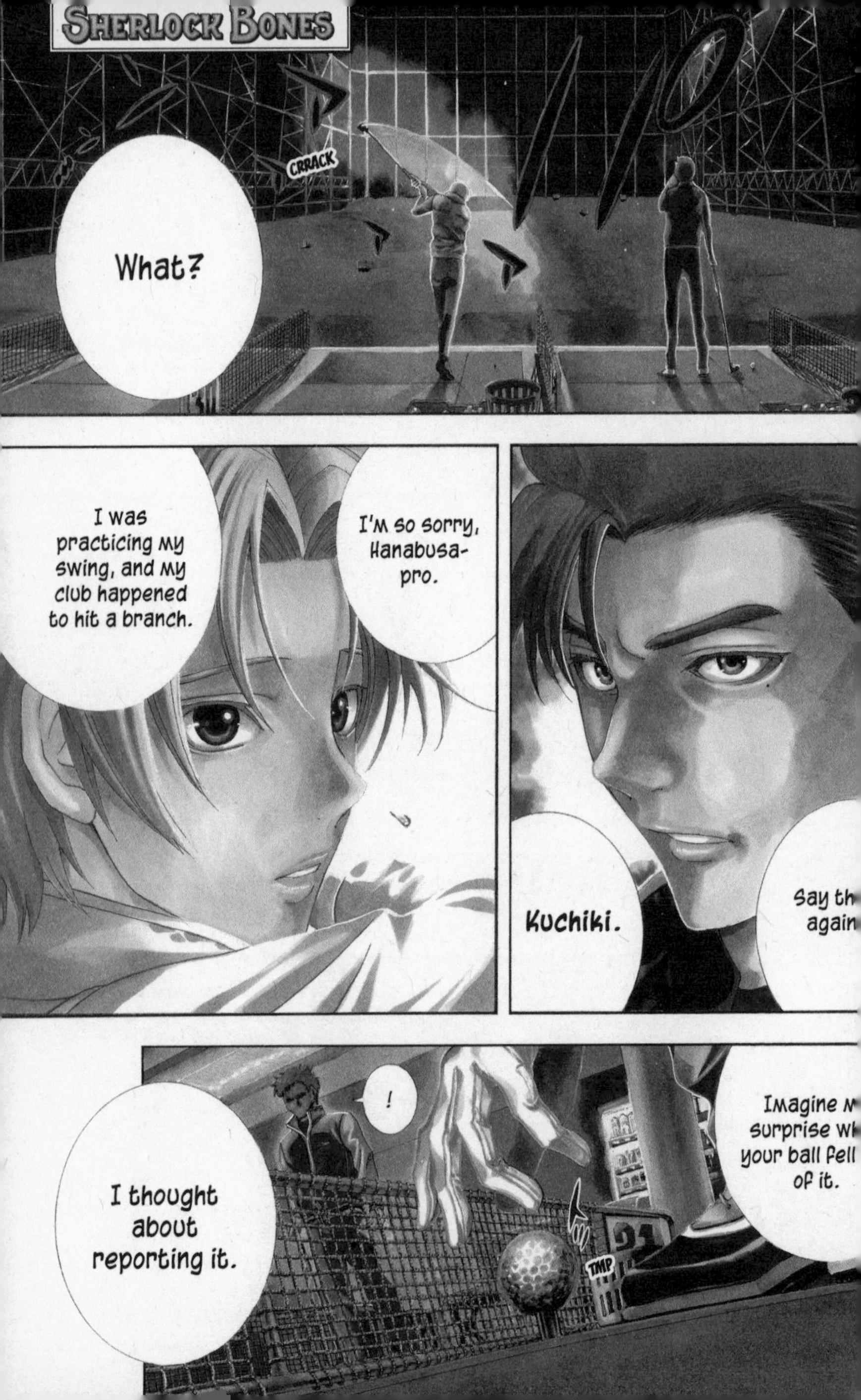
CRRACK
What?
Say th again
Kuchiki.
I'm so sorry, Hanabusa-pro.
I was practicing my swing, and my club happened to hit a branch.
Imagine m surprise w your ball fell of it.
!
TMP
I thought about reporting it.

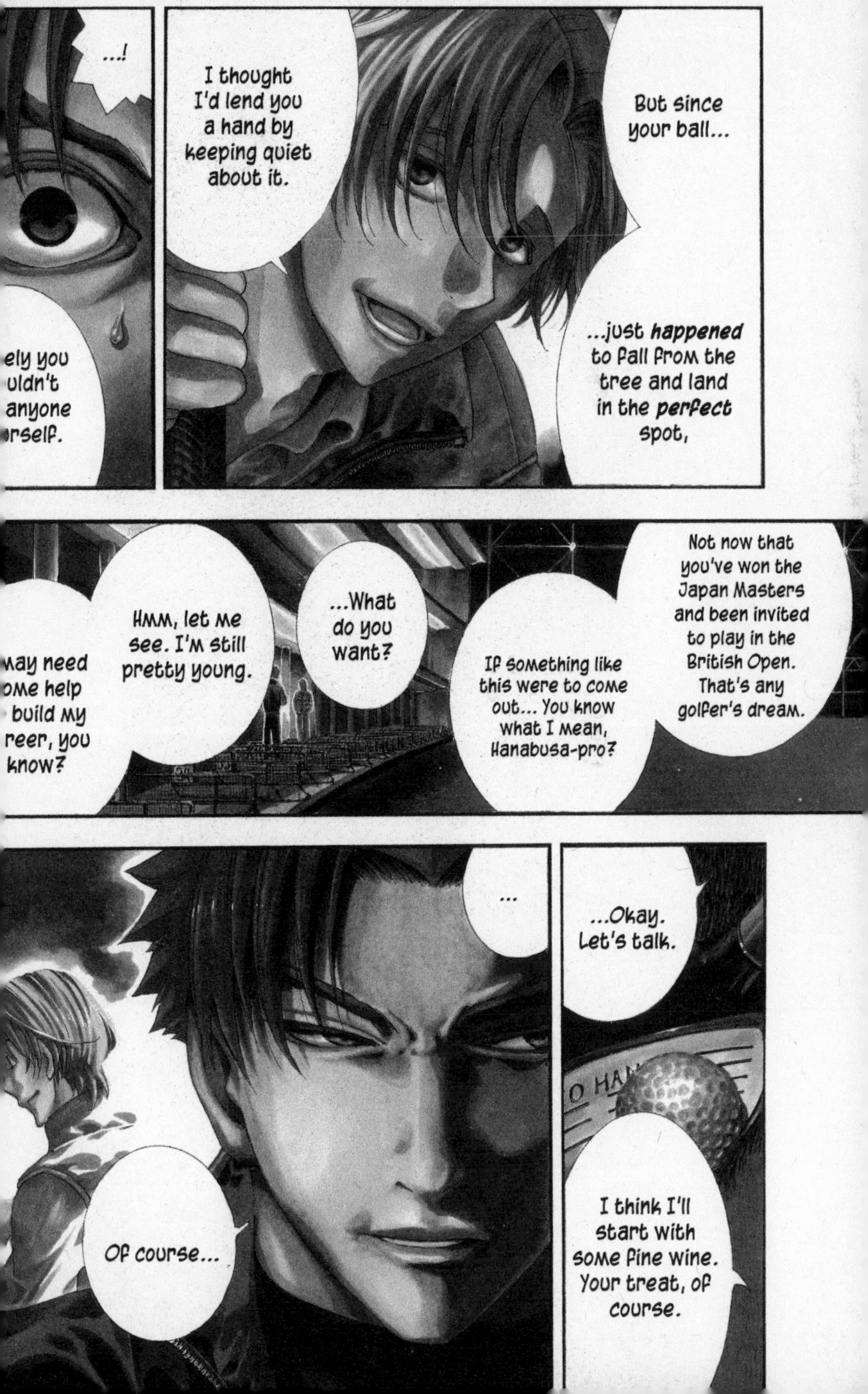
But since your ball...
...just *happened* to fall from the tree and land in the *perfect* spot,
I thought I'd lend you a hand by keeping quiet about it.
...!
ely you uldn't anyone rself.
Not now that you've won the Japan Masters and been invited to play in the British Open. That's any golfer's dream.
If something like this were to come out... You know what I mean, Hanabusa-pro?
...What do you want?
Hmm, let me see. I'm still pretty young.
ay need ome help build my reer, you know?
...Okay. Let's talk.
I think I'll start with some fine wine. Your treat, of course.
...
Of course...

Case 3: ⚜ A Golfer's Glory, Part 1

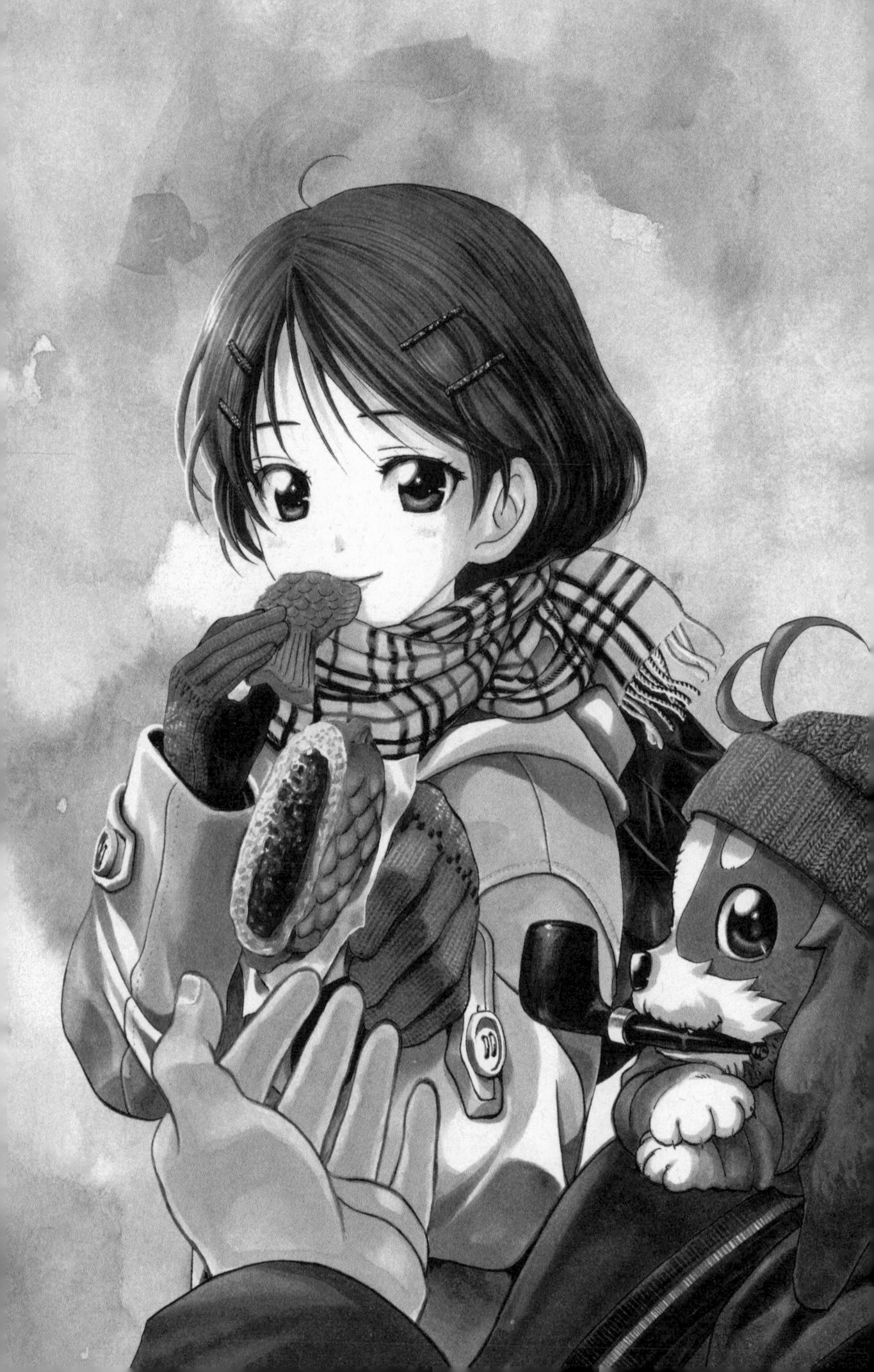

SHERLOCK
BONES

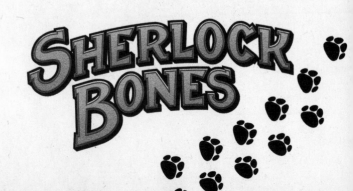

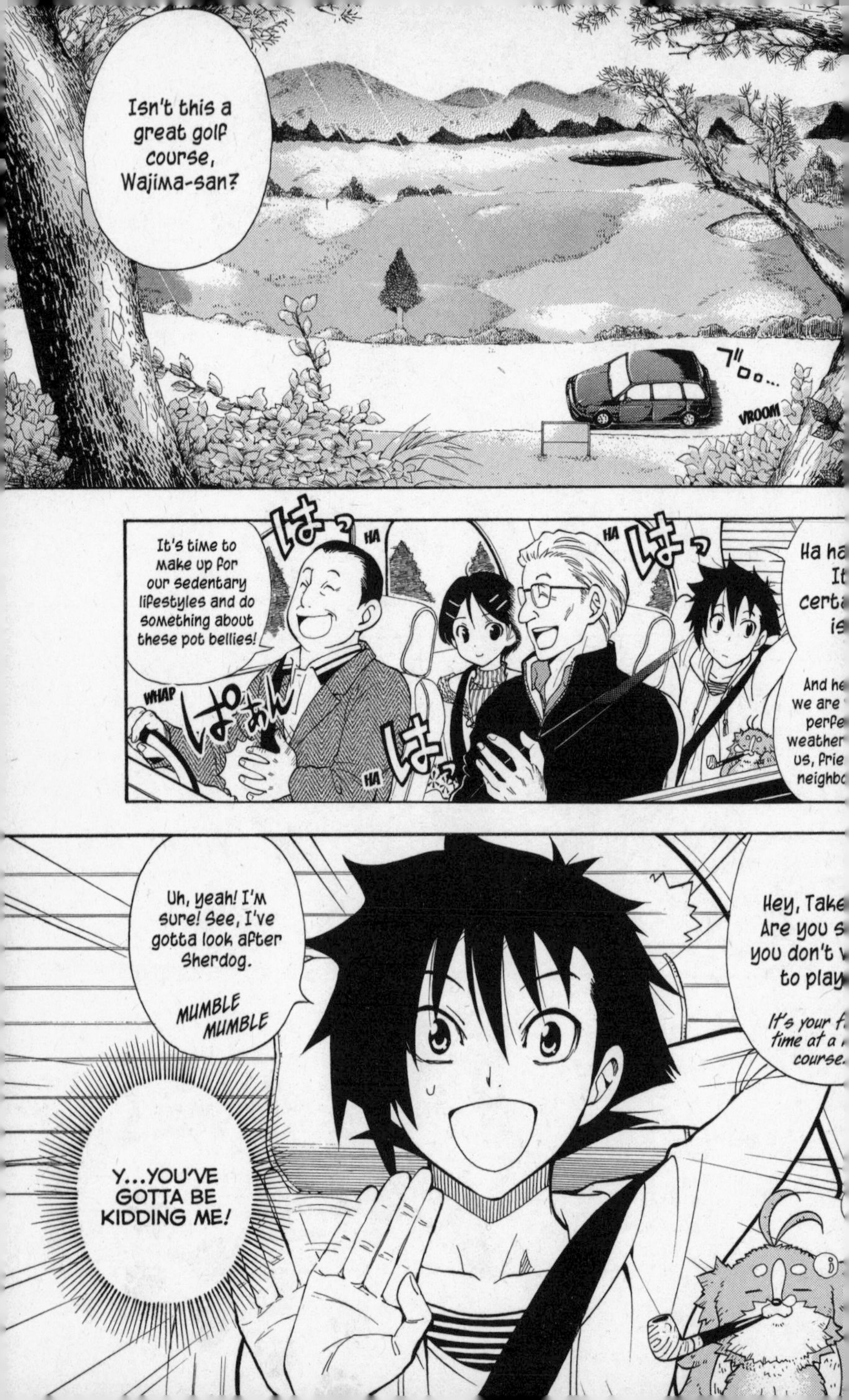

Isn't this a great golf course, Wajima-san?
ブロロ…
VROOM
Ha ha It certa is
And he we are perfe weather us, frie neighbo
はっ
HA
It's time to make up for our sedentary lifestyles and do something about these pot bellies!
はっ
HA
はっ
HA
ぱあん
WHAP
Hey, Take Are you s you don't to play
It's your f time at a course.
Uh, yeah! I'm sure! See, I've gotta look after Sherdog.
MUMBLE MUMBLE
Y...YOU'VE GOTTA BE KIDDING ME!

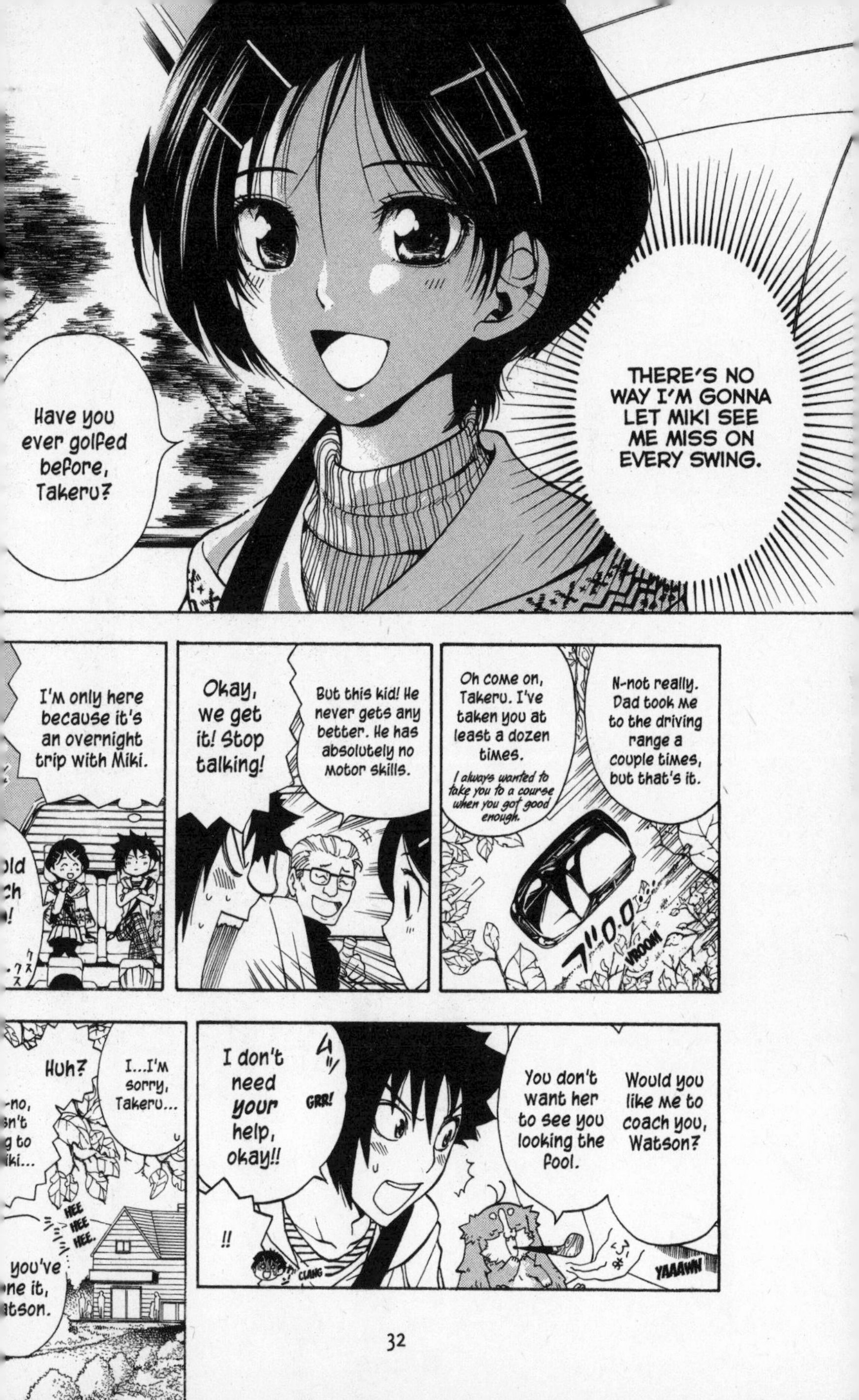
THERE'S NO WAY I'M GONNA LET MIKI SEE ME MISS ON EVERY SWING.
Have you ever golfed before, Takeru?
N-not really. Dad took me to the driving range a couple times, but that's it.
Oh come on, Takeru. I've taken you at least a dozen times.
I always wanted to take you to a course when you got good enough.
VROOM
But this kid! He never gets any better. He has absolutely no motor skills.
Okay, we get it! Stop talking!
I'm only here because it's an overnight trip with Miki.
Would you like me to coach you, Watson?
You don't want her to see you looking the fool.
GRR!
I don't need your help, okay!!
!!
CLANG
YAAAWN
I...I'm sorry, Takeru...
Huh?
HEE HEE HEE.

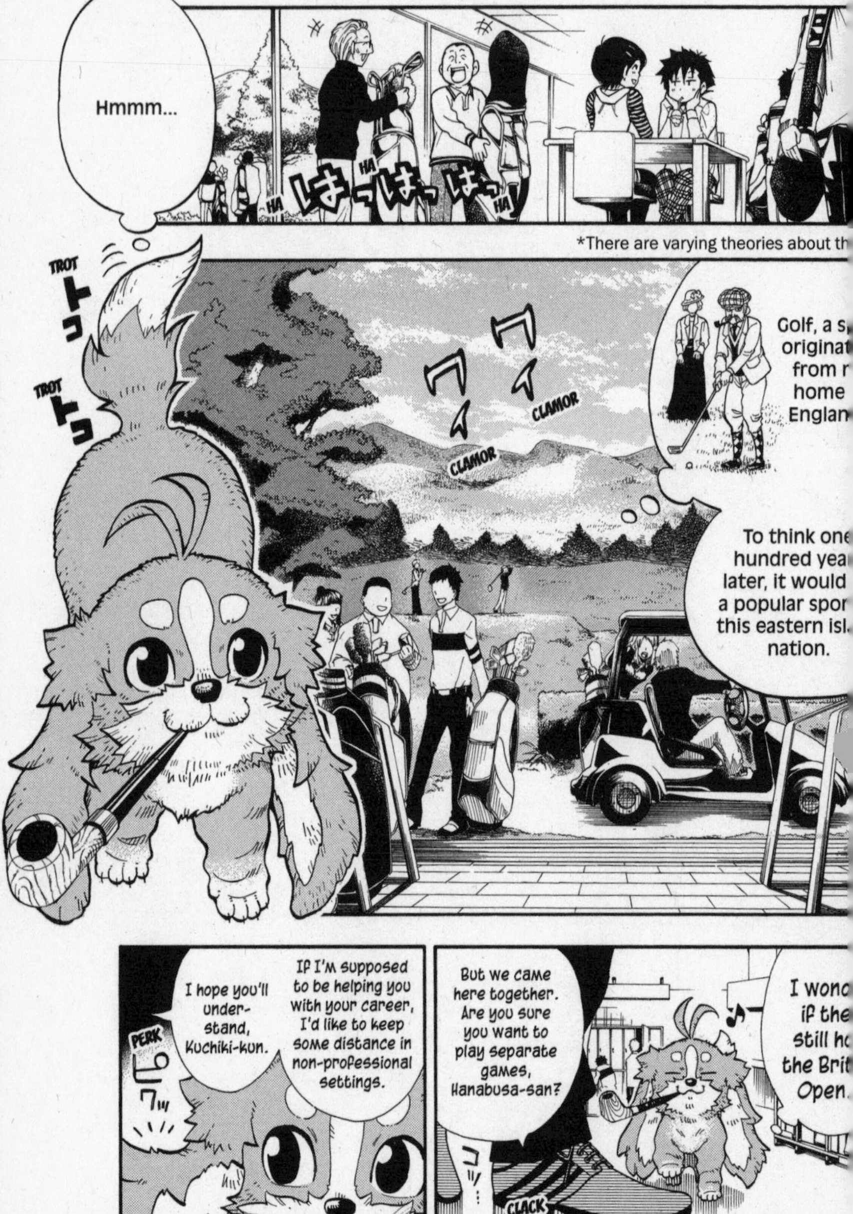
HA
はっはっはっ
HA
HA
HA
Hmmm...
*There are varying theories about th
Golf, a sp originat from r home Englan
To think one hundred yea later, it would a popular spor this eastern isl nation.
ワイワイ
CLAMOR
CLAMOR
TROT
トッ
TROT
トコ
I wonc if the still hc the Brit Open.
But we came here together. Are you sure you want to play separate games, Hanabusa-san?
CLACK
If I'm supposed to be helping you with your career, I'd like to keep some distance in non-professional settings.
I hope you'll under-stand, Kuchiki-kun.
PERK

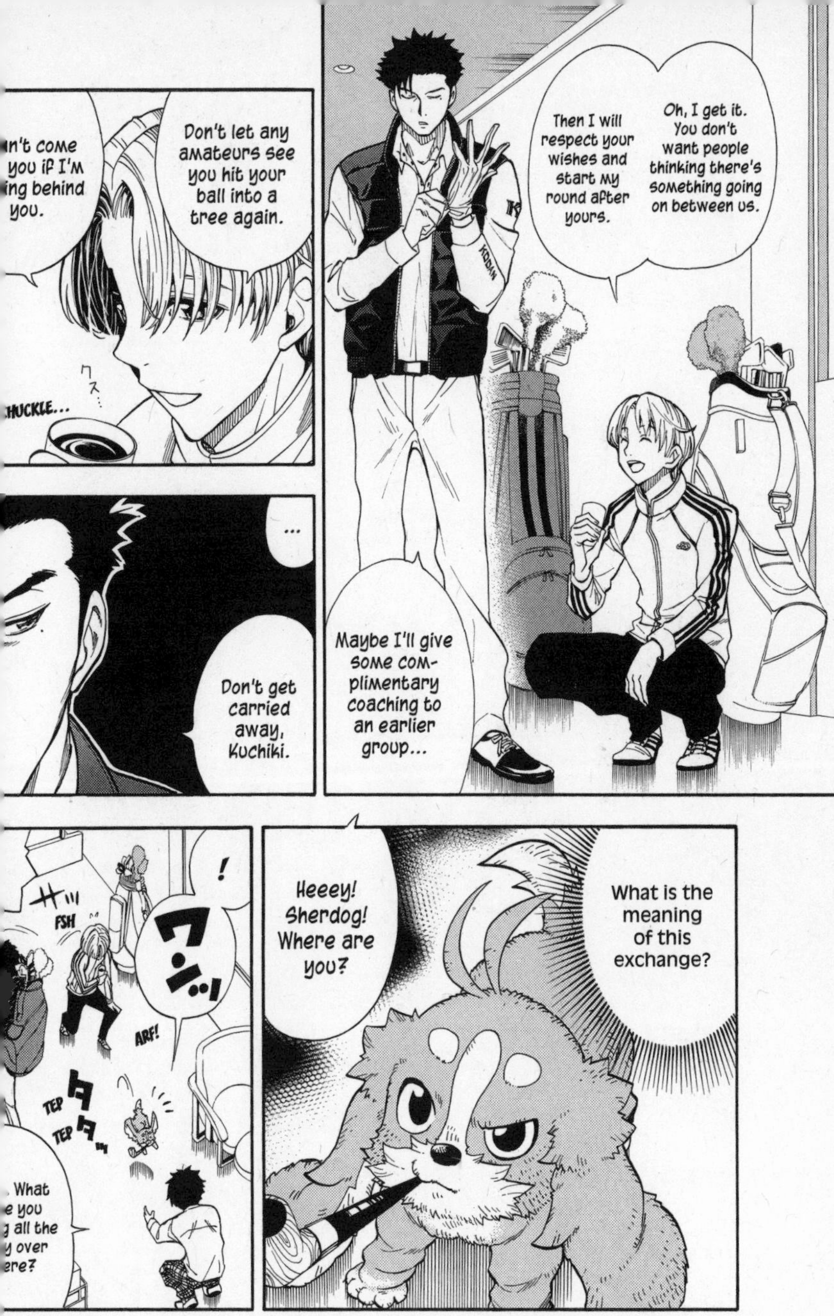

Oh, I get it. You don't want people thinking there's something going on between us.
Then I will respect your wishes and start my round after yours.
Maybe I'll give some complimentary coaching to an earlier group...
Don't let any amateurs see you hit your ball into a tree again.
n't come you if I'm ing behind you.
クス…
CHUCKLE...
...
Don't get carried away, Kuchiki.
What is the meaning of this exchange?
Heeey! Sherdog! Where are you?
!
ワン!
ARF!
サッ
FSH
TEP タ
TEP タ
What e you g all the y over ere?

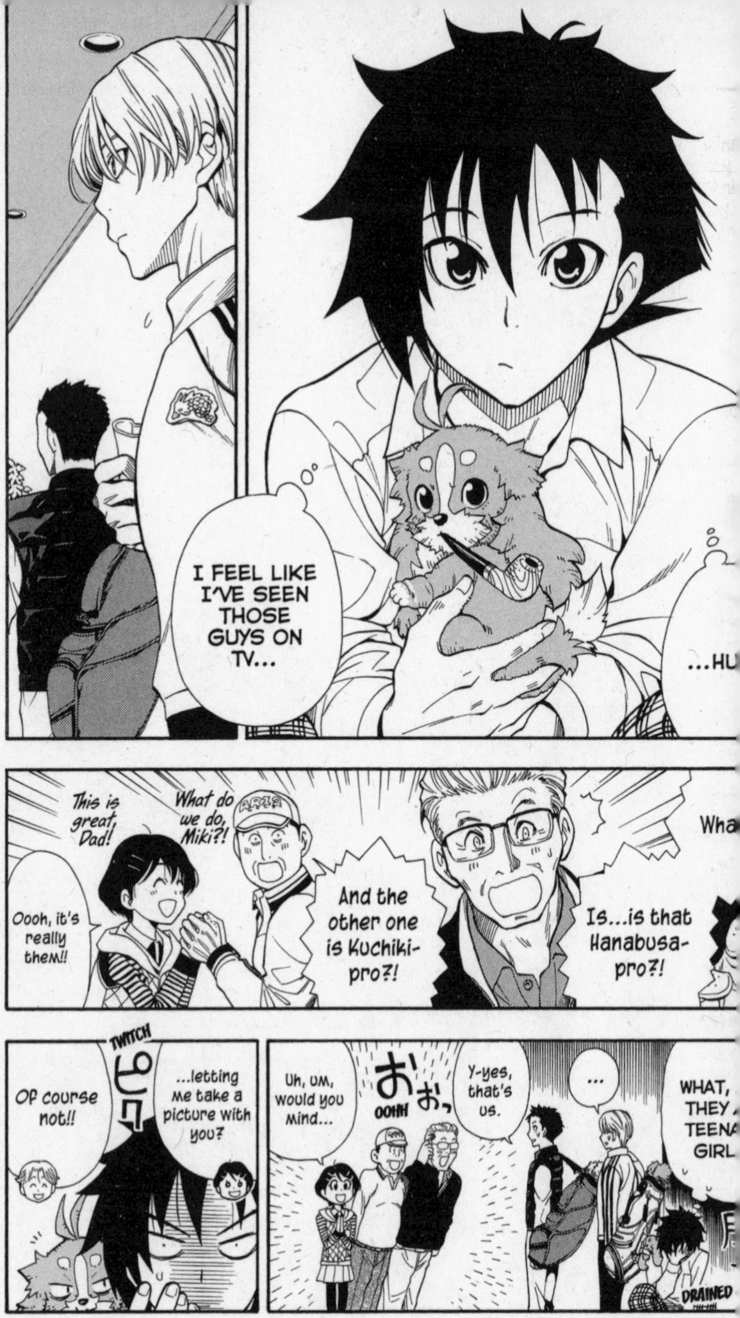
...HU
I FEEL LIKE I'VE SEEN THOSE GUYS ON TV...
Wha
Is...is that Hanabusa-pro?!
And the other one is Kuchiki-pro?!
What do we do, Miki?!
This is great, Dad!
Oooh, it's really them!!
WHAT, THEY
TEENA
GIRL
DRAINED
...
Y-yes, that's us.
おおっ
OOHH
Uh, um, would you mind...
...letting me take a picture with you?
ピク
TWITCH
Of course not!!

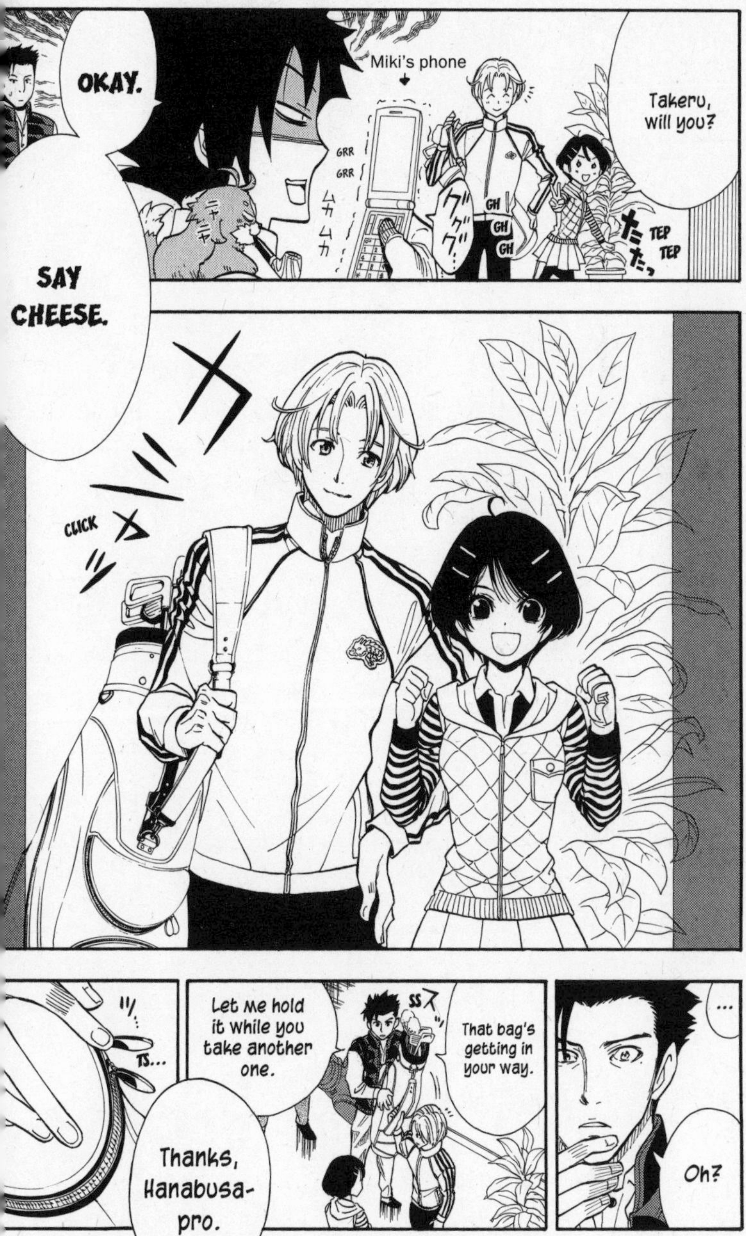
Takeru, will you?
TEP TEP
GH GH GH
Miki's phone
GRR GRR
ムカムカ
OKAY.
SAY CHEESE.
CLICK
...
Oh?
That bag's getting in your way.
SS
Let me hold it while you take another one.
Thanks, Hanabusa-pro.
TS...

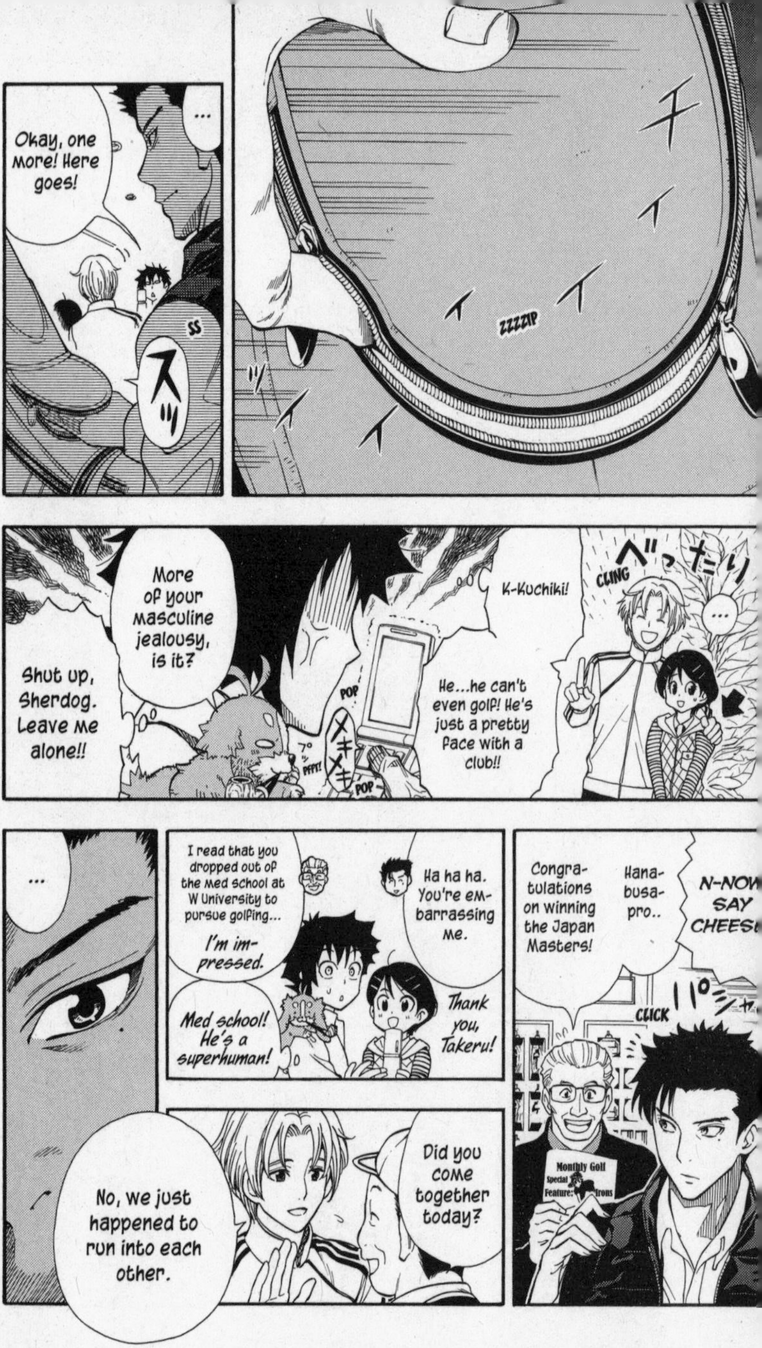
ZZZZIP
...
Okay, one more! Here goes!
SS
CLING
...
K-Kuchiki!
He...he can't even golf! He's just a pretty face with a club!!
POP
PFFT!
POP
More of your masculine jealousy, is it?
Shut up, Sherdog. Leave me alone!!
N-NOW SAY CHEES
Hana-busa-pro..
Congratulations on winning the Japan Masters!
CLICK
Monthly Golf
Special Feature: Irons
I read that you dropped out of the med school at W University to pursue golfing... I'm impressed.
Ha ha ha. You're embarrassing me.
Thank you, Takeru!
Med school! He's a superhuman!
Did you come together today?
No, we just happened to run into each other.
...

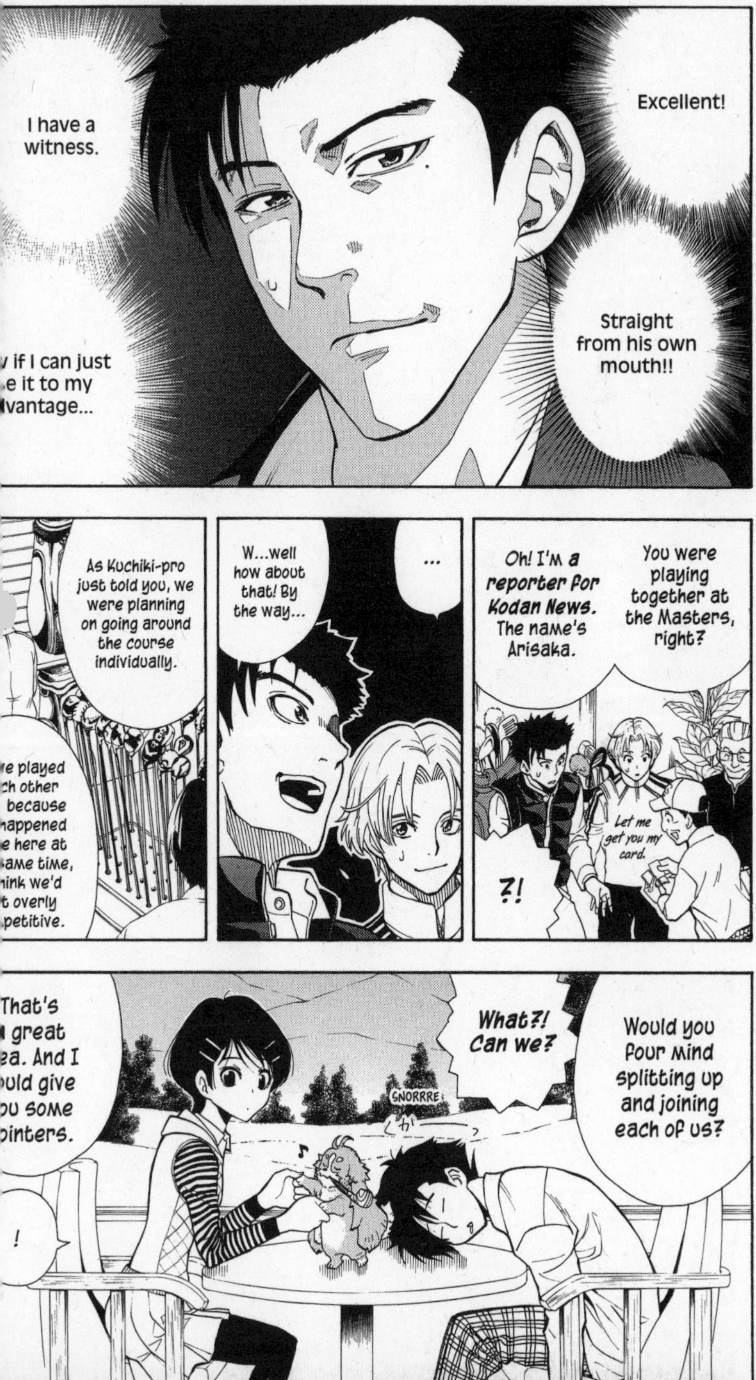
Excellent!
Straight from his own mouth!!
I have a witness.
y if I can just e it to my dvantage...
You were playing together at the Masters, right?
Oh! I'm a reporter for Kodan News. The name's Arisaka.
Let me get you my card.
?!
...
W...well how about that! By the way...
As Kuchiki-pro just told you, we were planning on going around the course individually.
e played ch other because happened e here at ame time, hink we'd t overly petitive.
Would you four mind splitting up and joining each of us?
What?! Can we?
SNORRRE
That's great ea. And I ould give ou some ointers.
!

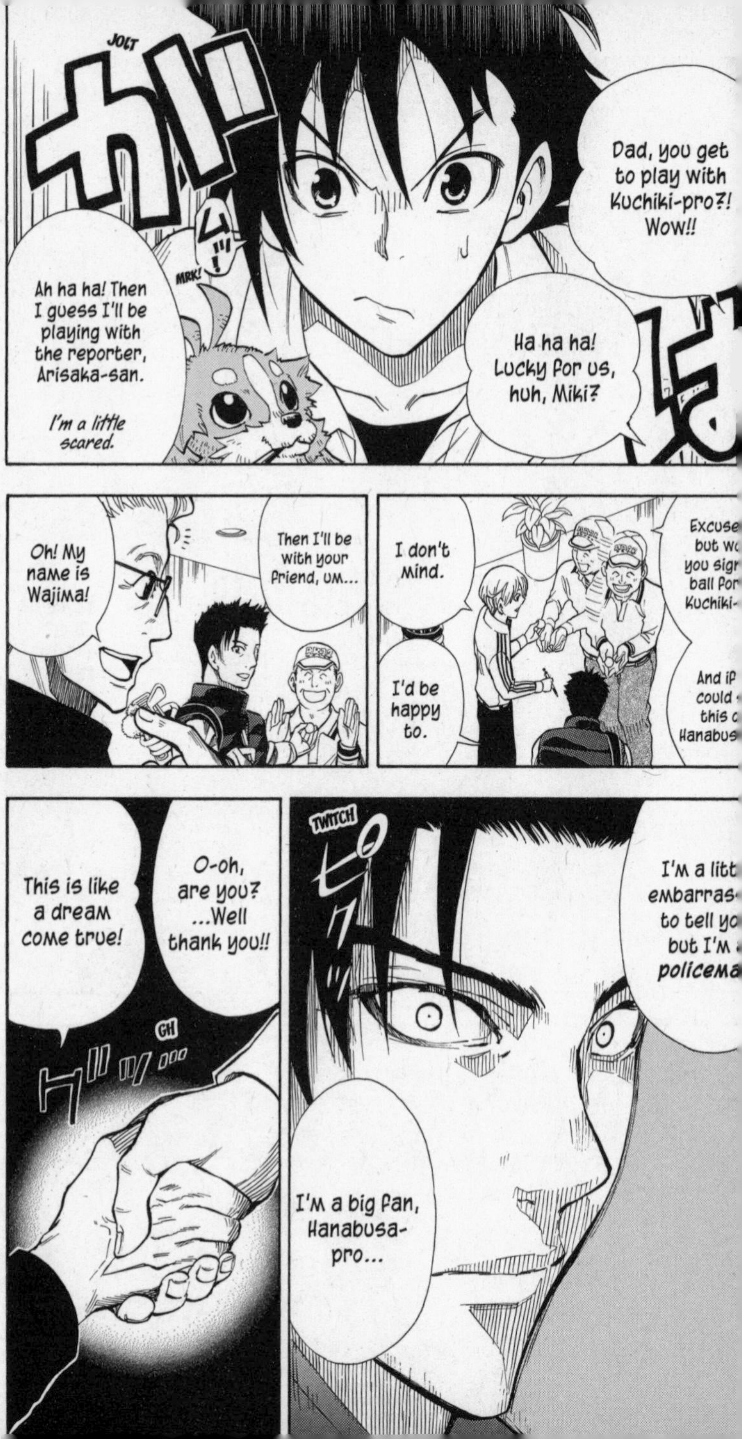

JOLT
Dad, you get to play with Kuchiki-pro?! Wow!!
Ha ha ha! Lucky for us, huh, Miki?
MRK!
Ah ha ha! Then I guess I'll be playing with the reporter, Arisaka-san.
I'm a little scared.
Excuse but wo you sig ball for Kuchiki-
And if could this c Hanabus
I don't mind.
I'd be happy to.
Then I'll be with your friend, um...
Oh! My name is Wajima!
I'm a litt embarras to tell yo but I'm ***policema***
TWITCH
I'm a big fan, Hanabusa-pro...
O-oh, are you? ...Well thank you!!
This is like a dream come true!
GH

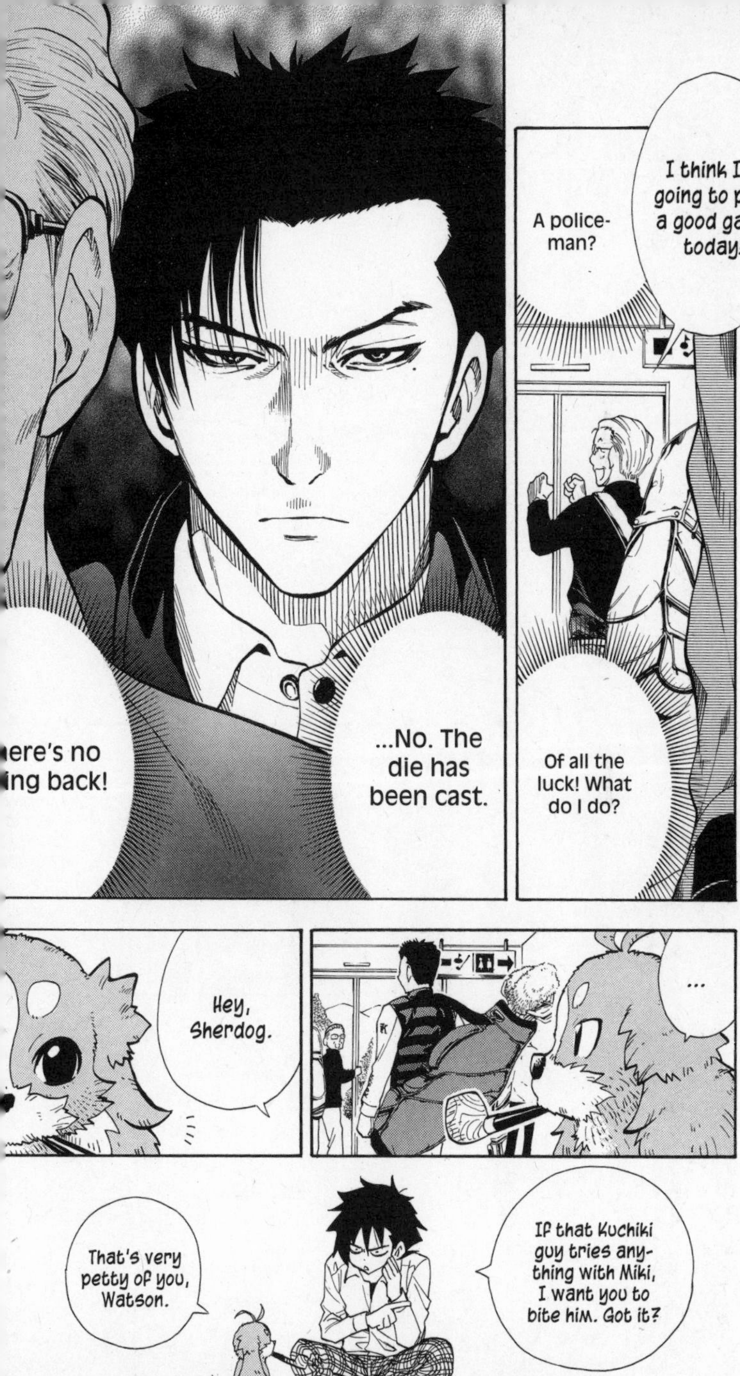
I think I'M going to play a good game today!
A police-man?
Of all the luck! What do I do?
...No. The die has been cast.
ere's no
ing back!
...
Hey, Sherdog.
If that Kuchiki guy tries any-thing with Miki, I want you to bite him. Got it?
That's very petty of you, Watson.

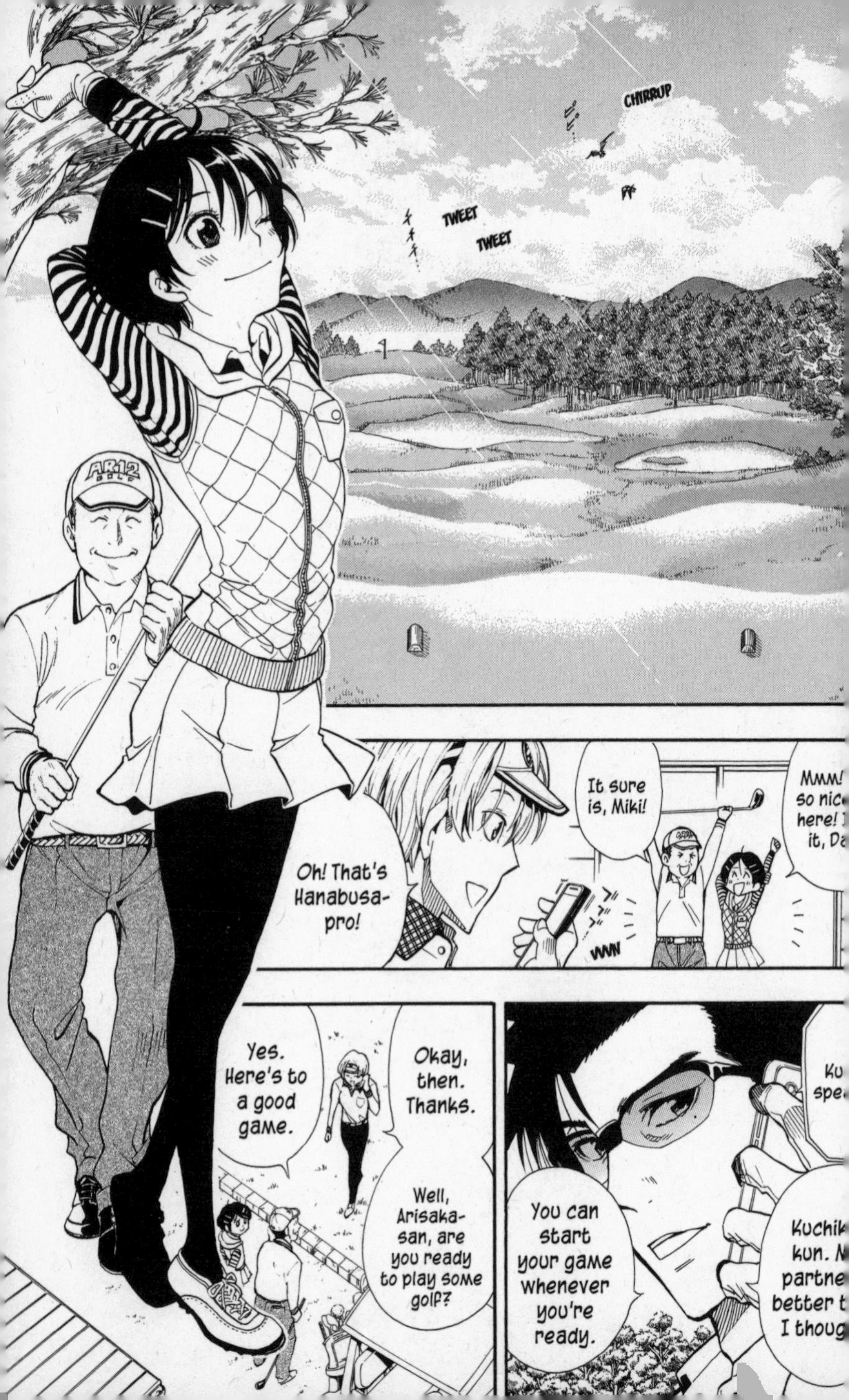
CHIRRUP
TWEET
TWEET
Mmm! so nic here! it, Da
It sure is, Miki!
Oh! That's Hanabusa-pro!
WWN
Ku spe
Kuchik kun. M partne better t I thoug
You can start your game whenever you're ready.
Okay, then. Thanks.
Yes. Here's to a good game.
Well, Arisaka-san, are you ready to play some golf?

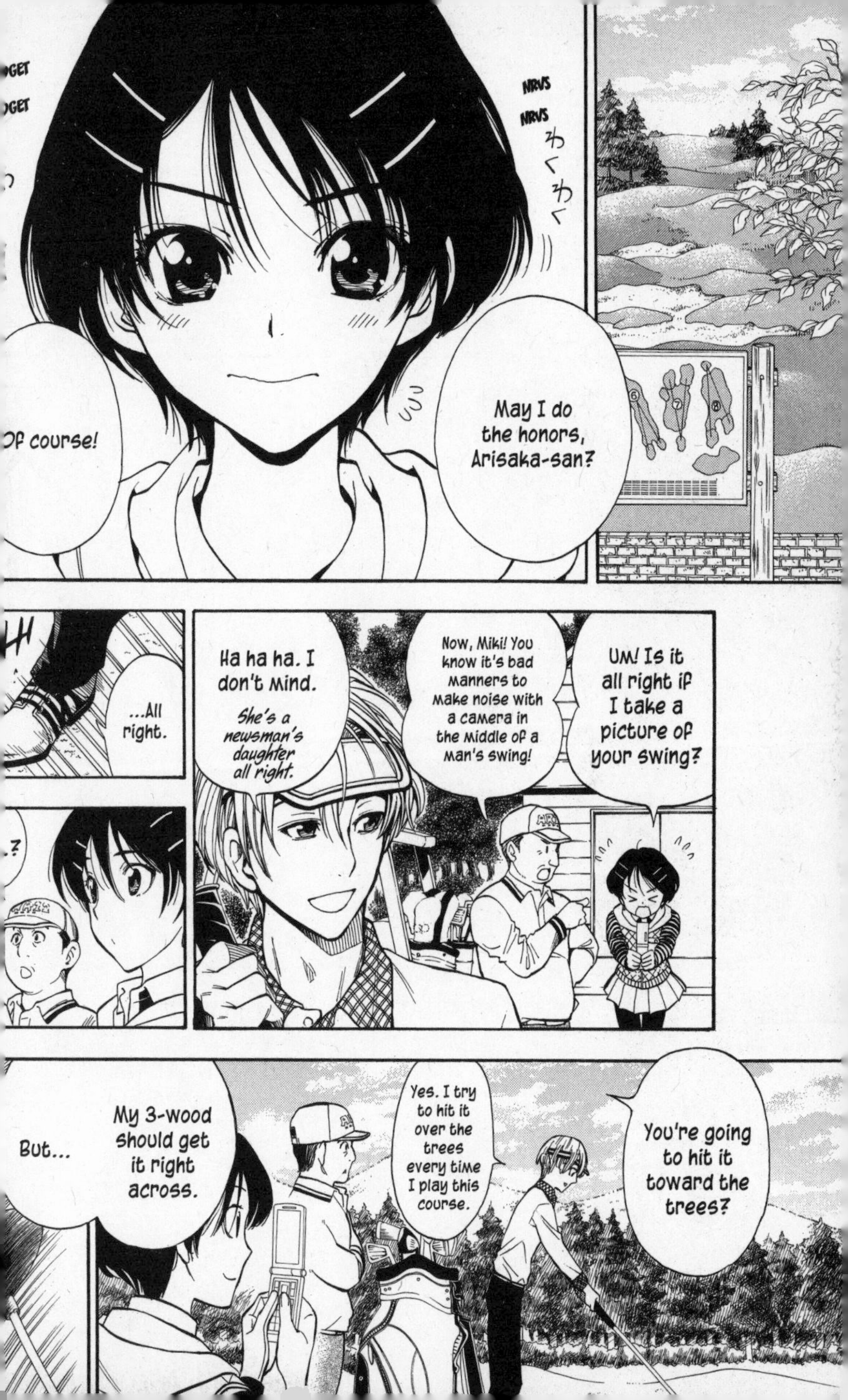
NRVS
NRVS
わくわく
May I do the honors, Arisaka-san?
Of course!
Um! Is it all right if I take a picture of your swing?
Now, Miki! You know it's bad manners to make noise with a camera in the middle of a man's swing!
Ha ha ha. I don't mind.
She's a newsman's daughter all right.
...All right.
You're going to hit it toward the trees?
Yes. I try to hit it over the trees every time I play this course.
My 3-wood should get it right across.
But...

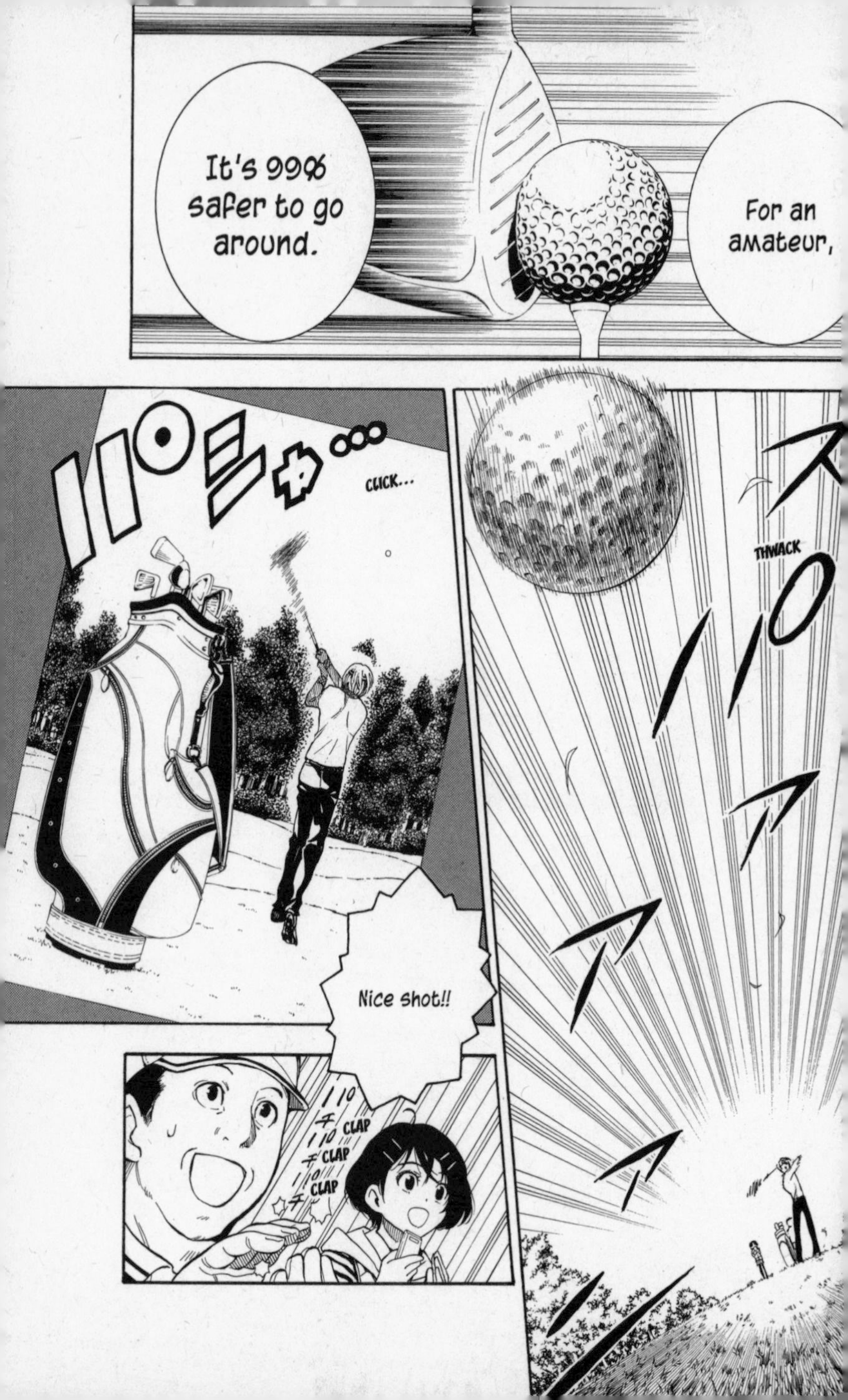
For an amateur,
It's 99% safer to go around.
THWACK
CLICK...
Nice shot!!
CLAP
CLAP
CLAP

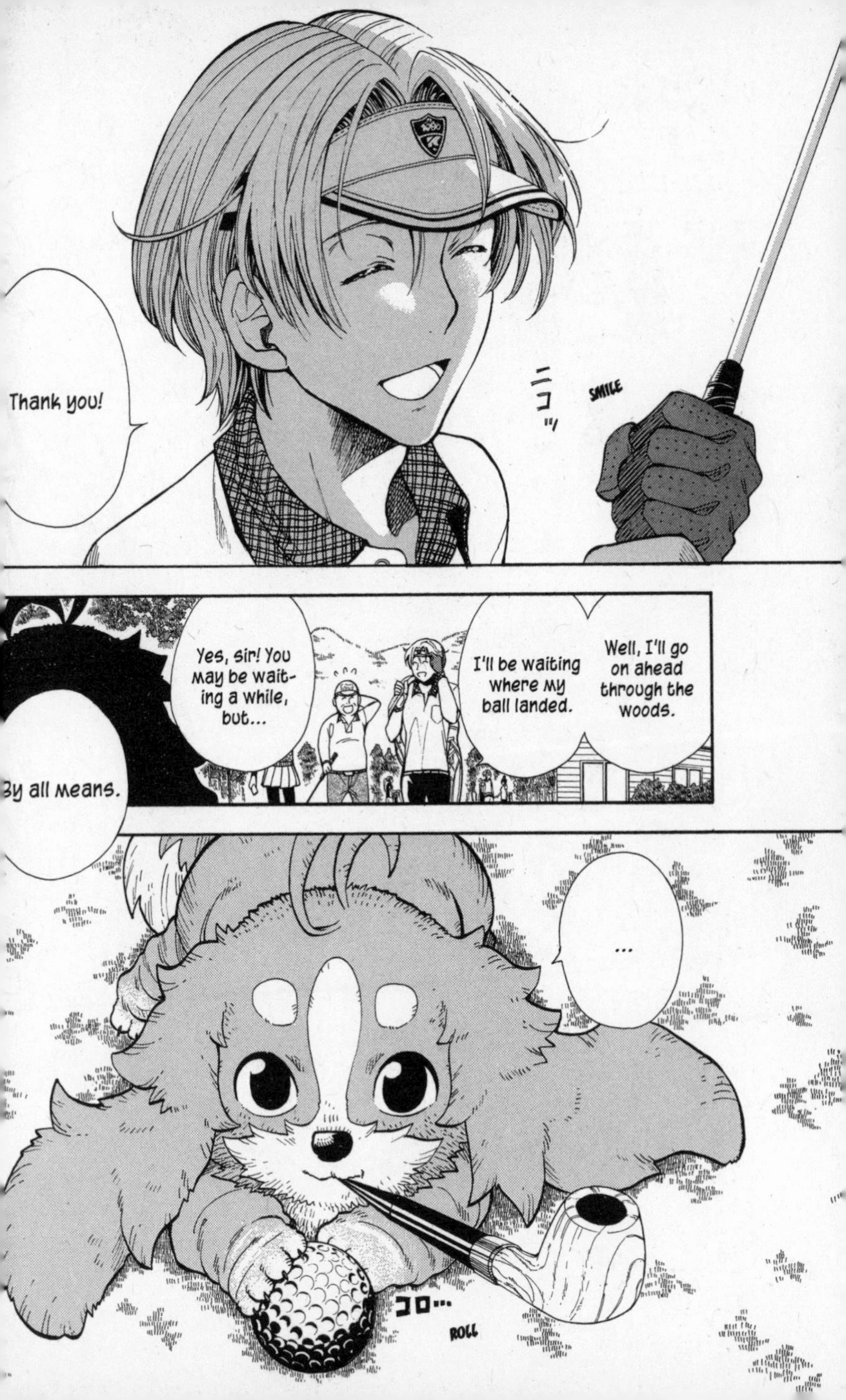
ニコッ
SMILE
Thank you!
Well, I'll go on ahead through the woods.
I'll be waiting where my ball landed.
Yes, sir! You may be waiting a while, but...
By all means.
...
コロ…
ROLL

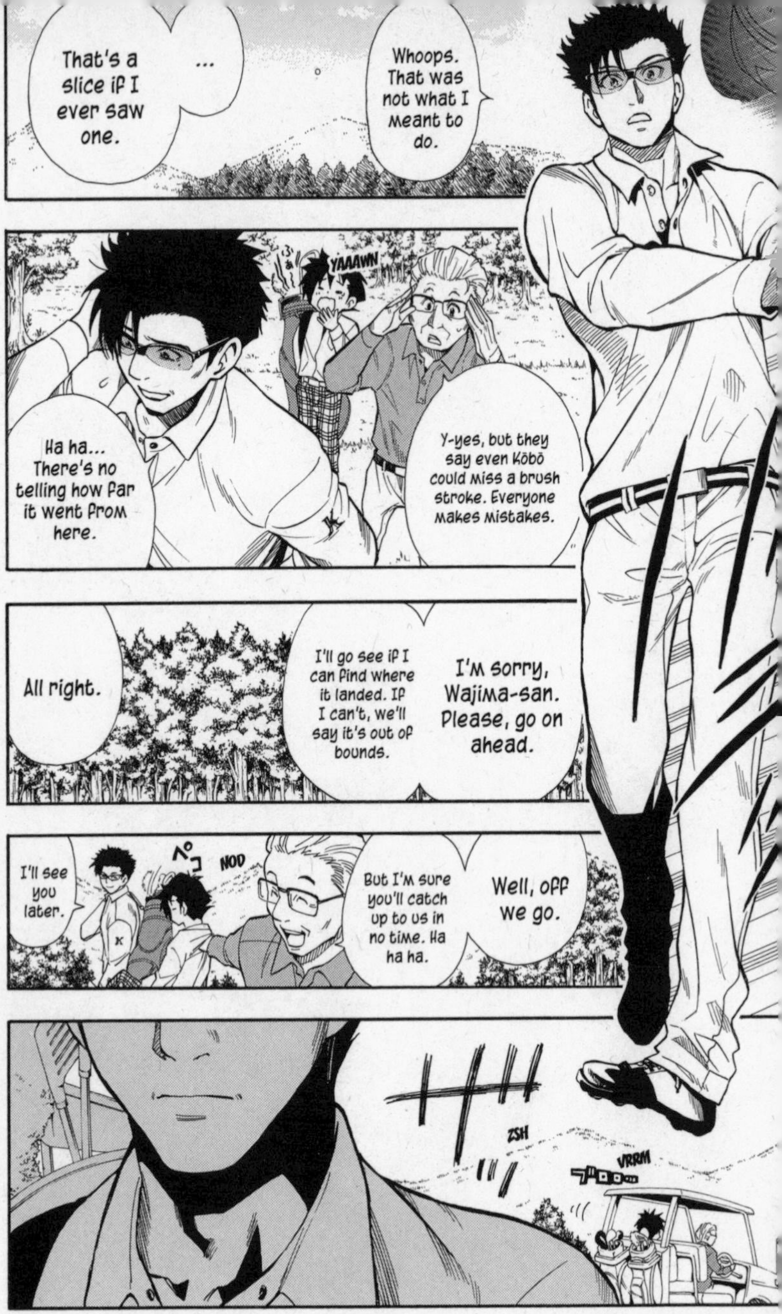
Whoops. That was not what I meant to do.
...
That's a slice if I ever saw one.
YAAAWN
Y-yes, but they say even Kōbō could miss a brush stroke. Everyone makes mistakes.
Ha ha... There's no telling how far it went from here.
I'm sorry, Wajima-san. Please, go on ahead.
I'll go see if I can find where it landed. If I can't, we'll say it's out of bounds.
All right.
Well, off we go.
But I'm sure you'll catch up to us in no time. Ha ha ha.
NOD
I'll see you later.
ZSH
VRRM

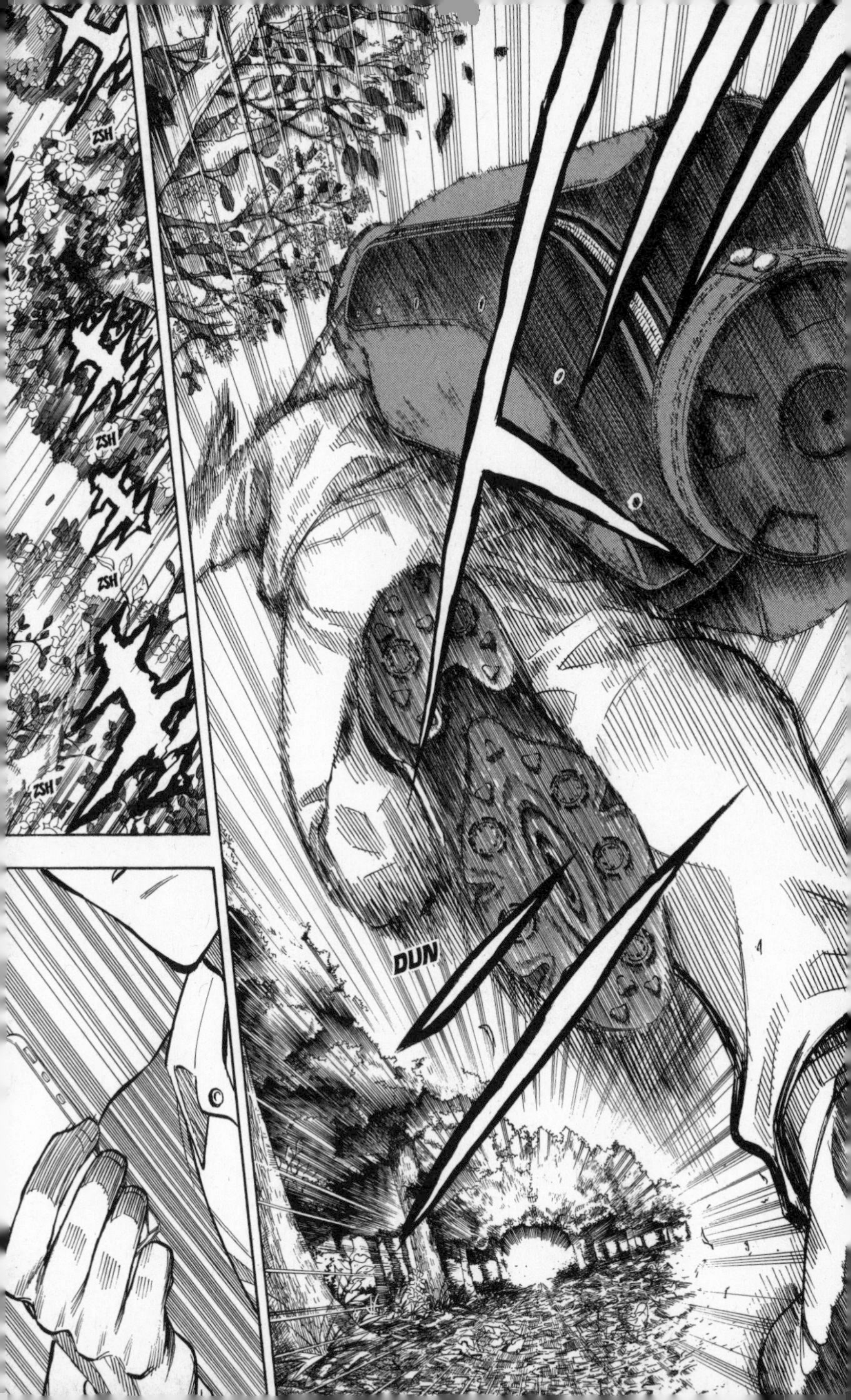
ZSH
ZSH
ZSH
ZSH
DUN

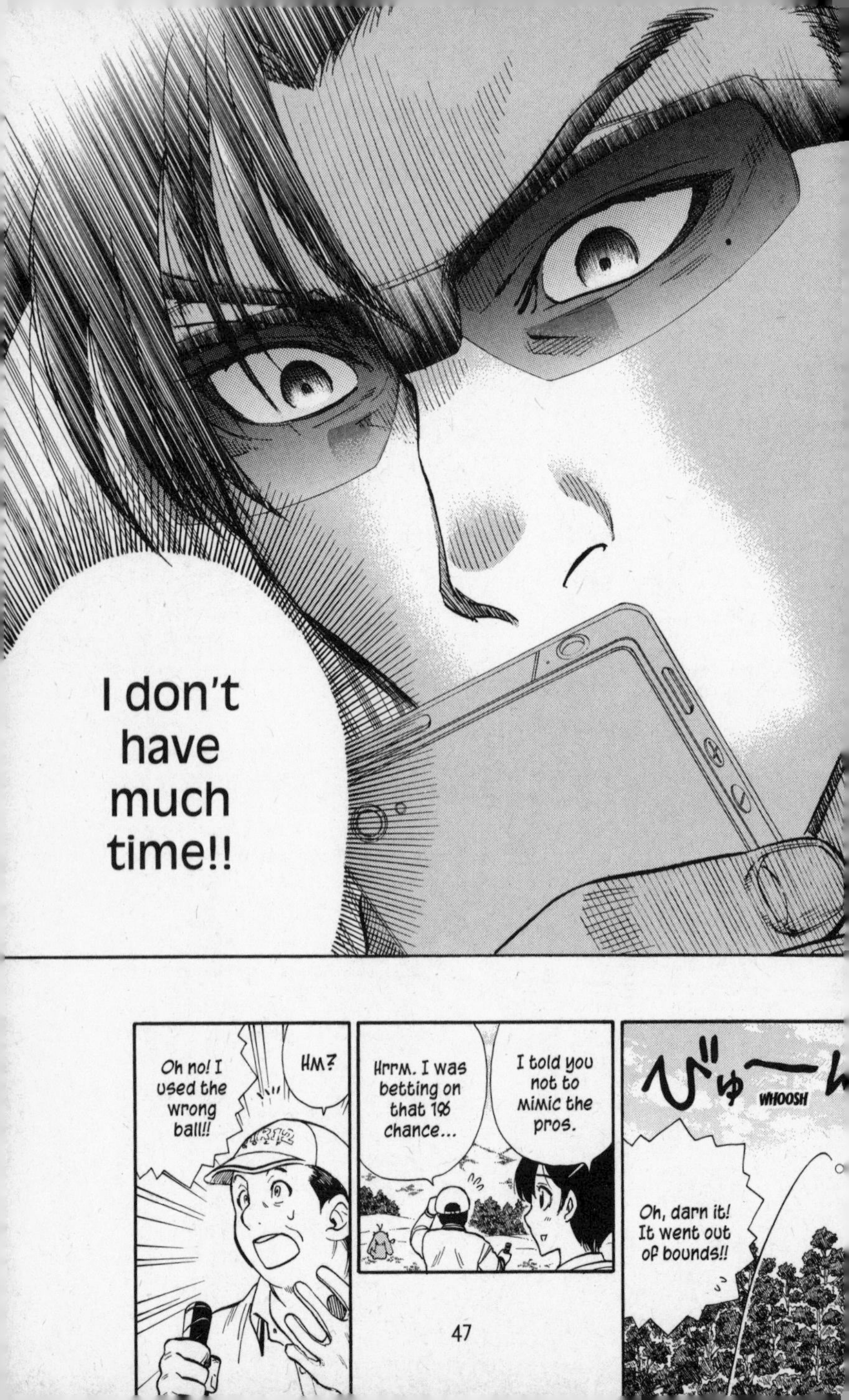
I don't have much time!!
びゅ〜ん
WHOOSH
Oh, darn it! It went out of bounds!!
I told you not to mimic the pros.
Hrrm. I was betting on that 1% chance...
HM?
Oh no! I used the wrong ball!!

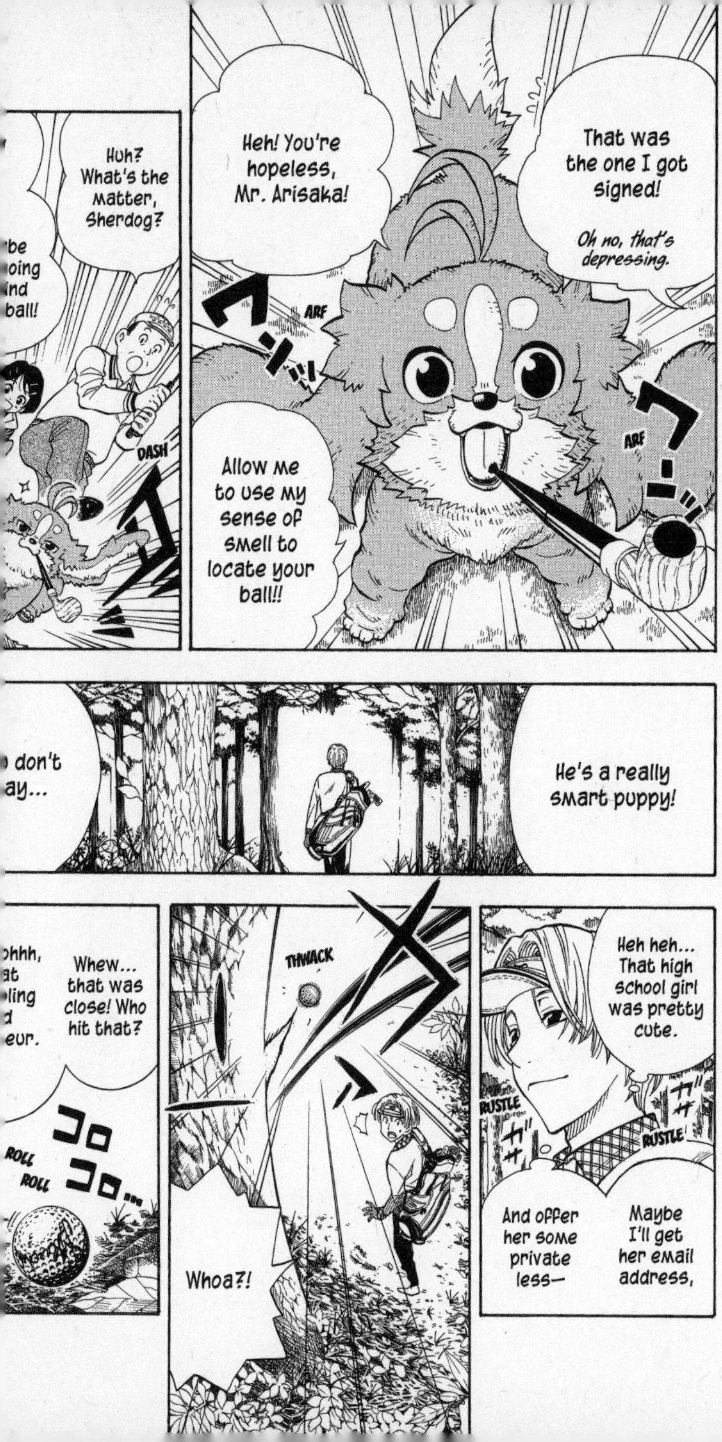
That was the one I got signed!
Oh no, that's depressing.
Heh! You're hopeless, Mr. Arisaka!
ARF
ARF
Allow me to use my sense of smell to locate your ball!!
Huh? What's the matter, Sherdog?
DASH
He's a really smart puppy!
Heh heh... That high school girl was pretty cute.
RUSTLE
RUSTLE
Maybe I'll get her email address,
And offer her some private less—
THWACK
Whoa?!
Whew... that was close! Who hit that?
ROLL
ROLL

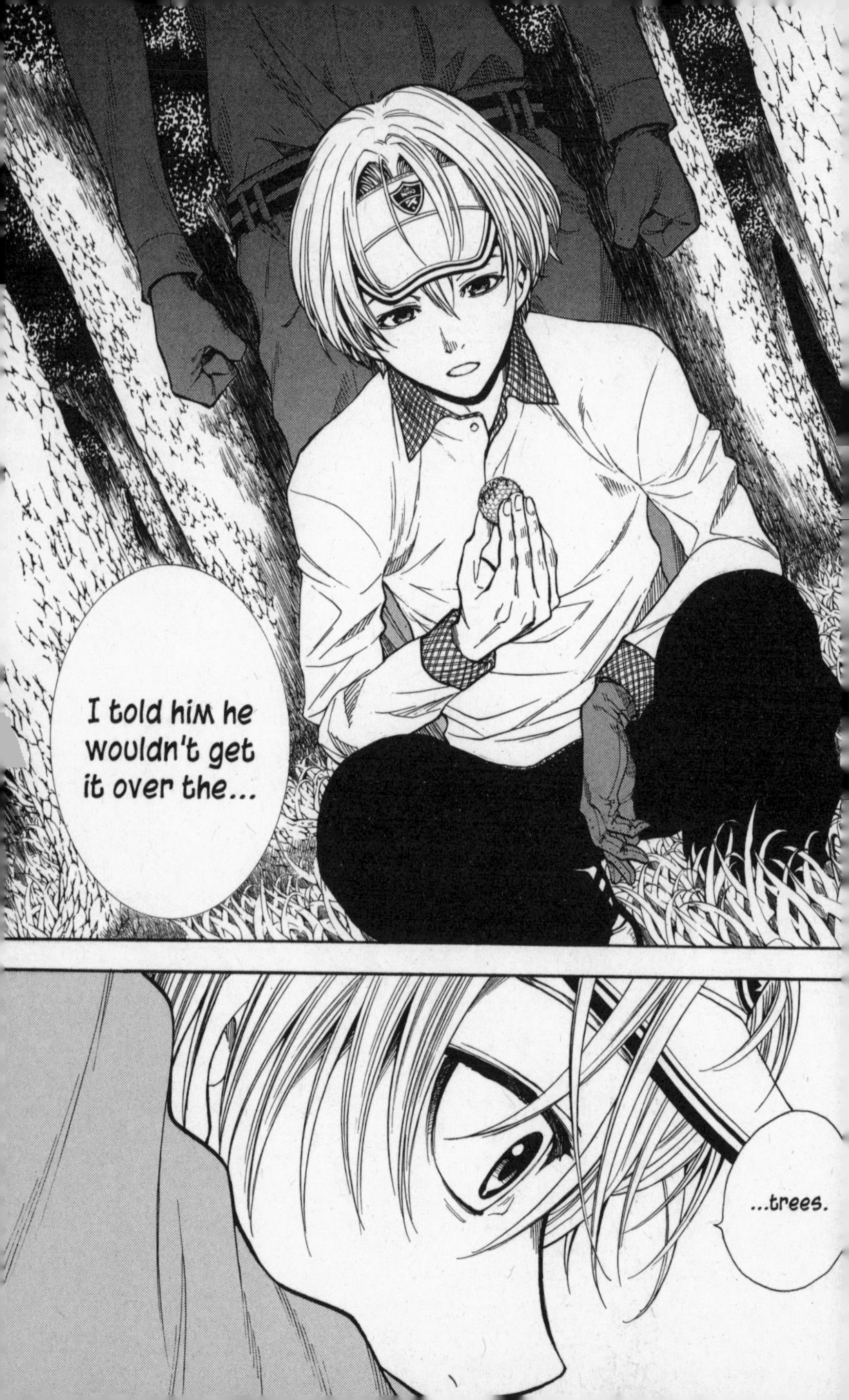
I told him he wouldn't get it over the...
...trees.

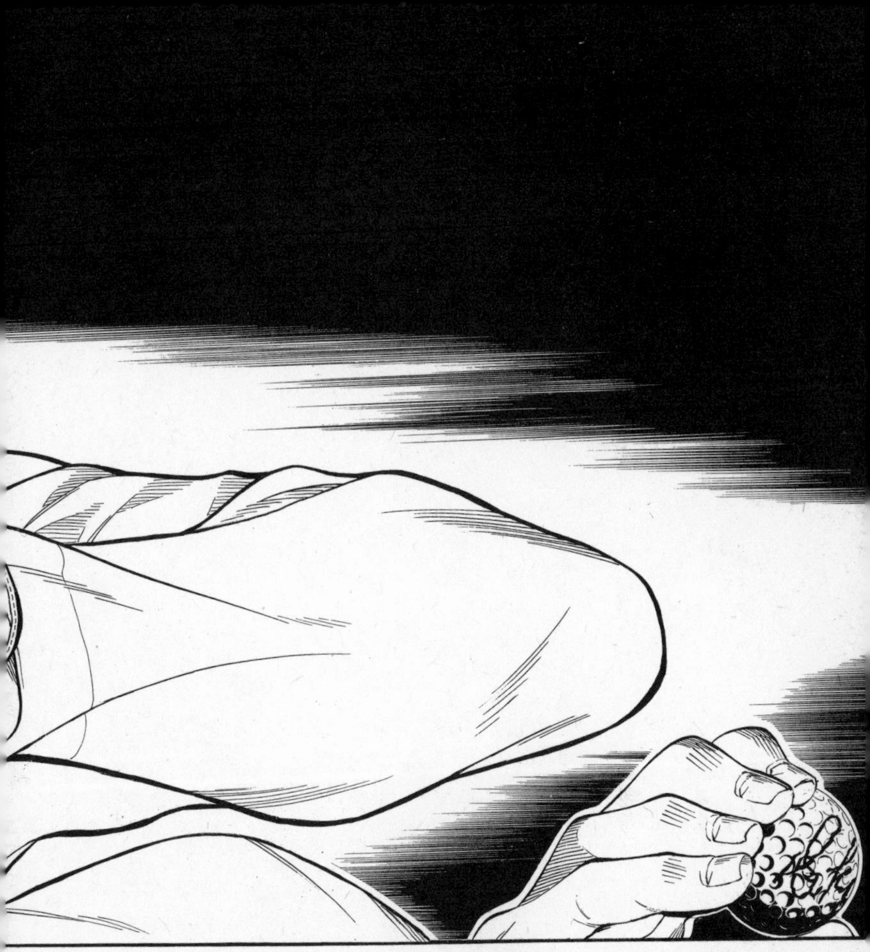

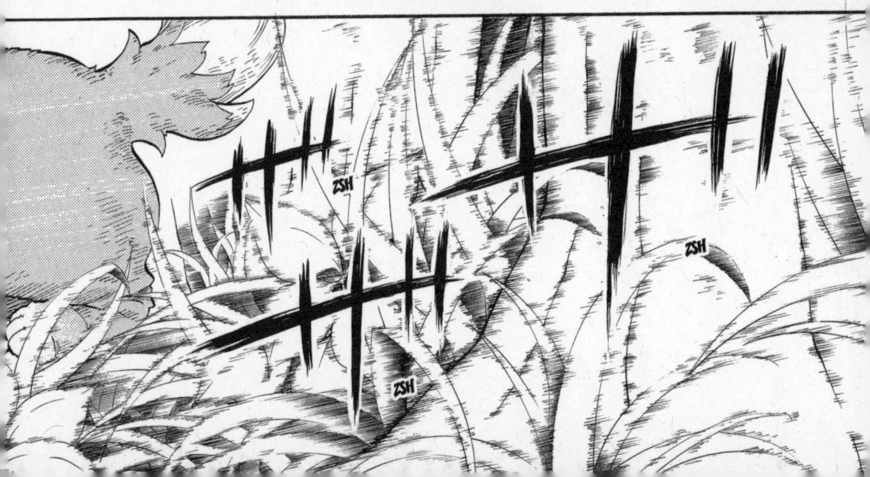
ZSH
ZSH
ZSH

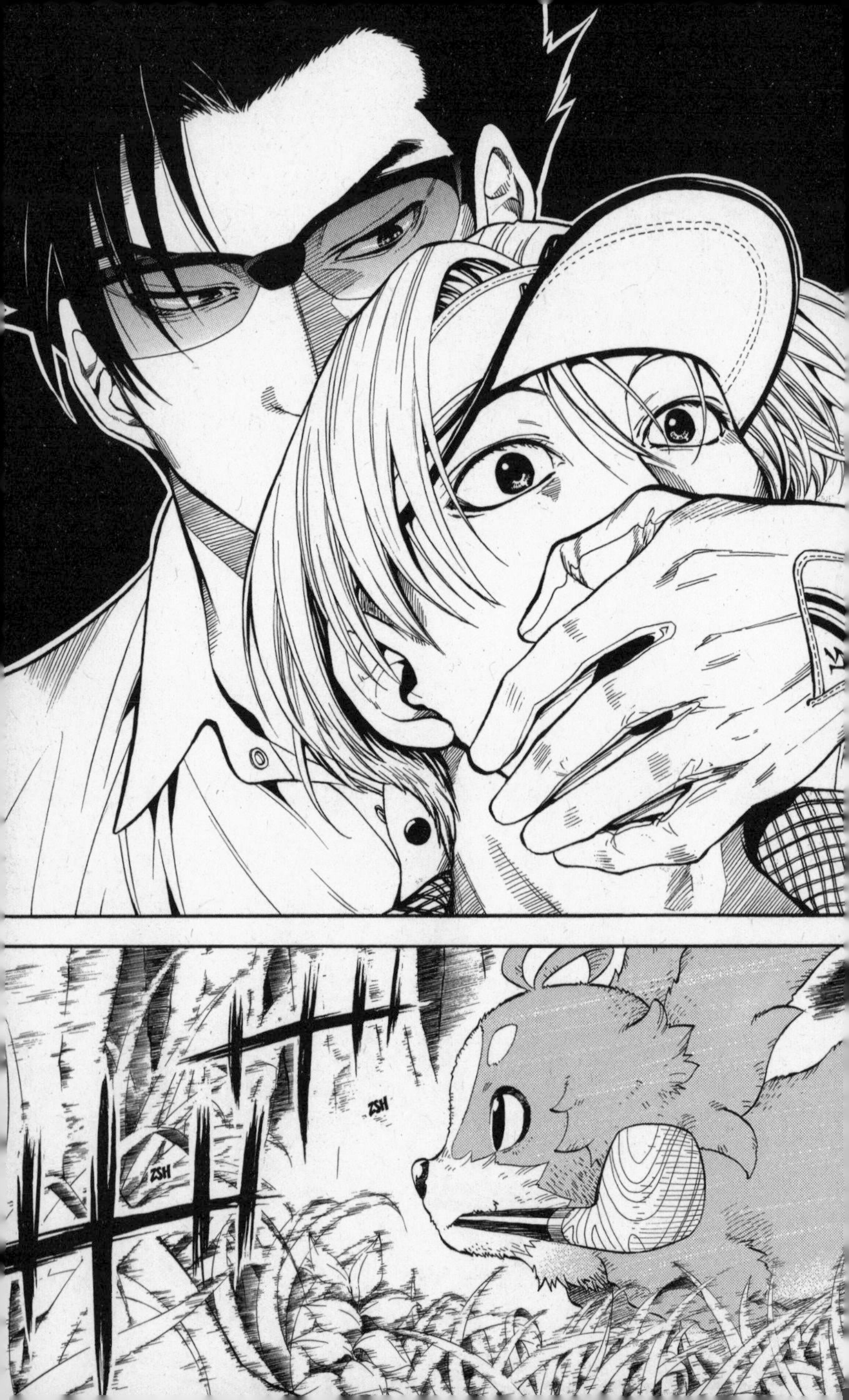
ZSH
ZSH

SHERLOCK BONES

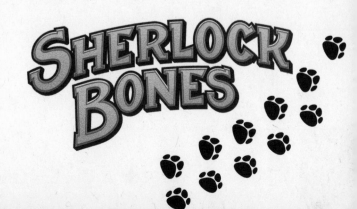

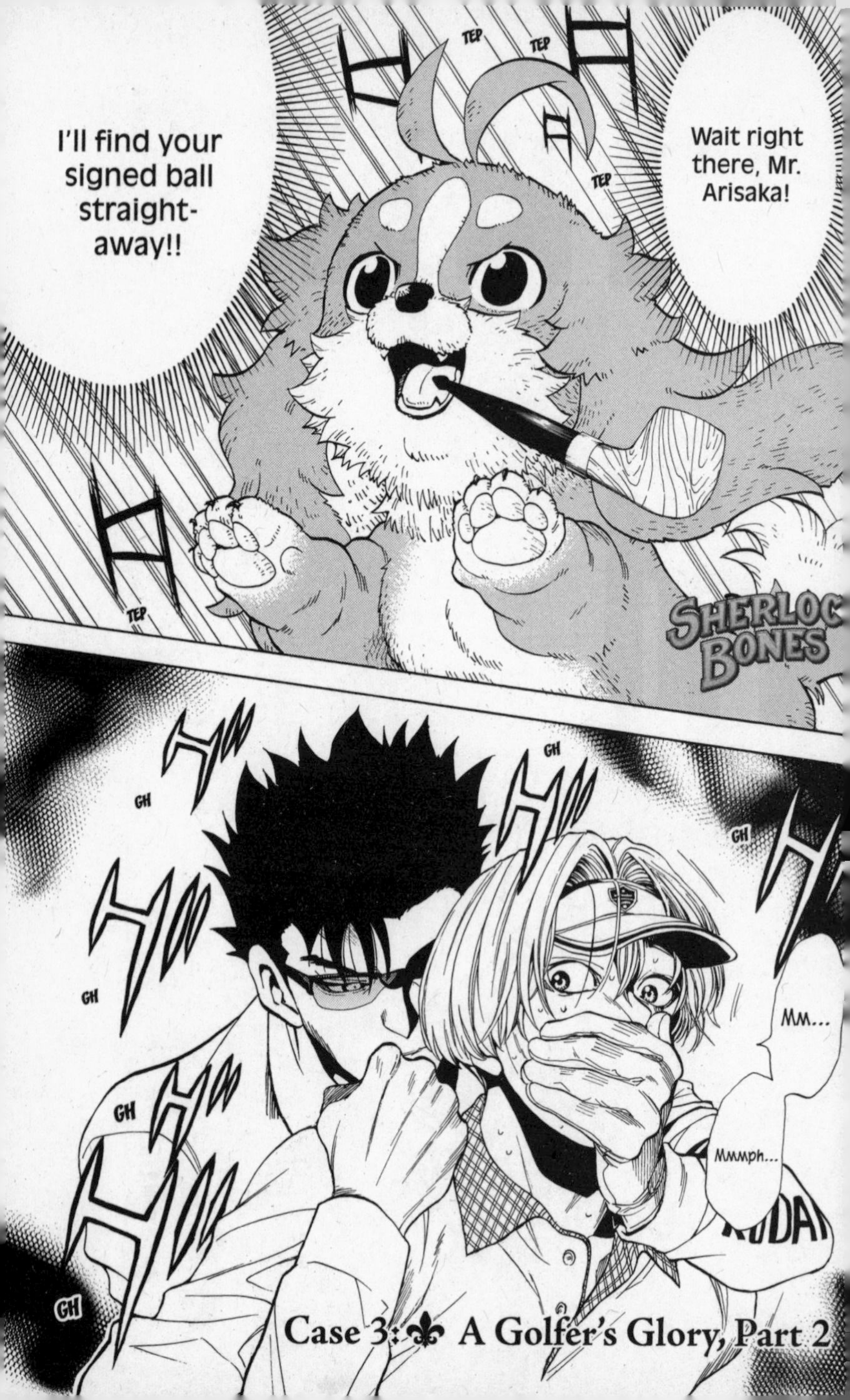
Wait right there, Mr. Arisaka!
TEP TEP
TEP
I'll find your signed ball straight-away!!
TEP
SHERLOC BONES
GH
Mm...
Mmmph...
GH
GH
GH
GH
GH
Case 3: A Golfer's Glory, Part 2

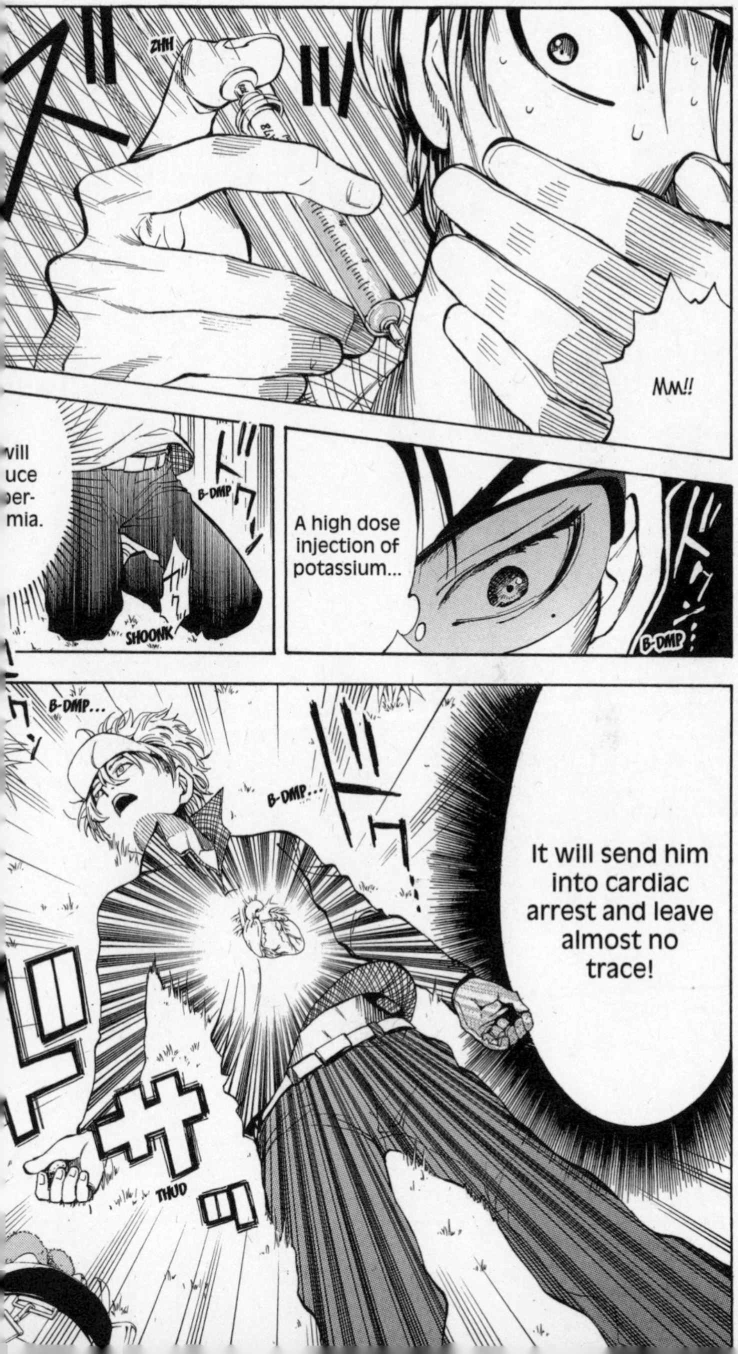
ZHH
MM!!
A high dose injection of potassium...
B-DMP
vill uce per- mia.
B-DMP
SHOONK
It will send him into cardiac arrest and leave almost no trace!
B-DMP...
B-DMP...
THUD

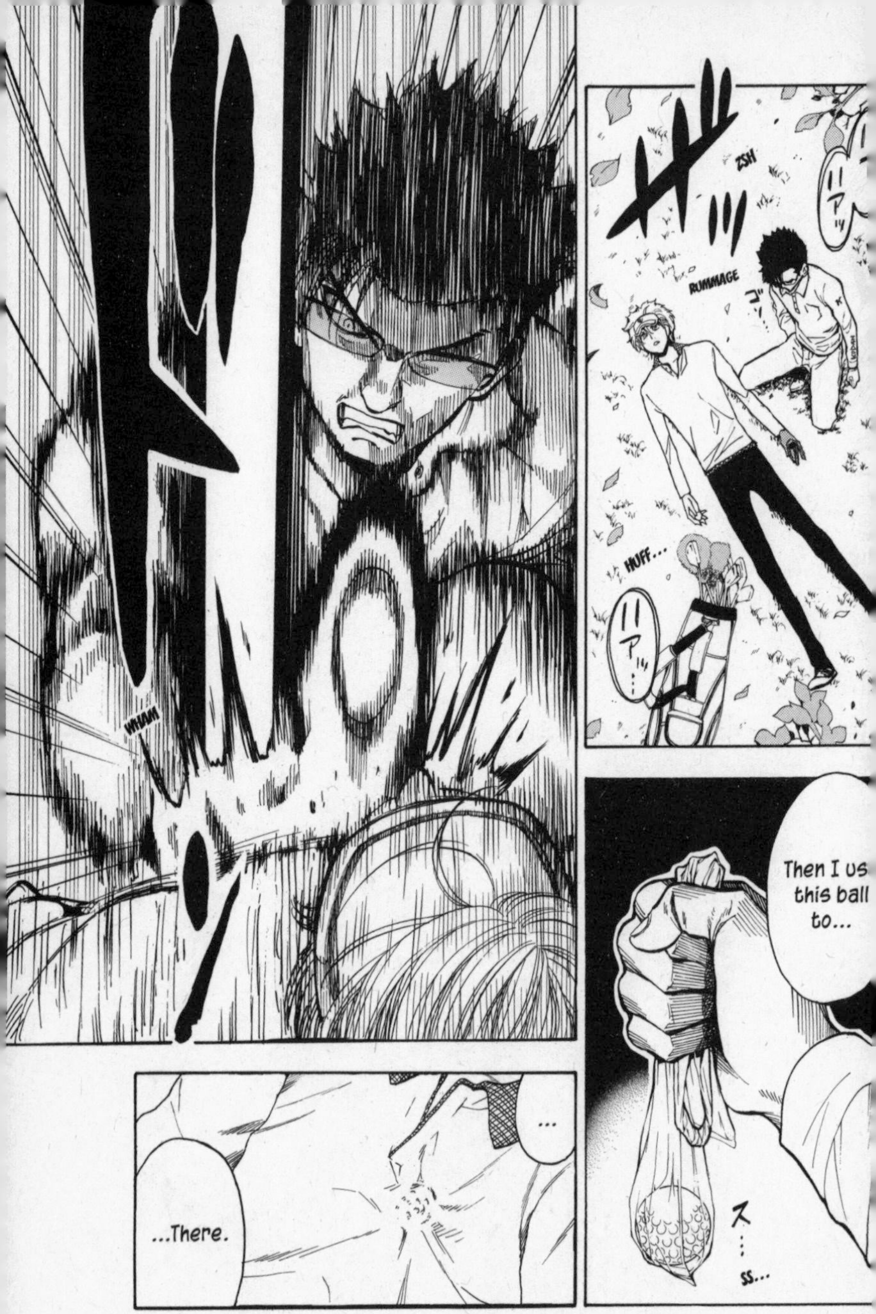
ザザッ
ZSH
ハァッ
RUMMAGE
ゴソ…
HUFF…
ハァッ…
Then I us this ball to...
ス…
SS...
WHAM
...
...There.

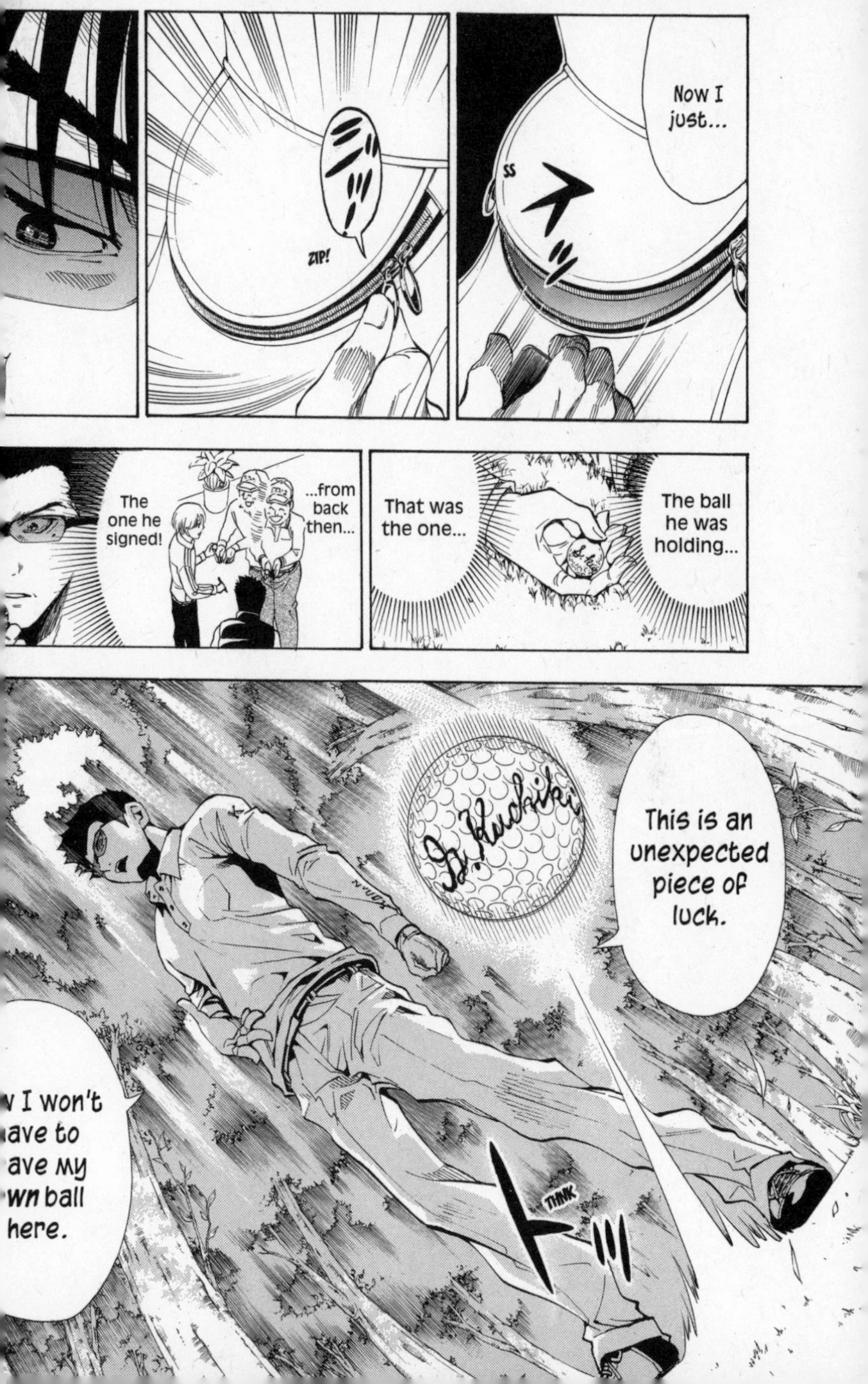

Now I just...
SS
ZIP!
The ball he was holding...
That was the one...
...from back then...
The one he signed!
This is an unexpected piece of luck.
THNK
v I won't
ave to
ave my
wn ball
here.

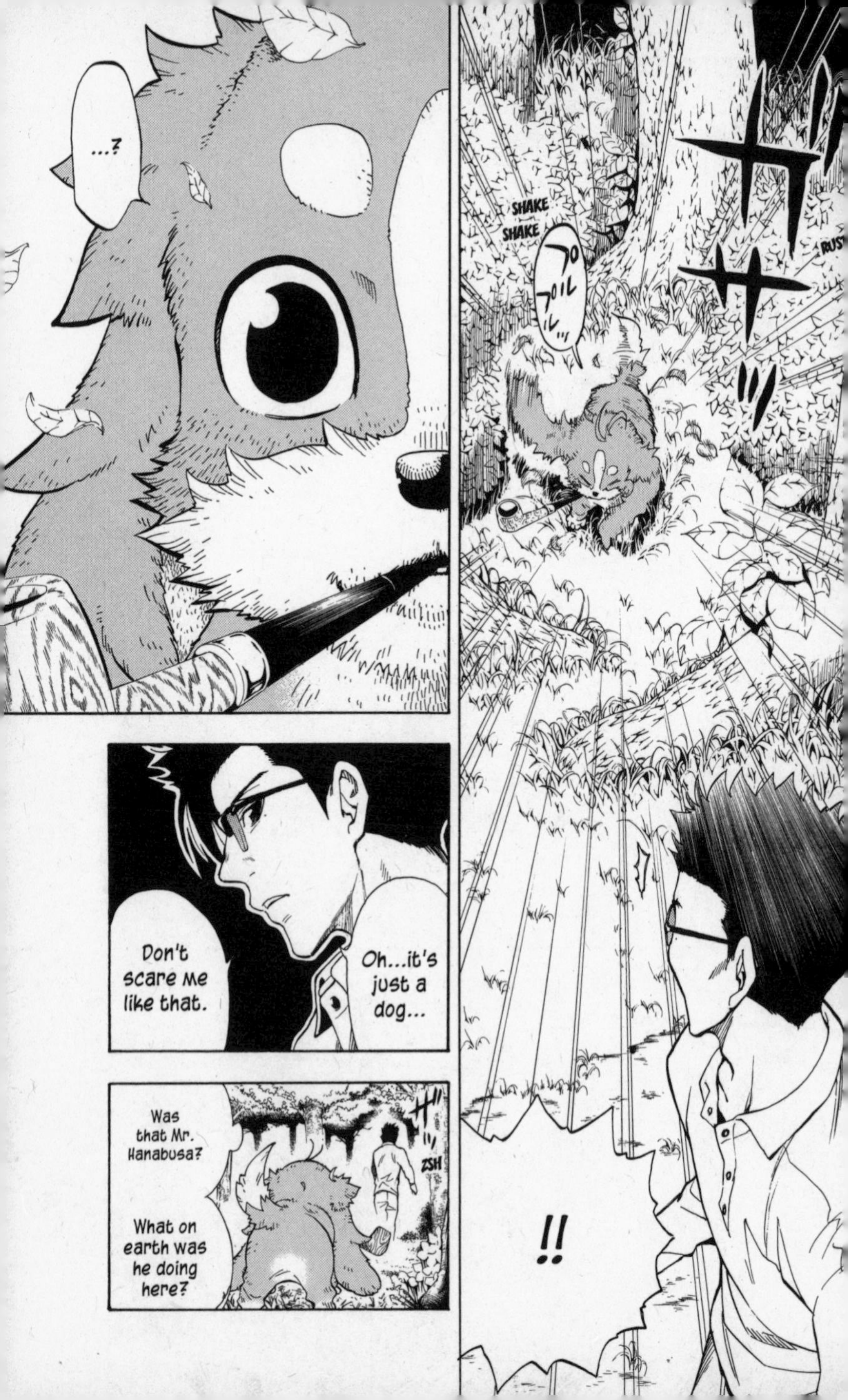
SHAKE
SHAKE
RUST
!!
...?
Oh...it's just a dog...
Don't scare me like that.
ZSH
Was that Mr. Hanabusa?
What on earth was he doing here?

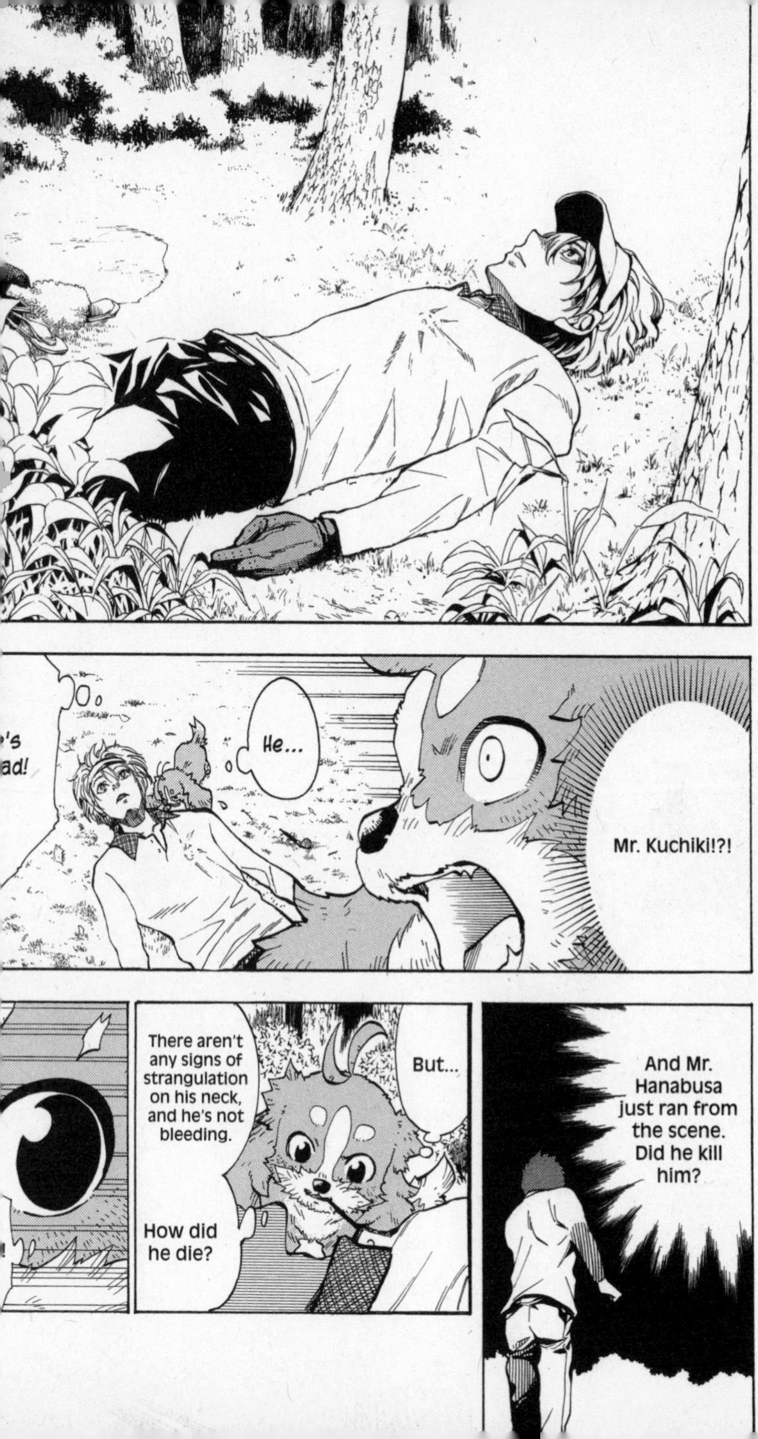
Mr. Kuchiki!?!
He...
And Mr. Hanabusa just ran from the scene. Did he kill him?
But...
There aren't any signs of strangulation on his neck, and he's not bleeding.
How did he die?

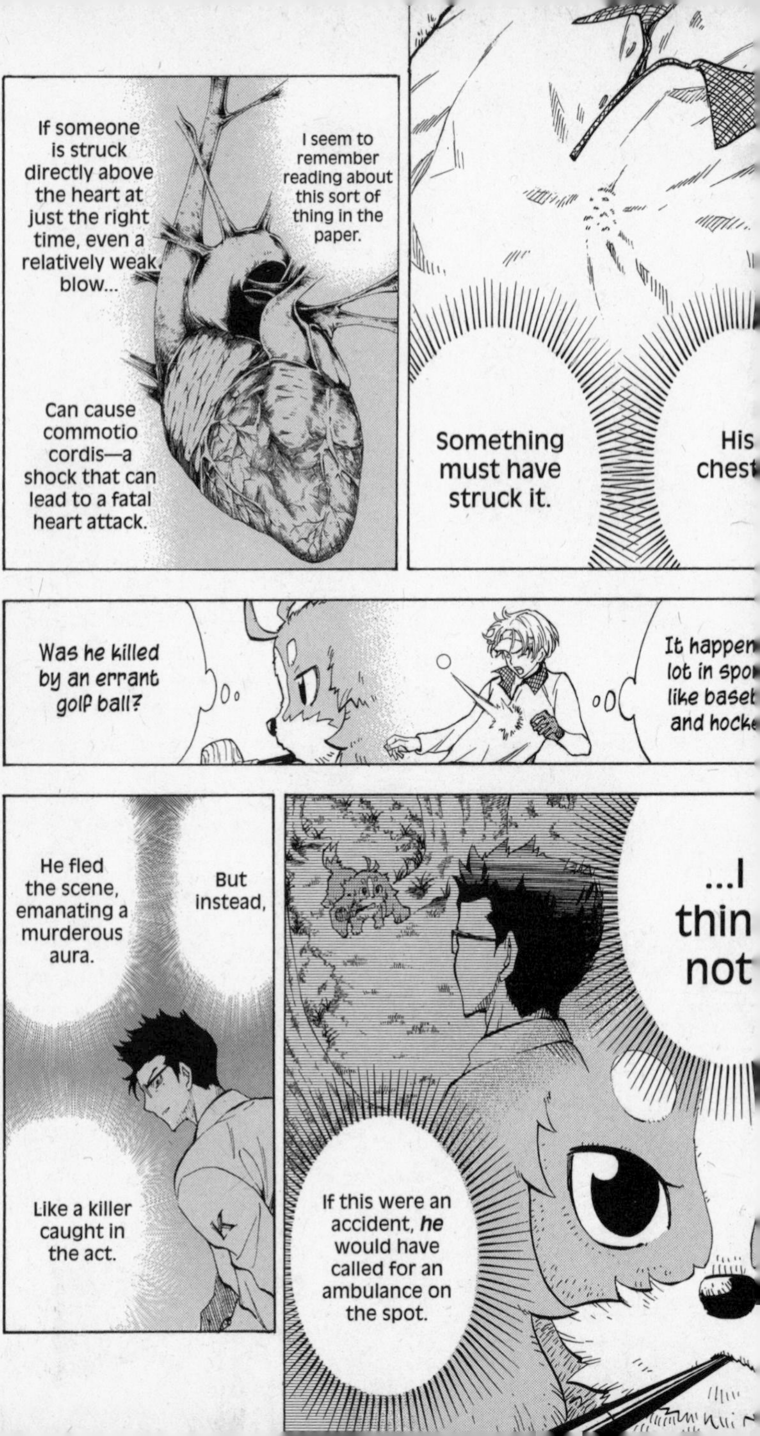

His chest
Something must have struck it.
I seem to remember reading about this sort of thing in the paper.
If someone is struck directly above the heart at just the right time, even a relatively weak blow...
Can cause commotio cordis—a shock that can lead to a fatal heart attack.
It happen lot in spo like baset and hocke
Was he killed by an errant golf ball?
...I thin not
If this were an accident, *he* would have called for an ambulance on the spot.
But instead,
He fled the scene, emanating a murderous aura.
Like a killer caught in the act.

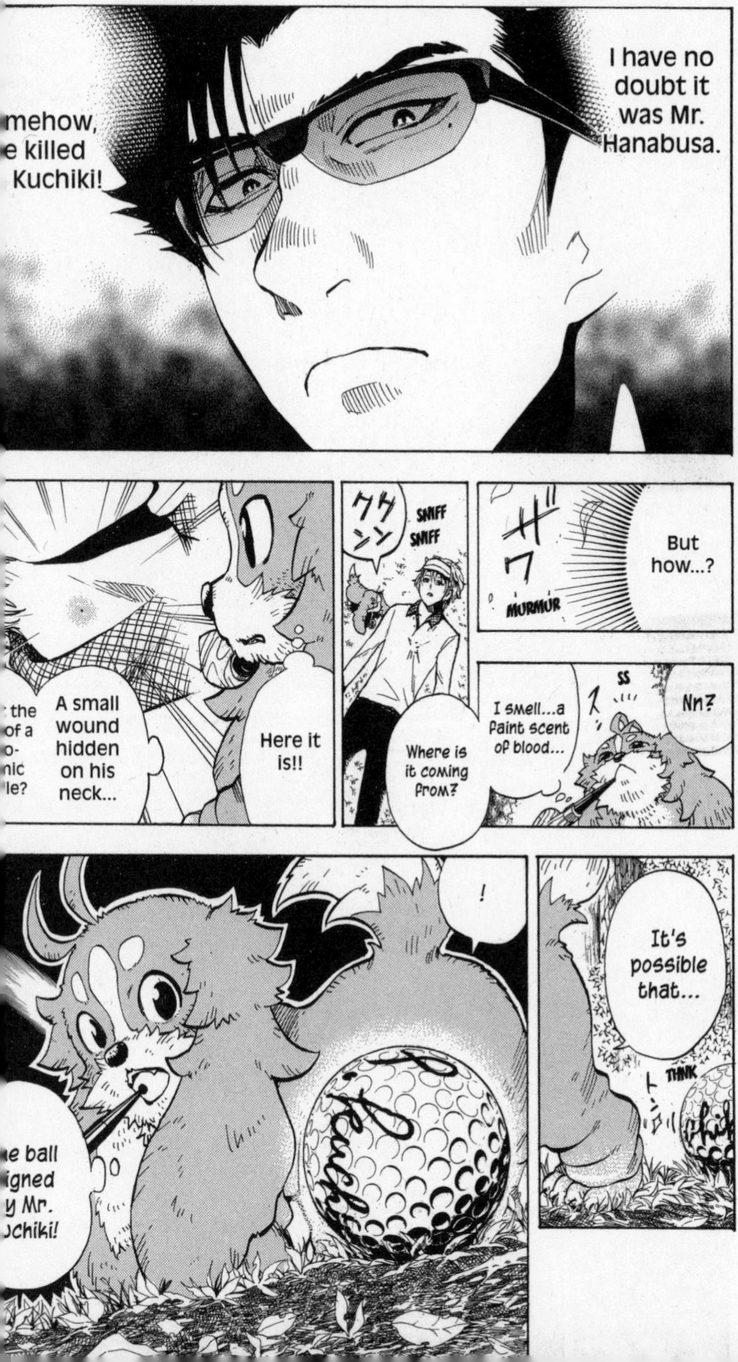
I have no doubt it was Mr. Hanabusa.
mehow, e killed Kuchiki!
ザワ
MURMUR
But how...?
SS
Nn?
I smell...a faint scent of blood...
クンクン
SNIFF SNIFF
Where is it coming from?
Here it is!!
A small wound hidden on his neck...
the of a o- nic le?
THINK
It's possible that...
!
e ball igned y Mr. uchiki!

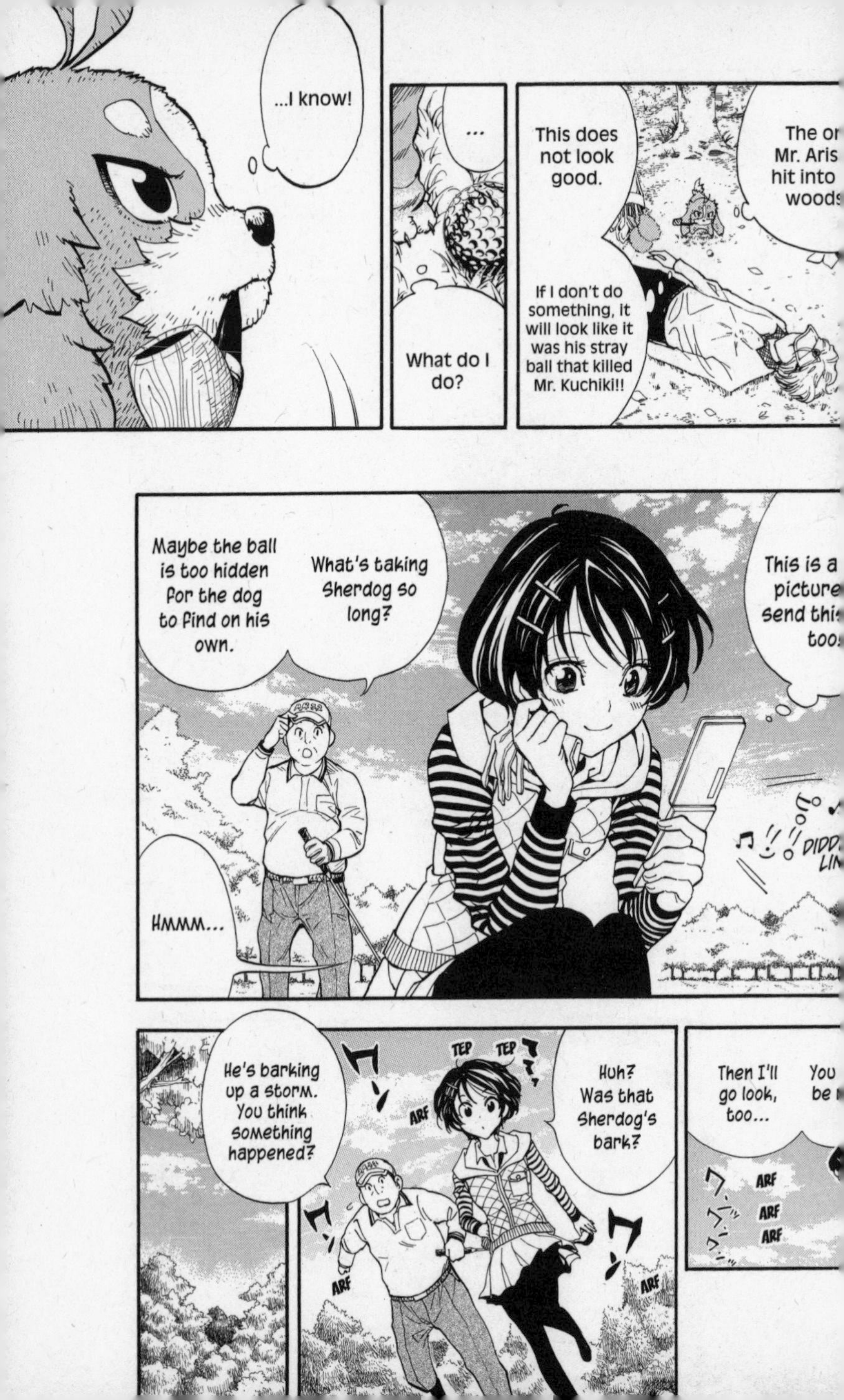
The or Mr. Aris hit into woods
This does not look good.
If I don't do something, it will look like it was his stray ball that killed Mr. Kuchiki!!
...
What do I do?
...I know!
This is a picture send thi too
DIDD LIN
What's taking Sherdog so long?
Maybe the ball is too hidden for the dog to find on his own.
HMMM...
You be
Then I'll go look, too...
ARF
ARF
ARF
TEP TEP
Huh? Was that Sherdog's bark?
ARF
He's barking up a storm. You think something happened?
ARF
ARF

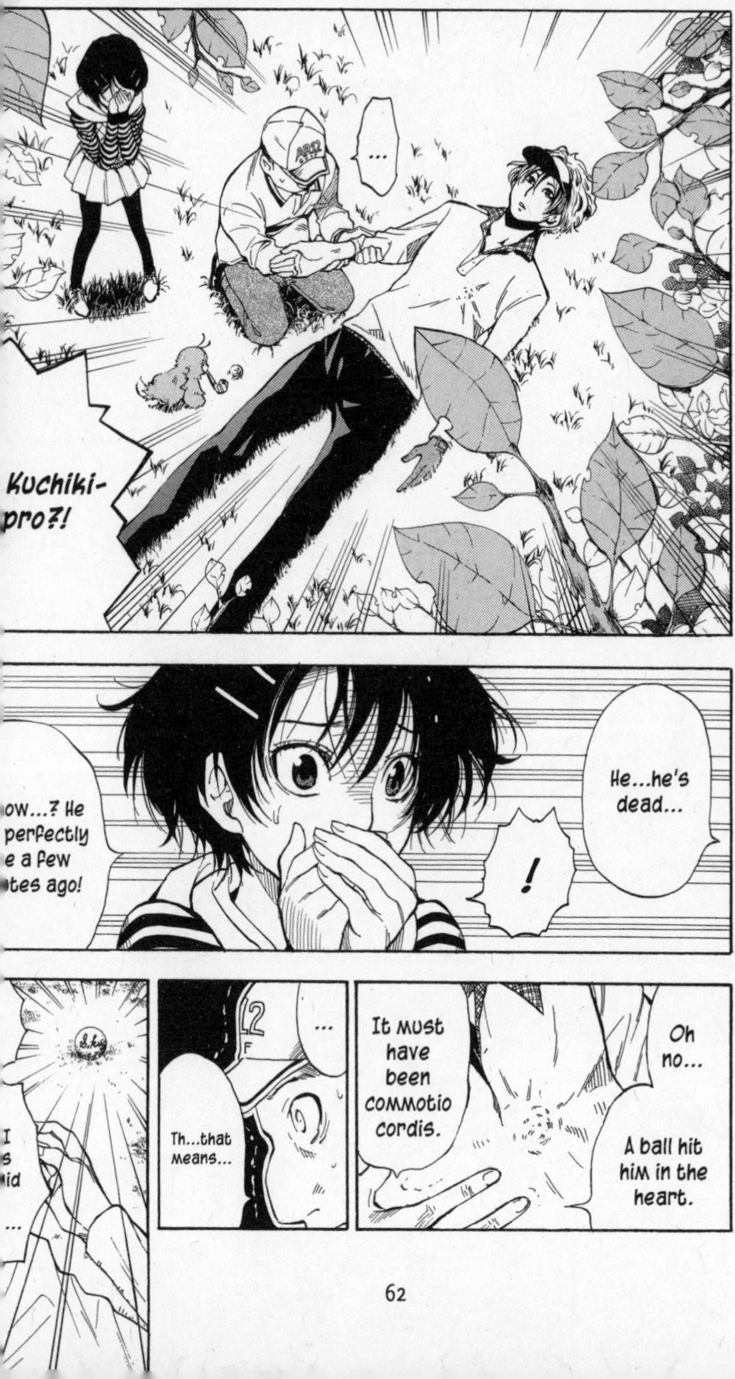

...
Kuchiki-pro?!
He...he's dead...
!
ow...? He
perfectly
e a few
otes ago!
Oh no...
A ball hit him in the heart.
It must have been commotio cordis.
...
Th...that means...
I
s
id
...

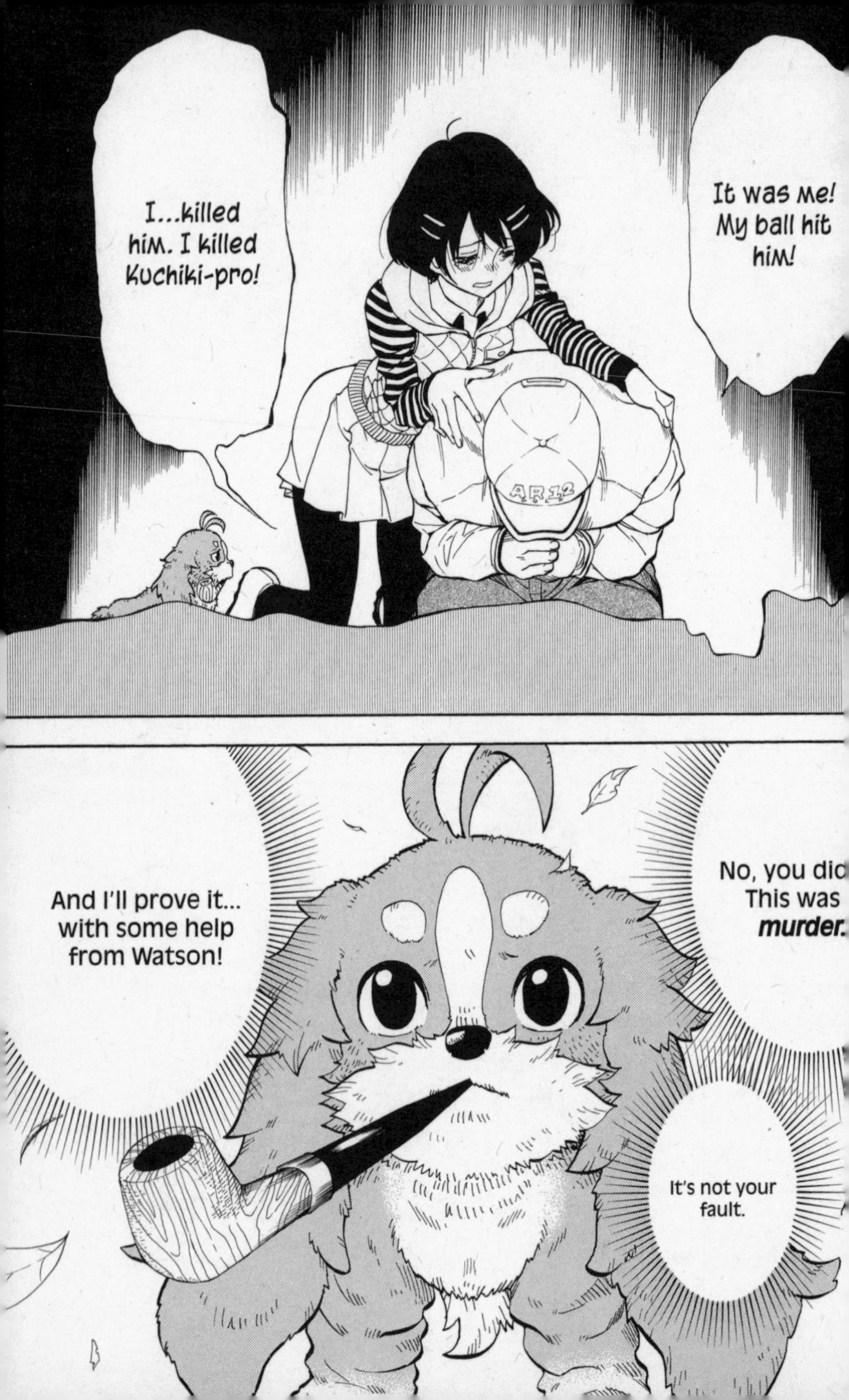
It was me! My ball hit him!
I...killed him. I killed Kuchiki-pro!
No, you did
This was *murder.*
It's not your fault.
And I'll prove it... with some help from Watson!

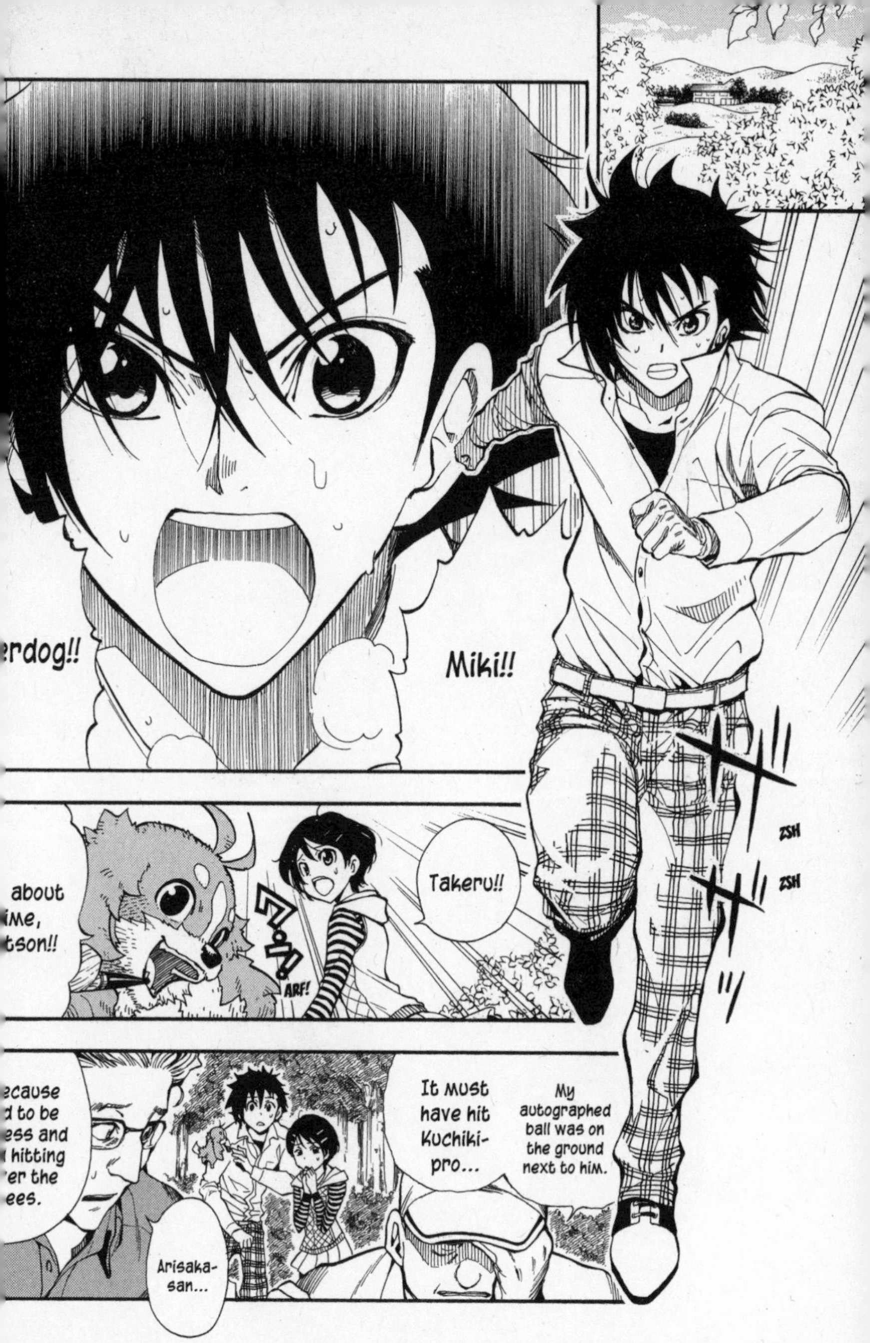
ZSH
ZSH
Miki!!
erdog!!
Takeru!!
?!
ARF!
about
ime,
tson!!
My autographed ball was on the ground next to him.
It must have hit Kuchiki-pro...
Arisaka-san...
ecause
d to be
ess and
hitting
er the
ees.

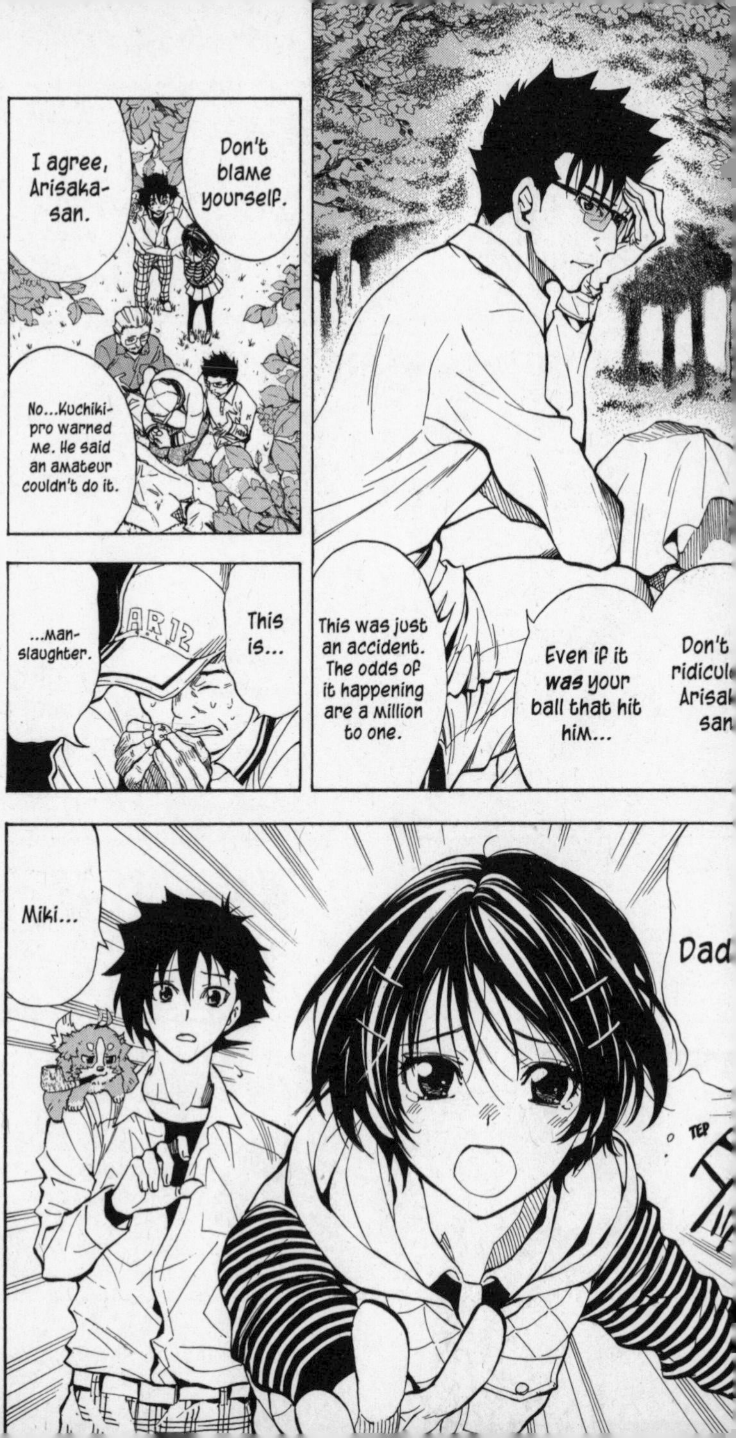

Don't ridicul Arisak san
Even if it was your ball that hit him...
This was just an accident. The odds of it happening are a million to one.
Don't blame yourself.
I agree, Arisaka-san.
No...Kuchiki-pro warned me. He said an amateur couldn't do it.
This is...
...man-slaughter.
Dad
TEP
Miki...

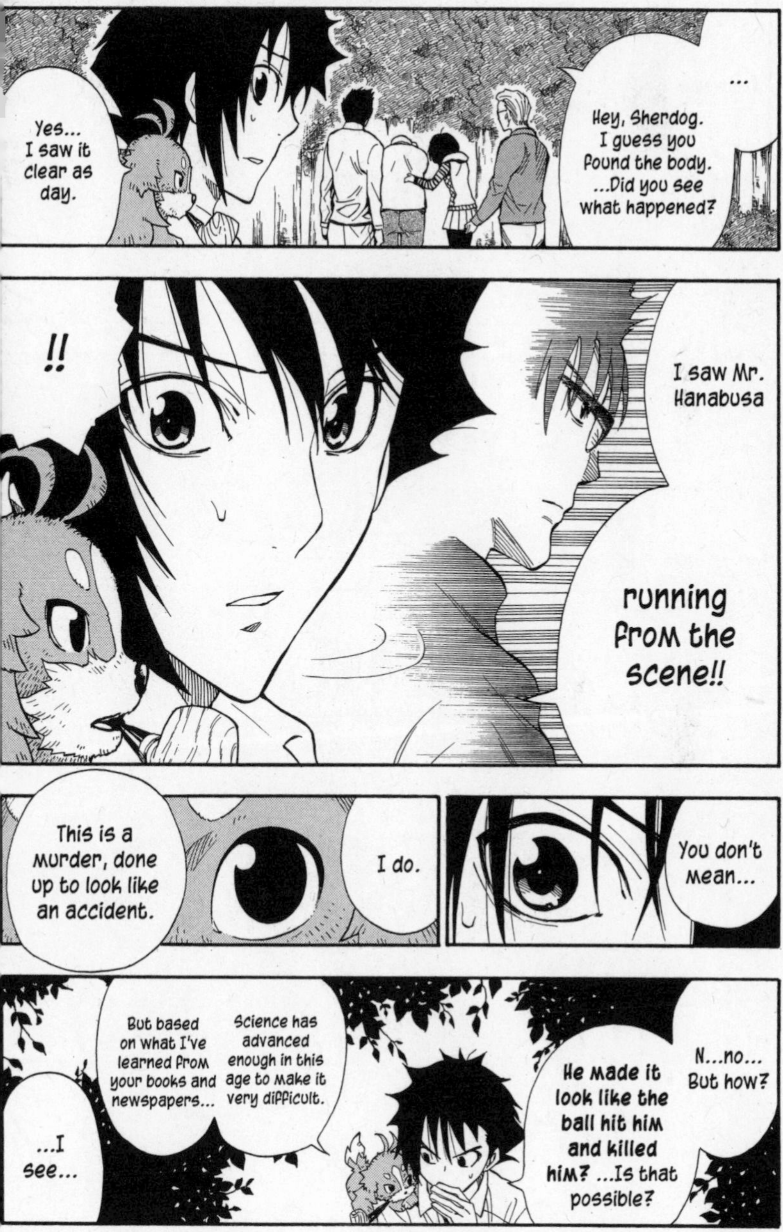
...
Hey, Sherdog. I guess you found the body. ...Did you see what happened?
Yes... I saw it clear as day.
I saw Mr. Hanabusa
running from the scene!!
!!
You don't mean...
I do.
This is a murder, done up to look like an accident.
N...no... But how?
He made it look like the ball hit him and killed him? ...Is that possible?
Science has advanced enough in this age to make it very difficult.
But based on what I've learned from your books and newspapers...
...I see...

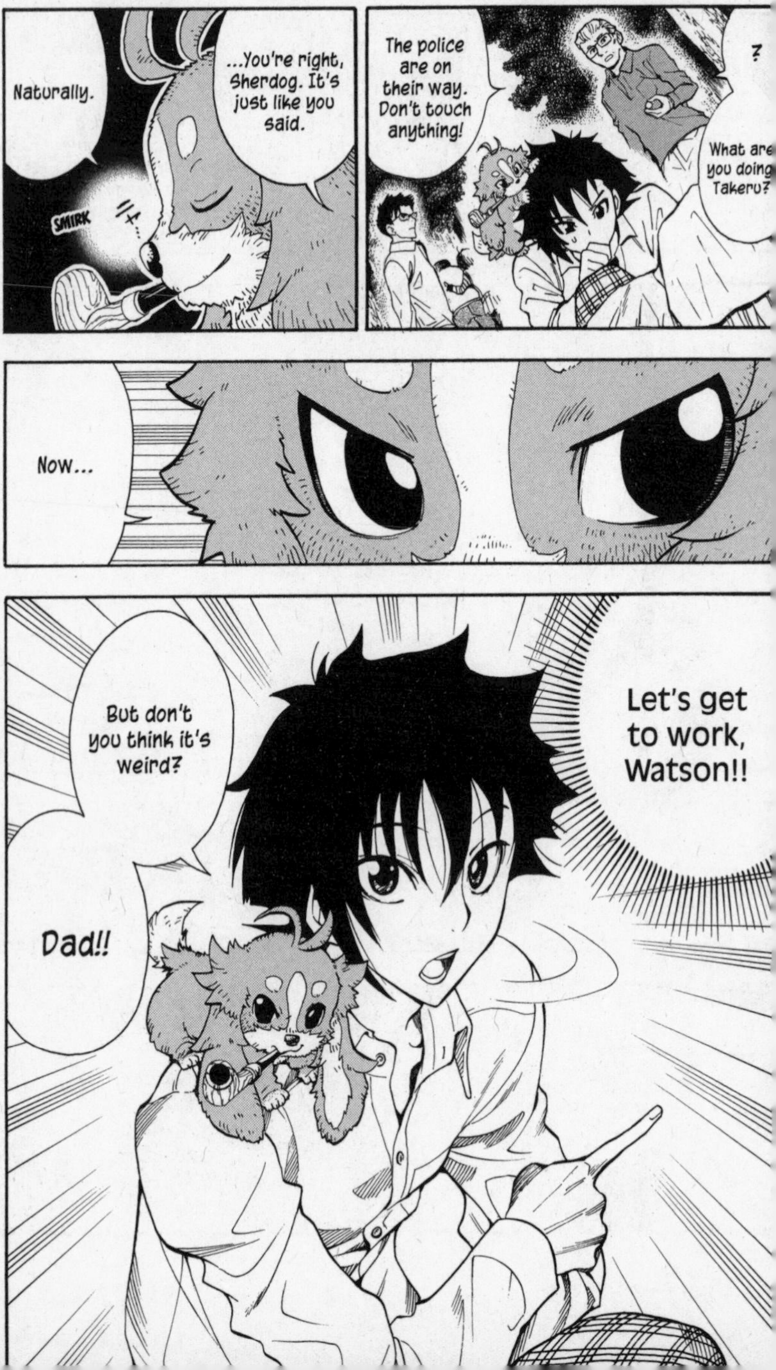
?
What are you doing Takeru?
The police are on their way. Don't touch anything!
...You're right, Sherdog. It's just like you said.
Naturally.
SMIRK
Now...
Let's get to work, Watson!!
But don't you think it's weird?
Dad!!

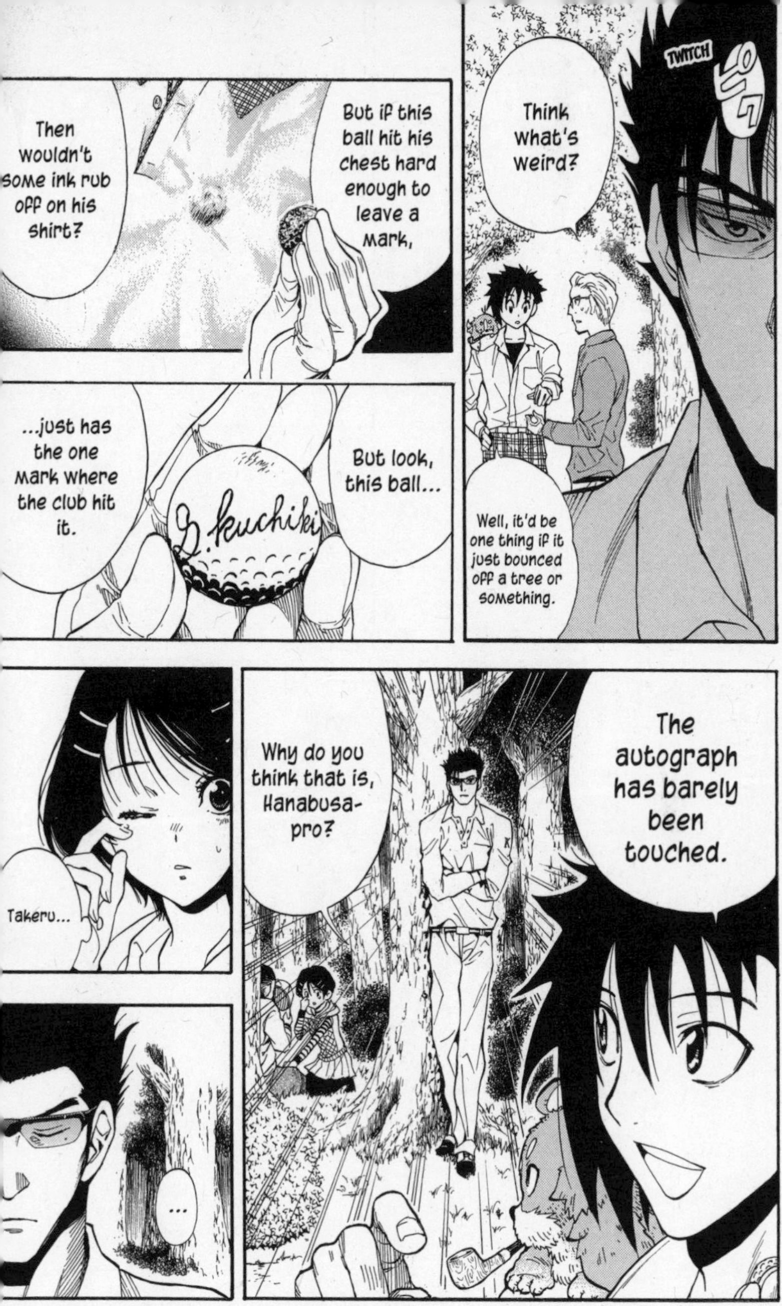
TWITCH
Think what's weird?
Well, it'd be one thing if it just bounced off a tree or something.
But if this ball hit his chest hard enough to leave a mark,
Then wouldn't some ink rub off on his shirt?
But look, this ball...
G. kuchiki
...just has the one mark where the club hit it.
The autograph has barely been touched.
Why do you think that is, Hanabusa-pro?
Takeru...
...

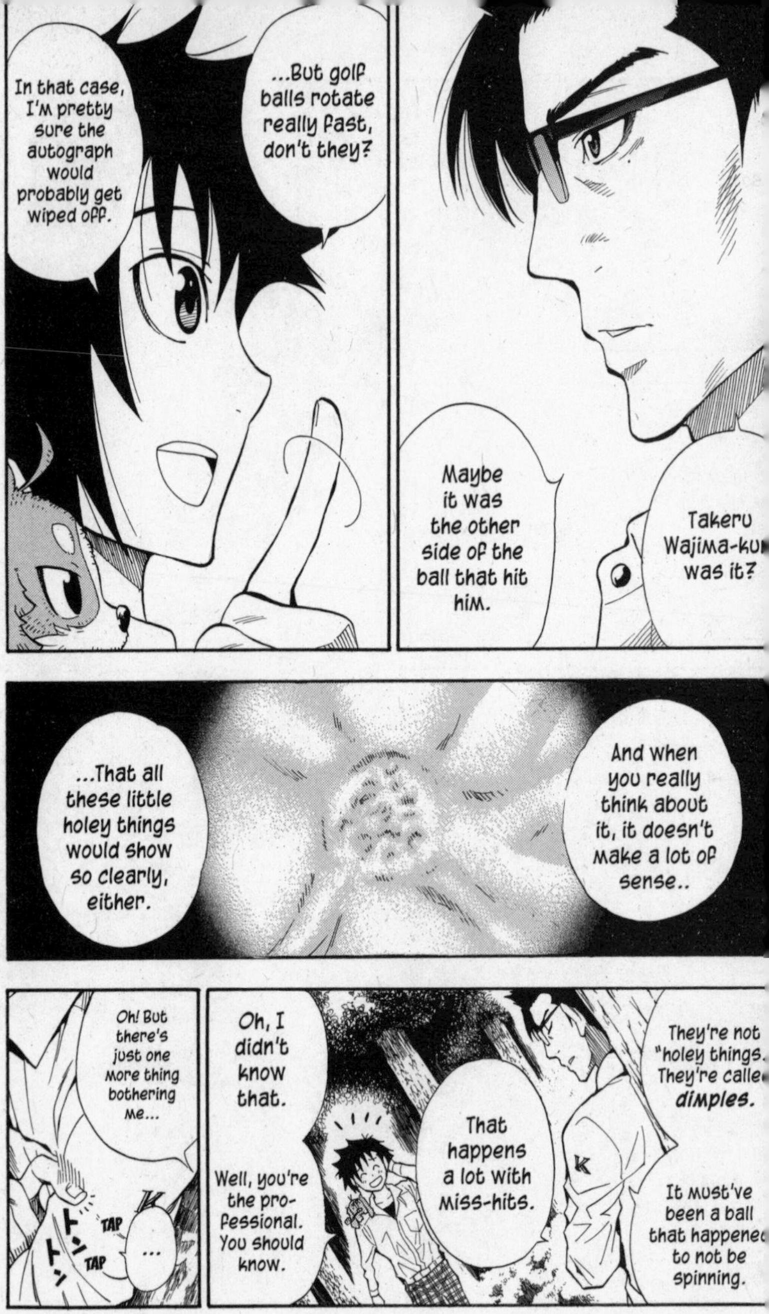
Takeru Wajima-ku was it?
Maybe it was the other side of the ball that hit him.
...But golf balls rotate really fast, don't they?
In that case, I'm pretty sure the autograph would probably get wiped off.
And when you really think about it, it doesn't make a lot of sense..
...That all these little holey things would show so clearly, either.
They're not "holey things. They're callec dimples.
It must've been a ball that happenec to not be spinning.
That happens a lot with miss-hits.
Oh, I didn't know that.
Well, you're the pro-fessional. You should know.
Oh! But there's just one more thing bothering me...
...
TAP
TAP

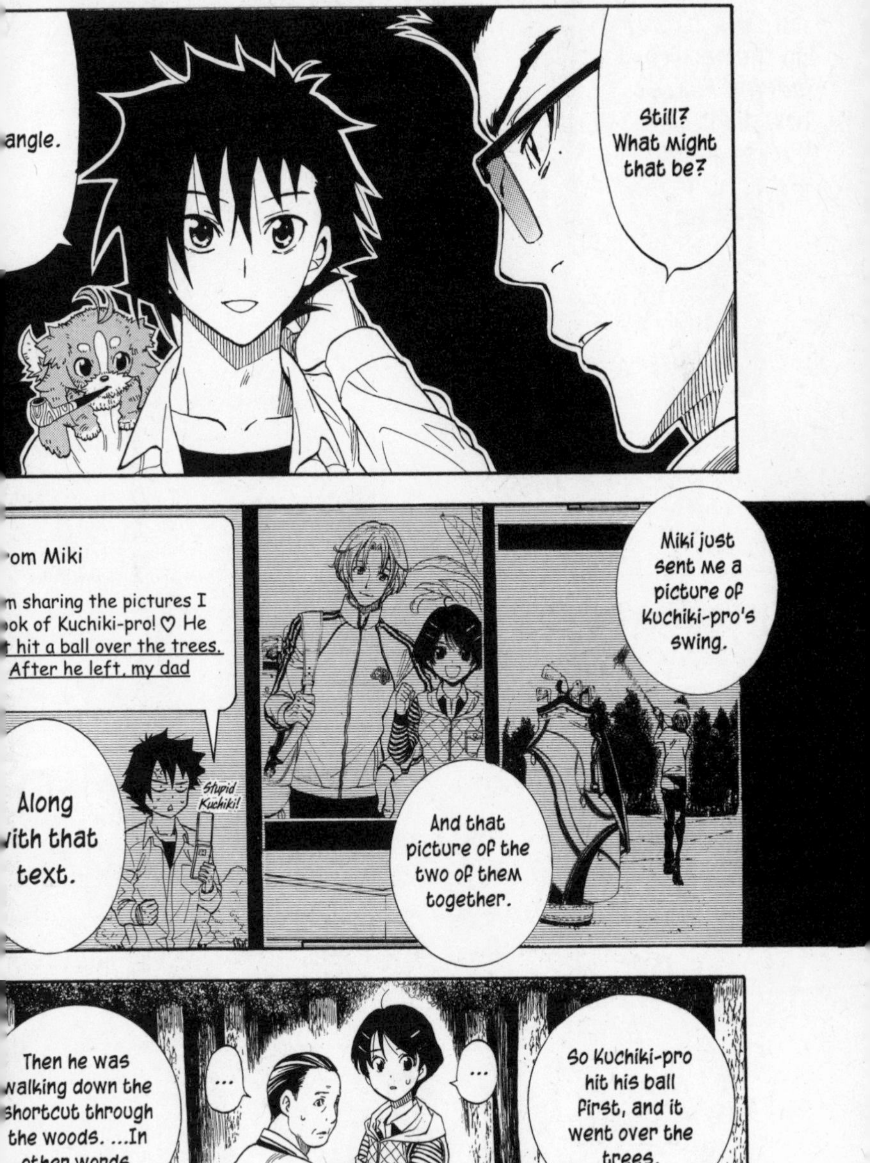
Still? What might that be?
angle.
Miki just sent me a picture of Kuchiki-pro's swing.
And that picture of the two of them together.
rom Miki
n sharing the pictures I
ook of Kuchiki-pro! ♡ He
hit a ball over the trees.
After he left, my dad
Stupid Kuchiki!
Along
ith that
text.
So Kuchiki-pro hit his ball first, and it went over the trees.
...
...
Then he was
alking down the
hortcut through
the woods. ...In
other words,

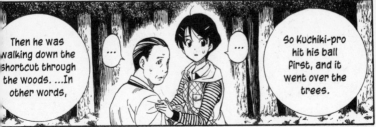

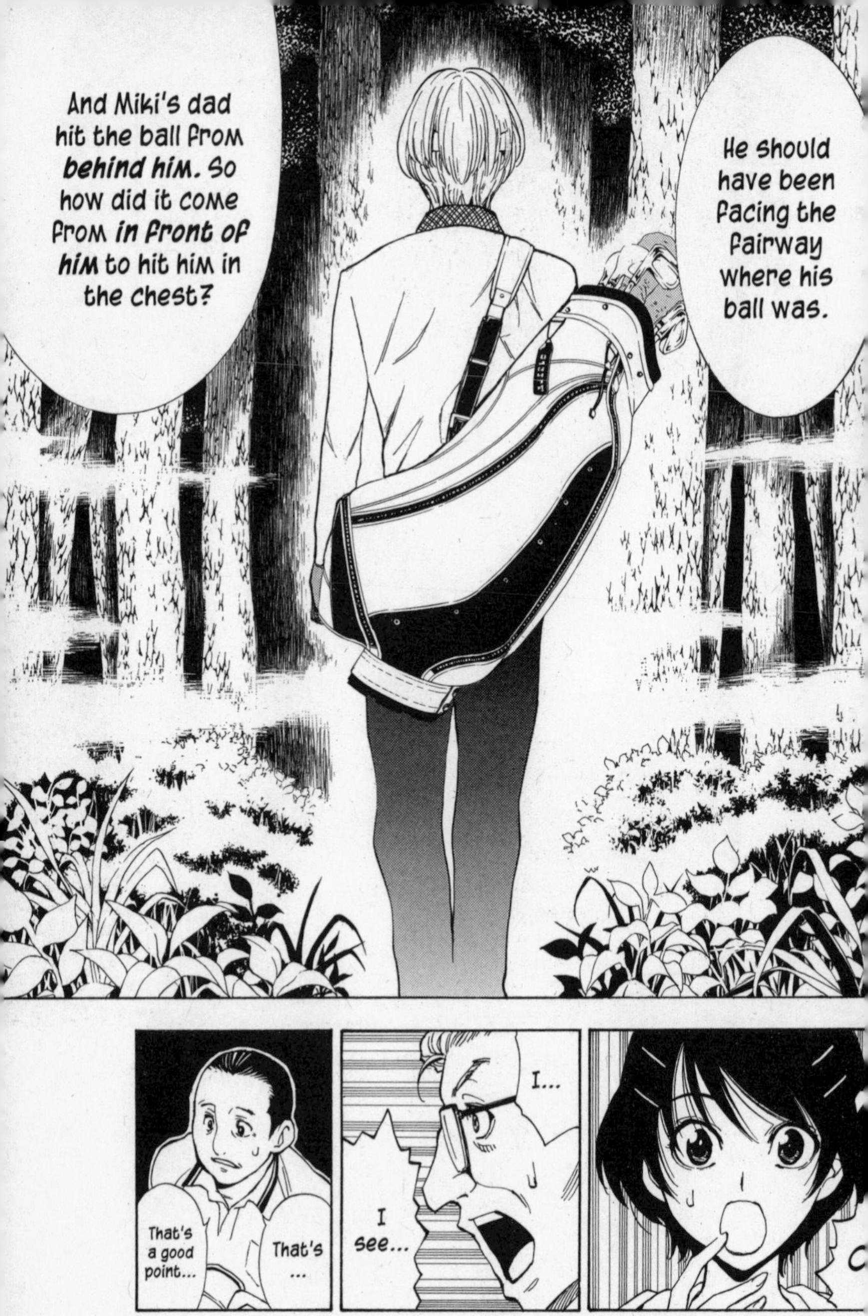
He should have been facing the fairway where his ball was.
And Miki's dad hit the ball from ***behind him.*** So how did it come from ***in front of him*** to hit him in the chest?
C
I...
I see...
That's...
That's a good point...

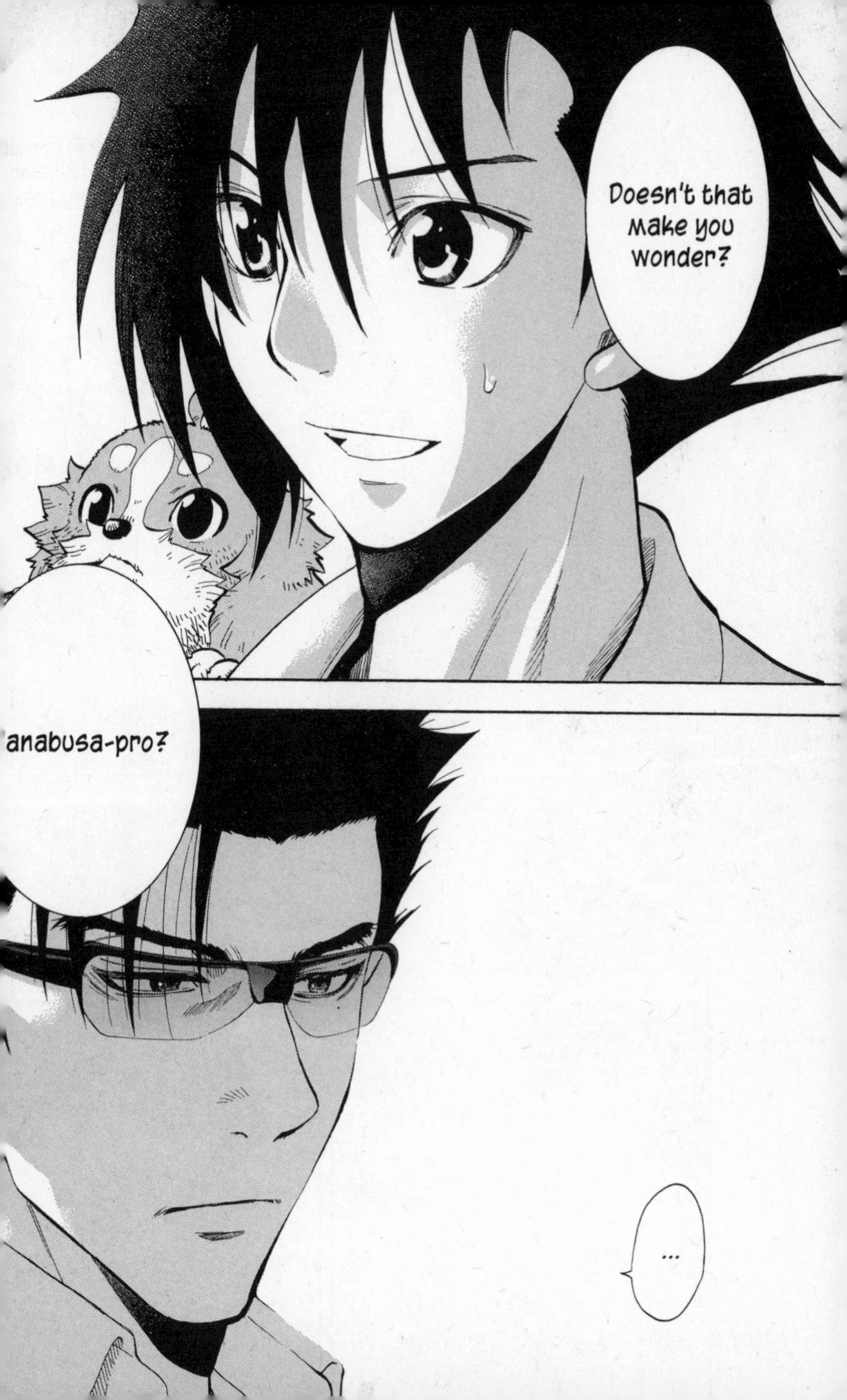
Doesn't that make you wonder?
anabusa-pro?
...

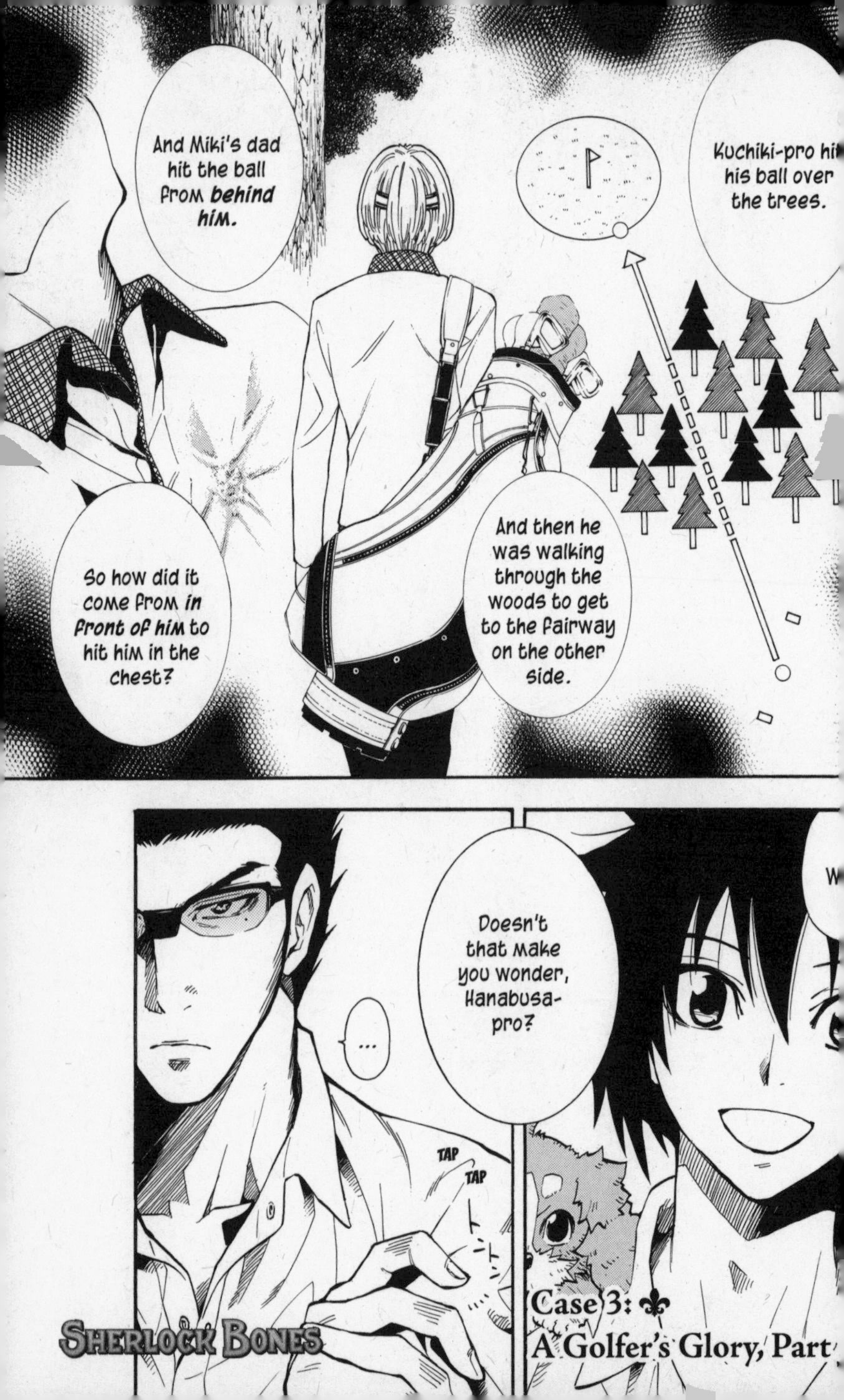
Kuchiki-pro hi his ball over the trees.
And then he was walking through the woods to get to the fairway on the other side.
And Miki's dad hit the ball from *behind him.*
So how did it come from *in front of him* to hit him in the chest?
Doesn't that make you wonder, Hanabusa-pro?
Case 3:
A Golfer's Glory, Part
...
TAP
TAP
Sherlock Bones

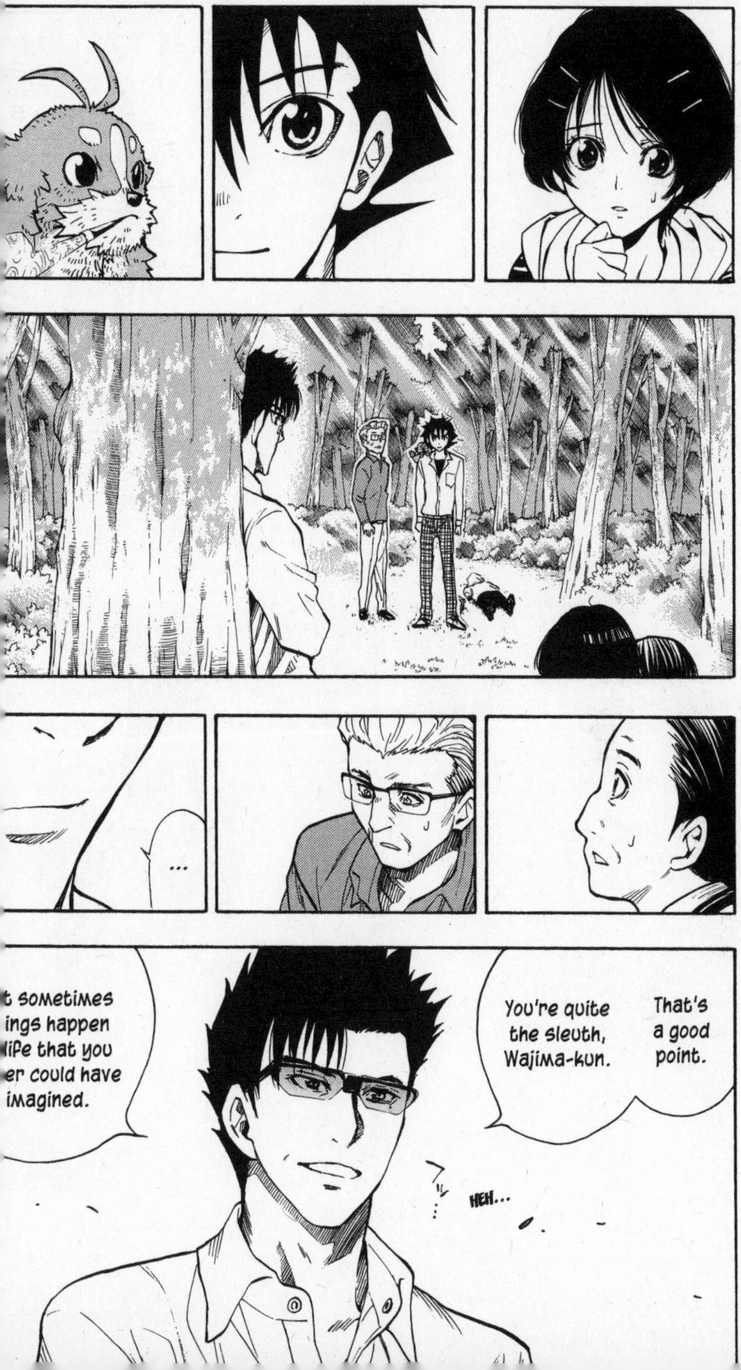
...
That's a good point.
You're quite the sleuth, Wajima-kun.
t sometimes ings happen life that you er could have imagined.
HEH...

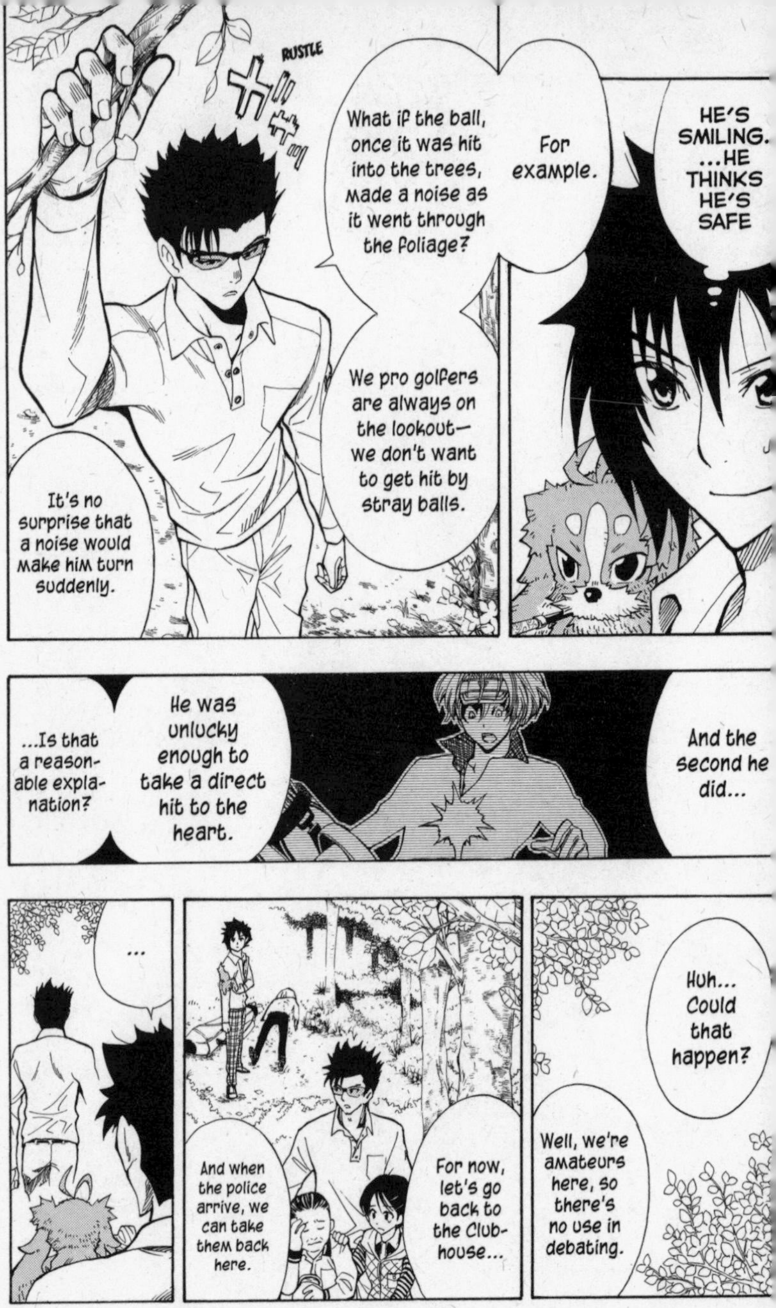
HE'S SMILING. ...HE THINKS HE'S SAFE
For example.
What if the ball, once it was hit into the trees, made a noise as it went through the foliage?
RUSTLE
We pro golfers are always on the lookout— we don't want to get hit by stray balls.
It's no surprise that a noise would make him turn suddenly.
And the second he did...
He was unlucky enough to take a direct hit to the heart.
...Is that a reason-able expla-nation?
Huh... Could that happen?
Well, we're amateurs here, so there's no use in debating.
For now, let's go back to the Club-house...
And when the police arrive, we can take them back here.
...

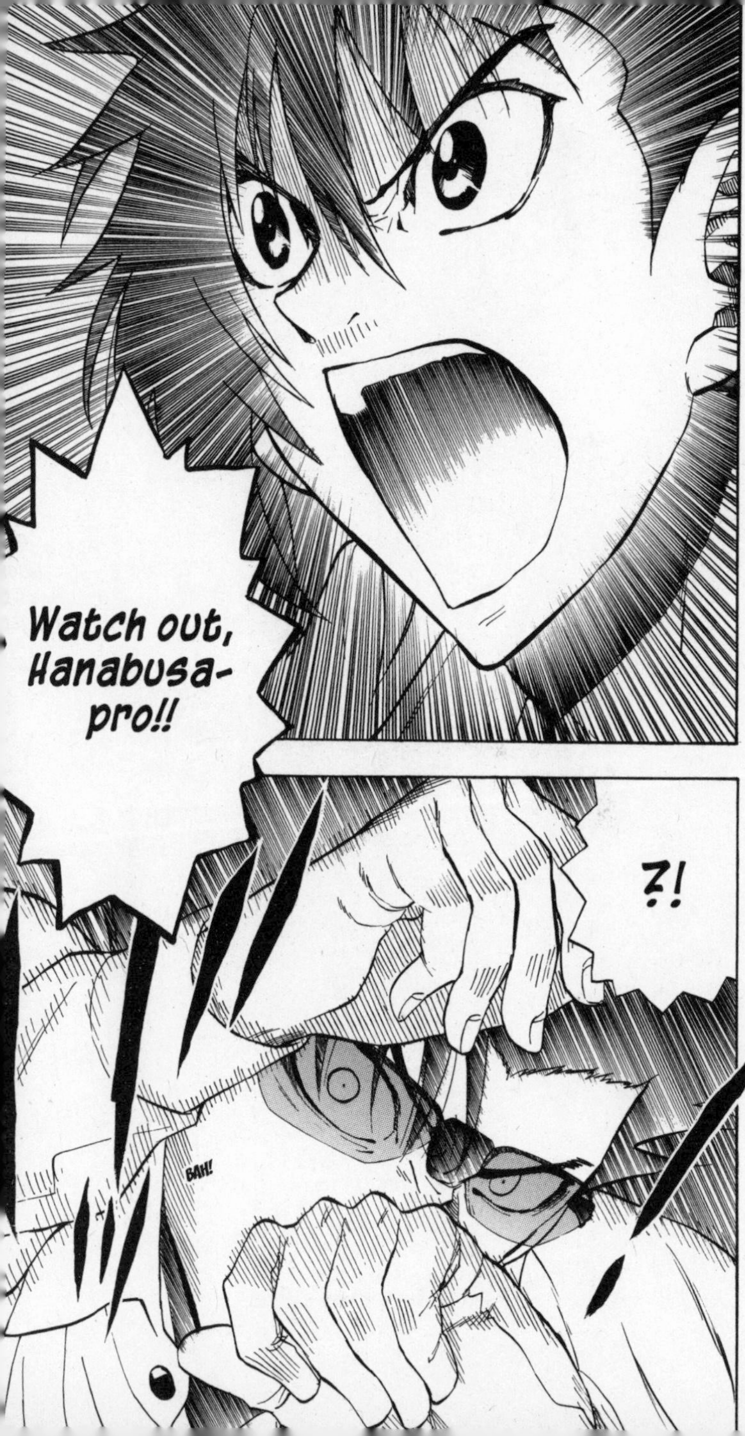
Watch out, Hanabusa-pro!!
?!
BAH!

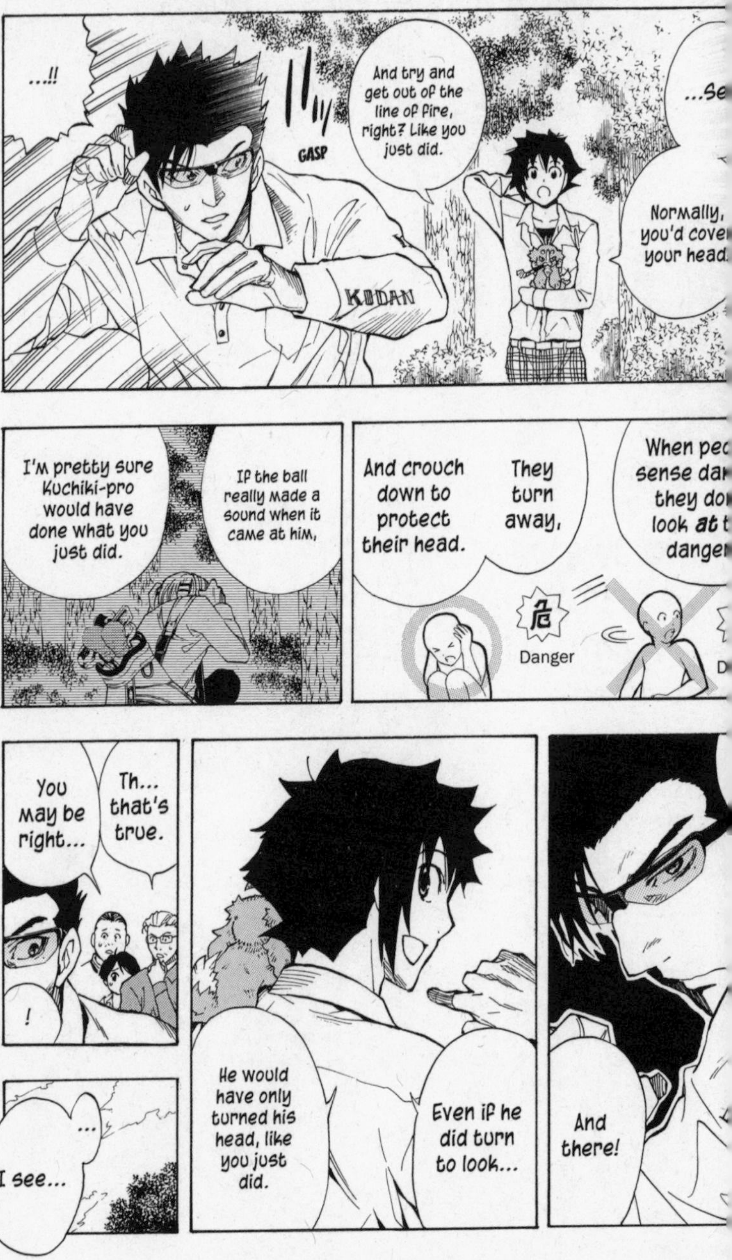
...Se
Normally, you'd cove your head.
And try and get out of the line of fire, right? Like you just did.
GASP
...!!
KODAN
When peo sense dan they do look at t danger
They turn away,
And crouch down to protect their head.
危
Danger
D
If the ball really made a sound when it came at him,
I'm pretty sure Kuchiki-pro would have done what you just did.
And there!
Even if he did turn to look...
He would have only turned his head, like you just did.
Th... that's true.
You may be right...
!
...
I see...

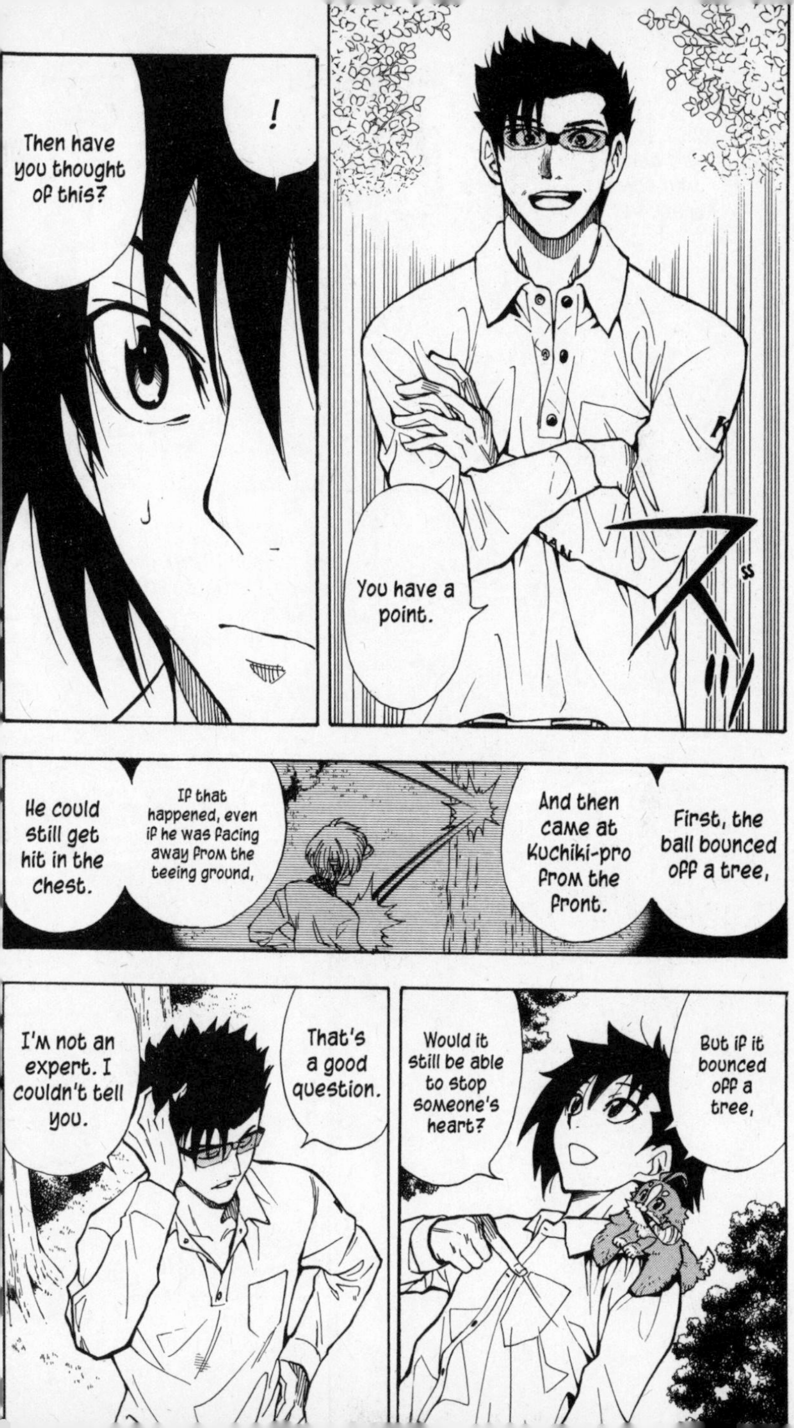
You have a point.
SS
!
Then have you thought of this?
First, the ball bounced off a tree,
And then came at Kuchiki-pro from the front.
If that happened, even if he was facing away from the teeing ground,
He could still get hit in the chest.
But if it bounced off a tree,
Would it still be able to stop someone's heart?
That's a good question.
I'm not an expert. I couldn't tell you.

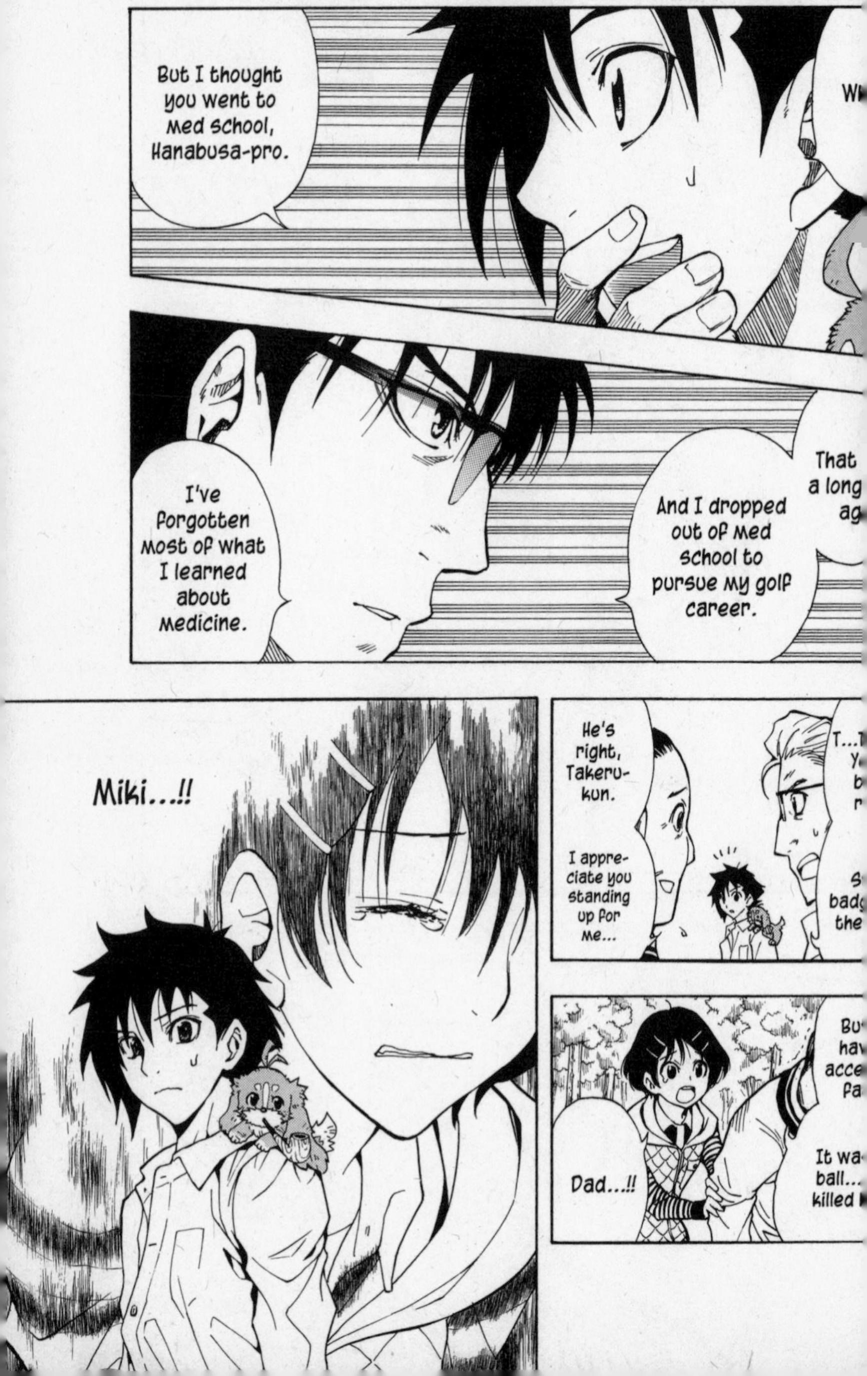

But I thought you went to med school, Hanabusa-pro.
And I dropped out of med school to pursue my golf career.
I've forgotten most of what I learned about medicine.
He's right, Takeru-kun.
I appreciate you standing up for me...
Dad...!!
Miki...!!

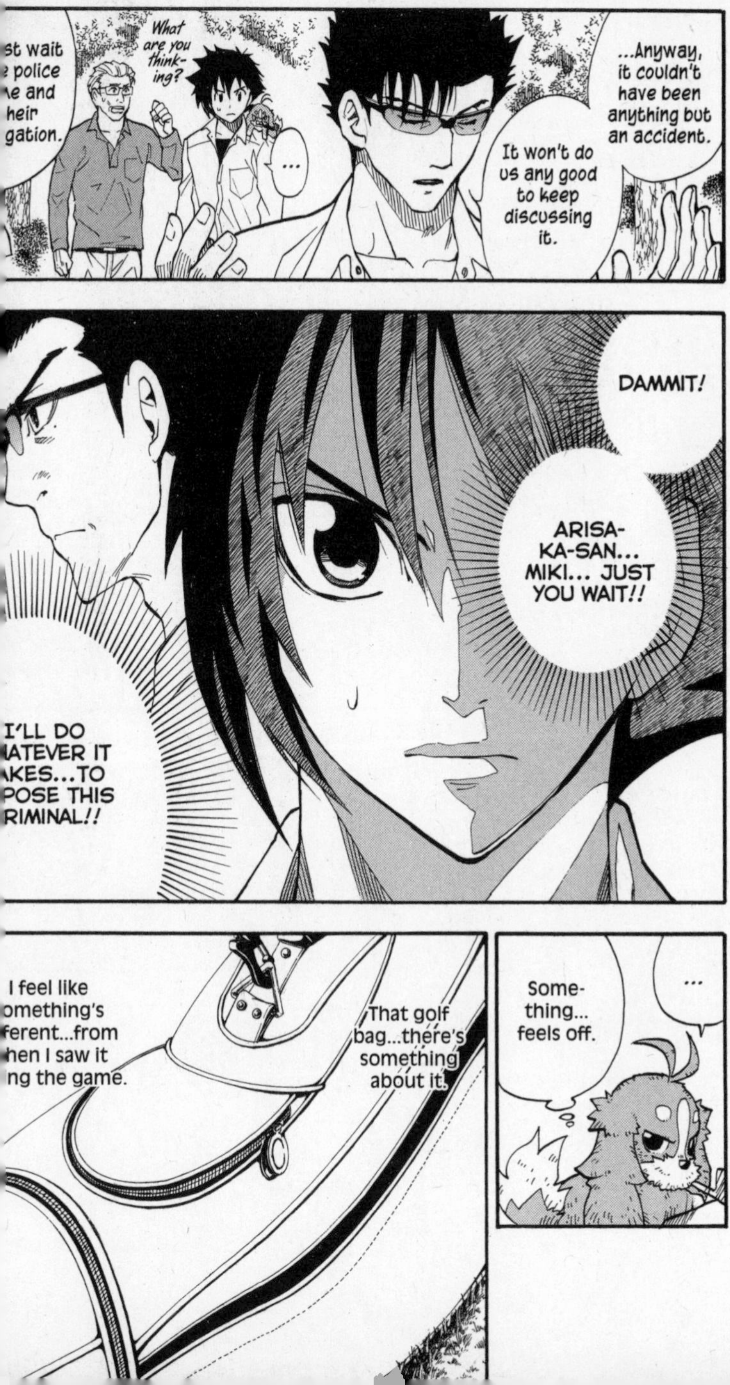
...Anyway, it couldn't have been anything but an accident.
It won't do us any good to keep discussing it.
...
What are you think- ing?
st wait e police ne and heir gation.
DAMMIT!
ARISA- KA-SAN... MIKI... JUST YOU WAIT!!
I'LL DO ATEVER IT KES...TO POSE THIS RIMINAL!!
...
Some- thing... feels off.
That golf bag...there's something about it.
I feel like omething's ferent...from hen I saw it ng the game.

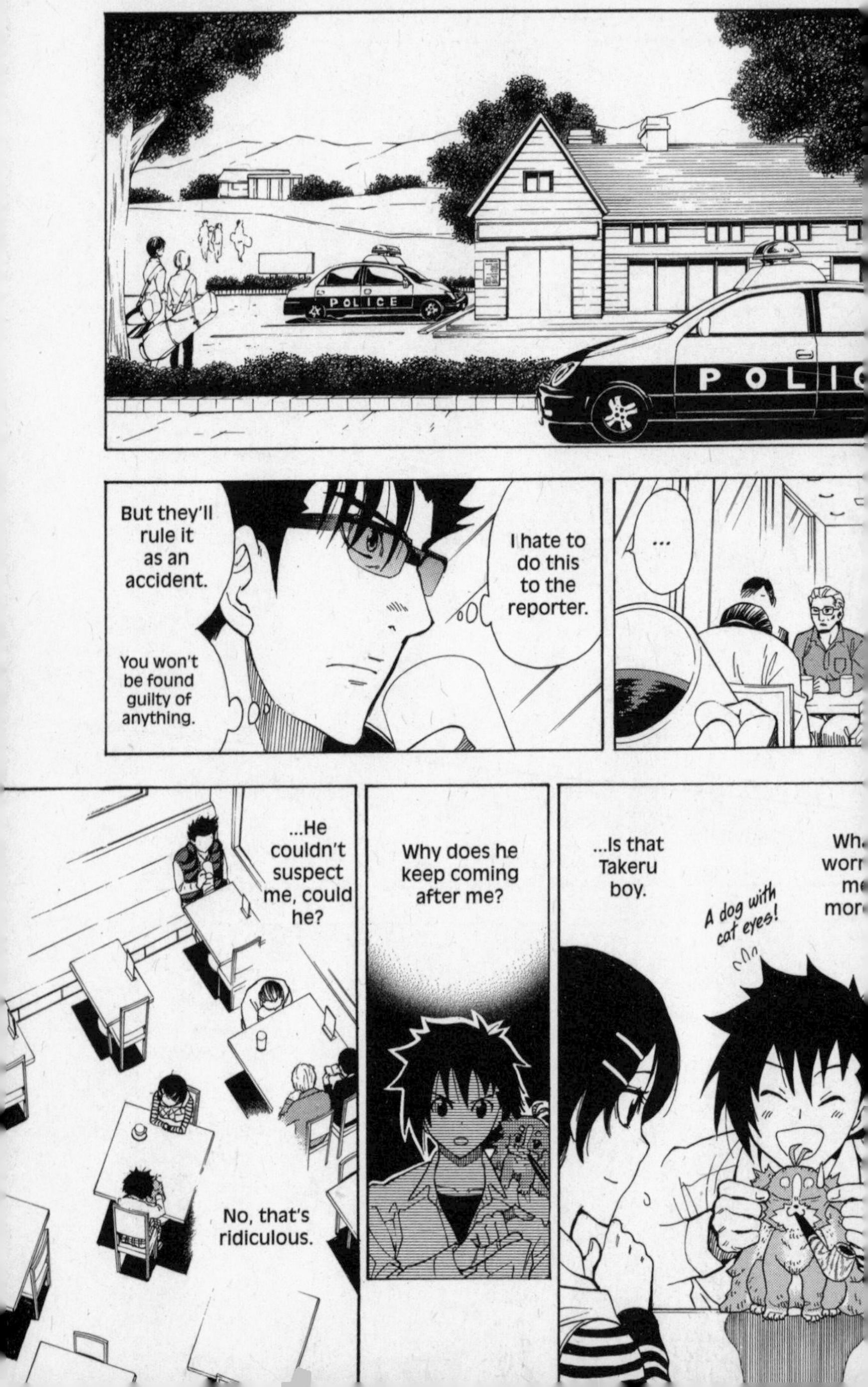
POLICE
...
I hate to do this to the reporter.
But they'll rule it as an accident.
You won't be found guilty of anything.
...Is that Takeru boy.
A dog with cat eyes!
Why does he keep coming after me?
...He couldn't suspect me, could he?
No, that's ridiculous.

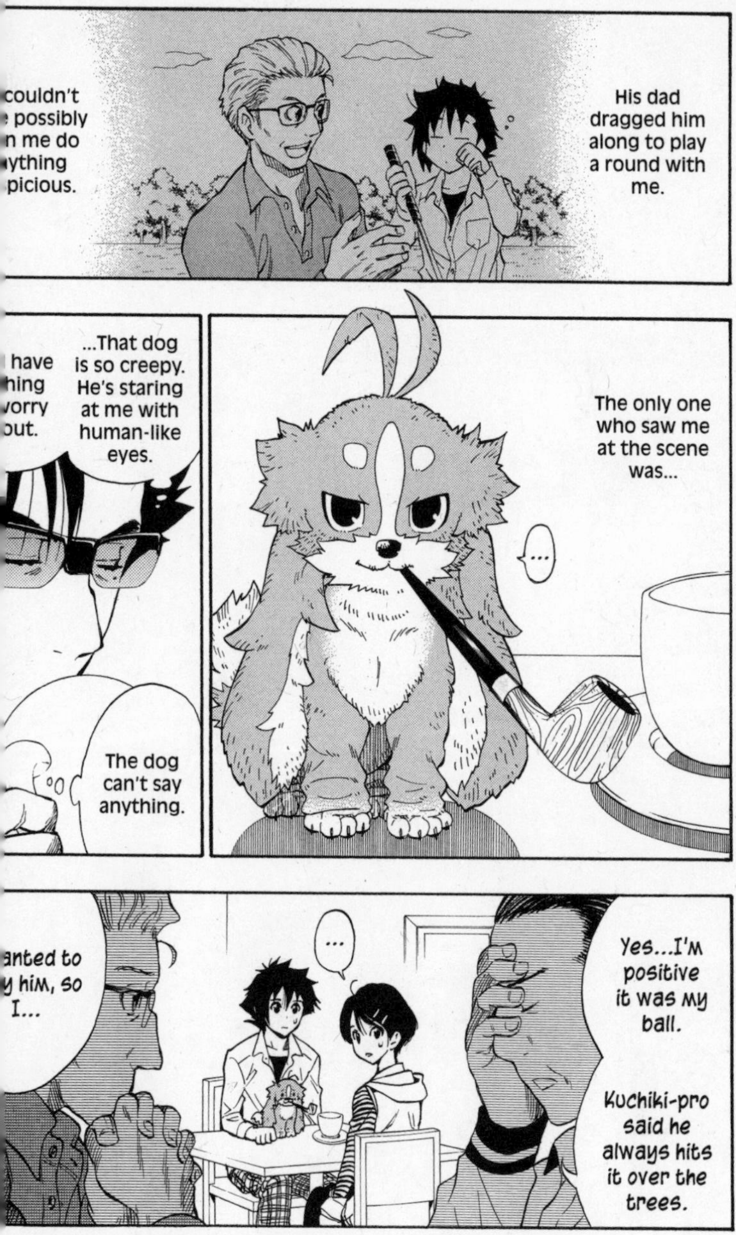
His dad dragged him along to play a round with me.
couldn't
possibly
n me do
ything
picious.
The only one who saw me at the scene was...
...
...That dog is so creepy. He's staring at me with human-like eyes.
have
hing
vorry
out.
The dog can't say anything.
Yes...I'm positive it was my ball.
Kuchiki-pro said he always hits it over the trees.
...
anted to
y him, so
I...

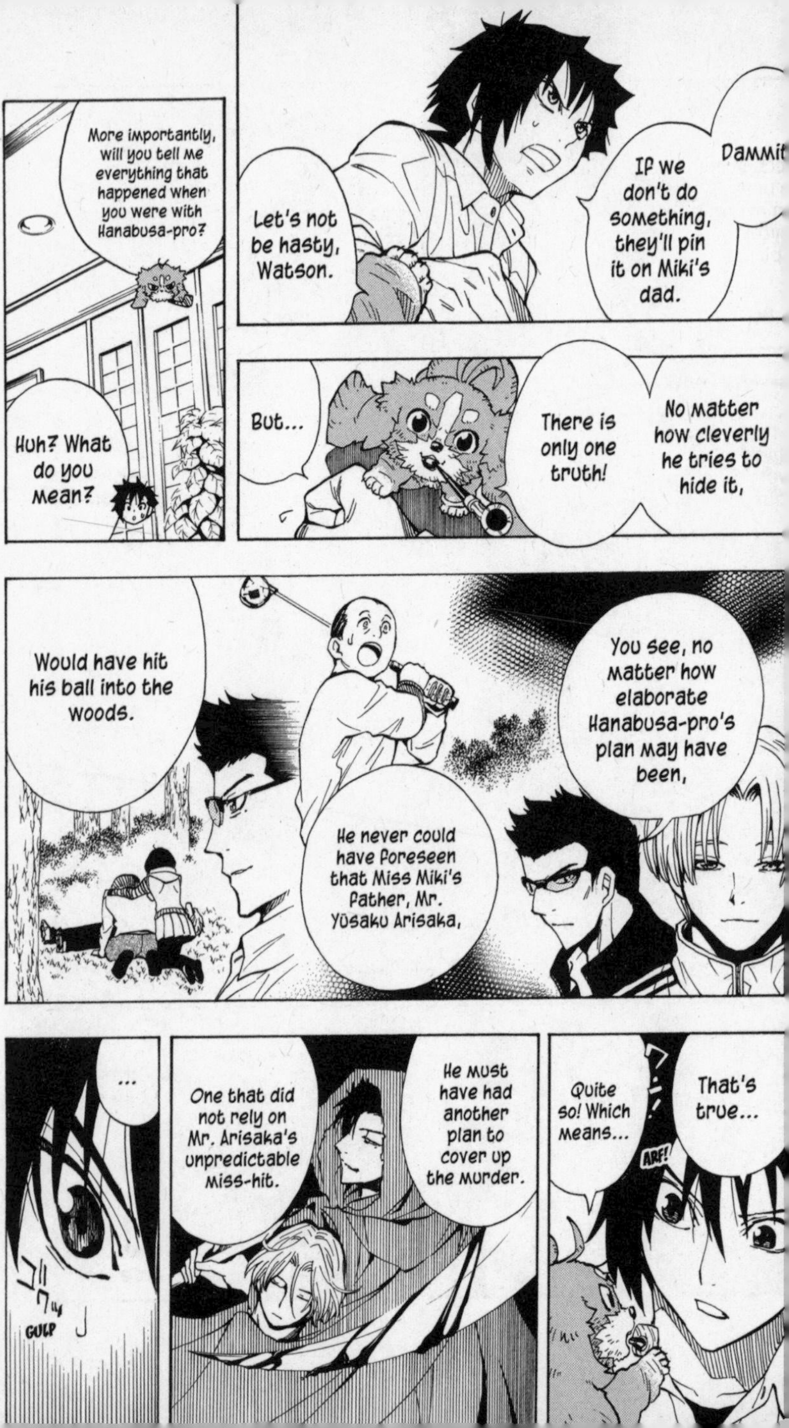
Dammit
If we don't do something, they'll pin it on Miki's dad.
Let's not be hasty, Watson.
No matter how cleverly he tries to hide it,
There is only one truth!
But...
More importantly, will you tell me everything that happened when you were with Hanabusa-pro?
Huh? What do you mean?
You see, no matter how elaborate Hanabusa-pro's plan may have been,
He never could have foreseen that Miss Miki's father, Mr. Yūsaku Arisaka,
Would have hit his ball into the woods.
That's true...
Quite so! Which means...
ARF!
He must have had another plan to cover up the murder.
One that did not rely on Mr. Arisaka's unpredictable miss-hit.
...
GULP

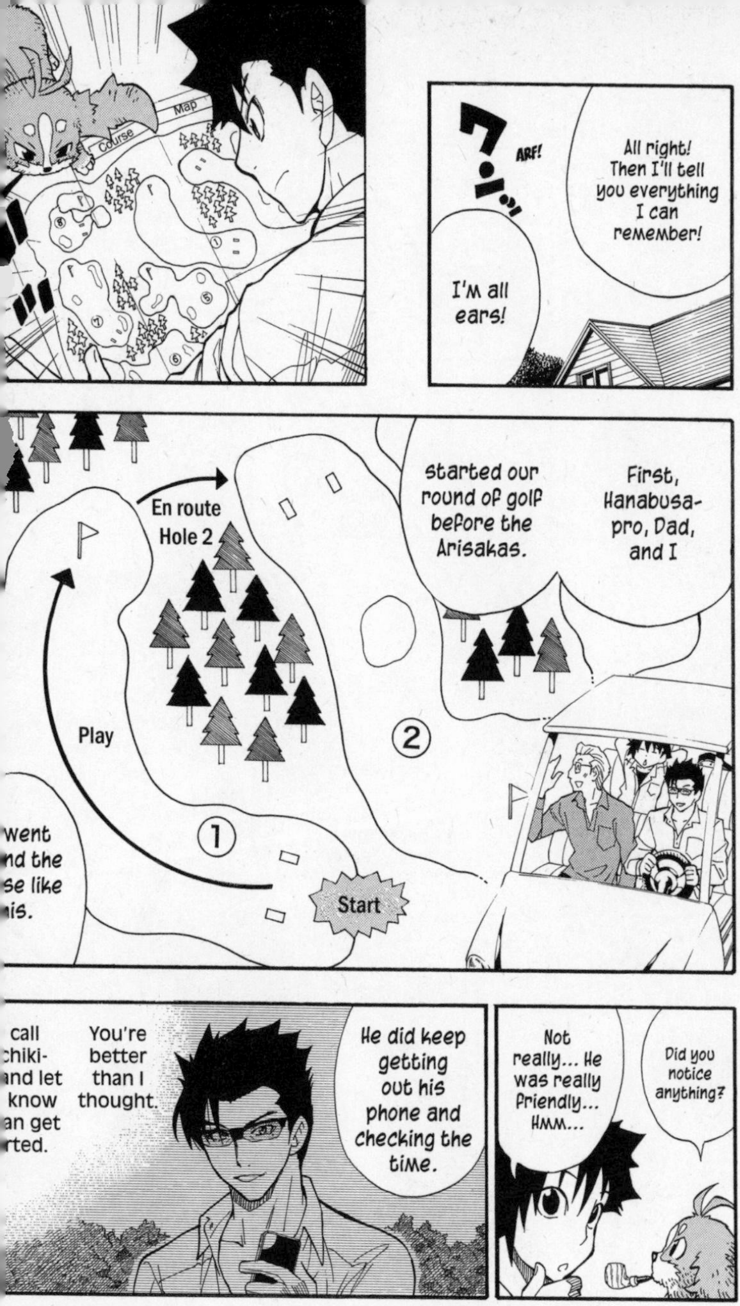
All right! Then I'll tell you everything I can remember!
ARF!
I'm all ears!
Course Map
First, Hanabusa-pro, Dad, and I
started our round of golf before the Arisakas.
went nd the se like is.
En route Hole 2
Play
Start
Did you notice anything?
Not really... He was really friendly... Hmm...
He did keep getting out his phone and checking the time.
You're better than I thought.
call chiki- and let know an get rted.

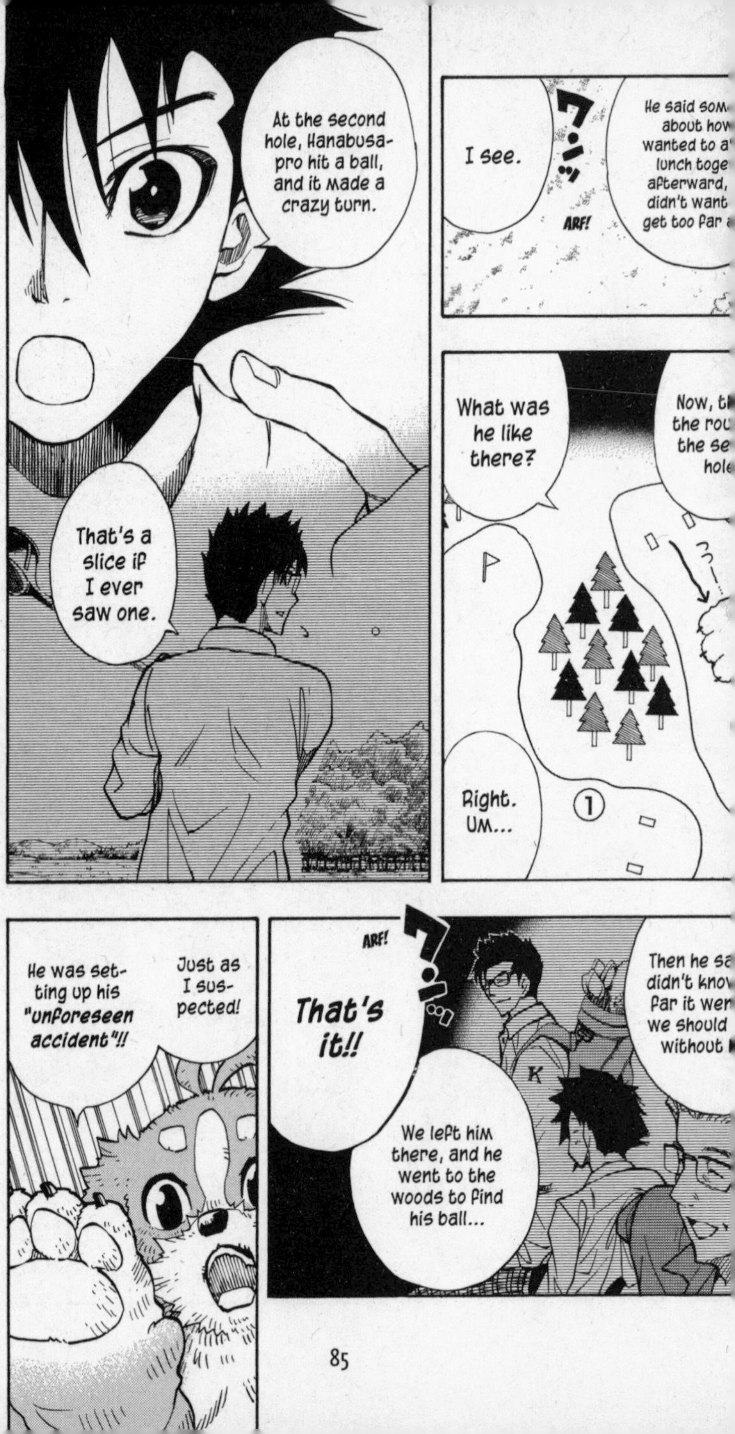
He said som
about how
wanted to a
lunch toge
afterward,
didn't want
get too far a
ARF!
I see.
Now, t
the rou
the se
hole
What was he like there?
Right. Um...
1
At the second hole, Hanabusa-pro hit a ball, and it made a crazy turn.
That's a slice if I ever saw one.
Then he sa
didn't know
far it wen
we should
without
ARF!
That's it!!
We left him there, and he went to the woods to find his ball...
Just as I suspected!
He was setting up his "unforeseen accident"!!

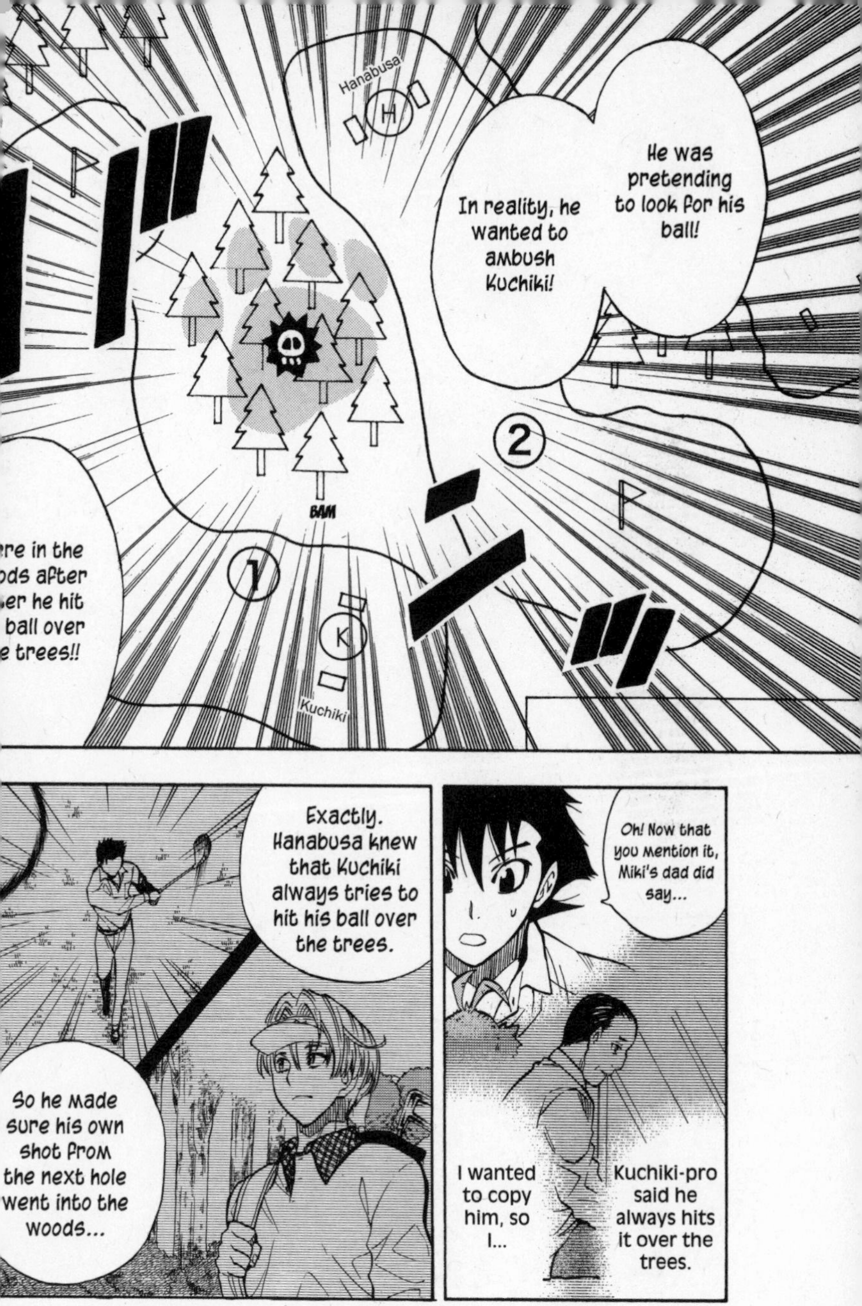
He was pretending to look for his ball!
In reality, he wanted to ambush Kuchiki!
Hanabusa
BAM
Kuchiki
re in the
ods after
er he hit
ball over
e trees!!
Oh! Now that you mention it, Miki's dad did say...
Kuchiki-pro said he always hits it over the trees.
I wanted to copy him, so I...
Exactly. Hanabusa knew that Kuchiki always tries to hit his ball over the trees.
So he made sure his own shot from the next hole went into the woods...

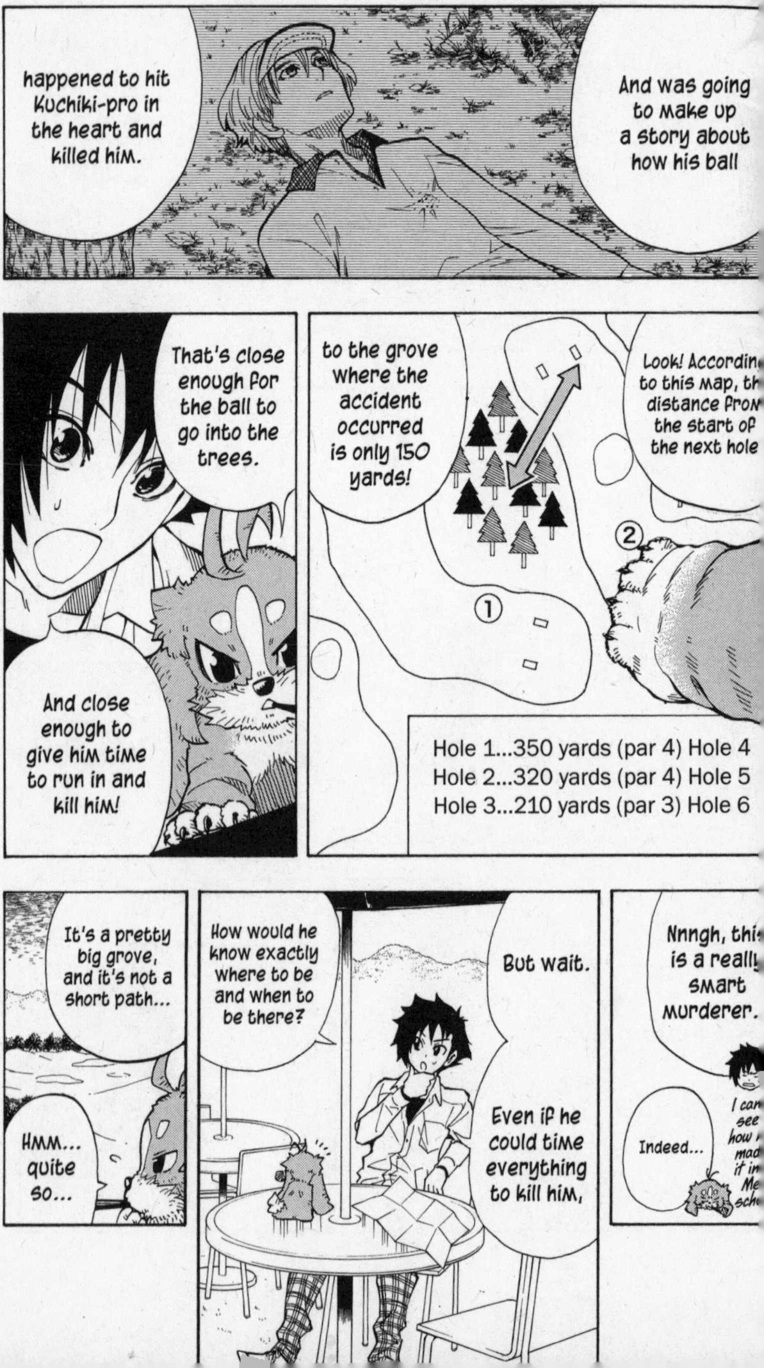

And was going to make up a story about how his ball
happened to hit Kuchiki-pro in the heart and killed him.
Look! Accordin to this map, th distance from the start of the next hole
to the grove where the accident occurred is only 150 yards!
①
②
Hole 1...350 yards (par 4) Hole 4
Hole 2...320 yards (par 4) Hole 5
Hole 3...210 yards (par 3) Hole 6
That's close enough for the ball to go into the trees.
And close enough to give him time to run in and kill him!
Nnngh, thi is a really smart murderer.
Indeed...
But wait.
Even if he could time everything to kill him,
How would he know exactly where to be and when to be there?
It's a pretty big grove, and it's not a short path...
Hmm... quite so...

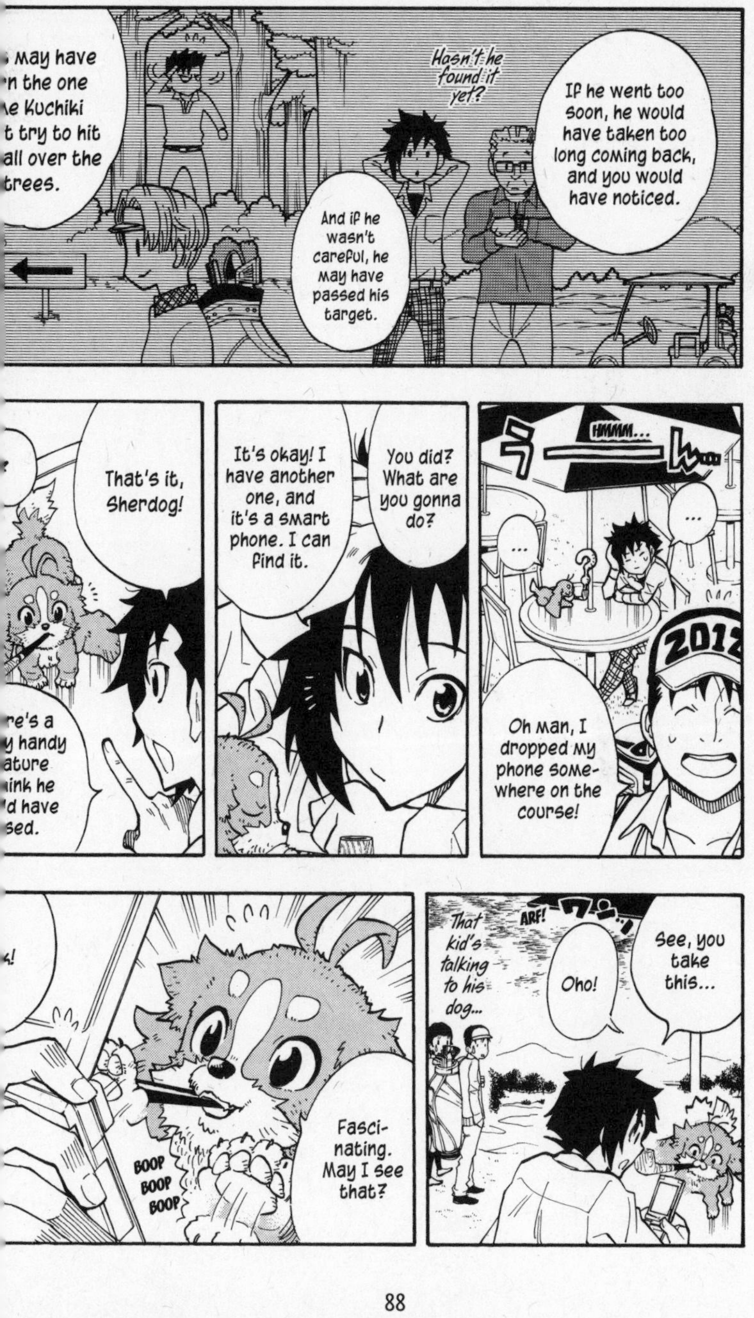
If he went too soon, he would have taken too long coming back, and you would have noticed.
Hasn't he found it yet?
And if he wasn't careful, he may have passed his target.
may have
n the one
e Kuchiki
t try to hit
all over the
trees.
HMMM...
...
...
Oh man, I dropped my phone somewhere on the course!
You did? What are you gonna do?
It's okay! I have another one, and it's a smart phone. I can find it.
That's it, Sherdog!
re's a
y handy
ature
iink he
'd have
sed.
See, you take this...
ARF!
Oho!
That kid's talking to his dog...
Fascinating. May I see that?
BOOP BOOP BOOP

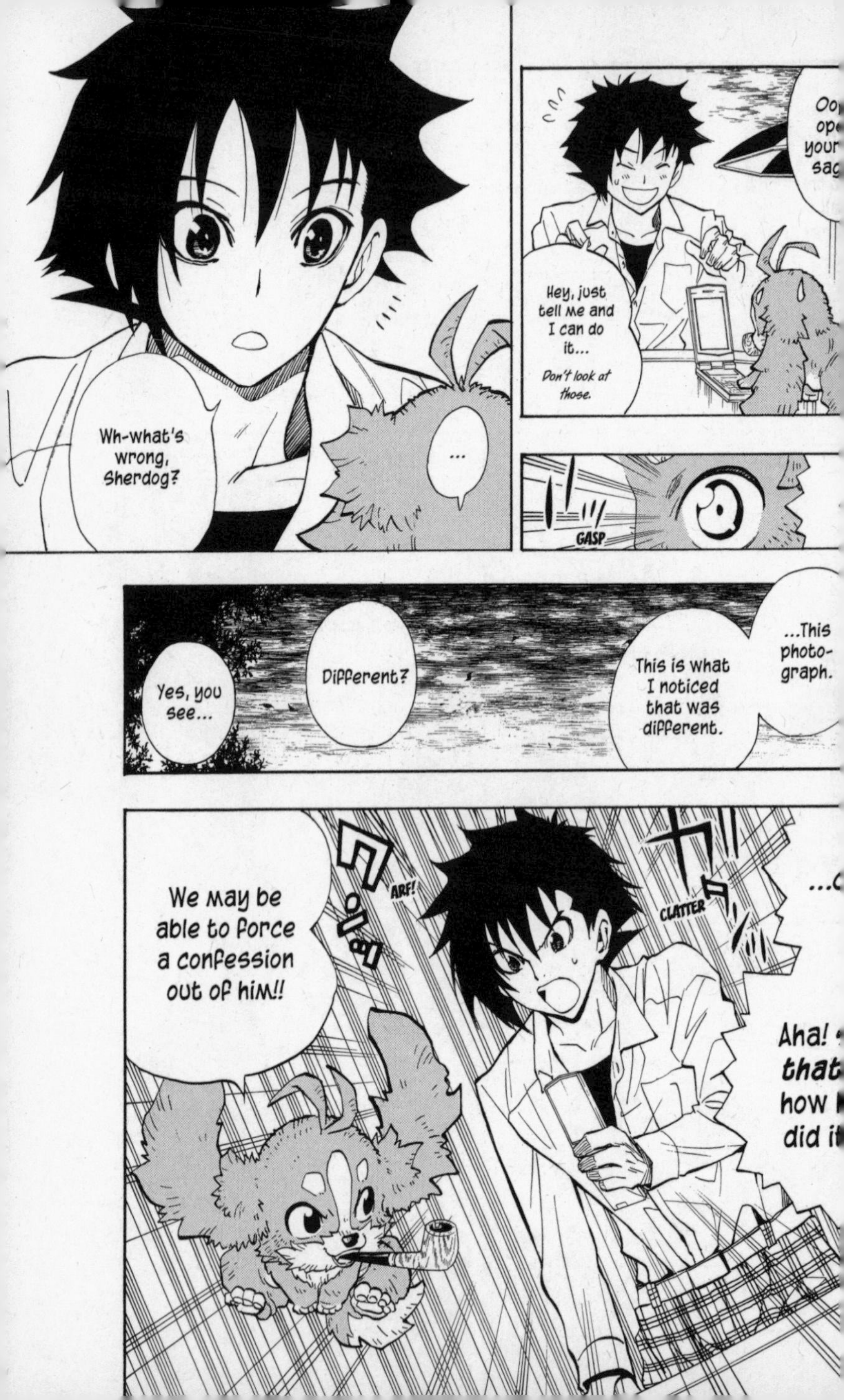
Hey, just tell me and I can do it...
Don't look at those.
GASP
...
Wh-what's wrong, Sherdog?
...This photograph.
This is what I noticed that was different.
Different?
Yes, you see...
CLATTER
ARF!
We may be able to force a confession out of him!!

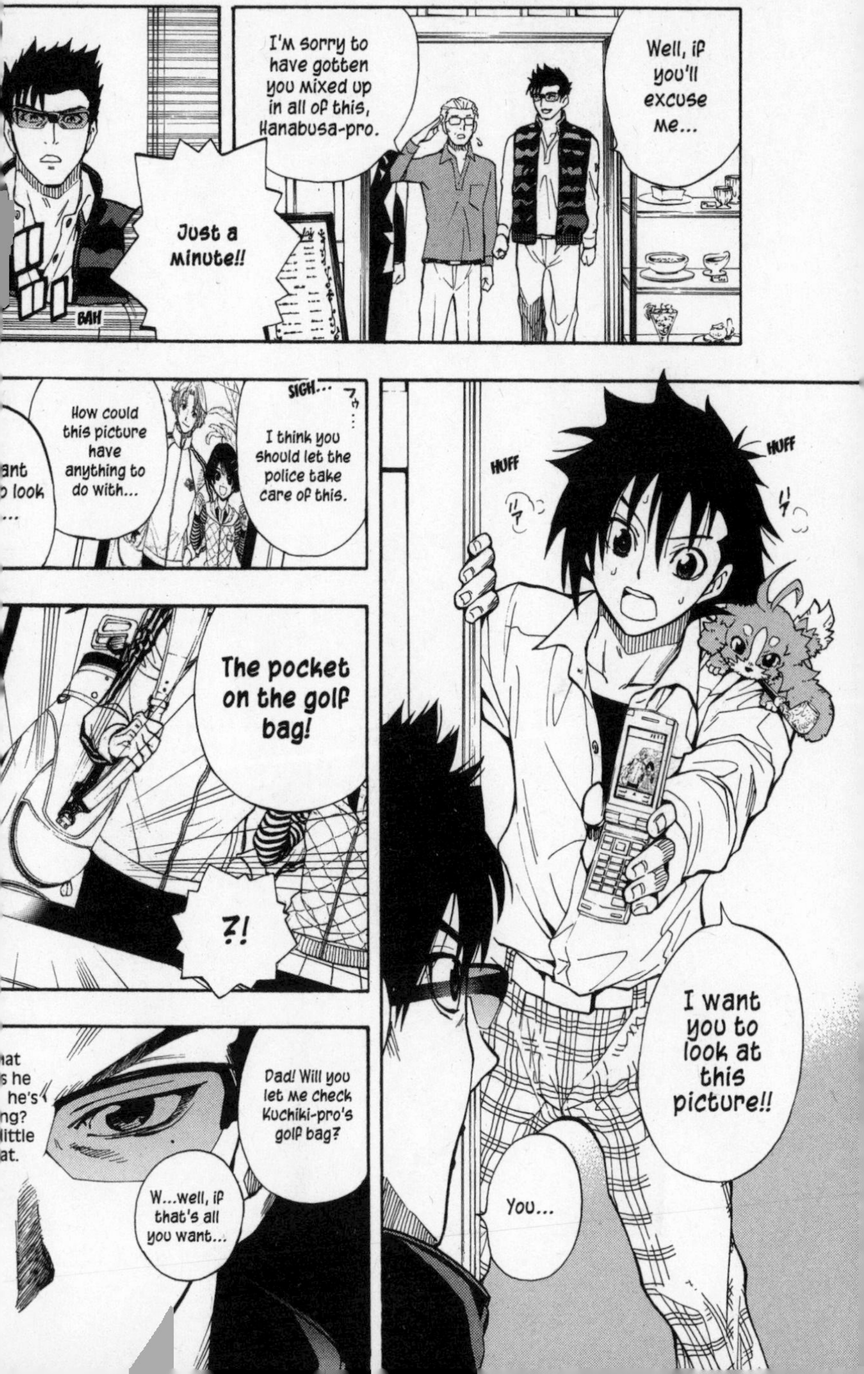
Well, if you'll excuse me...
I'm sorry to have gotten you mixed up in all of this, Hanabusa-pro.
Just a minute!!
BAH
HUFF
HUFF
I want you to look at this picture!!
You...
SIGH...
I think you should let the police take care of this.
How could this picture have anything to do with...
The pocket on the golf bag!
?!
Dad! Will you let me check Kuchiki-pro's golf bag?
W...well, if that's all you want...

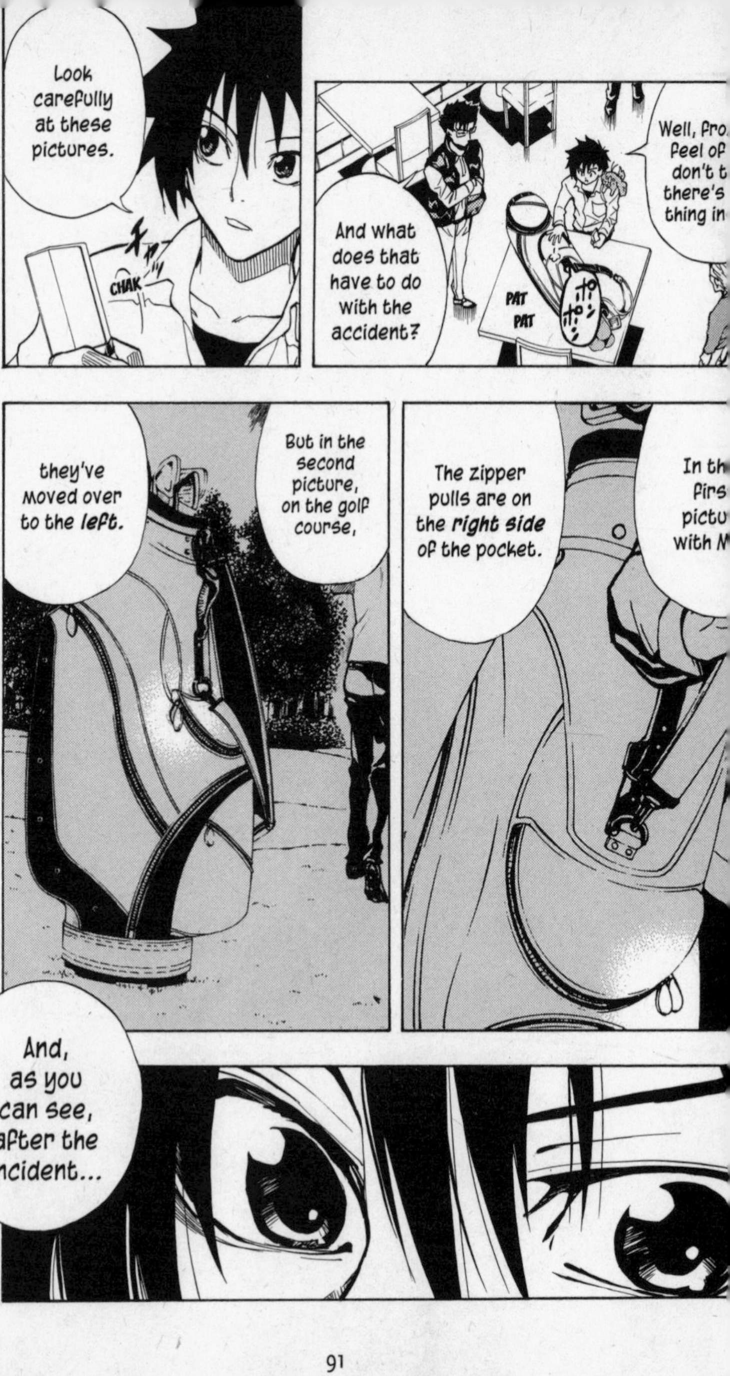

Well, fro
feel of
don't t
there's
thing in
PAT PAT
ポンポン
And what does that have to do with the accident?
Look carefully at these pictures.
CHAK
In th
firs
pictu
with M
The zipper pulls are on the ***right side*** of the pocket.
But in the second picture, on the golf course,
they've moved over to the ***left.***
And, as you can see, after the incident...

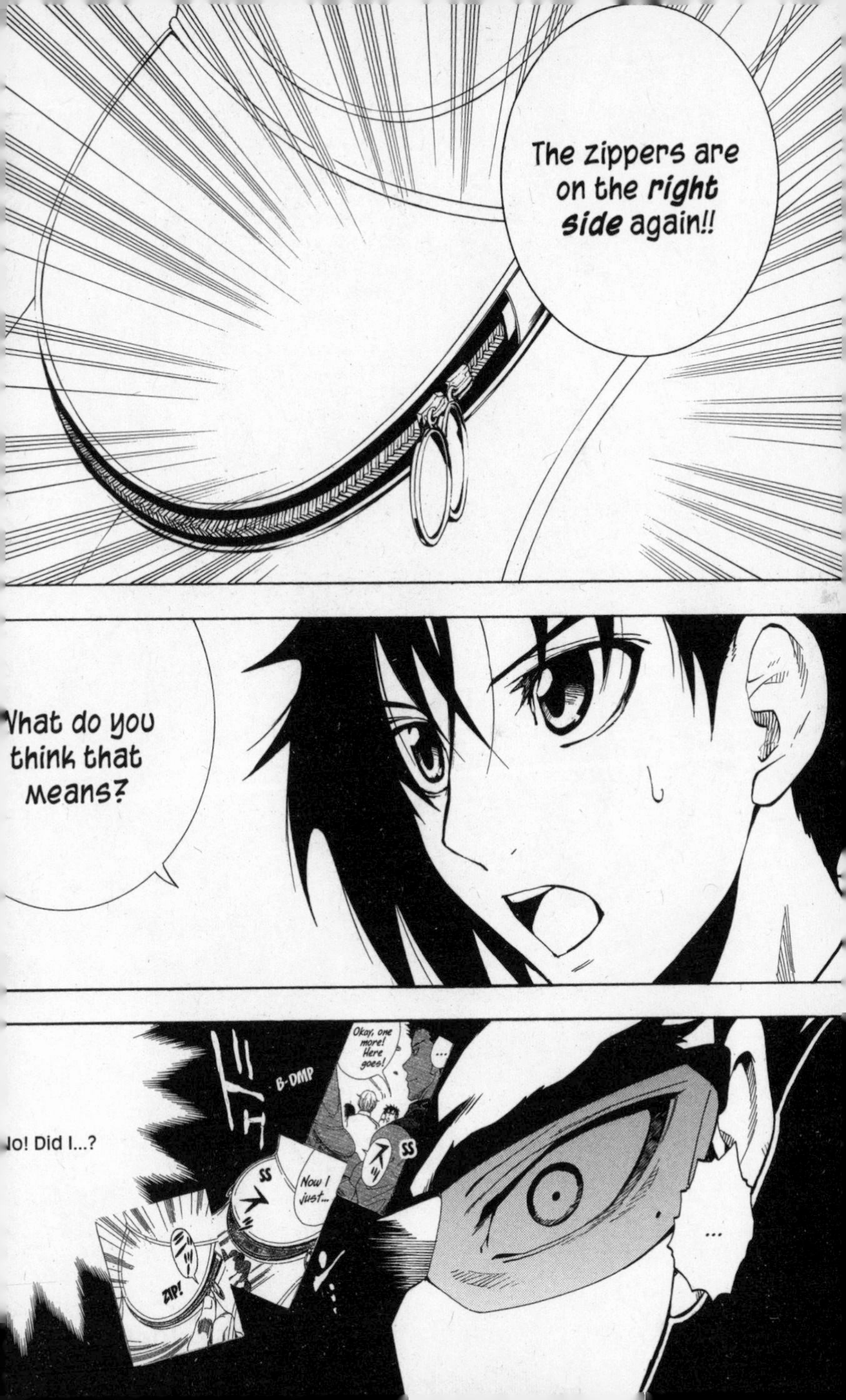
The zippers are on the **right side** again!!
Vhat do you think that means?
...
Okay, one more! Here goes!
...
B-DMP
SS
Now I just...
SS
ZIP!
lo! Did I...?

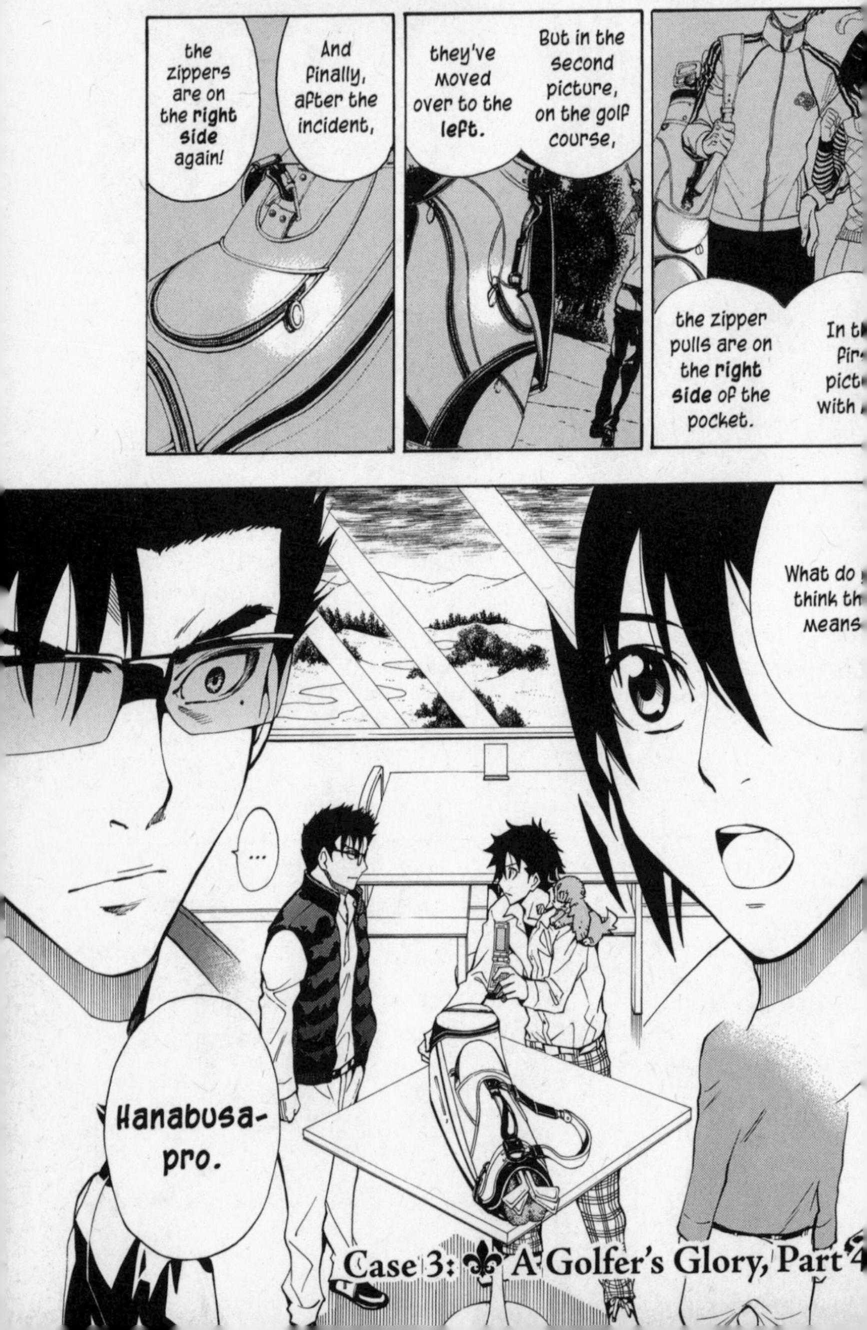
In th
fir
pict
with
the zipper pulls are on the right side of the pocket.
But in the second picture, on the golf course,
they've moved over to the left.
And finally, after the incident,
the zippers are on the right side again!
What do
think th
means
...
Hanabusa-pro.
Case 3: ⚜ A Golfer's Glory, Part 4

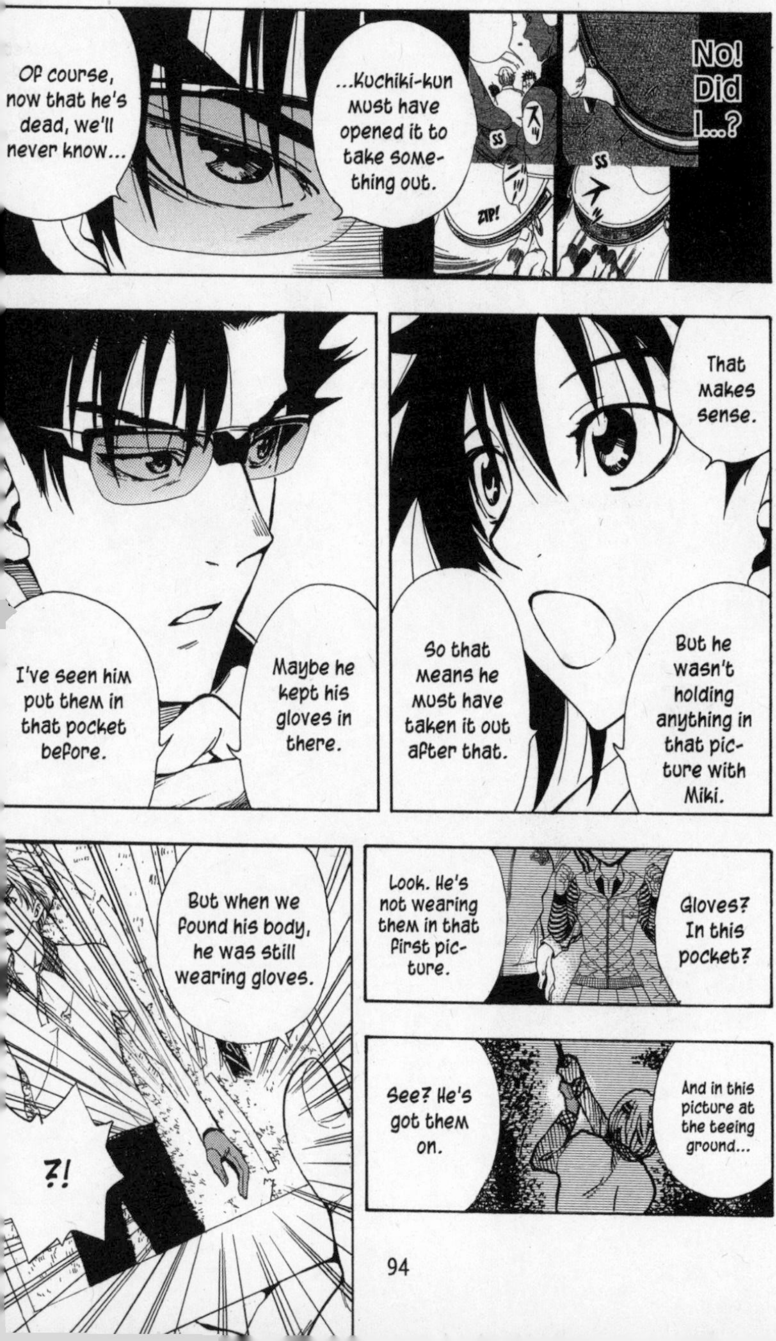
No! Did I...?
SS
SS
ZIP!
...Kuchiki-kun must have opened it to take some-thing out.
Of course, now that he's dead, we'll never know...
That makes sense.
But he wasn't holding anything in that pic-ture with Miki.
So that means he must have taken it out after that.
Maybe he kept his gloves in there.
I've seen him put them in that pocket before.
Gloves? In this pocket?
Look. He's not wearing them in that first pic-ture.
And in this picture at the teeing ground...
See? He's got them on.
But when we found his body, he was still wearing gloves.
?!

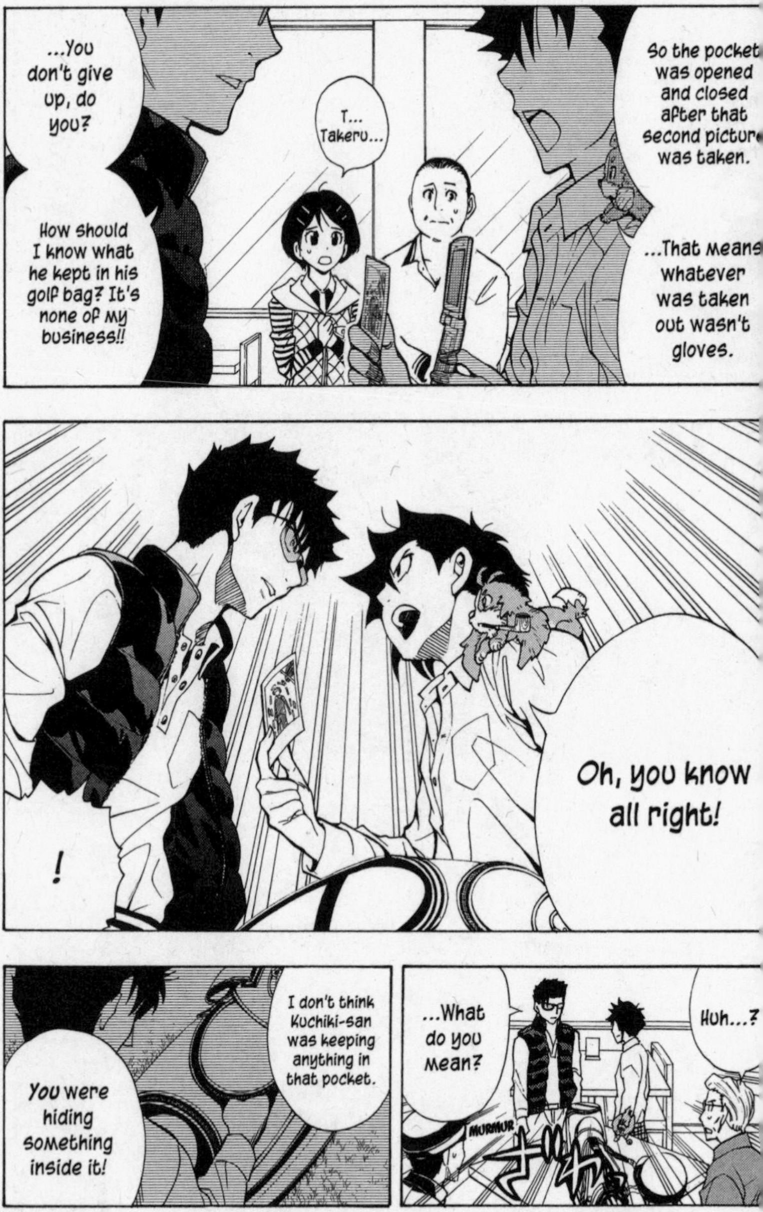
So the pocket was opened and closed after that second pictur was taken.
...That means whatever was taken out wasn't gloves.
T... Takeru...
...You don't give up, do you?
How should I know what he kept in his golf bag? It's none of my business!!
Oh, you know all right!
!
Huh...?
...What do you mean?
MURMUR
I don't think Kuchiki-san was keeping anything in that pocket.
You were hiding something inside it!

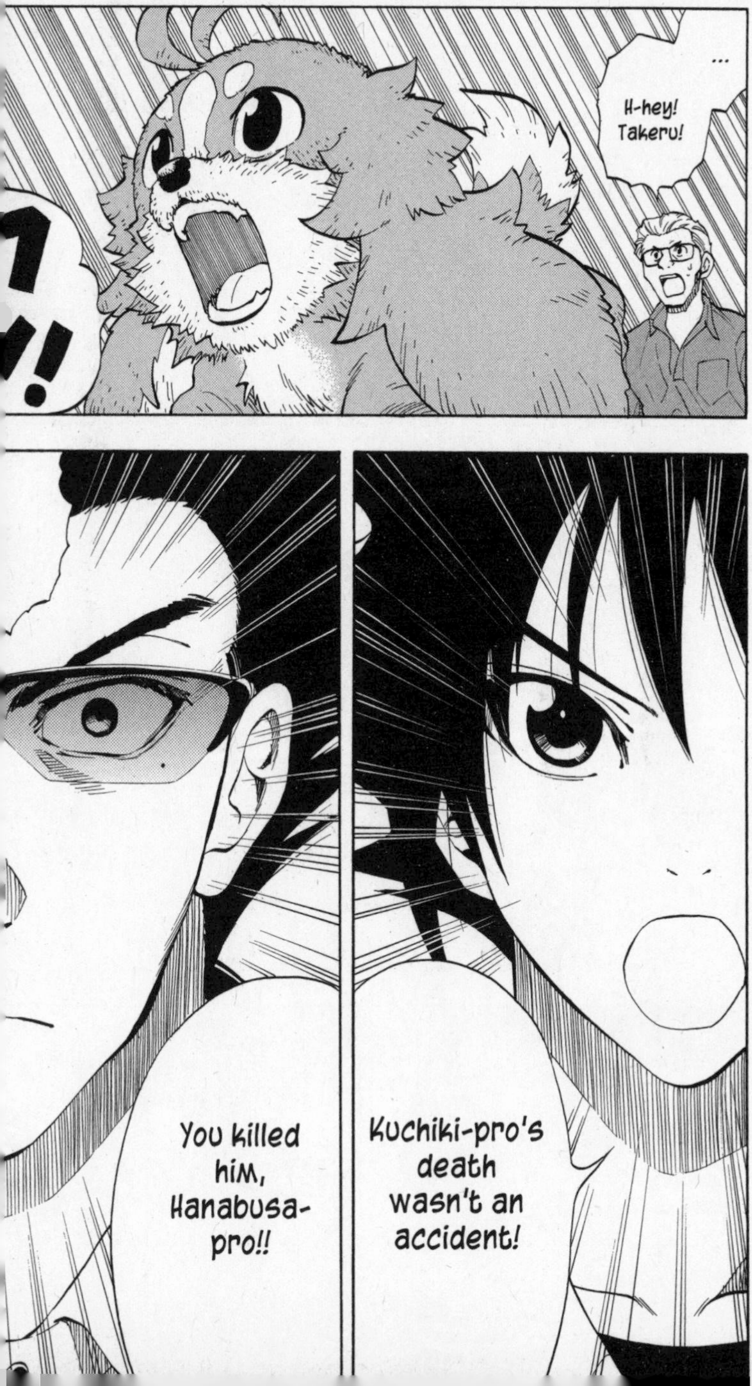
...
H-hey! Takeru!
Kuchiki-pro's death wasn't an accident!
You killed him, Hanabusa-pro!!

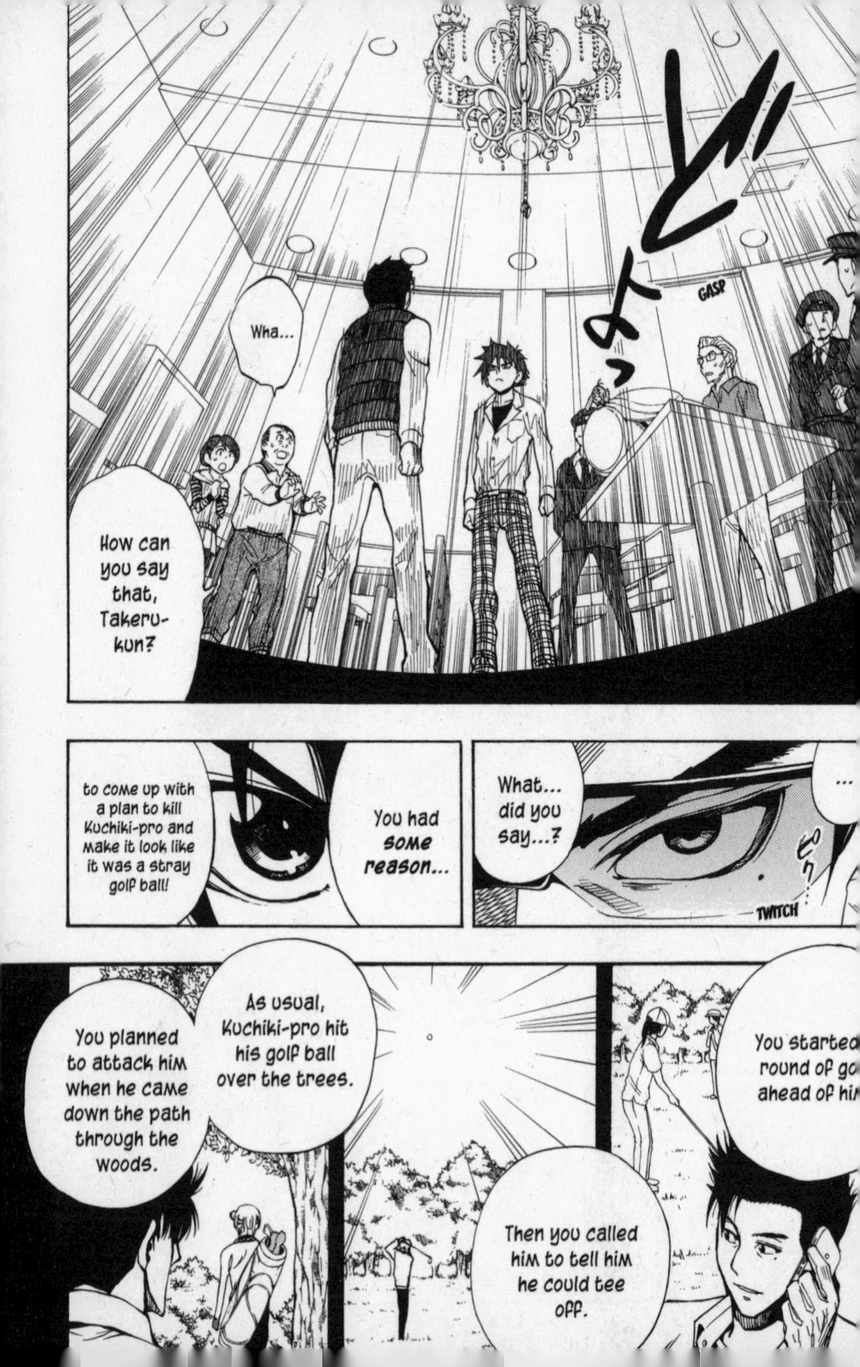
どよっ
GASP
Wha...
How can you say that, Takeru-kun?
...
TWITCH
What... did you say...?
You had some reason...
to come up with a plan to kill Kuchiki-pro and make it look like it was a stray golf ball!
You started round of ahead of
Then you called him to tell him he could tee off.
As usual, Kuchiki-pro hit his golf ball over the trees.
You planned to attack him when he came down the path through the woods.

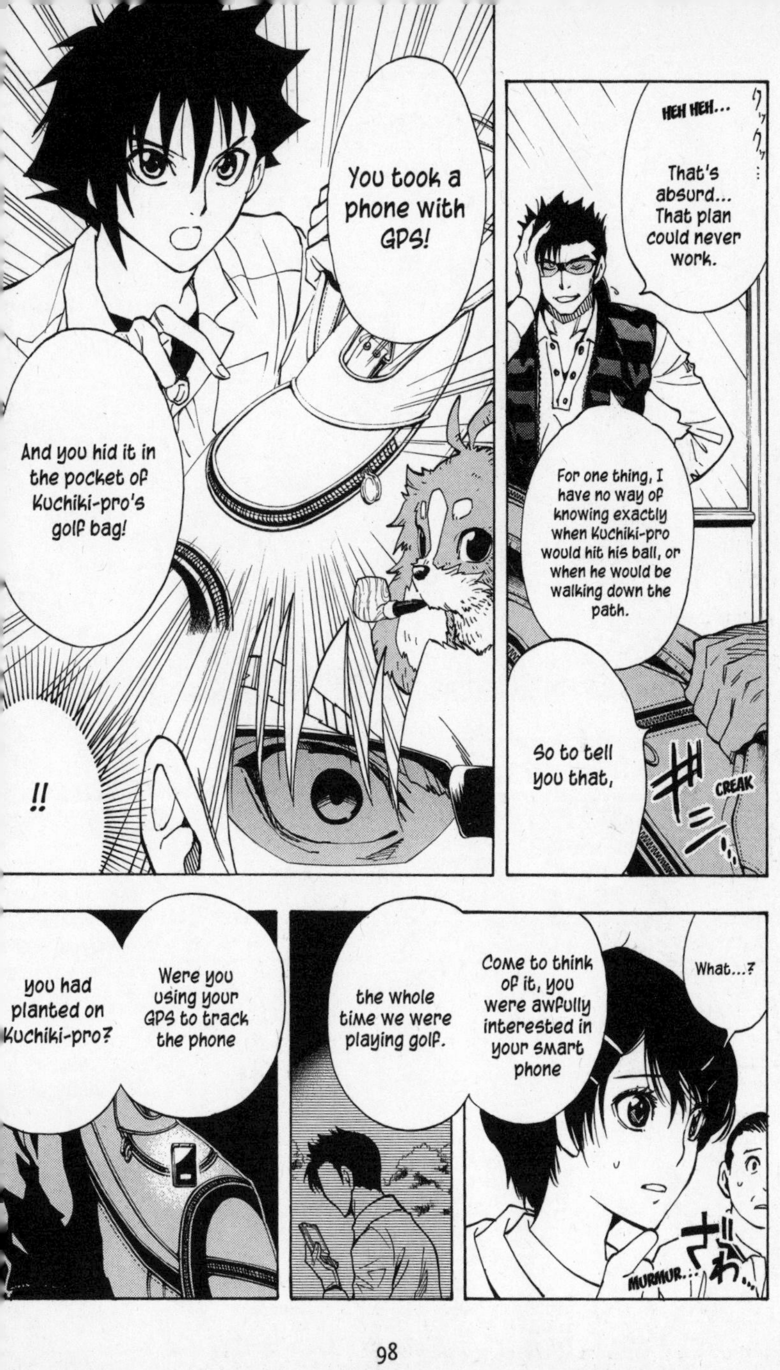
HEH HEH...
クックッ…
That's absurd... That plan could never work.
For one thing, I have no way of knowing exactly when Kuchiki-pro would hit his ball, or when he would be walking down the path.
So to tell you that,
CREAK
You took a phone with GPS!
And you hid it in the pocket of Kuchiki-pro's golf bag!
!!
What...?
Come to think of it, you were awfully interested in your smart phone
the whole time we were playing golf.
MURMUR...
ざわ...
Were you using your GPS to track the phone
you had planted on Kuchiki-pro?

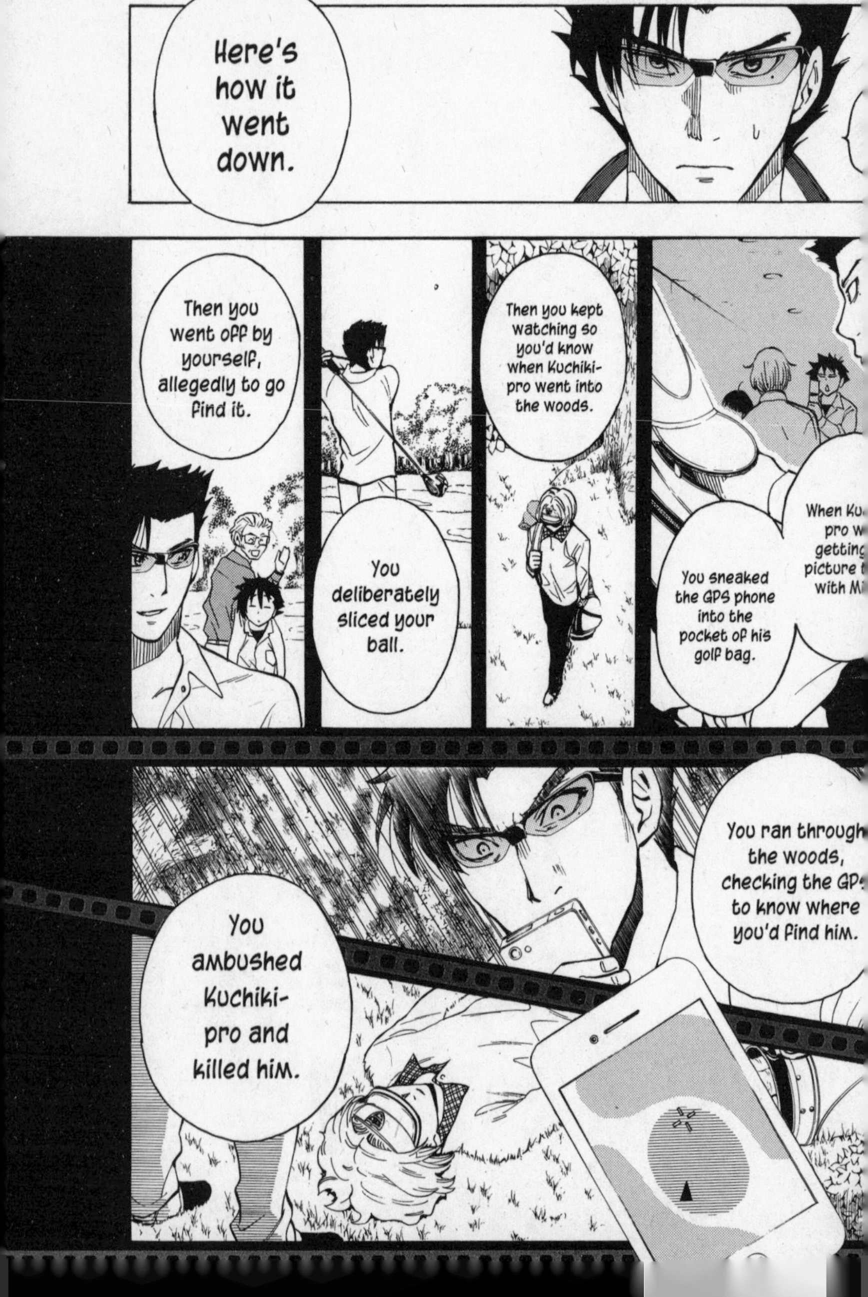
Here's how it went down.
When Ku
pro w
getting
picture
with M
You sneaked the GPS phone into the pocket of his golf bag.
Then you kept watching so you'd know when Kuchiki-pro went into the woods.
You deliberately sliced your ball.
Then you went off by yourself, allegedly to go find it.
You ran throug the woods, checking the GP to know where you'd find him.
You ambushed Kuchiki-pro and killed him.

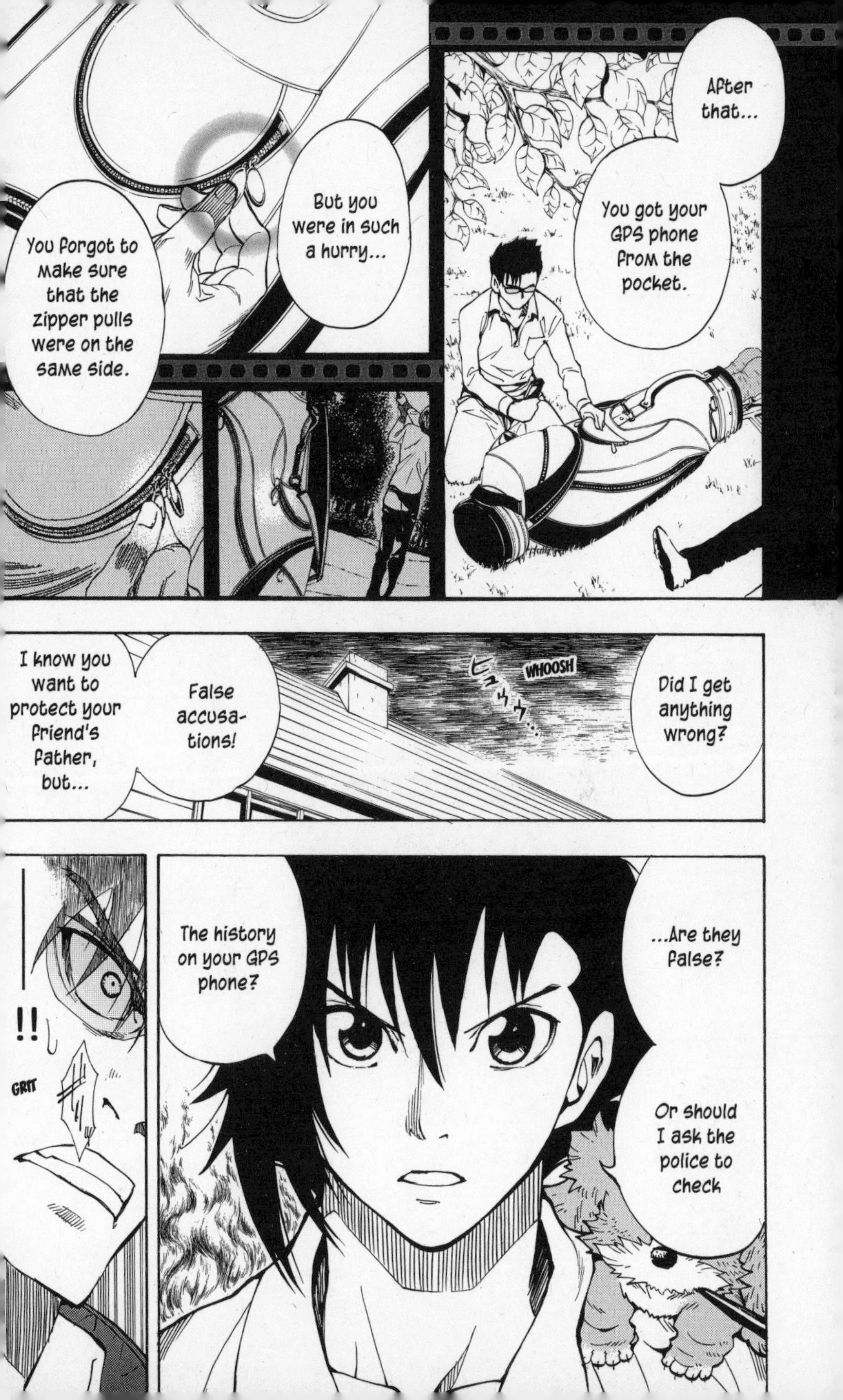
After that...
You got your GPS phone from the pocket.
But you were in such a hurry...
You forgot to make sure that the zipper pulls were on the same side.
Did I get anything wrong?
WHOOSH
False accusa-tions!
I know you want to protect your friend's father, but...
...Are they false?
Or should I ask the police to check
The history on your GPS phone?
!!
GRIT

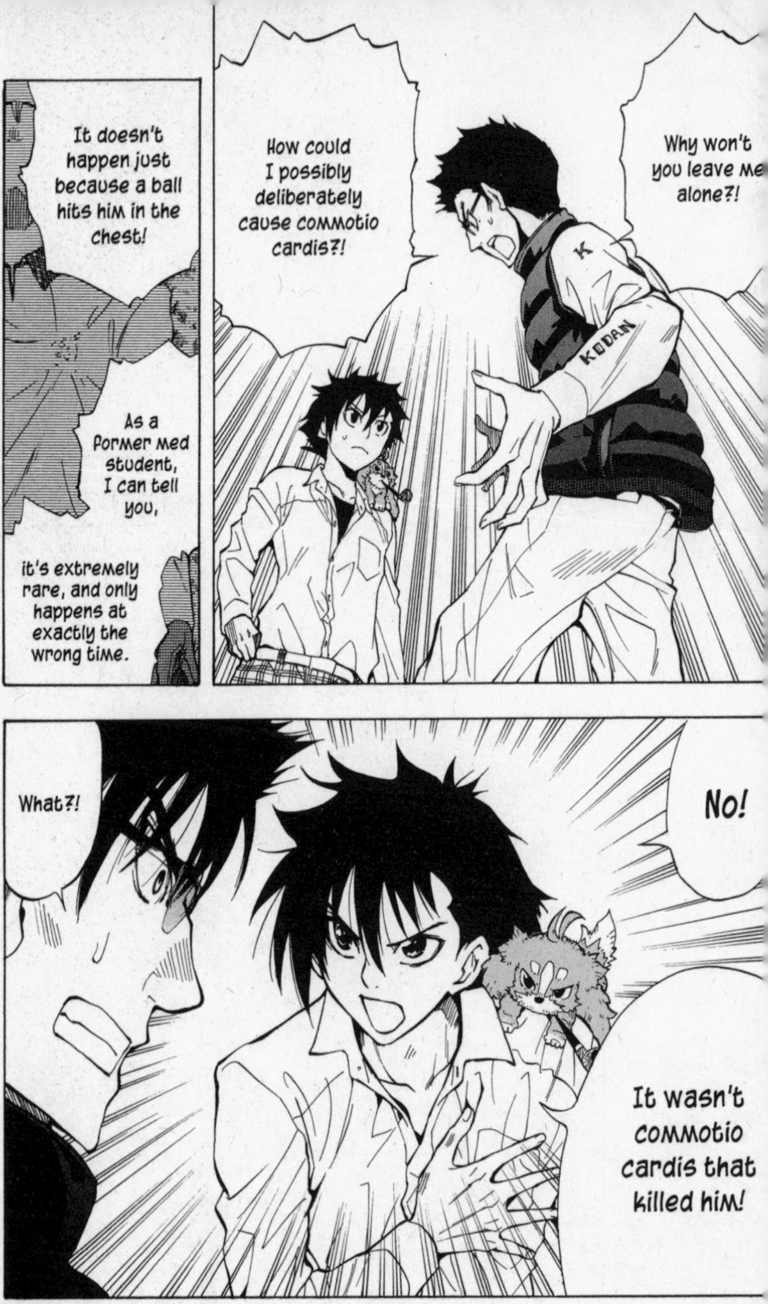
Why won't you leave me alone?!
How could I possibly deliberately cause commotio cardis?!
It doesn't happen just because a ball hits him in the chest!
As a former med student, I can tell you,
it's extremely rare, and only happens at exactly the wrong time.
No!
What?!
It wasn't commotio cardis that killed him!

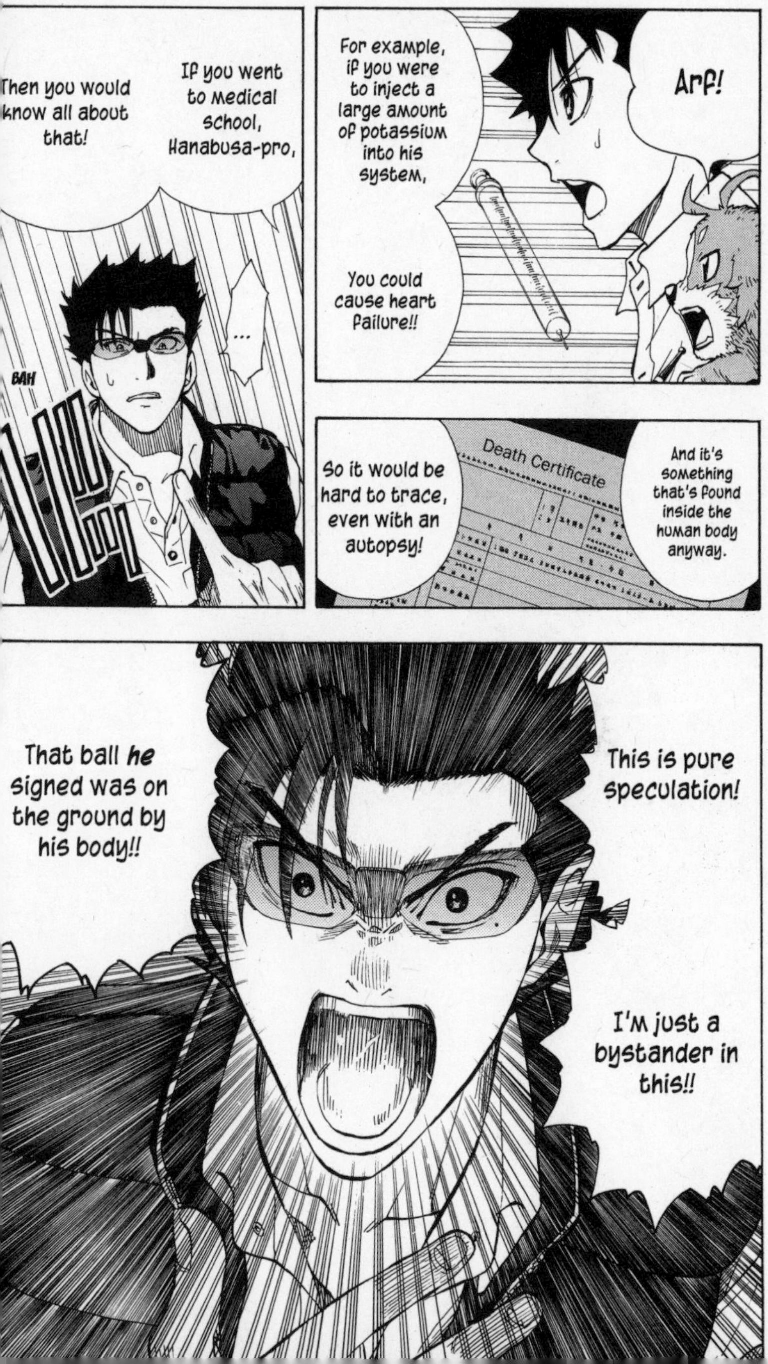
Arf!
For example, if you were to inject a large amount of potassium into his system,
You could cause heart failure!!
And it's something that's found inside the human body anyway.
Death Certificate
So it would be hard to trace, even with an autopsy!
If you went to medical school, Hanabusa-pro,
Then you would know all about that!
...
BAH
This is pure speculation!
I'm just a bystander in this!!
That ball *he* signed was on the ground by his body!!

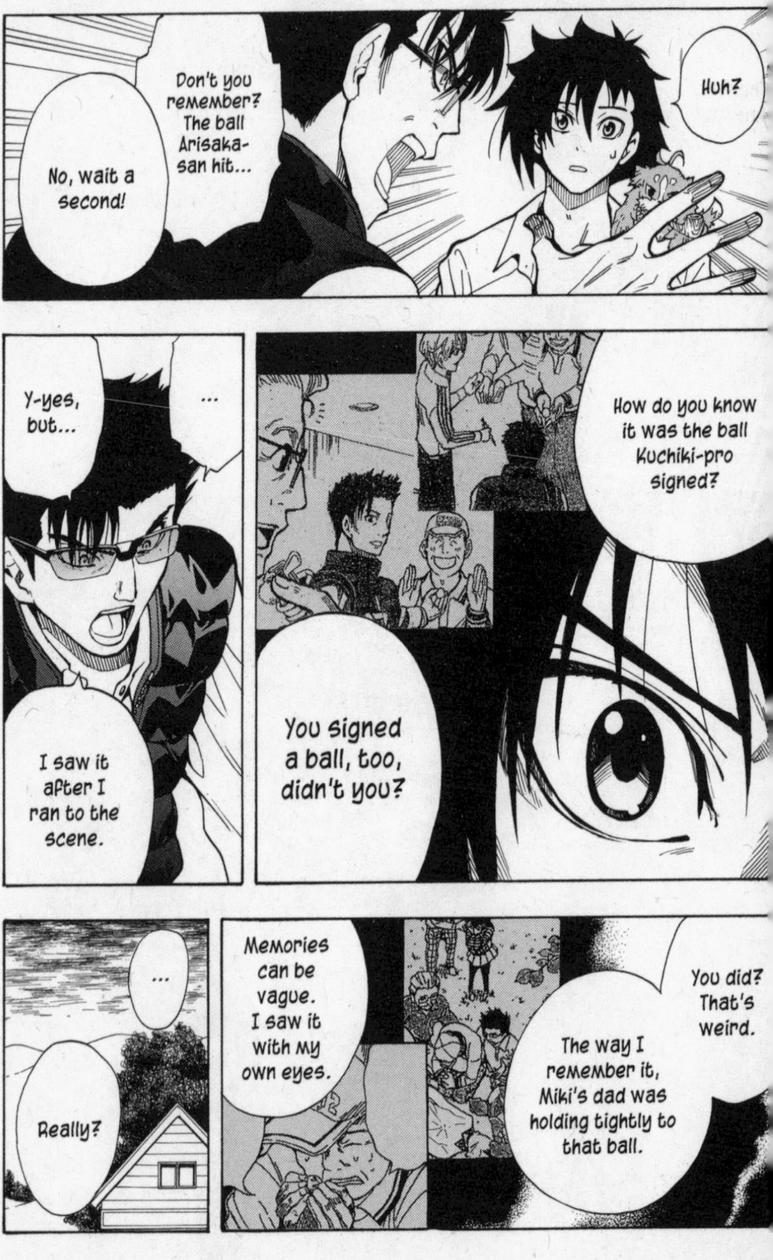
Huh?
Don't you remember? The ball Arisaka-san hit...
No, wait a second!
How do you know it was the ball Kuchiki-pro signed?
You signed a ball, too, didn't you?
...
Y-yes, but...
I saw it after I ran to the scene.
You did? That's weird.
The way I remember it, Miki's dad was holding tightly to that ball.
Memories can be vague. I saw it with my own eyes.
...
Really?

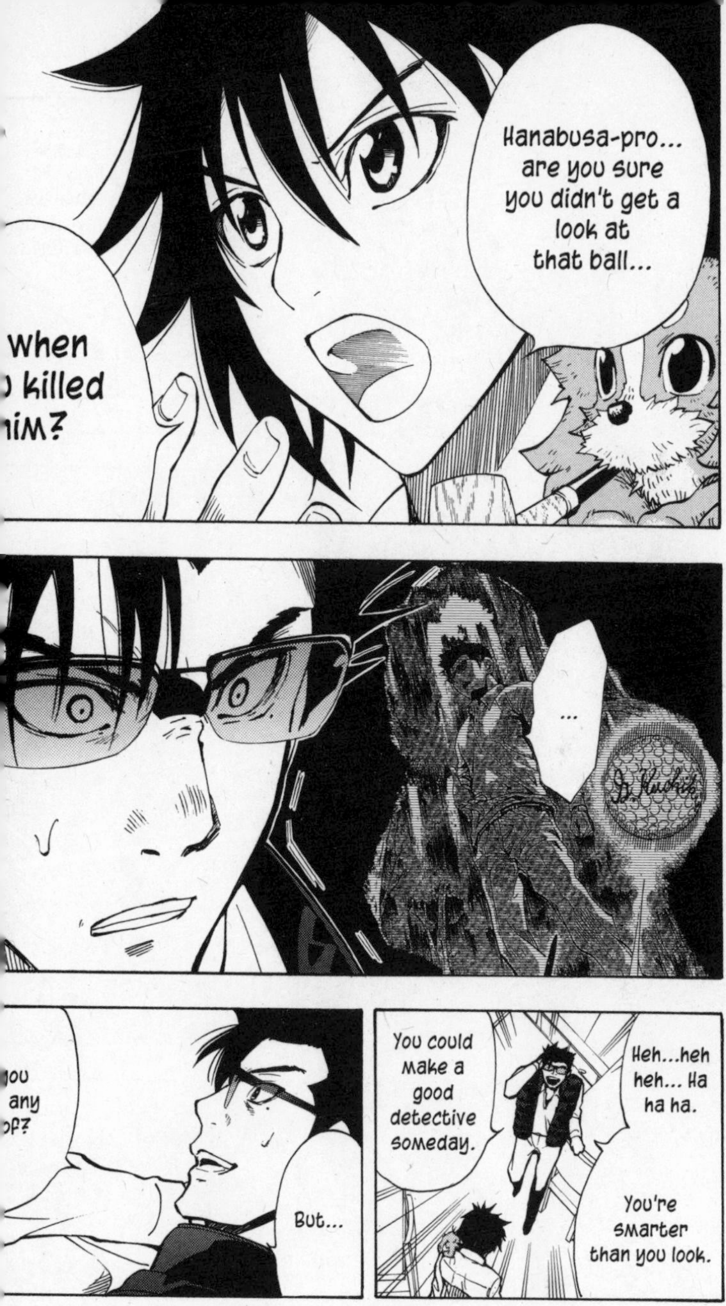
Hanabusa-pro... are you sure you didn't get a look at that ball...
when killed
...
Heh...heh heh... Ha ha ha.
You could make a good detective someday.
You're smarter than you look.
any
But...

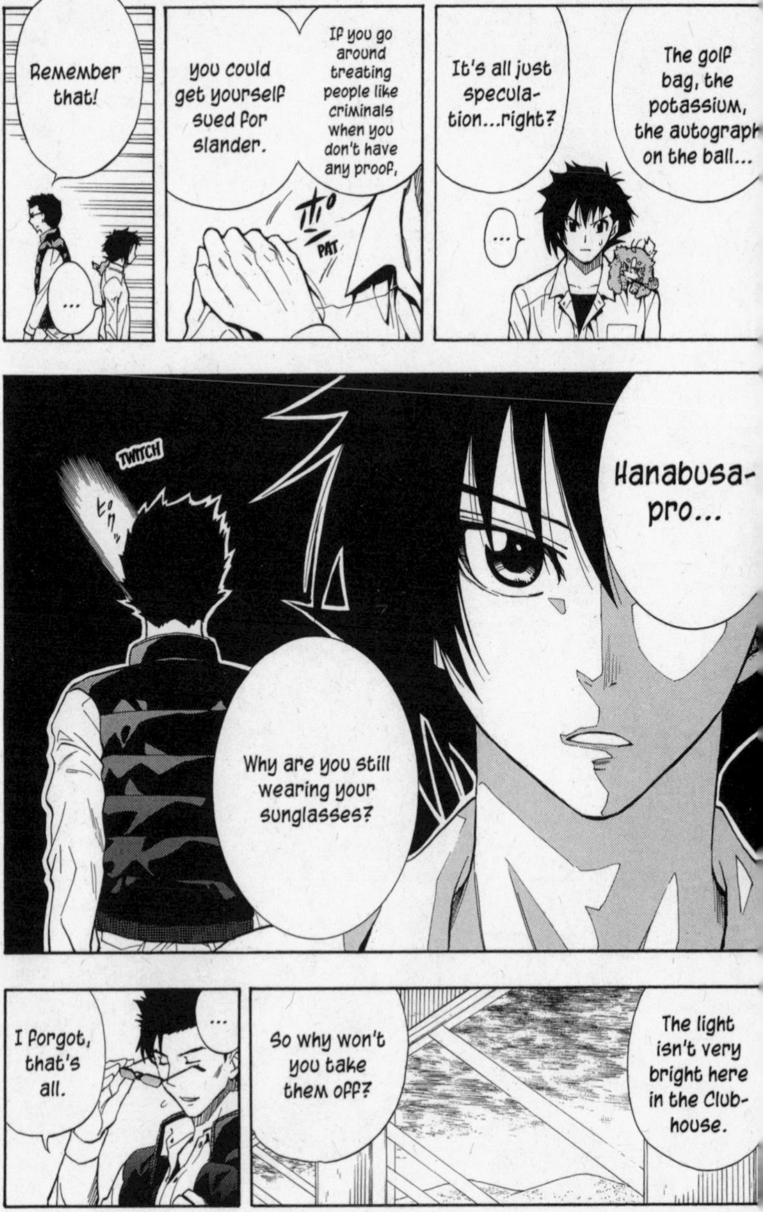

The golf bag, the potassium, the autograph on the ball...
It's all just specula-tion...right?
...
If you go around treating people like criminals when you don't have any proof,
you could get yourself sued for slander.
PAT
Remember that!
...
Hanabusa-pro...
TWITCH
Why are you still wearing your sunglasses?
The light isn't very bright here in the Club-house.
So why won't you take them off?
...
I forgot, that's all.

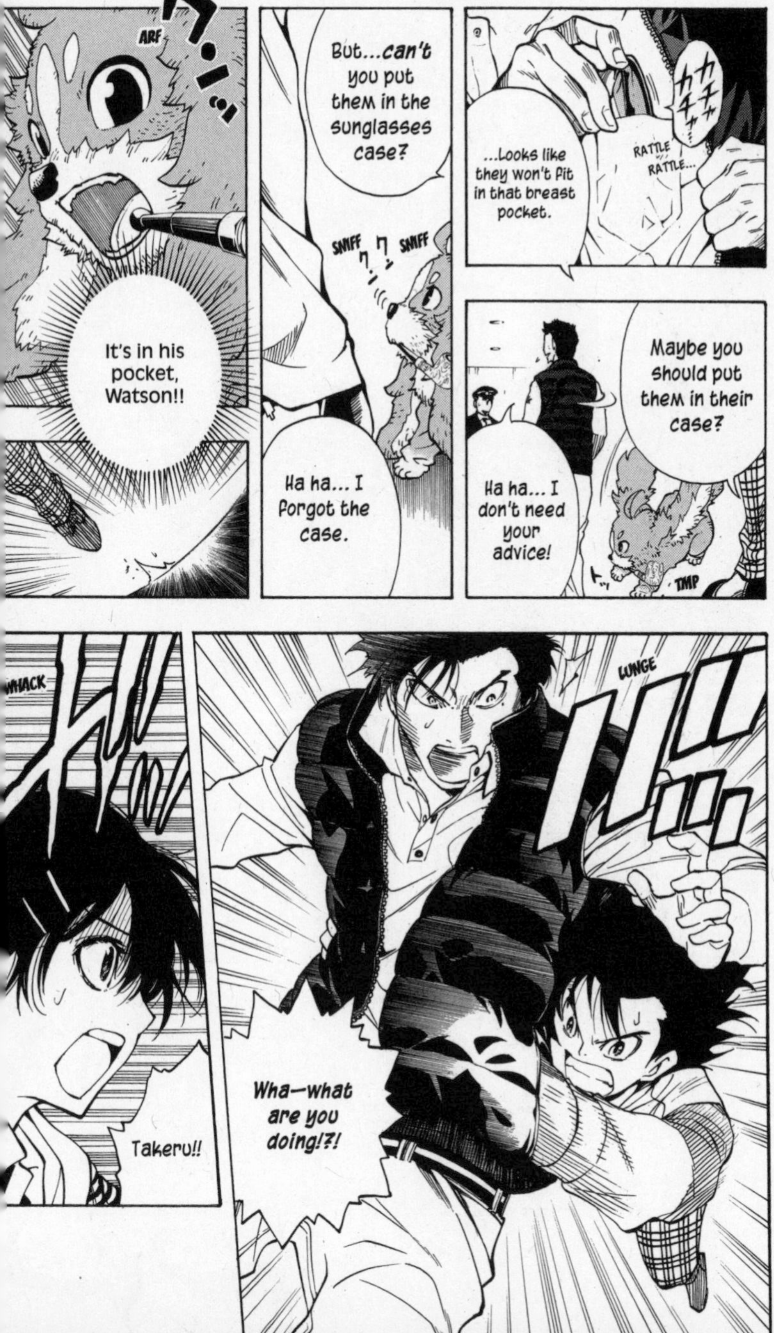
カチャカチャ
RATTLE RATTLE...
...Looks like they won't fit in that breast pocket.
Maybe you should put them in their case?
Ha ha... I don't need your advice!
TMP
But...can't you put them in the sunglasses case?
SNIFF SNIFF
Ha ha... I forgot the case.
ARF
It's in his pocket, Watson!!
LUNGE
Wha—what are you doing!?!
WHACK
Takeru!!

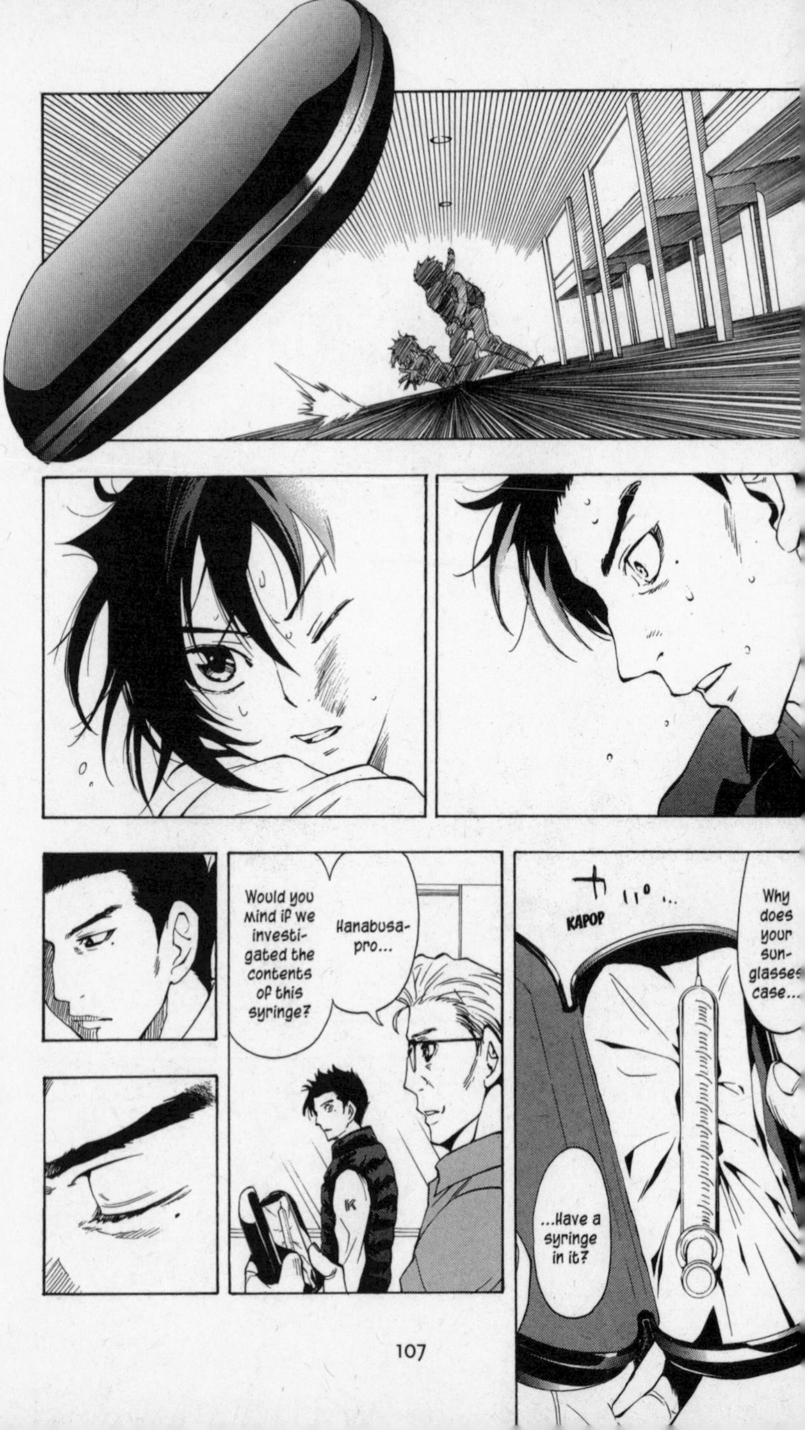
KAPOP
Why does your sunglasses case...
...Have a syringe in it?
Hanabusa-pro...
Would you mind if we investigated the contents of this syringe?

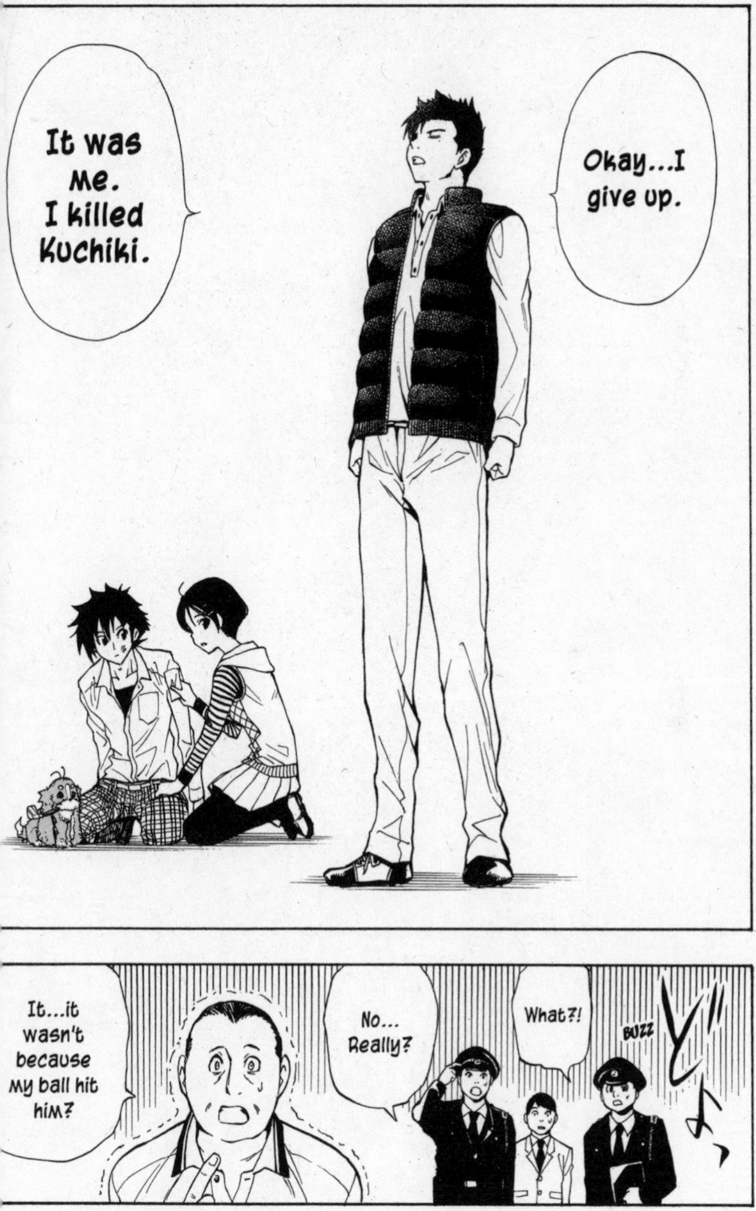
Okay...I give up.
It was me. I killed Kuchiki.
BUZZ
What?!
No... Really?
It...it wasn't because my ball hit him?

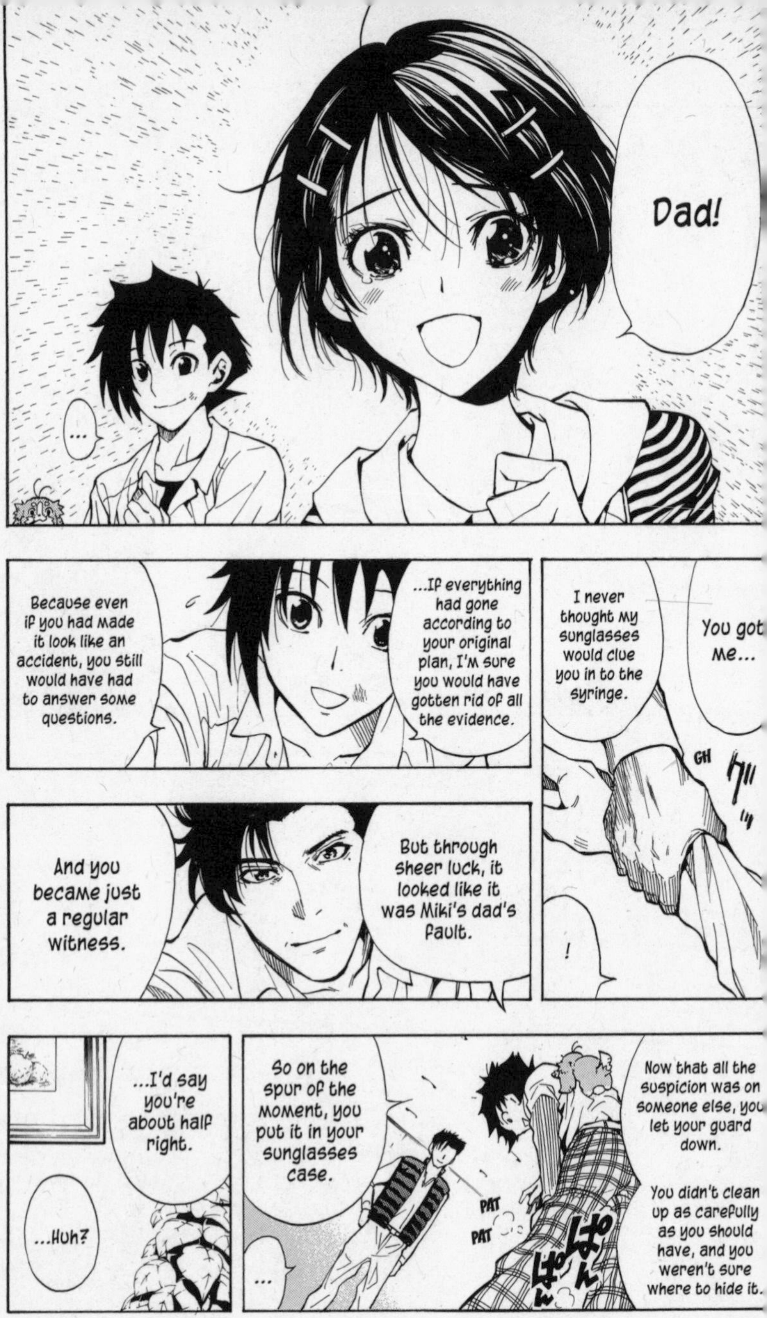

Dad!
...
You got me...
I never thought my sunglasses would clue you in to the syringe.
GH
!
...If everything had gone according to your original plan, I'm sure you would have gotten rid of all the evidence.
Because even if you had made it look like an accident, you still would have had to answer some questions.
But through sheer luck, it looked like it was Miki's dad's fault.
And you became just a regular witness.
Now that all the suspicion was on someone else, you let your guard down.
You didn't clean up as carefully as you should have, and you weren't sure where to hide it.
PAT
PAT
So on the spur of the moment, you put it in your sunglasses case.
...
...I'd say you're about half right.
...Huh?

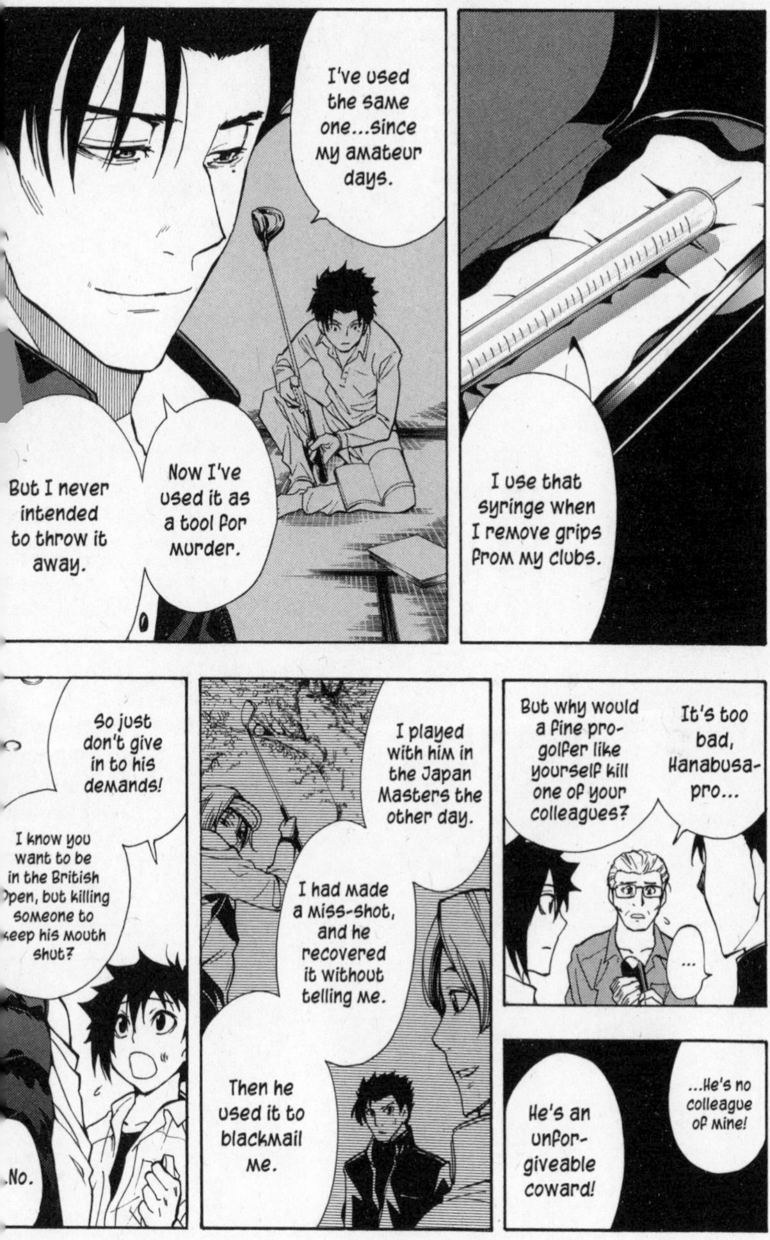
I use that syringe when I remove grips from my clubs.
I've used the same one...since my amateur days.
Now I've used it as a tool for murder.
But I never intended to throw it away.
It's too bad, Hanabusa-pro...
But why would a fine pro-golfer like yourself kill one of your colleagues?
...
...He's no colleague of mine!
He's an unforgiveable coward!
I played with him in the Japan Masters the other day.
I had made a miss-shot, and he recovered it without telling me.
Then he used it to blackmail me.
So just don't give in to his demands!
I know you want to be in the British pen, but killing someone to eep his mouth shut?
.No.

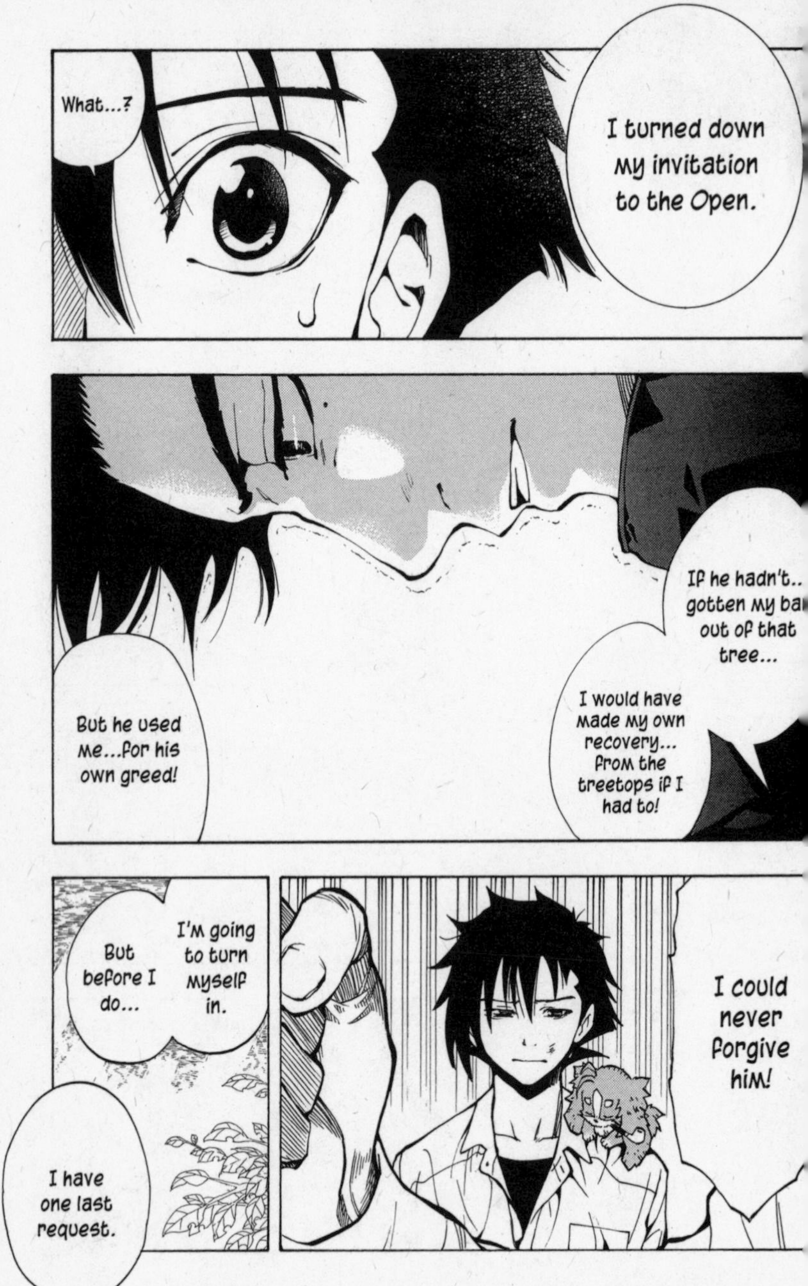
I turned down my invitation to the Open.
What...?
If he hadn't.. gotten my ba out of that tree...
I would have made my own recovery... from the treetops if I had to!
But he used me...for his own greed!
I could never forgive him!
I'm going to turn myself in.
But before I do...
I have one last request.

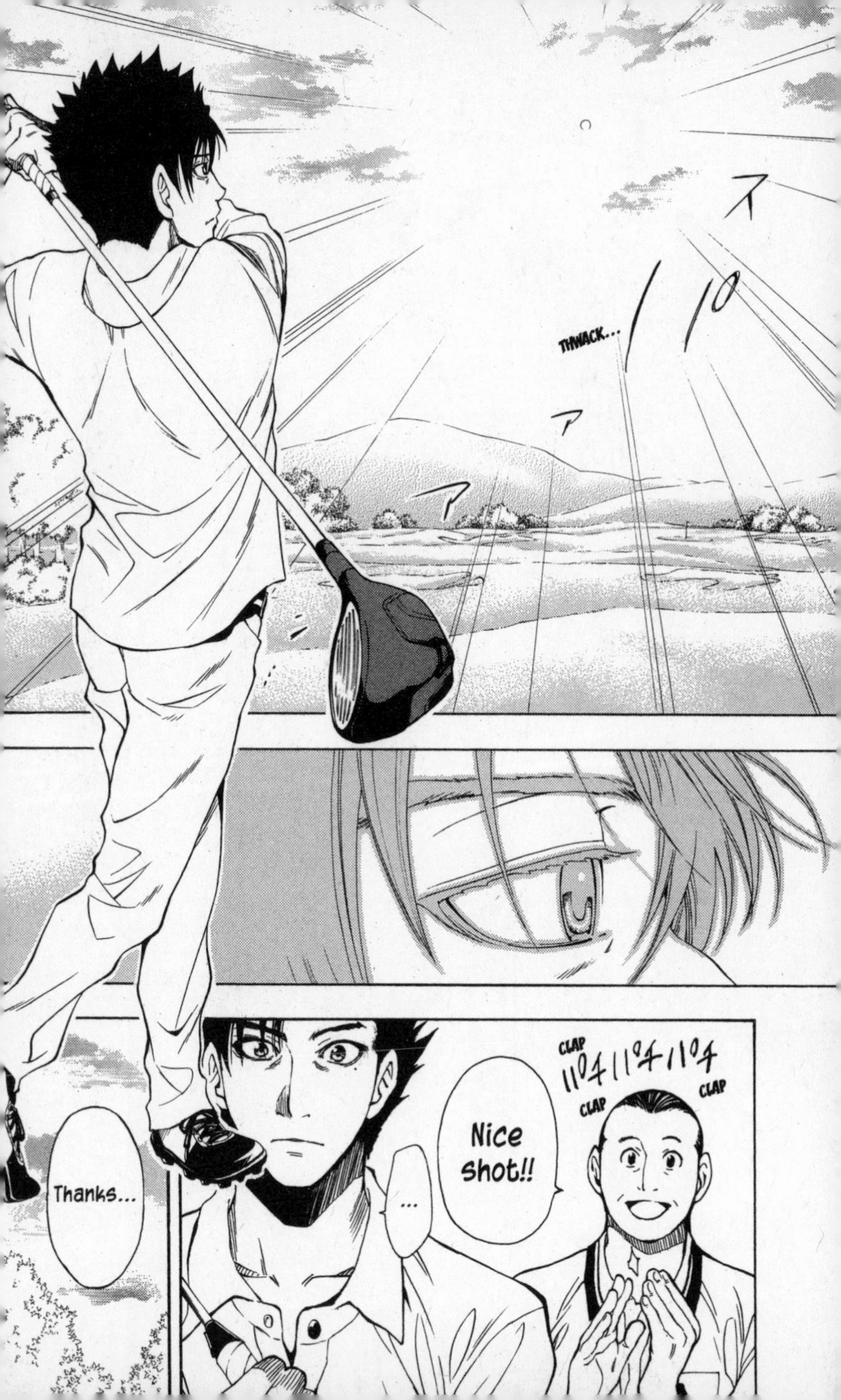

スパァァ
THWACK...
CLAP
パチパチパチ
CLAP
CLAP
Nice shot!!
...
Thanks...

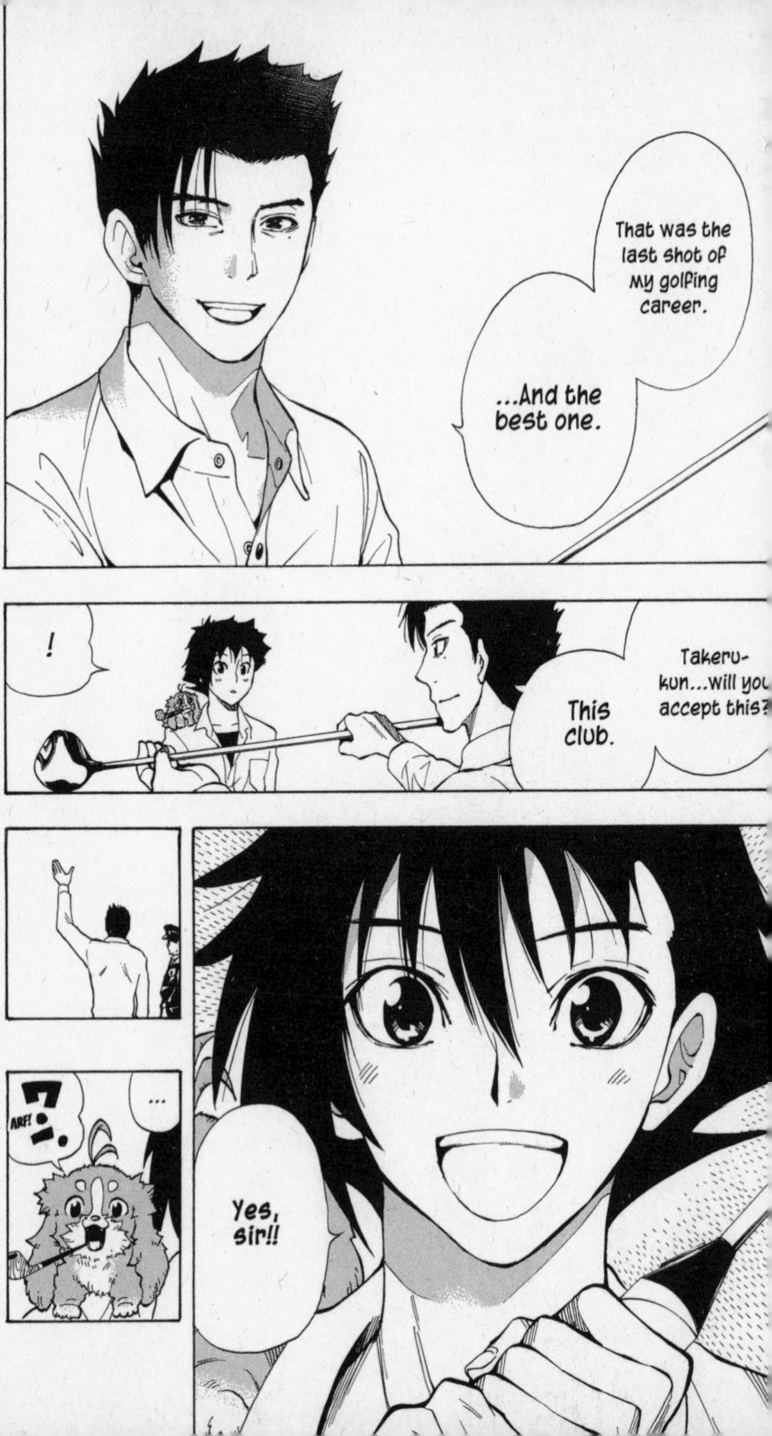
That was the last shot of my golfing career.
...And the best one.
Takeru-kun...will you accept this?
This club.
!
Yes, sir!!
...
?!
ARF!

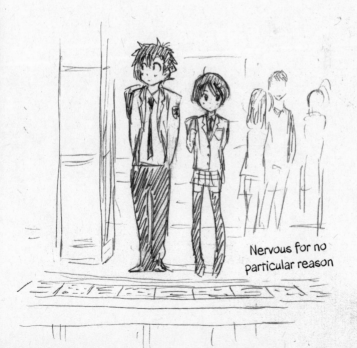

Nervous for no
particular reason

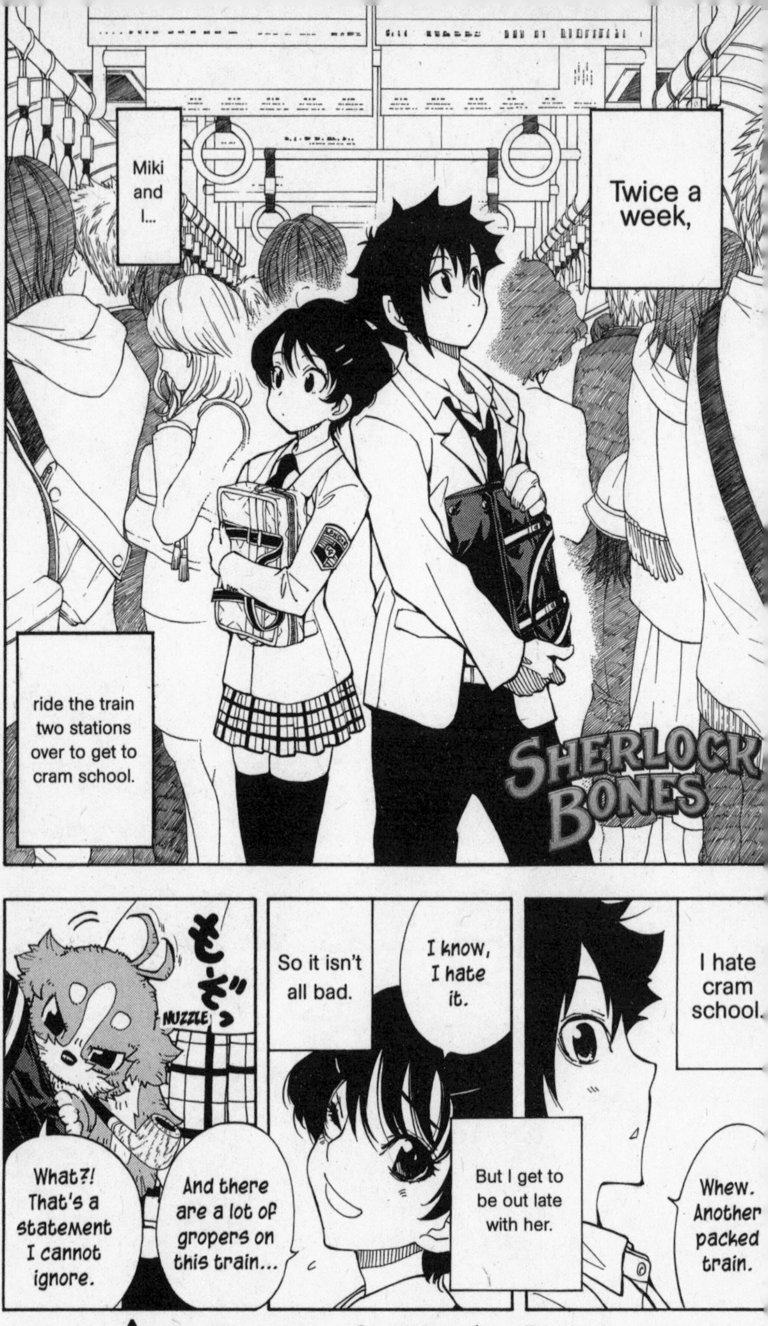
Twice a week,
Miki and I...
ride the train two stations over to get to cram school.
SHERLOCK BONES
I hate cram school.
Whew. Another packed train.
I know, I hate it.
So it isn't all bad.
But I get to be out late with her.
もぞっ
NUZZLE
And there are a lot of gropers on this train...
What?! That's a statement I cannot ignore.

Case 4: ⚜ An Equation for Murder, Part 1

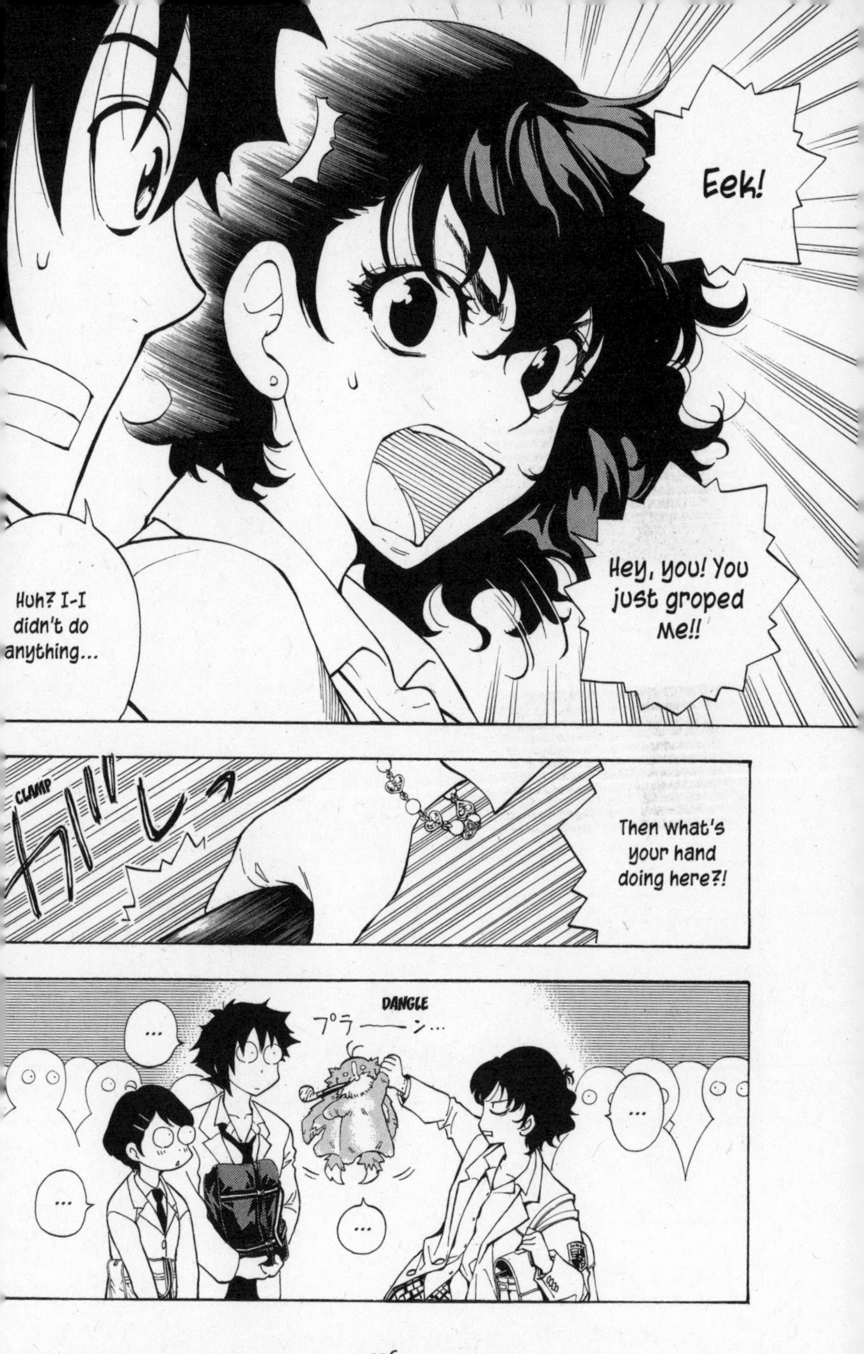

Eek!
Hey, you! You just groped me!!
Huh? I-I didn't do anything...
Then what's your hand doing here?!
CLAMP
...
DANGLE
プラ――ン…
...
...
...
...

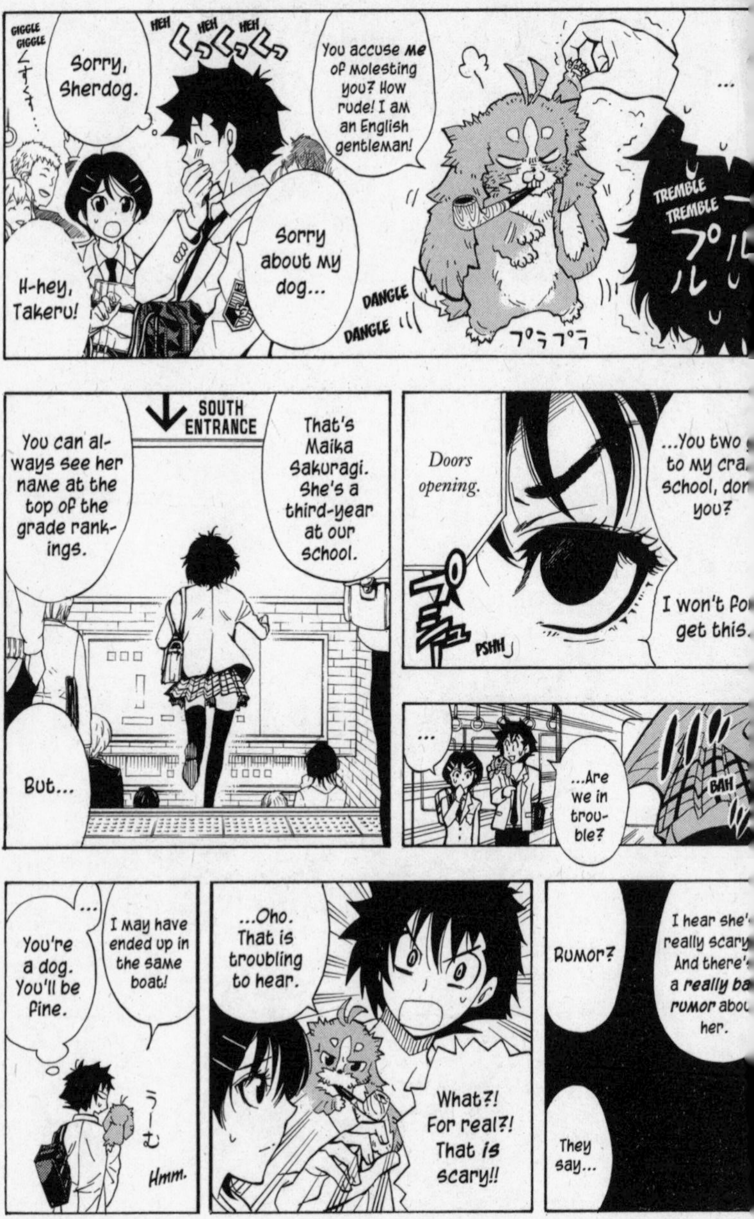
...
TREMBLE TREMBLE
プルプル
You accuse *me* of molesting you? How rude! I am an English gentleman!
HEH HEH HEH
くっくっくっ
Sorry about my dog...
DANGLE DANGLE
プラプラ
Sorry, Sherdog.
GIGGLE GIGGLE
くすくす...
H-hey, Takeru!
...You two
to my cra
school, dor
you?
I won't fo
get this.
Doors opening.
PSHH
プシュー
BAH
...Are we in trou-ble?
...
That's Maika Sakuragi. She's a third-year at our school.
SOUTH ENTRANCE
You can al-ways see her name at the top of the grade rank-ings.
But...
I hear she'
really scary
And there'
a *really* ba
rumor abou
her.
Rumor?
They say...
...Oho. That is troubling to hear.
What?! For real?! That *is* scary!!
I may have ended up in the same boat!
...
You're a dog. You'll be fine.
うーむ
Hmm.

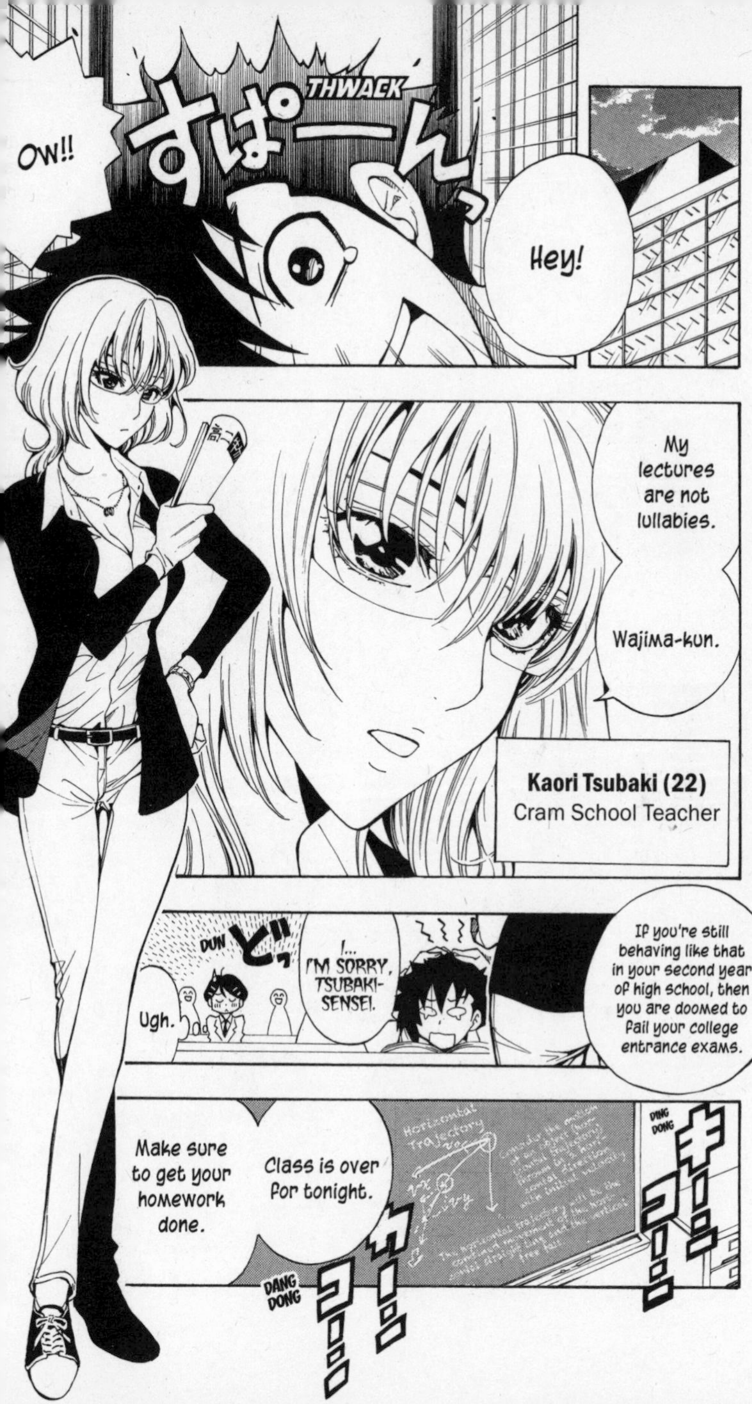

Hey!
すぱーんっ
THWACK
OW!!
My lectures are not lullabies.
Wajima-kun.
Kaori Tsubaki (22)
Cram School Teacher
If you're still behaving like that in your second year of high school, then you are doomed to fail your college entrance exams.
I... I'M SORRY, TSUBAKI-SENSEI.
DUN
どっ
Ugh.
DING DONG
キーンコーン
Class is over for tonight.
Make sure to get your homework done.
DANG DONG
カーンコーン

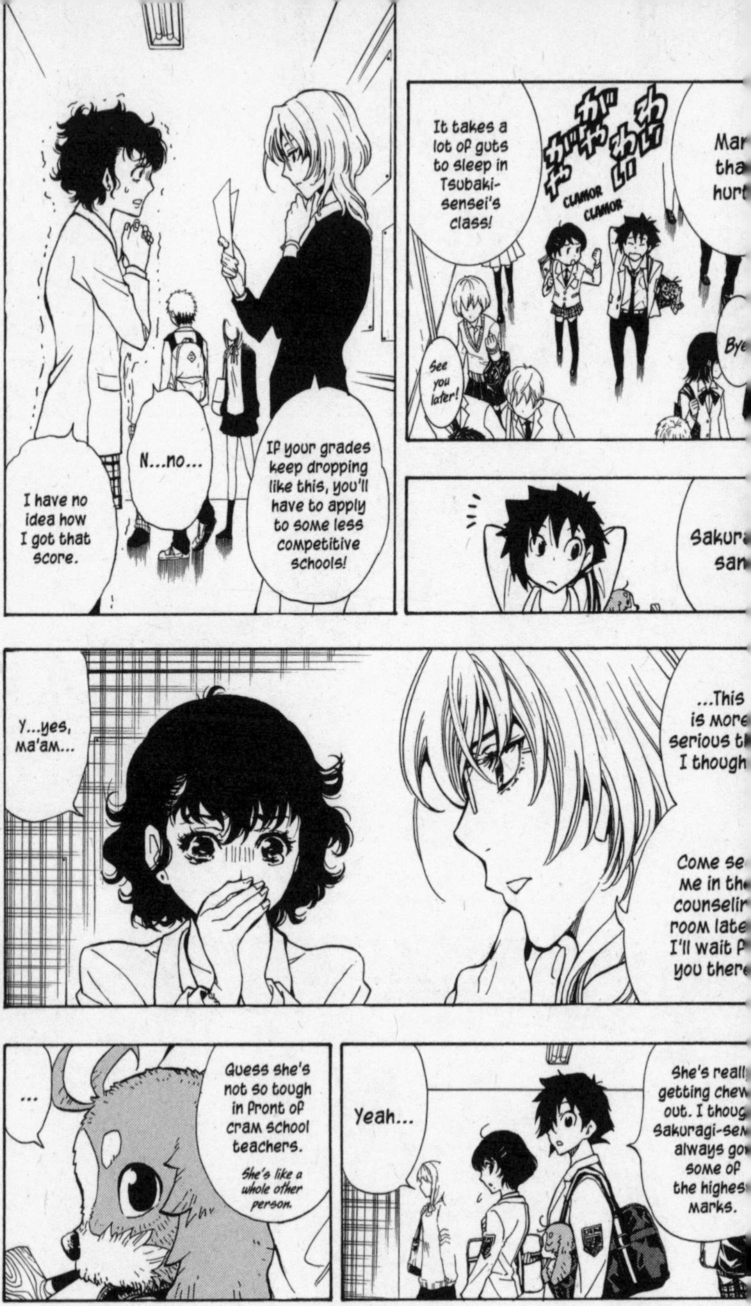

Mar
tha
hurt
がやがや
わいわい
CLAMOR
CLAMOR
It takes a lot of guts to sleep in Tsubaki-sensei's class!
Bye
See you later!
Sakura
san
If your grades keep dropping like this, you'll have to apply to some less competitive schools!
N...no...
I have no idea how I got that score.
...This is more serious t I though
Come se me in th counseli room late I'll wait f you there
Y...yes, ma'am...
She's reall getting chew out. I thoug Sakuragi-sen always go some of the highes marks.
Yeah...
Guess she's not so tough in front of cram school teachers.
She's like a whole other person.
...

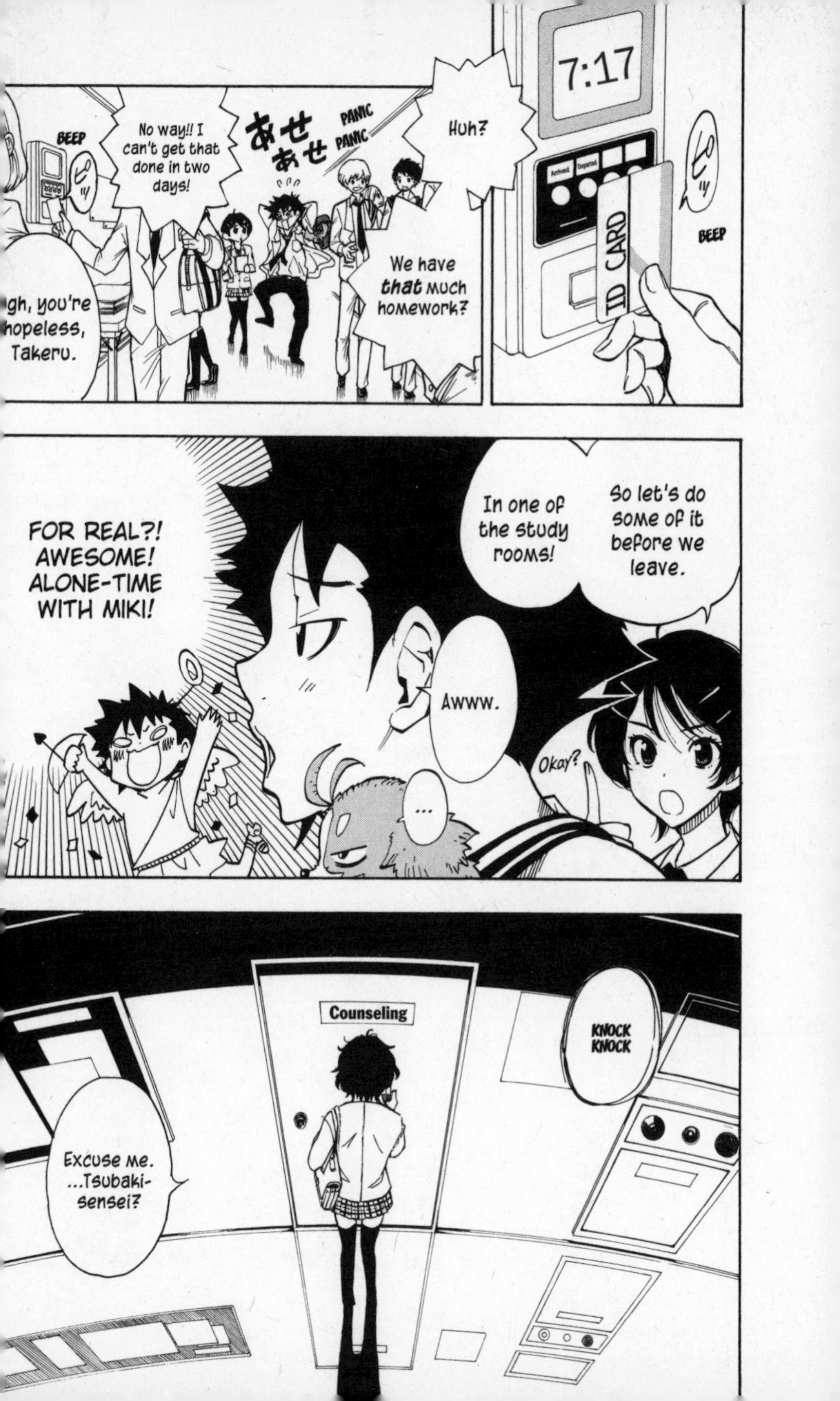
7:17
ID CARD
ピッ
BEEP
Huh?
We have *that* much homework?
あせ あせ
PANIC PANIC
No way!! I can't get that done in two days!
BEEP
ピッ
gh, you're hopeless, Takeru.
So let's do some of it before we leave.
In one of the study rooms!
Okay?
Awww.
...
FOR REAL?! AWESOME! ALONE-TIME WITH MIKI!
KNOCK KNOCK
Counseling
Excuse me. ...Tsubaki-sensei?

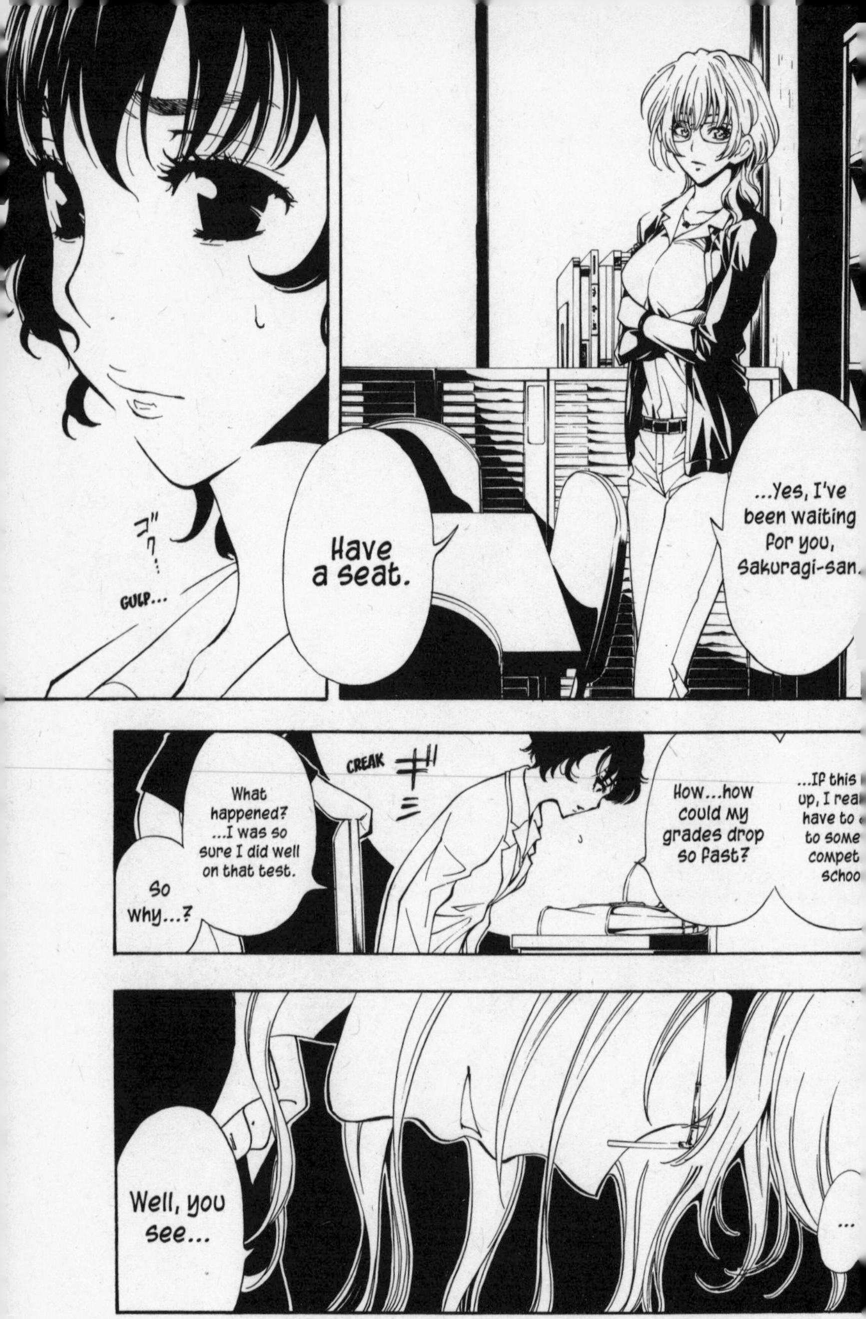
...Yes, I've been waiting for you, Sakuragi-san.
Have a seat.
ゴク…
GULP...
...If this
up, I rea
have to
to some
compet
schoo
How...how could my grades drop so fast?
CREAK
What happened? ...I was so sure I did well on that test.
So why...?
...
Well, you see...

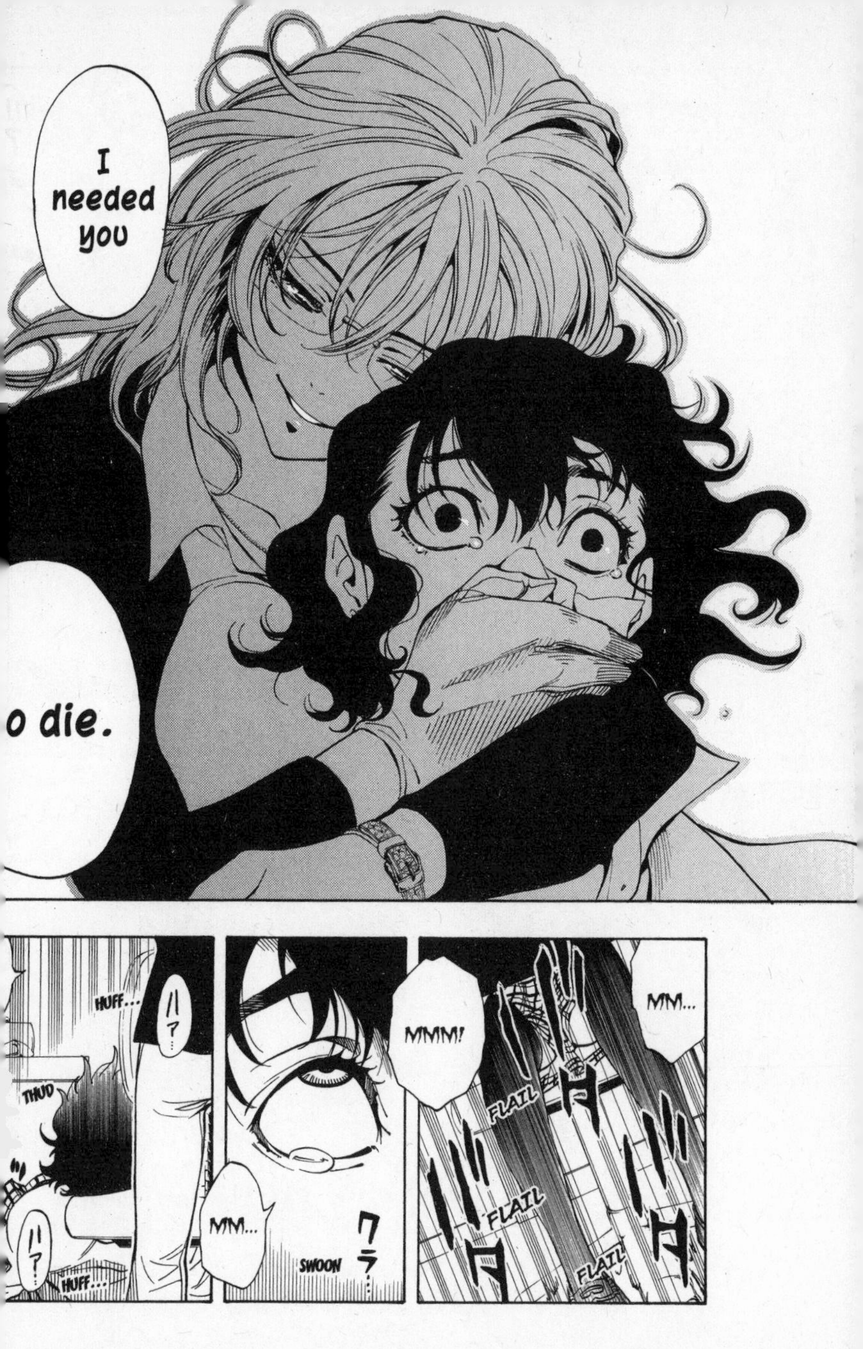

I needed you
o die.
MM...
MMM!
FLAIL
FLAIL
FLAIL
MM...
SWOON
クラ…
HUFF...
ハァ…
THUD
ハァ…
HUFF...

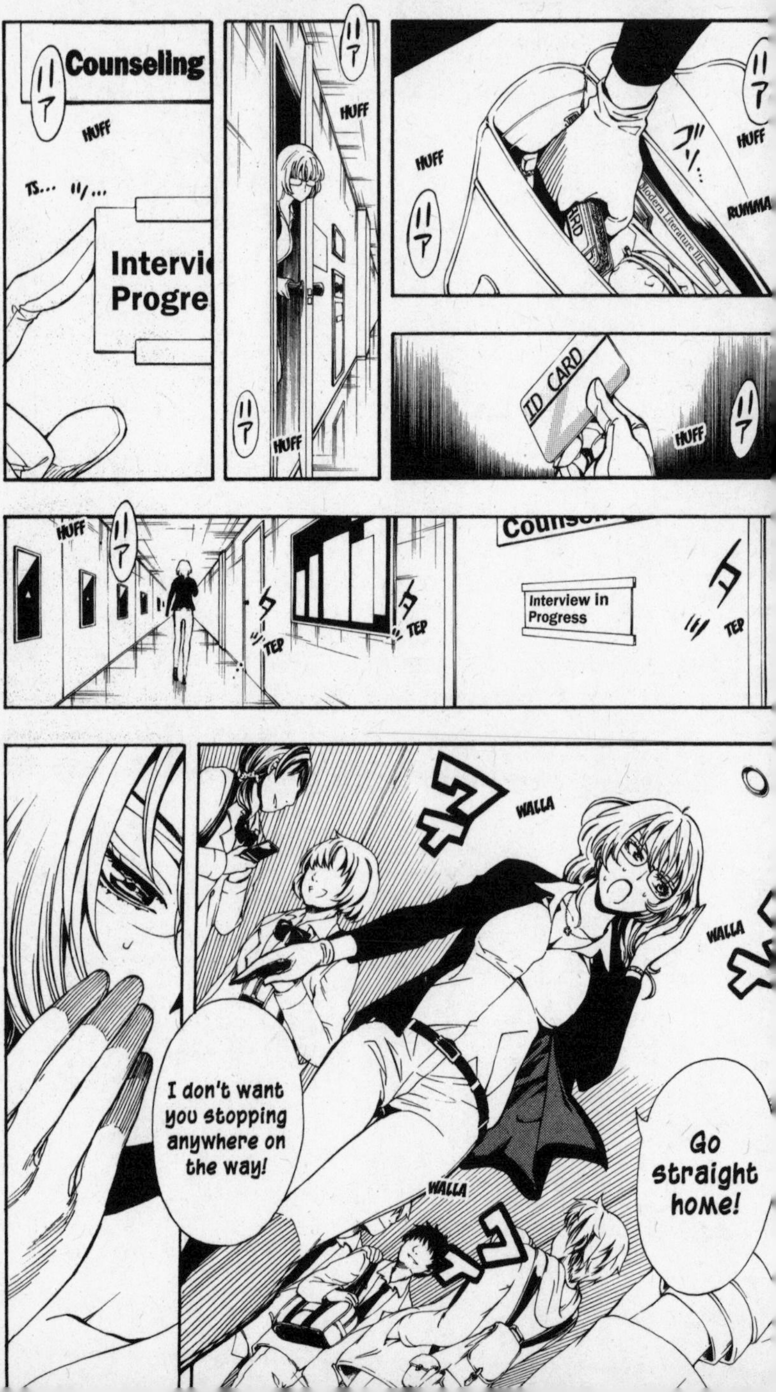
HUFF
RUMMA
Modern Literature III
HUFF
ID CARD
HUFF
HUFF
HUFF
Counseling
HUFF
TS...
Intervie
Progre
Interview in
Progress
TEP
TEP
TEP
HUFF
WALLA
WALLA
Go straight home!
I don't want you stopping anywhere on the way!
WALLA

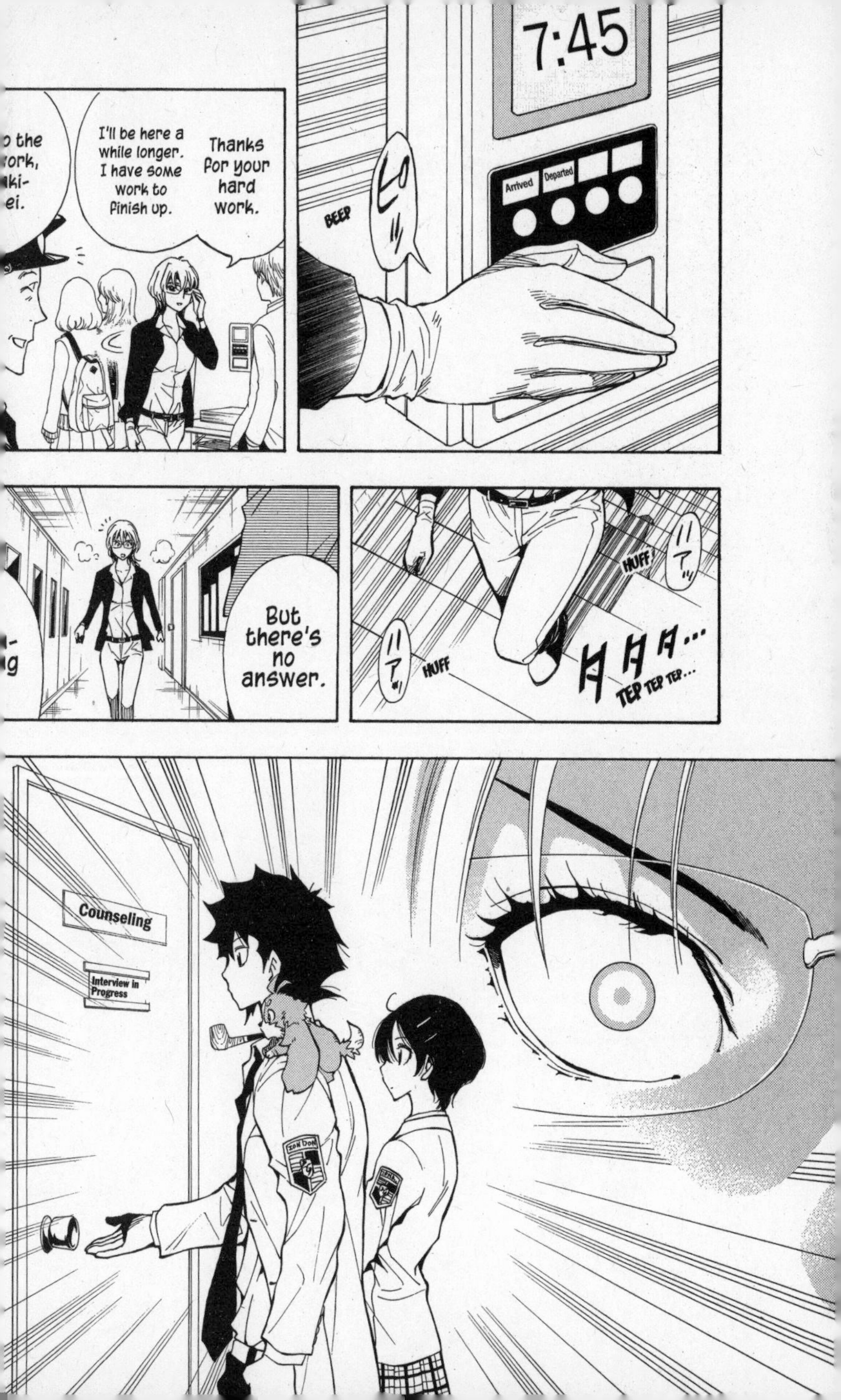
7:45
Arrived
Departed
BEEP
Thanks for your hard work.
I'll be here a while longer. I have some work to finish up.
HUFF
HUFF
TEP TEP TEP...
But there's no answer.
Counseling
Interview in Progress

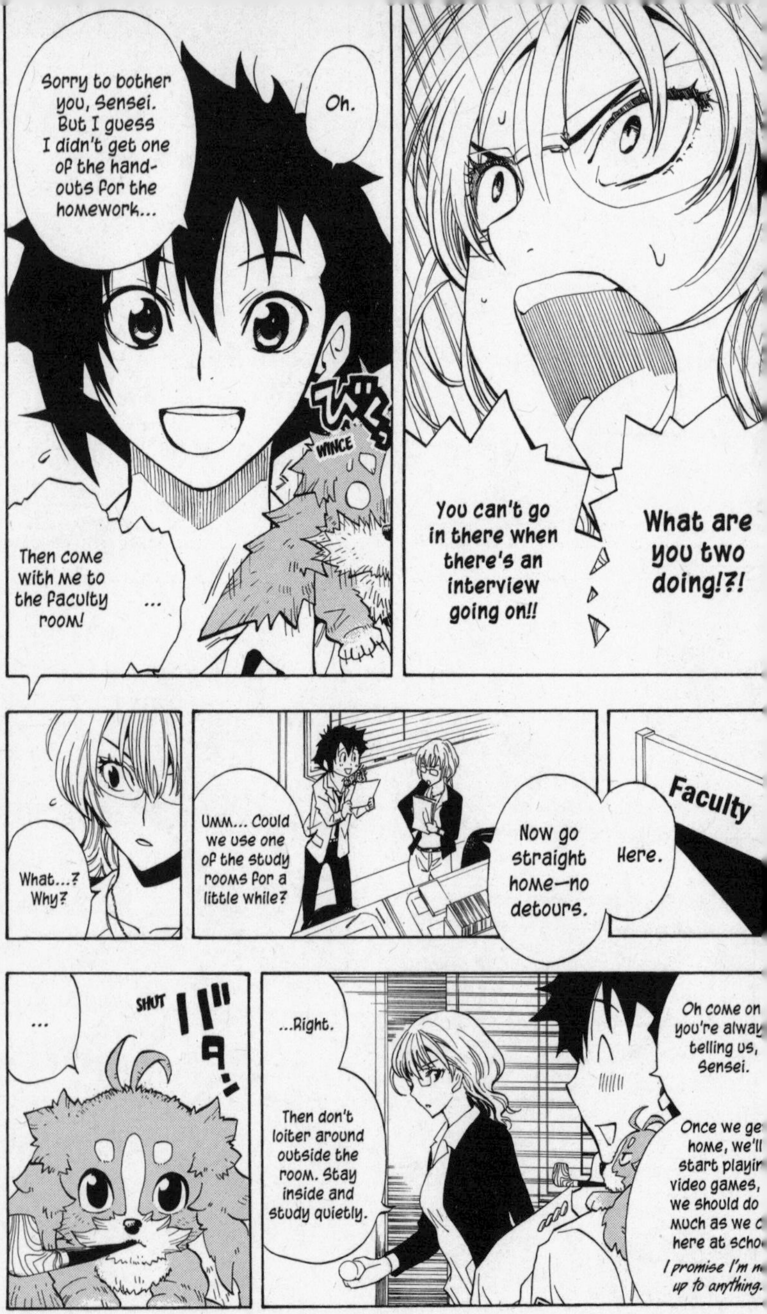
What are you two doing!?!
You can't go in there when there's an interview going on!!
Oh.
Sorry to bother you, Sensei. But I guess I didn't get one of the hand-outs for the homework...
WINCE
...
Then come with me to the faculty room!
Faculty
Here.
Now go straight home—no detours.
Umm... Could we use one of the study rooms for a little while?
What...? Why?
Oh come on you're alway telling us, Sensei.
Once we ge home, we'll start playir video games, we should do much as we c here at scho
I promise I'm n up to anything.
...Right.
Then don't loiter around outside the room. Stay inside and study quietly.
SHUT
...

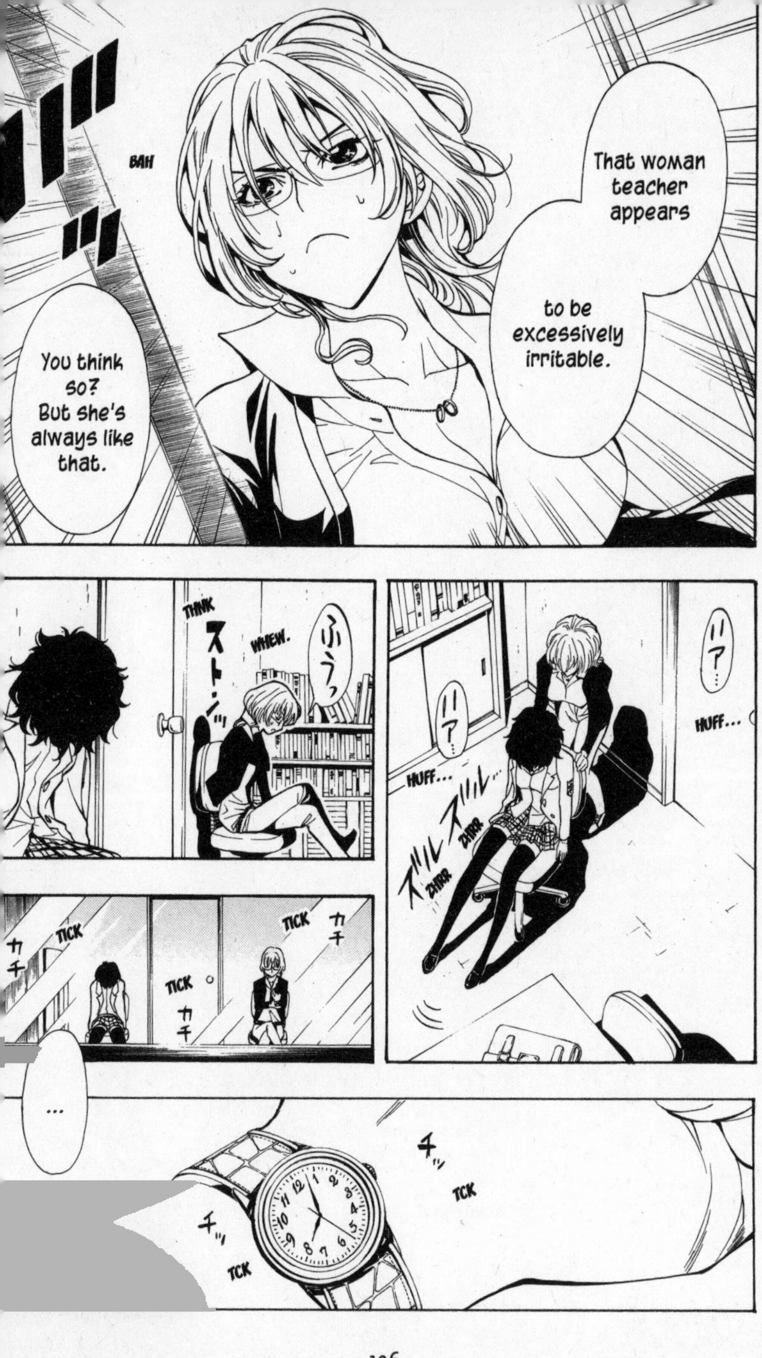

That woman teacher appears
to be excessively irritable.
BAH
You think so? But she's always like that.
ハア…
HUFF...
ハア…
HUFF...
ズルズル
ZHRR
ZHRR
ふうっ
WHEW.
ストンッ
THINK
カチ
TICK
カチ
TICK
カチ
TICK
...
チッ
TCK
チッ
TCK

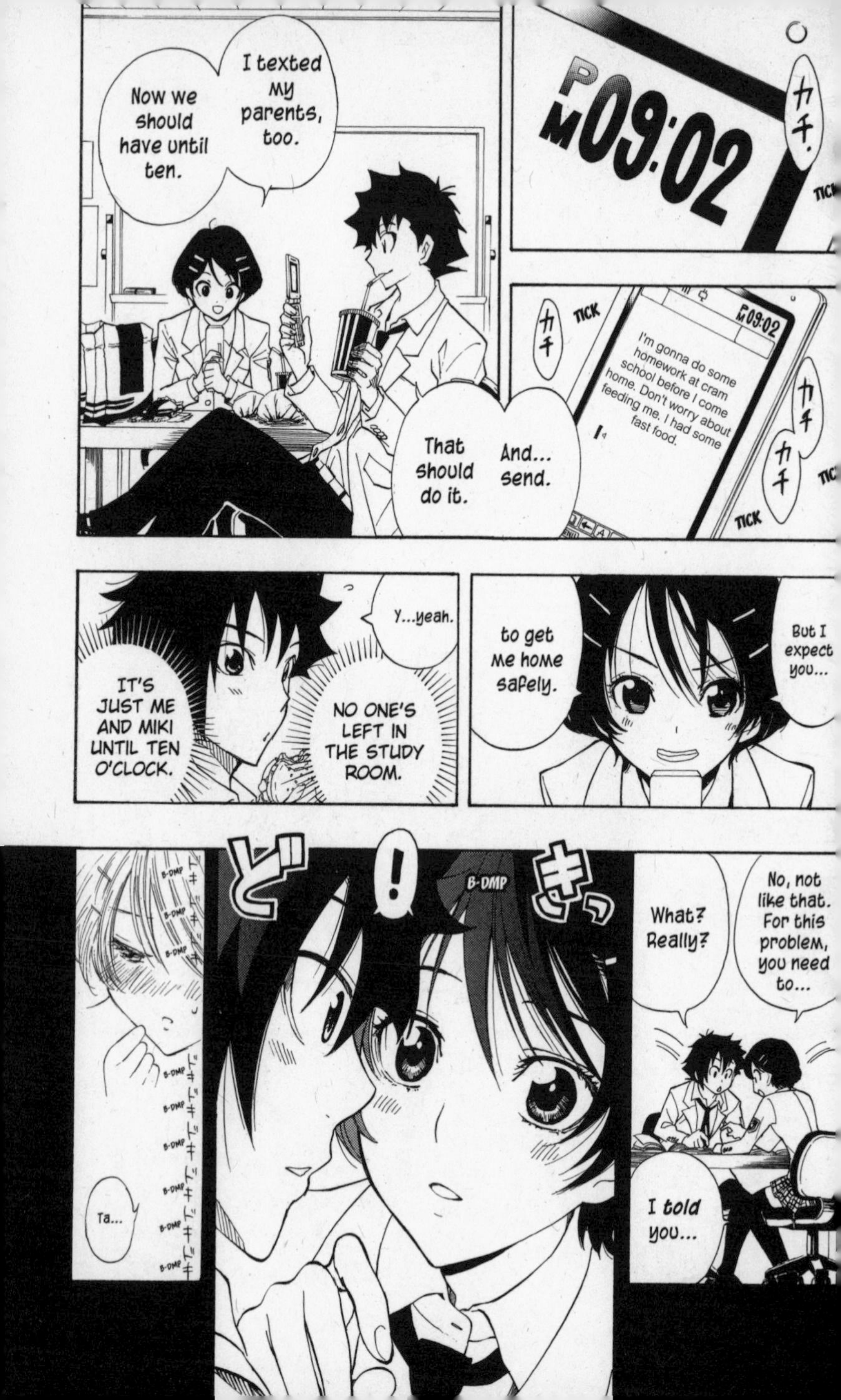
カチ.
TICK
PM 09:02
カチ
カチ
TICK
PM 09:02
I'm gonna do some homework at cram school before I come home. Don't worry about feeding me. I had some fast food.
TICK
カチ
TICK
And... send.
I texted my parents, too.
Now we should have until ten.
That should do it.
But I expect you...
to get me home safely.
Y...yeah.
NO ONE'S LEFT IN THE STUDY ROOM.
IT'S JUST ME AND MIKI UNTIL TEN O'CLOCK.
No, not like that. For this problem, you need to...
What? Really?
I told you...
きっ
B-DMP
!
ど
B-DMP ドキ
B-DMP ドキ
B-DMP ドキ
B-DMP ドキ
B-DMP ドキ
B-DMP ドキ
B-DMP ドキ
B-DMP ドキ
B-DMP ドキ
Ta...

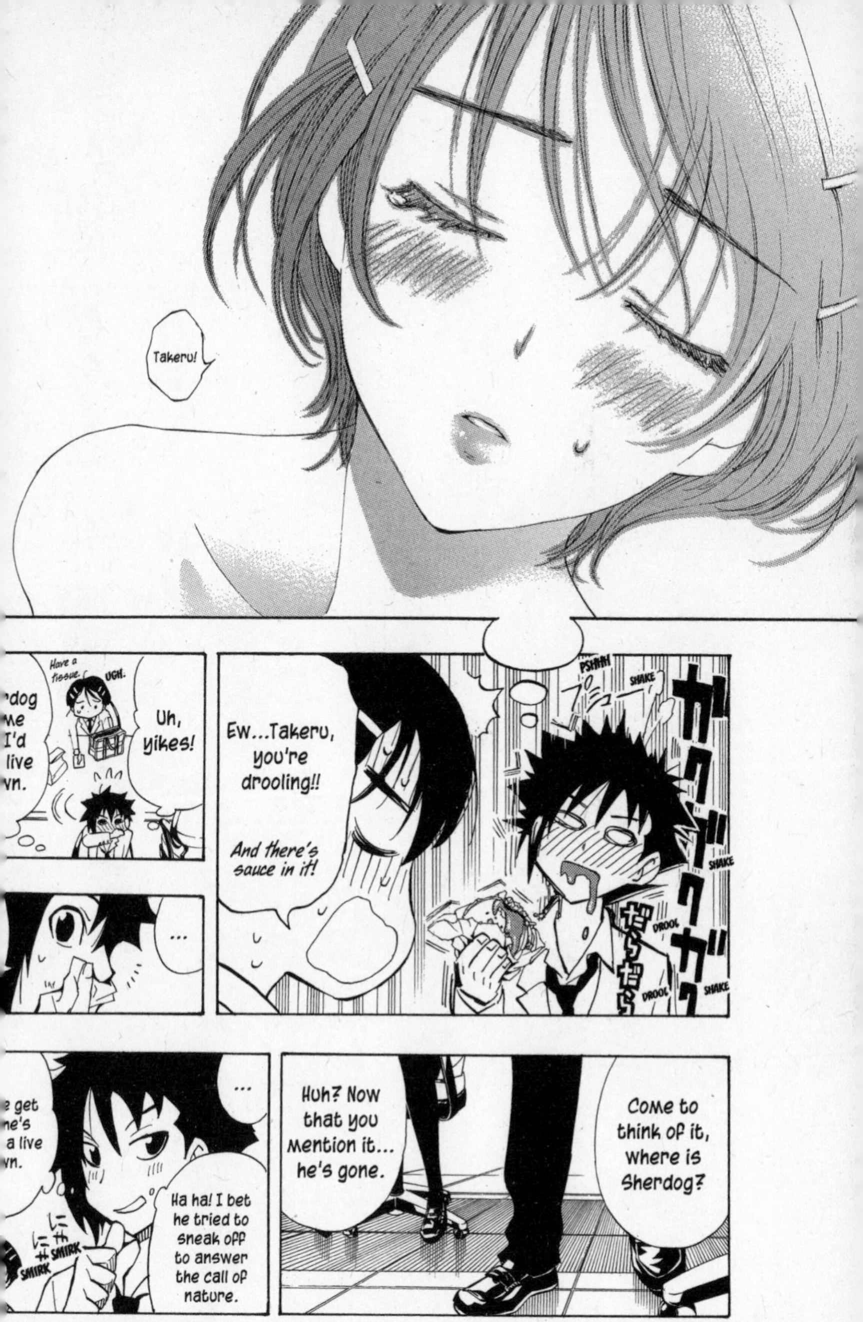
Takeru!
PSHHH
SHAKE
Ew...Takeru, you're drooling!!
And there's sauce in it!
SHAKE
DROOL
DROOL
SHAKE
Have a tissue.
UGH.
Uh, yikes!
...
Come to think of it, where is Sherdog?
Huh? Now that you mention it... he's gone.
...
Ha ha! I bet he tried to sneak off to answer the call of nature.
SMIRK
SMIRK

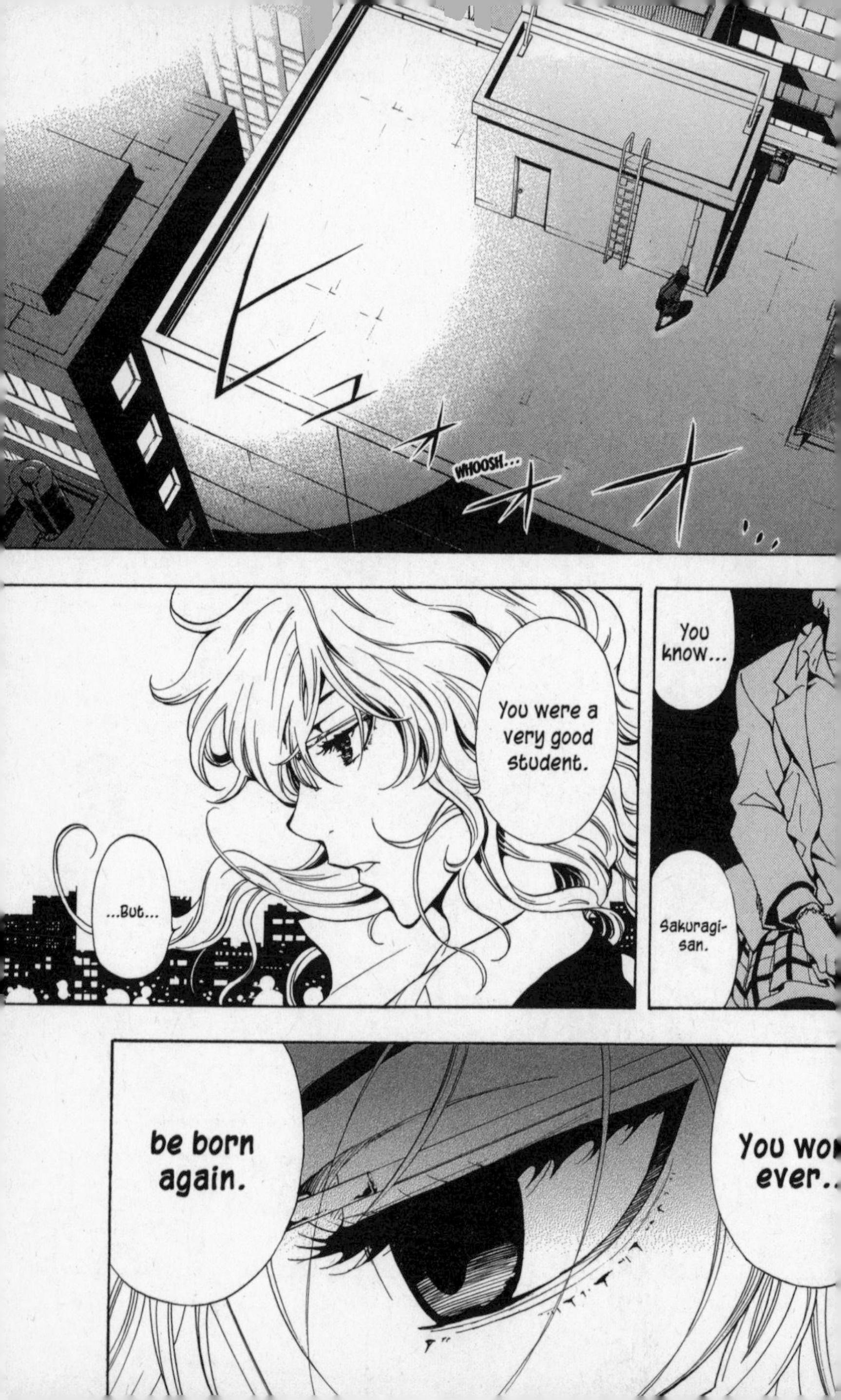

WHOOSH...
You know...
Sakuragi-san.
You were a very good student.
...But...
You wo ever..
be born again.

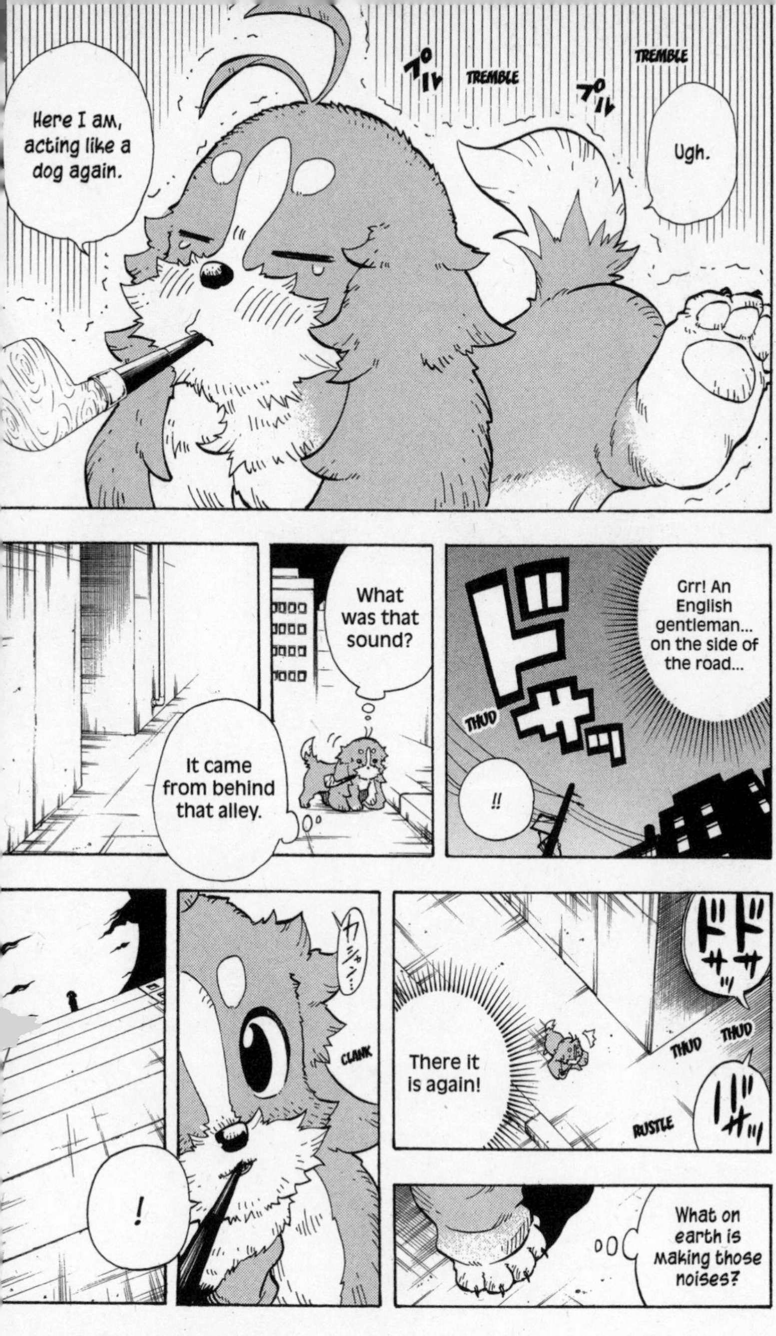

TREMBLE
Ugh.
TREMBLE
Here I am, acting like a dog again.
Grr! An English gentleman... on the side of the road...
THUD
!!
What was that sound?
It came from behind that alley.
THUD
THUD
There it is again!
RUSTLE
What on earth is making those noises?
CLANK
!

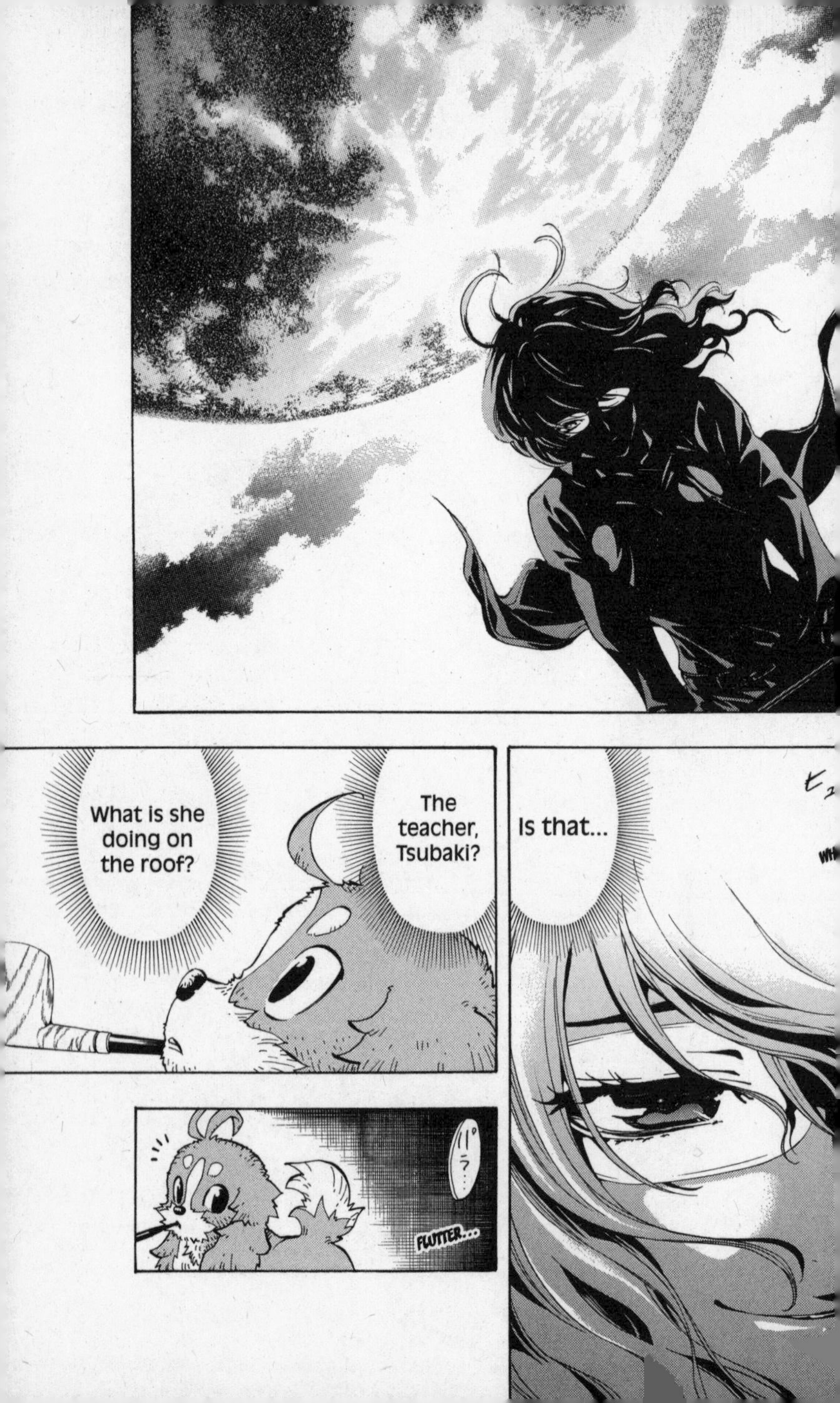

Is that...
The teacher, Tsubaki?
What is she doing on the roof?
パラ…
FLUTTER...

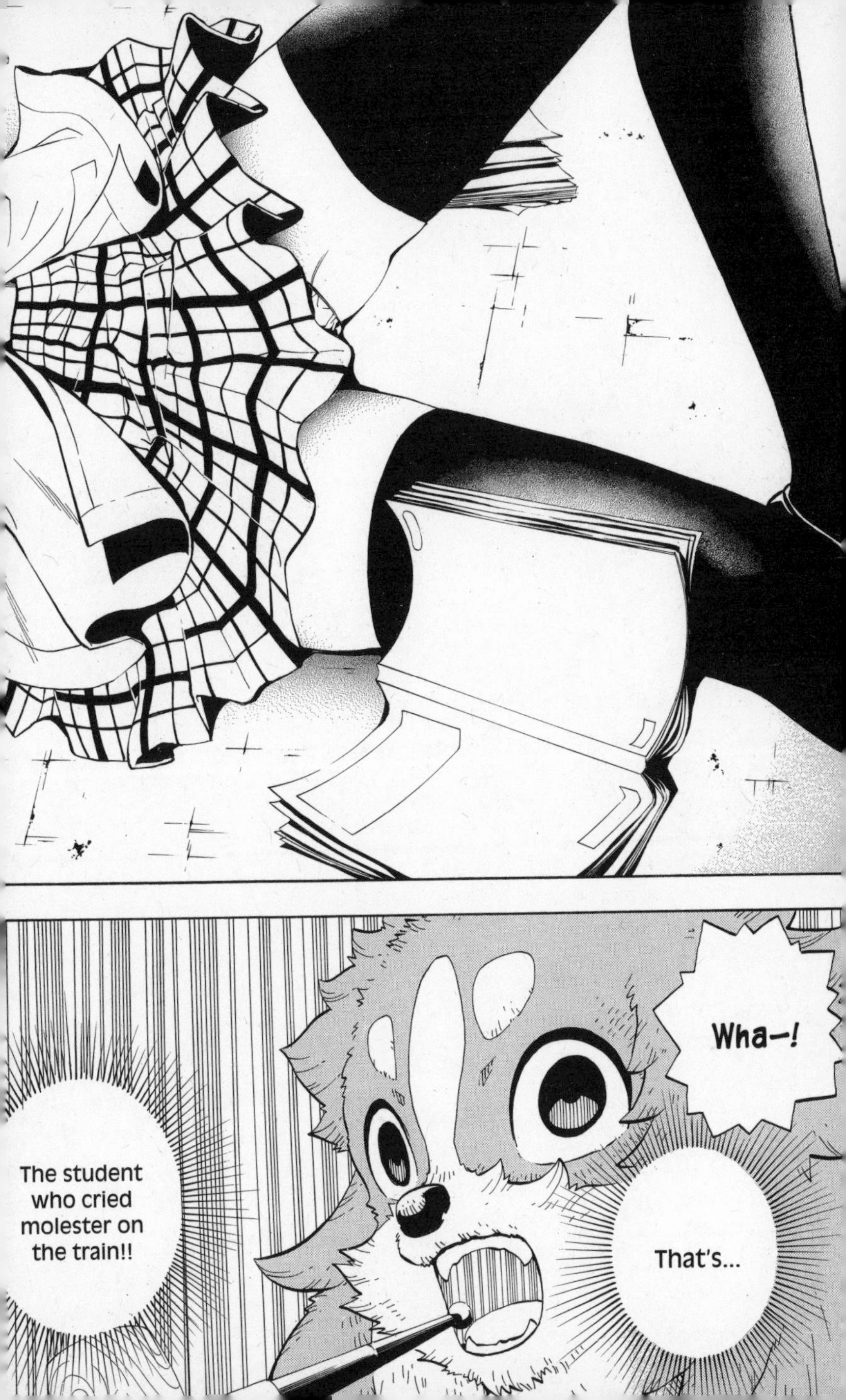
Wha–!
That's...
The student who cried molester on the train!!

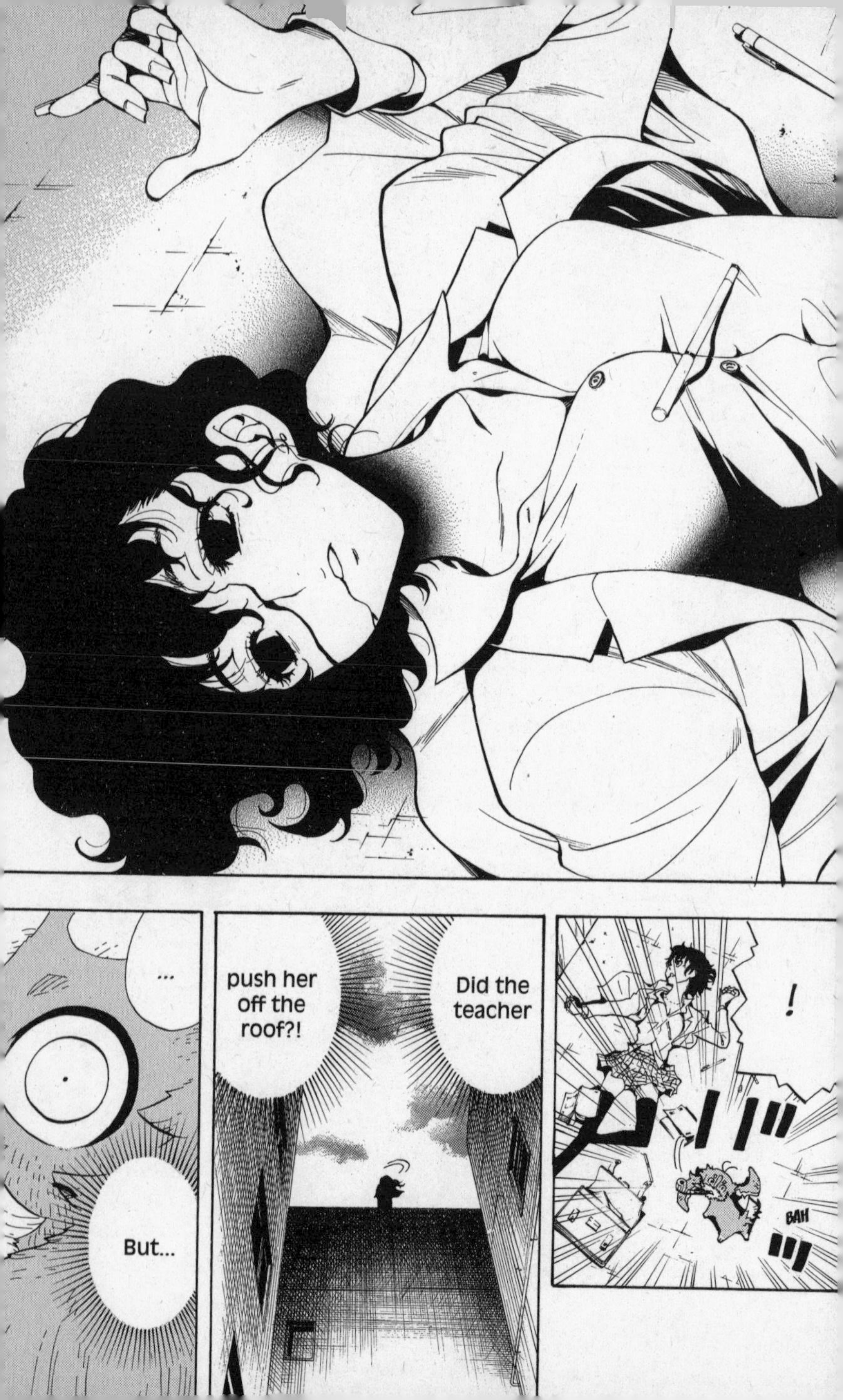
!
BAH
Did the teacher
push her off the roof?!
...
But...

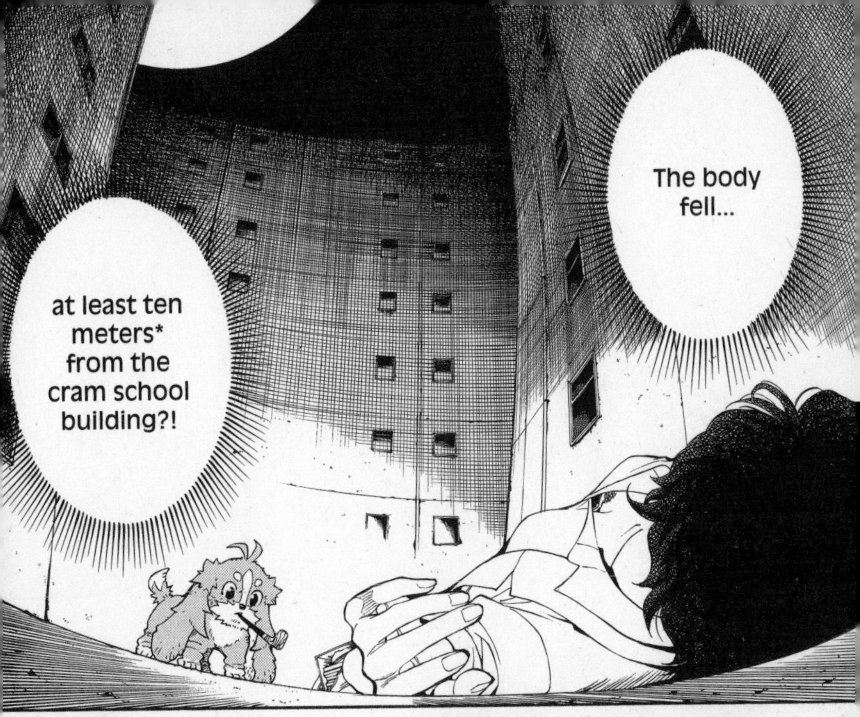
The body fell...
at least ten meters* from the cram school building?!

*About 30 feet.

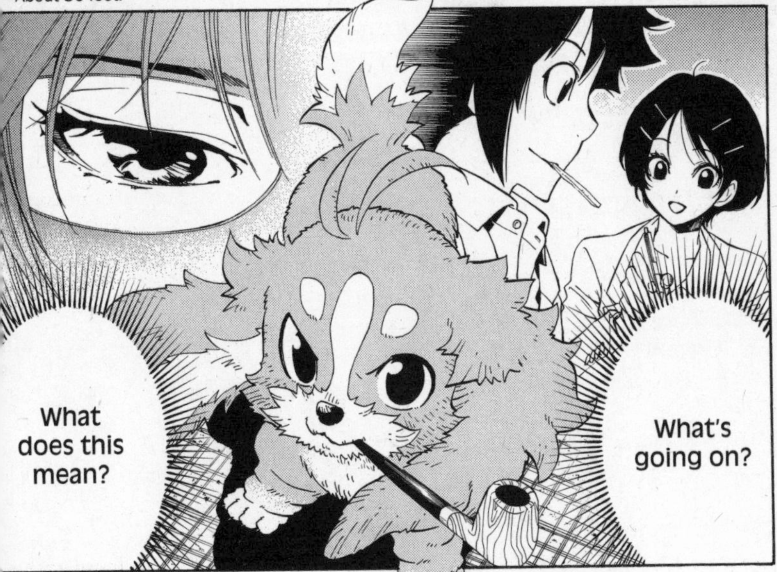
What's going on?
What does this mean?

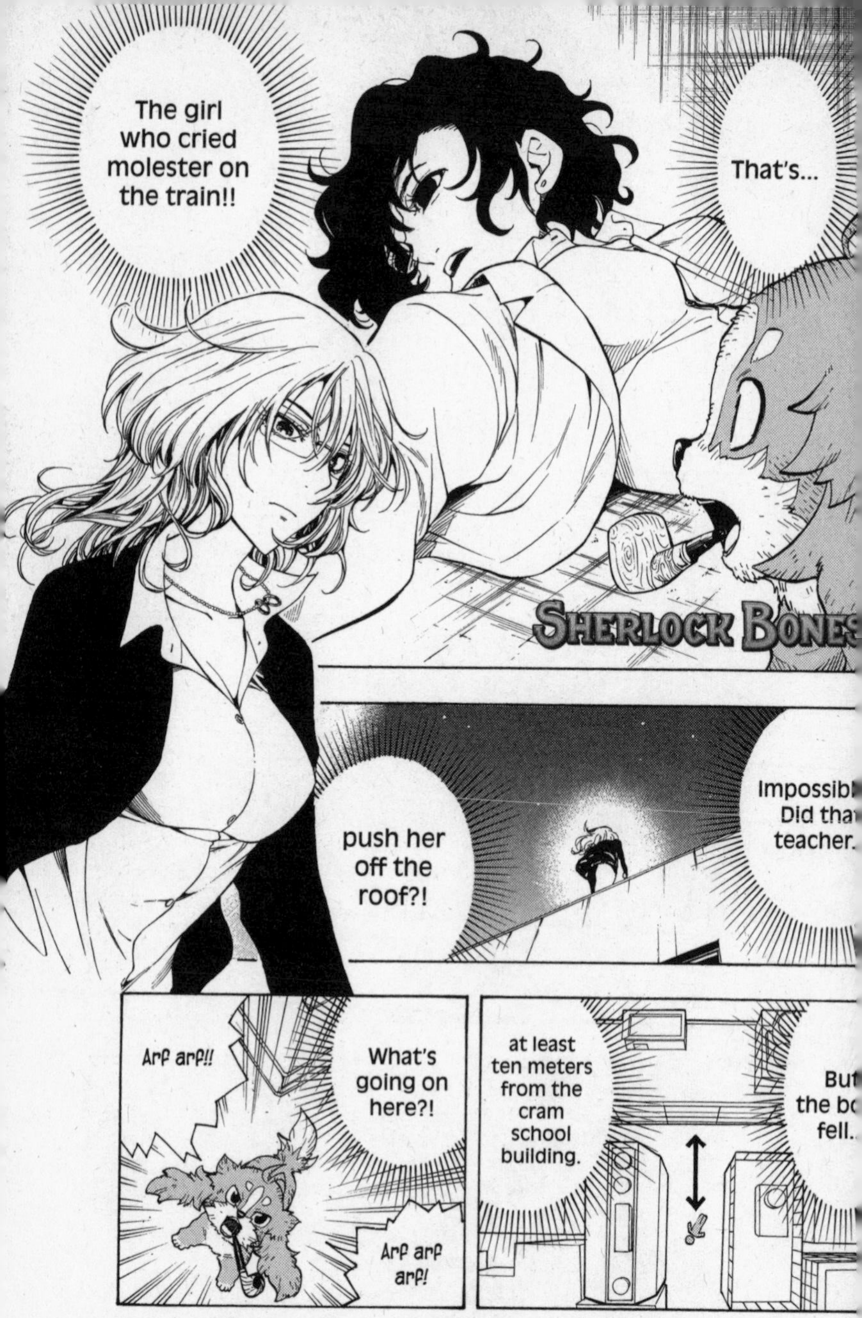
That's...
The girl who cried molester on the train!!
SHERLOCK BONES
Impossib Did tha teacher.
push her off the roof?!
But the bo fell..
at least ten meters from the cram school building.
What's going on here?!
Arf arf!!
Arf arf arf!

Case 4: ⚜ An Equation for Murder, Part 2

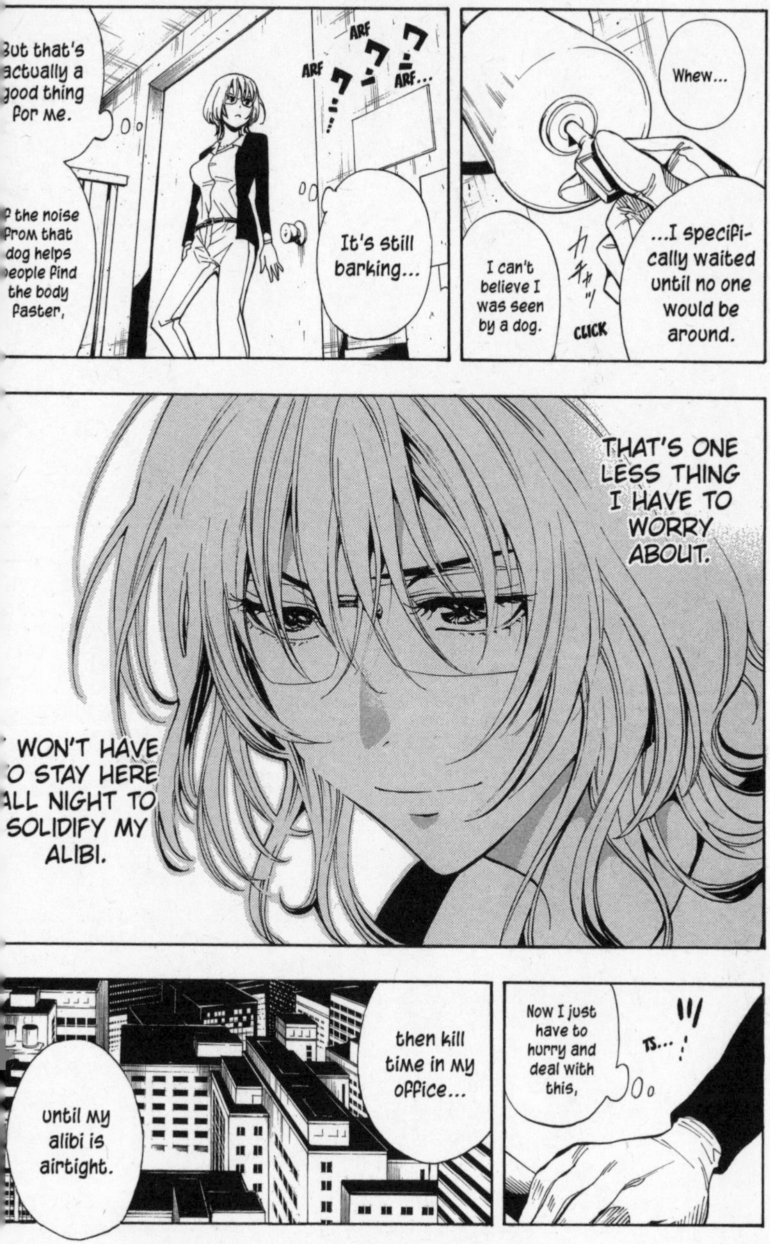

Whew...
...I specifi-cally waited until no one would be around.
カチャッ
CLICK
I can't believe I was seen by a dog.
ARF ARF...
ARF
It's still barking...
But that's actually a good thing for me.
If the noise from that dog helps people find the body faster,
THAT'S ONE LESS THING I HAVE TO WORRY ABOUT.
I WON'T HAVE TO STAY HERE ALL NIGHT TO SOLIDIFY MY ALIBI.
TS...
Now I just have to hurry and deal with this,
then kill time in my office...
until my alibi is airtight.

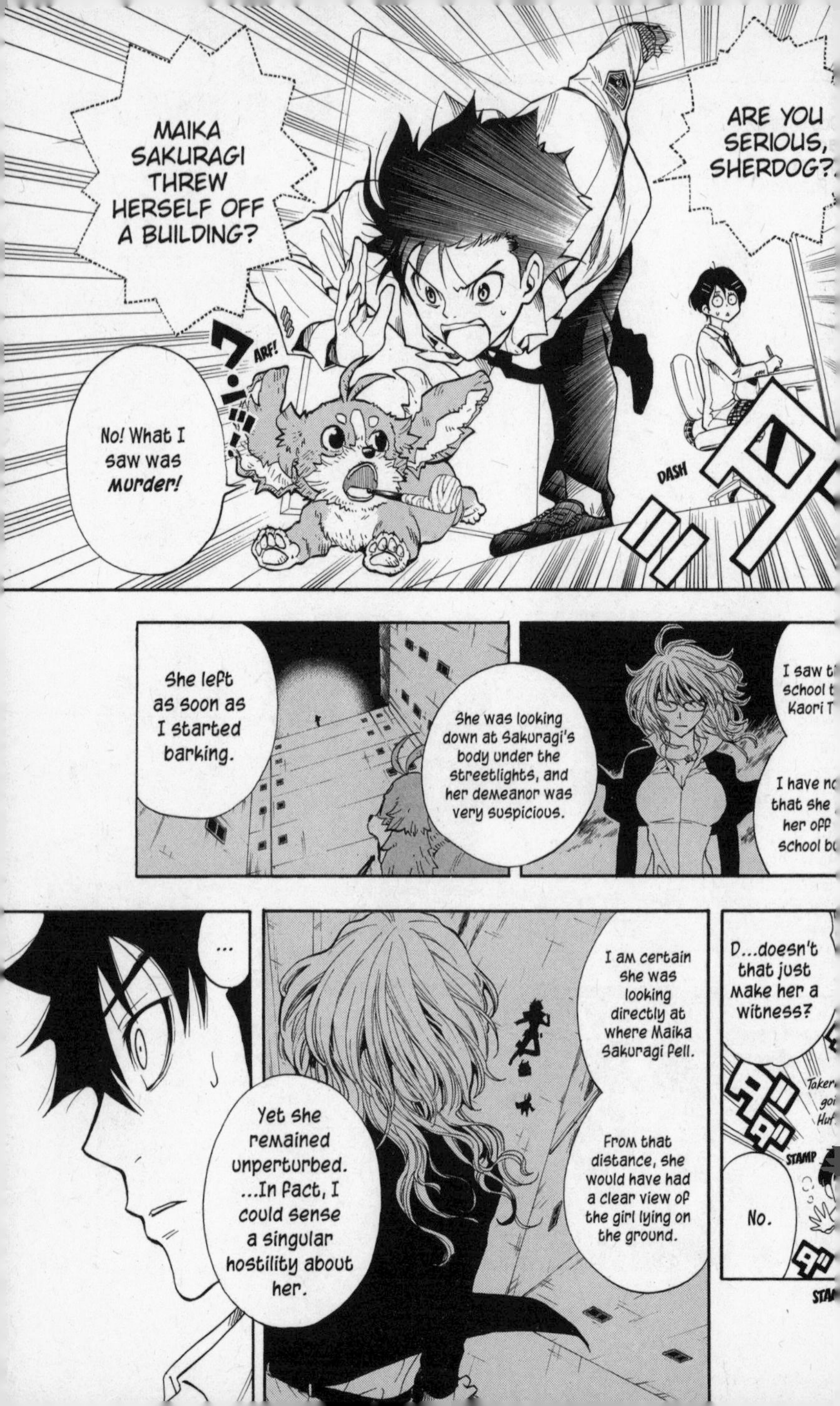
ARE YOU SERIOUS, SHERDOG?!
MAIKA SAKURAGI THREW HERSELF OFF A BUILDING?
ARF!
DASH
No! What I saw was murder!
She was looking down at Sakuragi's body under the streetlights, and her demeanor was very suspicious.
She left as soon as I started barking.
D...doesn't that just make her a witness?
STAMP
No.
I am certain she was looking directly at where Maika Sakuragi fell.
From that distance, she would have had a clear view of the girl lying on the ground.
Yet she remained unperturbed. ...In fact, I could sense a singular hostility about her.
...

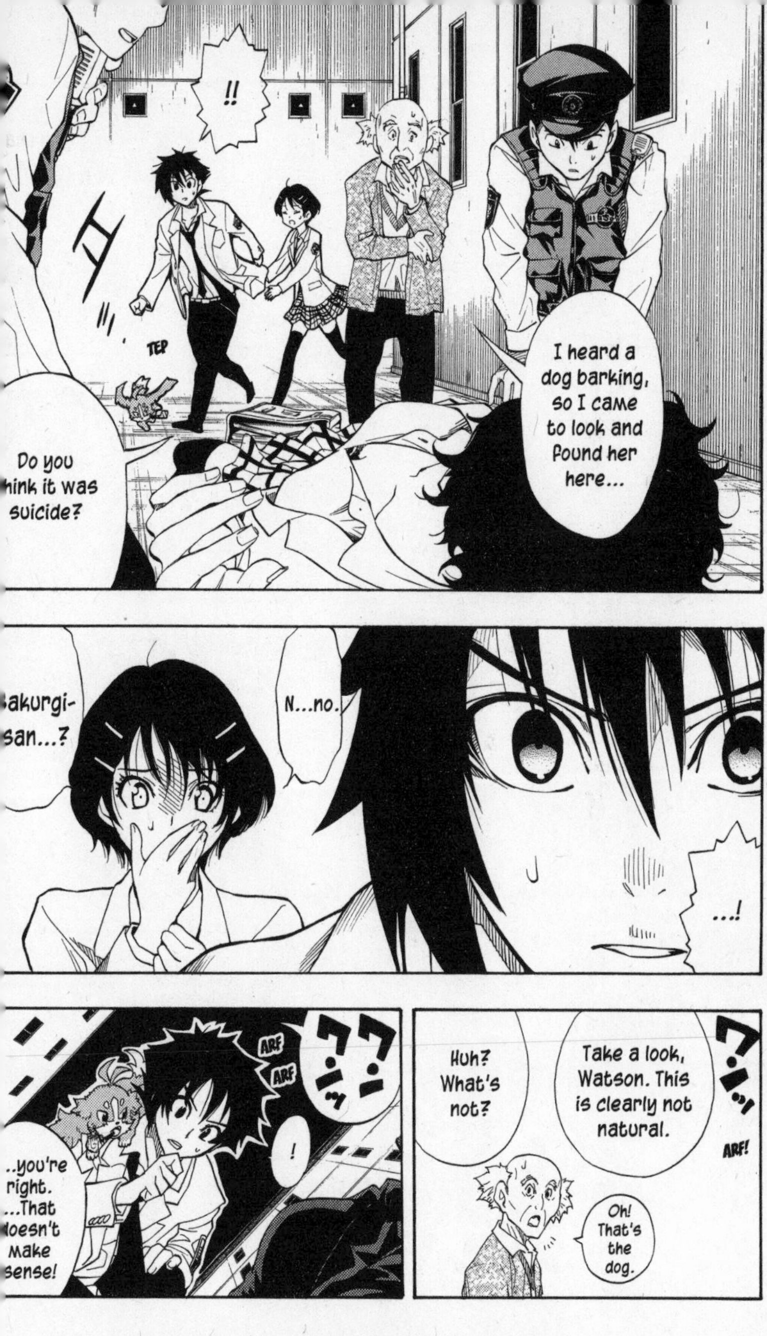
!!
I heard a dog barking, so I came to look and found her here...
TEP
Do you hink it was suicide?
...!
N...no.
akurgi-san...?
Take a look, Watson. This is clearly not natural.
Huh? What's not?
ARF!
Oh! That's the dog.
ARF
ARF
!
..you're right. ...That oesn't make sense!

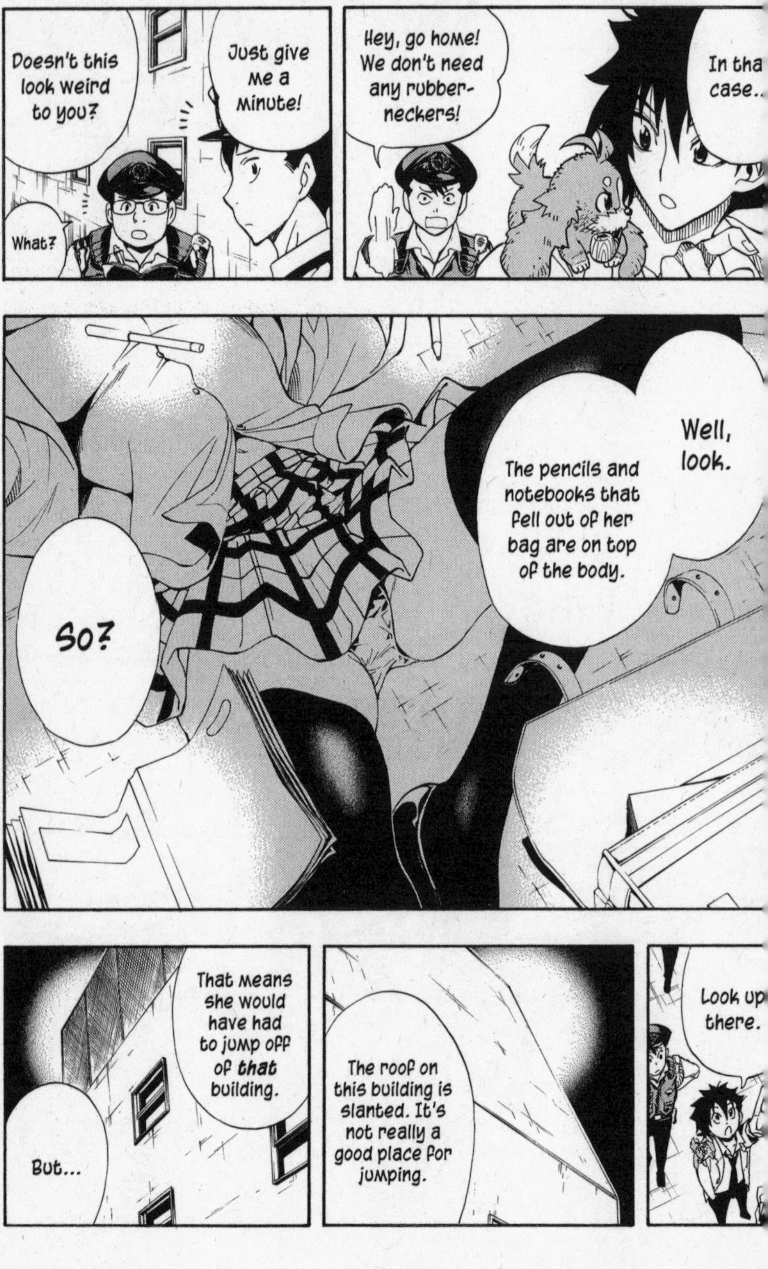
In tha
case..
Hey, go home! We don't need any rubber-neckers!
Just give me a minute!
Doesn't this look weird to you?
What?
Well, look.
The pencils and notebooks that fell out of her bag are on top of the body.
So?
Look up there.
The roof on this building is slanted. It's not really a good place for jumping.
That means she would have had to jump off of *that* building.
But...

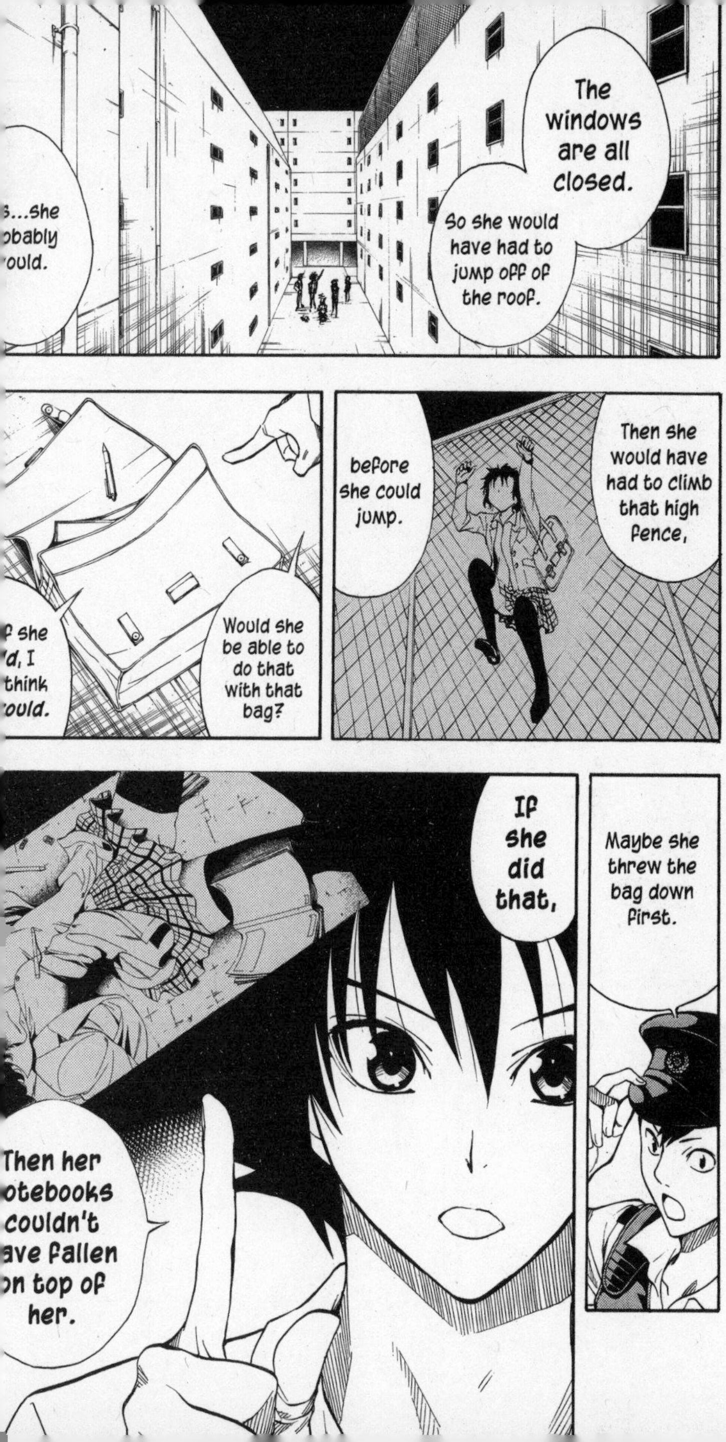
The windows are all closed.
So she would have had to jump off of the roof.
s...she obably ould.
Then she would have had to climb that high fence,
before she could jump.
Would she be able to do that with that bag?
f she 'd, I think ould.
Maybe she threw the bag down first.
If she did that,
Then her otebooks couldn't ave fallen on top of her.

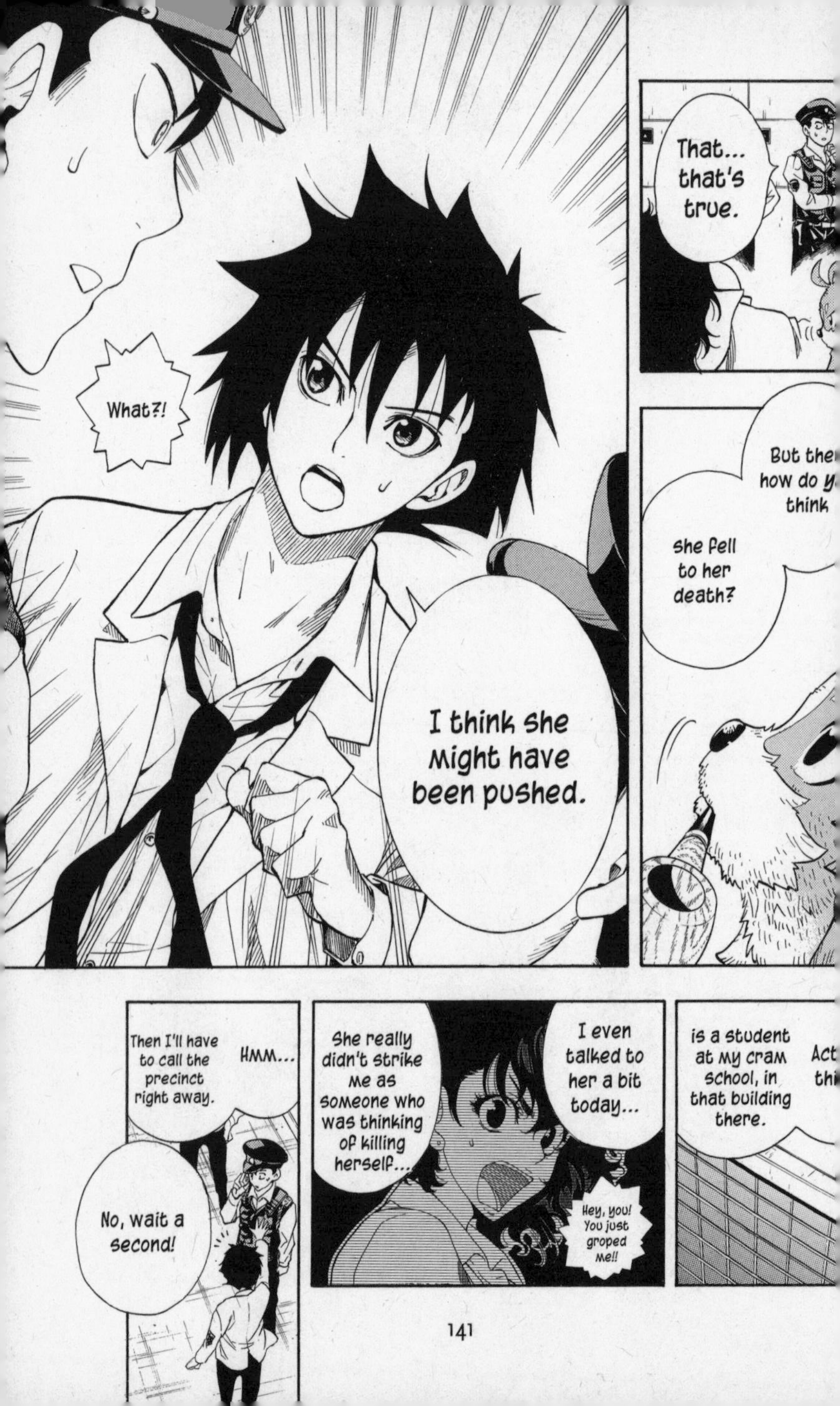

That... that's true.
But the how do y think
she fell to her death?
I think she might have been pushed.
What?!
Act thi
is a student at my cram school, in that building there.
I even talked to her a bit today...
She really didn't strike me as someone who was thinking of killing herself...
Hey, you! You just groped me!!
Hmm...
Then I'll have to call the precinct right away.
No, wait a second!

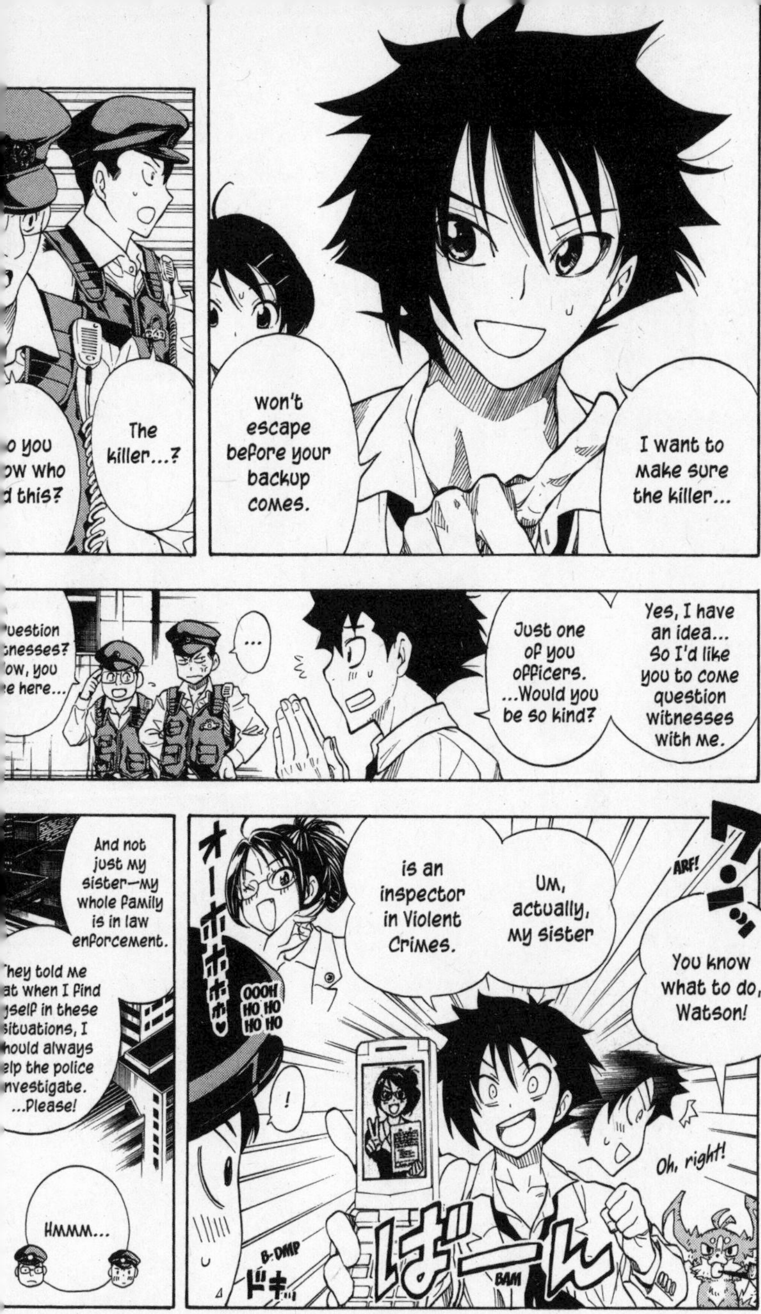
I want to make sure the killer...
won't escape before your backup comes.
The killer...?
o you ow who d this?
Yes, I have an idea... So I'd like you to come question witnesses with me.
Just one of you officers. ...Would you be so kind?
...
uestion tnesses? ow, you e here...
?!
ARF!
You know what to do, Watson!
Oh, right!
Um, actually, my sister
is an inspector in Violent Crimes.
オーホホホ♥
OOOH HO HO HO HO
!
ばーん
BAM
ドキ
B-DMP
And not just my sister—my whole family is in law enforcement.
hey told me at when I find yself in these situations, I hould always elp the police nvestigate. ...Please!
HMMM...

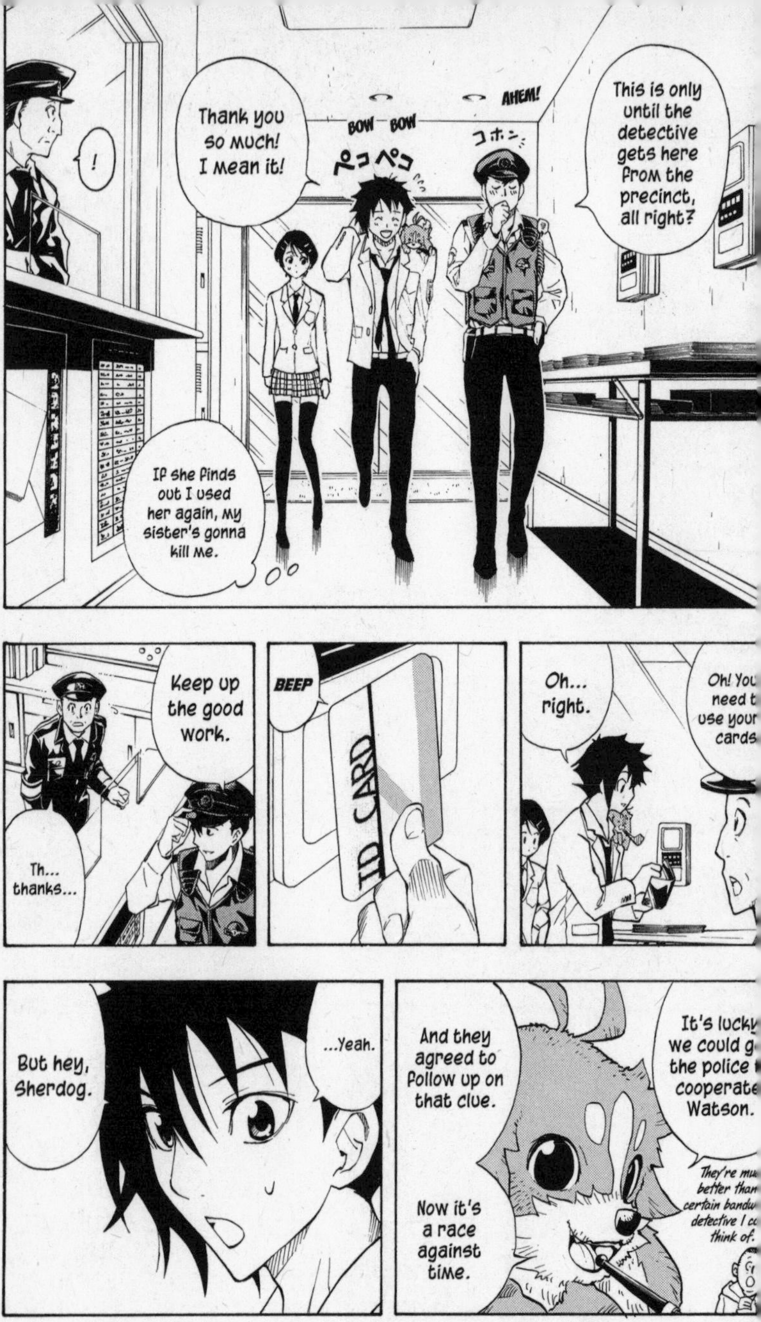
This is only until the detective gets here from the precinct, all right?
AHEM!
コホン
BOW BOW
ペコペコ
Thank you so much! I mean it!
!
If she finds out I used her again, my sister's gonna kill me.
Oh! You need t use your cards
Oh... right.
BEEP
ID CARD
Keep up the good work.
Th... thanks...
It's lucky we could g the police cooperate Watson.
And they agreed to follow up on that clue.
They're mu better than certain bandu detective I c think of.
Now it's a race against time.
...Yeah.
But hey, Sherdog.

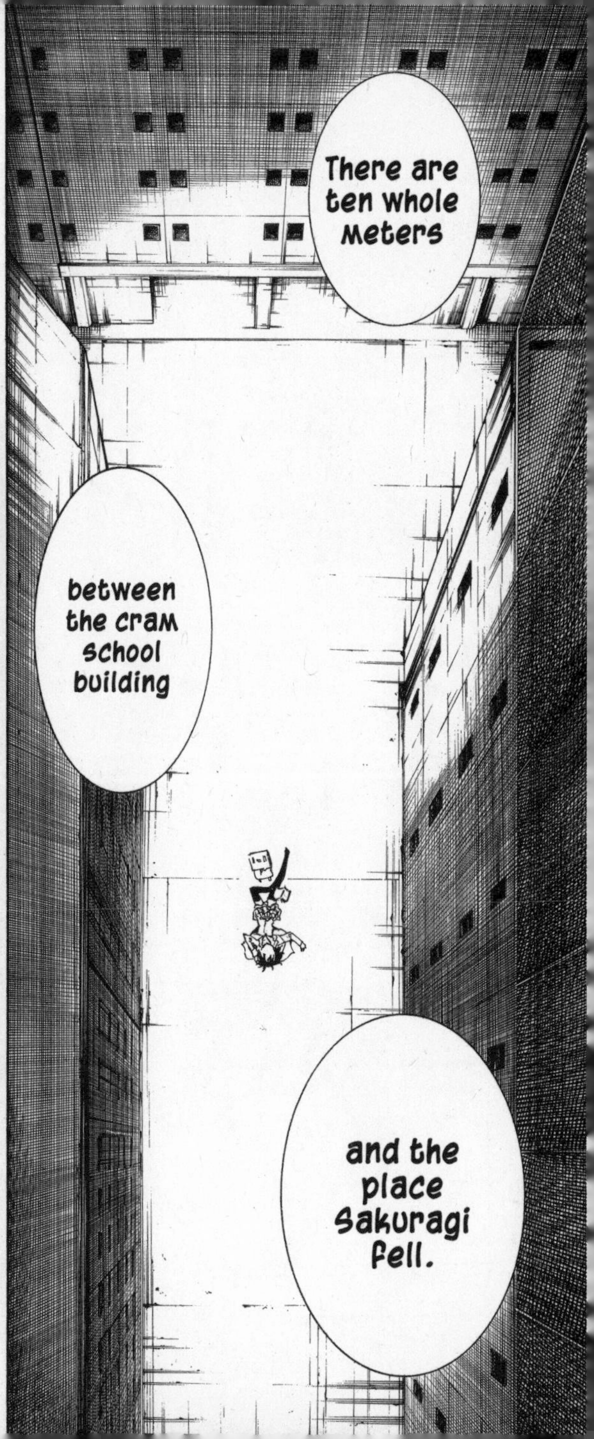
There are ten whole meters
between the cram school building
and the place Sakuragi fell.
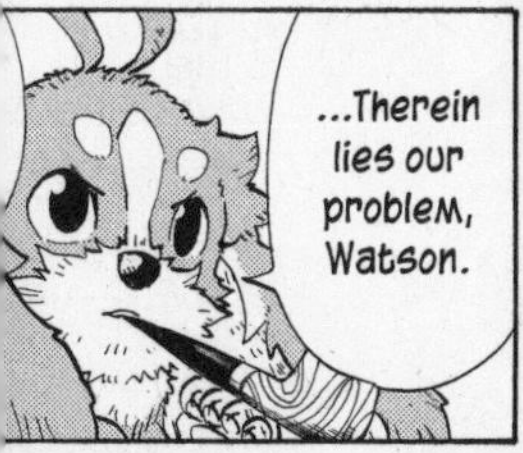
...Therein lies our problem, Watson.
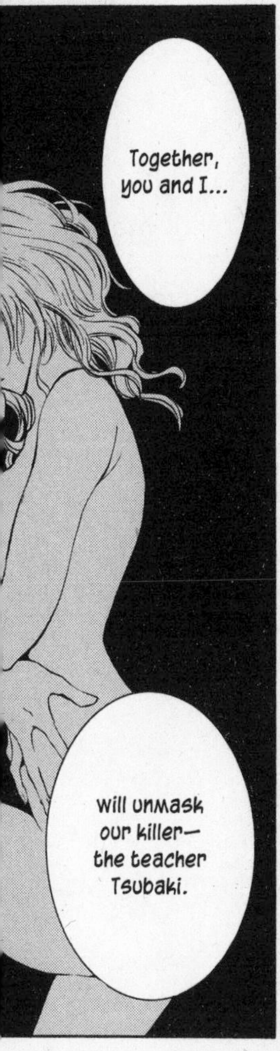
Together, you and I...
will unmask our killer—the teacher Tsubaki.

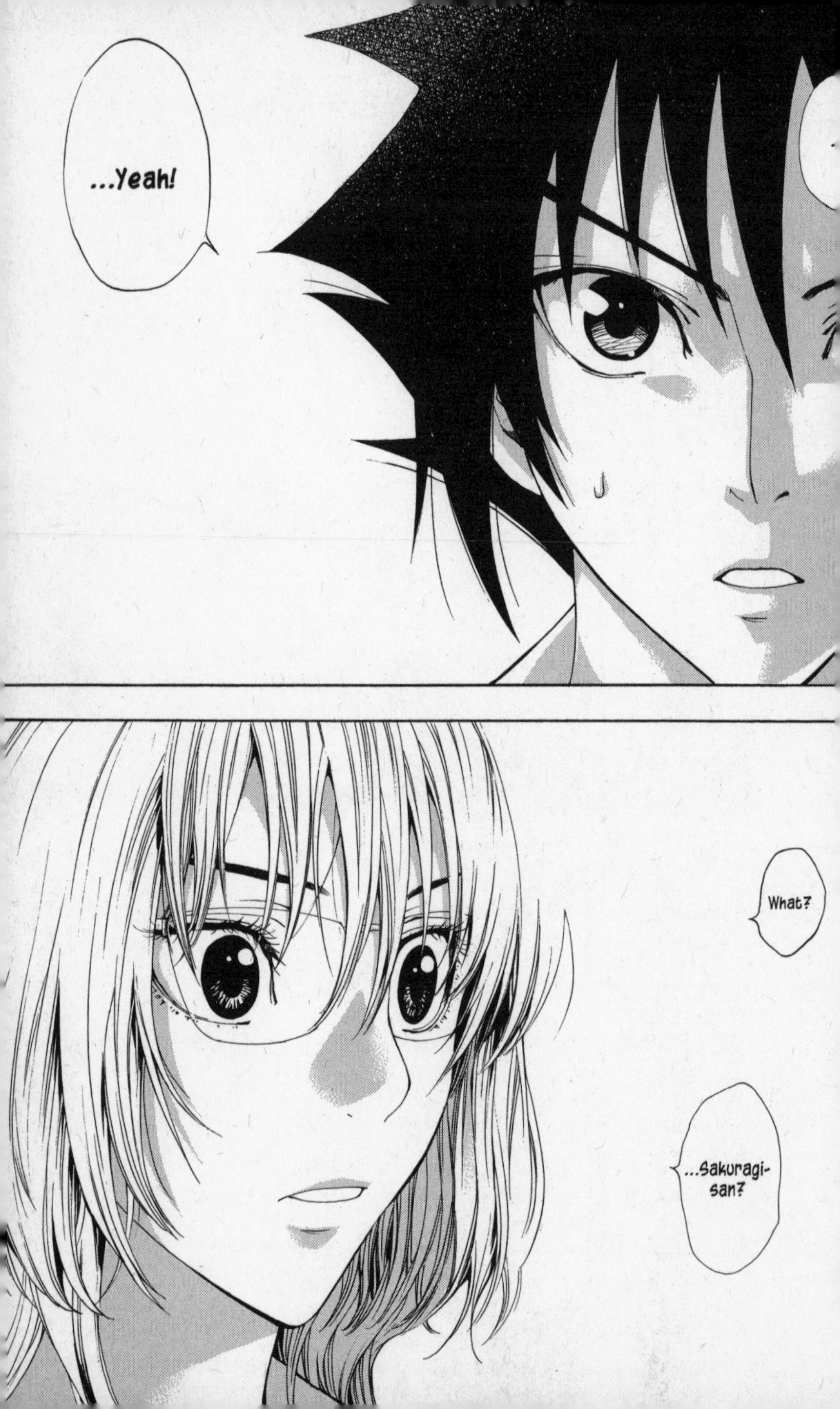
...Yeah!
What?
...Sakuragi-san?

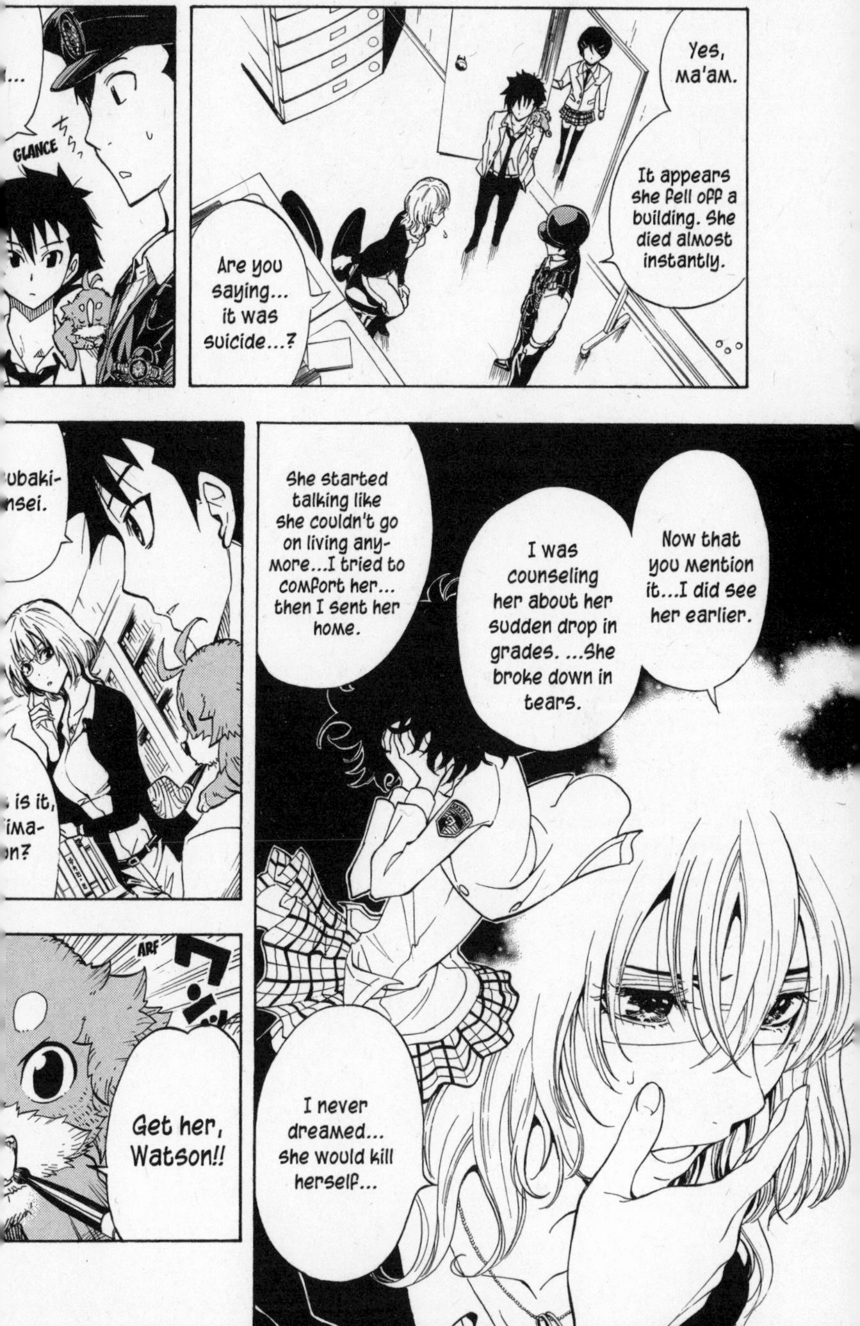

Yes, ma'am.
It appears she fell off a building. She died almost instantly.
Are you saying... it was suicide...?
GLANCE
Now that you mention it...I did see her earlier.
I was counseling her about her sudden drop in grades. ...She broke down in tears.
She started talking like she couldn't go on living any-more...I tried to comfort her... then I sent her home.
I never dreamed... she would kill herself...
ubaki-nsei.
is it, ima-on?
ARF
Get her, Watson!!

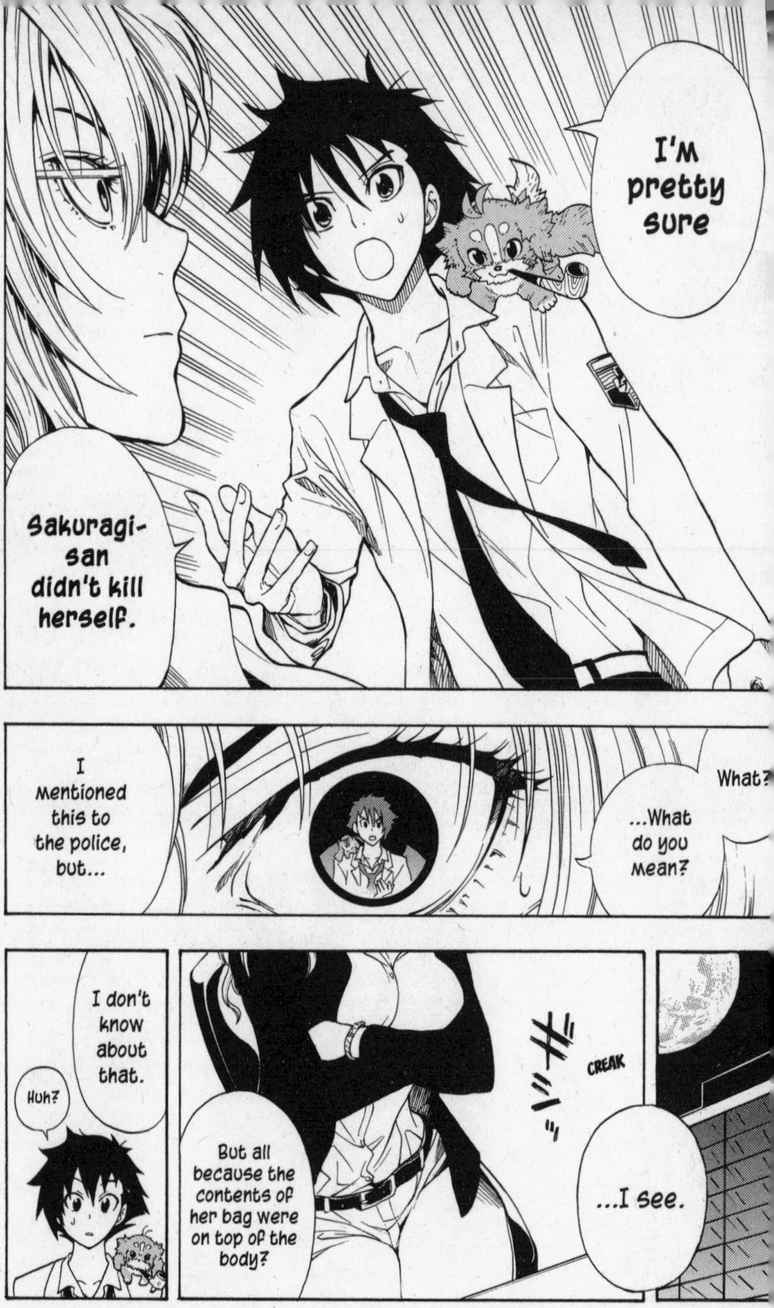
I'm pretty sure
Sakuragi-san didn't kill herself.
What?
...What do you mean?
I mentioned this to the police, but...
...I see.
CREAK
But all because the contents of her bag were on top of the body?
I don't know about that.
Huh?

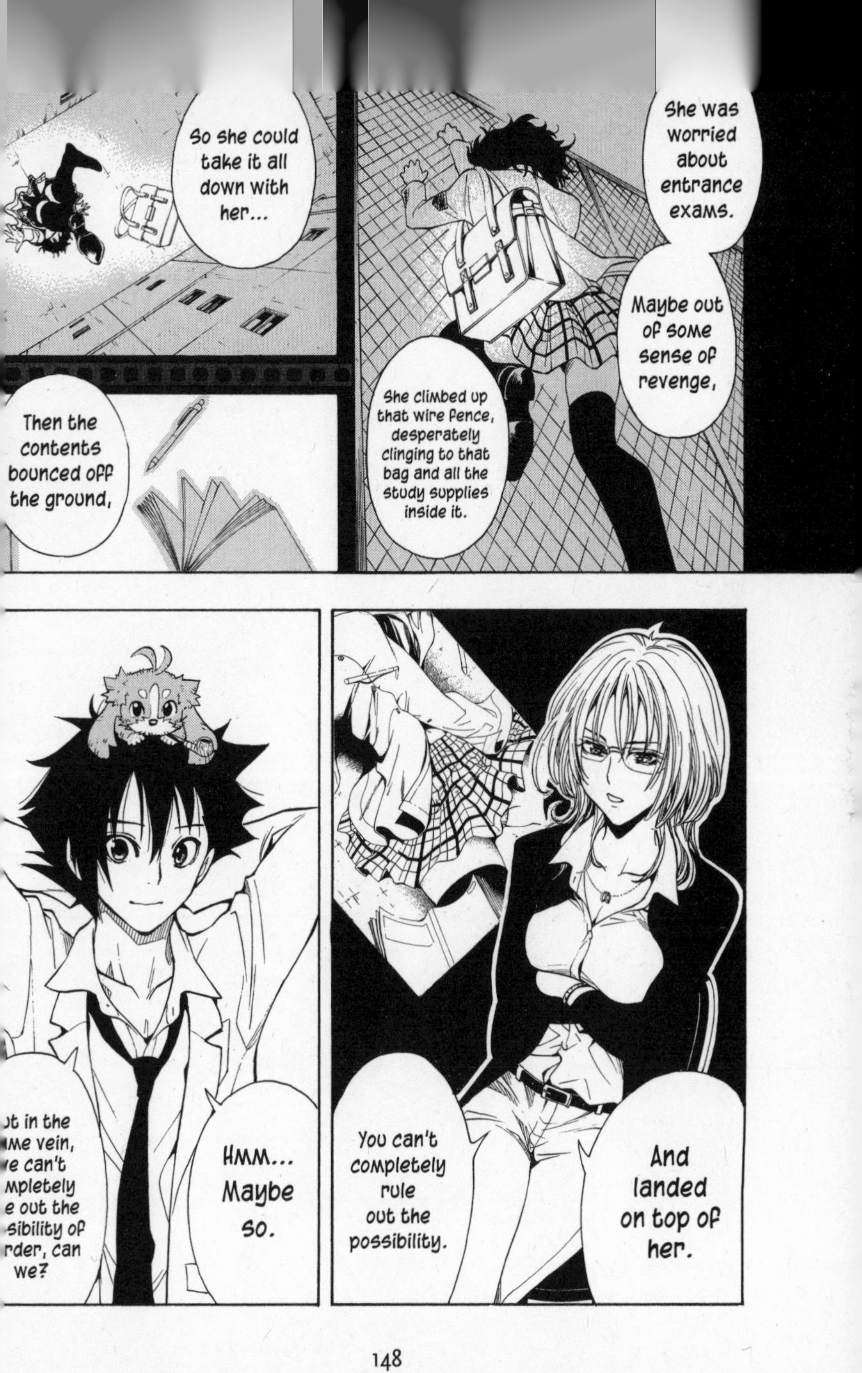
She was worried about entrance exams.
Maybe out of some sense of revenge,
She climbed up that wire fence, desperately clinging to that bag and all the study supplies inside it.
So she could take it all down with her...
Then the contents bounced off the ground,
And landed on top of her.
You can't completely rule out the possibility.
HMM... Maybe so.
ut in the me vein, e can't mpletely e out the sibility of rder, can we?

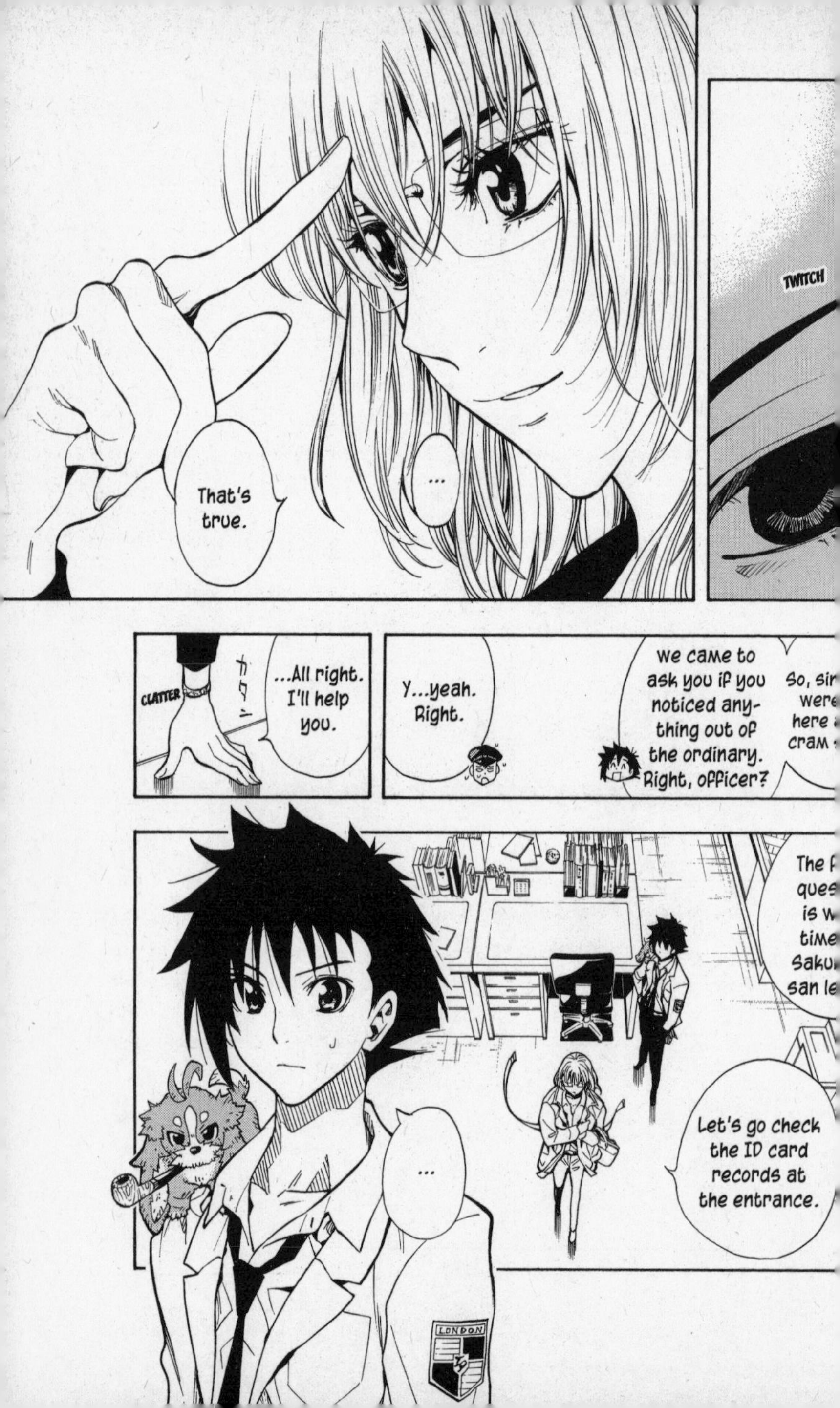
TWITCH
...
That's true.
So, sir were here cram
we came to ask you if you noticed anything out of the ordinary. Right, officer?
Y...yeah. Right.
...All right. I'll help you.
CLATTER
The
ques
is
time
Saku
san le
Let's go check the ID card records at the entrance.
...

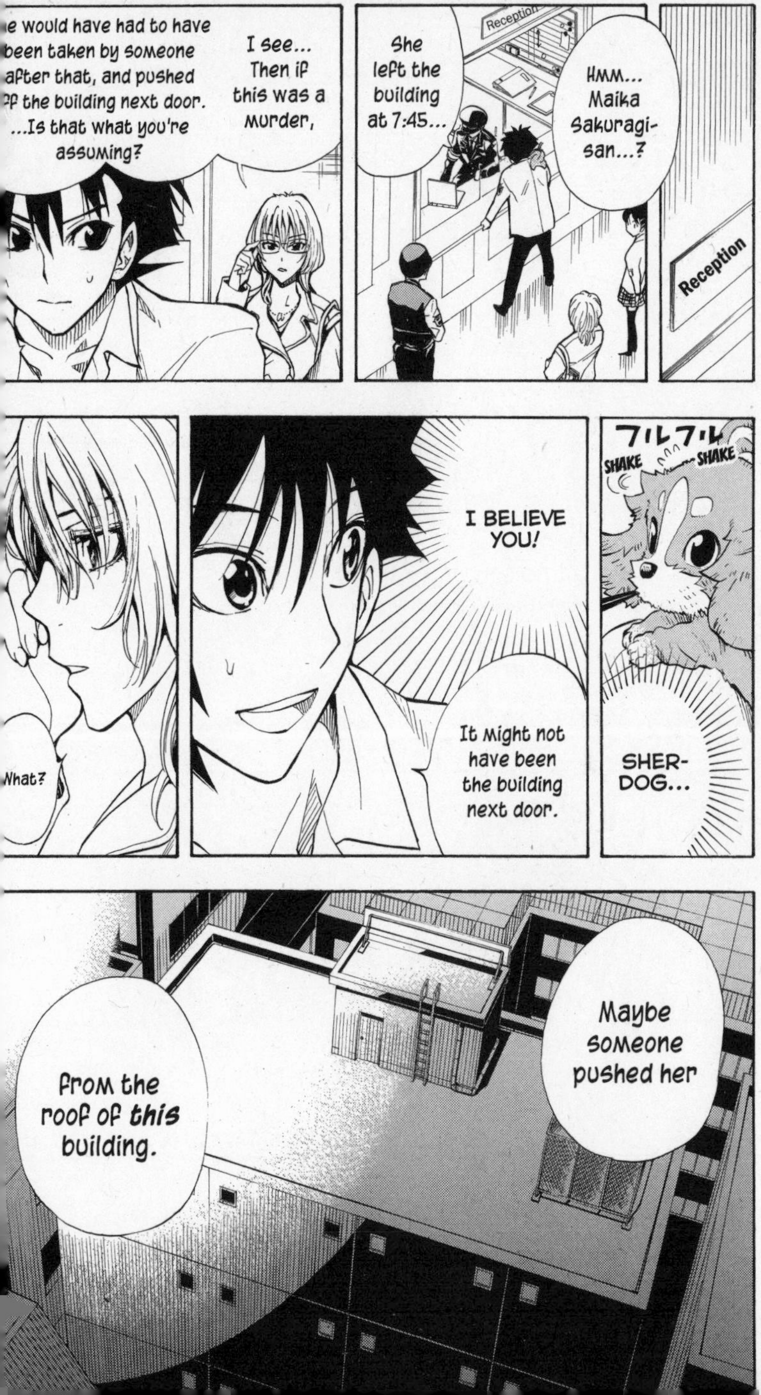
Reception
Reception
HMM... Maika Sakuragi-san...?
She left the building at 7:45...
I see... Then if this was a murder,
e would have had to have been taken by someone after that, and pushed ff the building next door. ...Is that what you're assuming?
フルフル
SHAKE SHAKE
SHER-DOG...
I BELIEVE YOU!
It might not have been the building next door.
What?
Maybe someone pushed her
from the roof of this building.

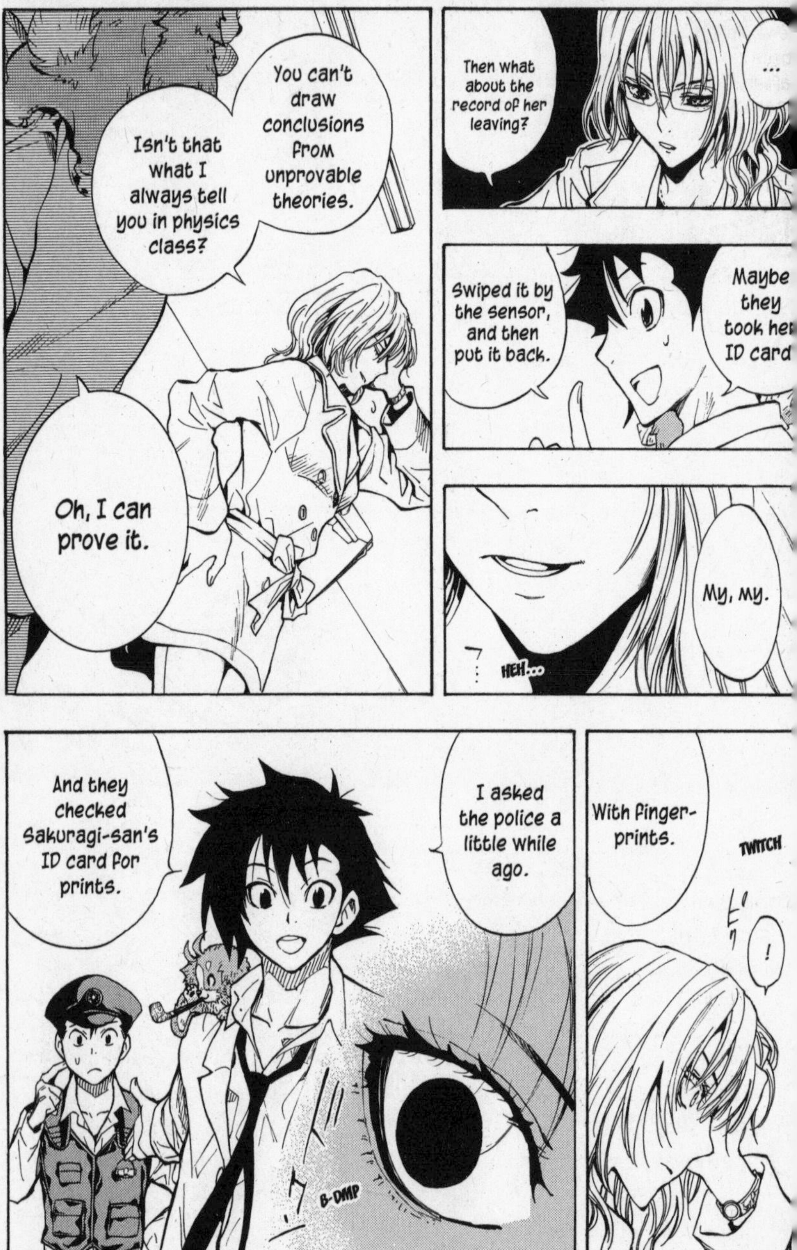
...
Then what about the record of her leaving?
Maybe they took he ID card
Swiped it by the sensor, and then put it back.
My, my.
HEH...
You can't draw conclusions from unprovable theories.
Isn't that what I always tell you in physics class?
Oh, I can prove it.
TWITCH
!
With finger-prints.
I asked the police a little while ago.
And they checked Sakuragi-san's ID card for prints.
B-DMP

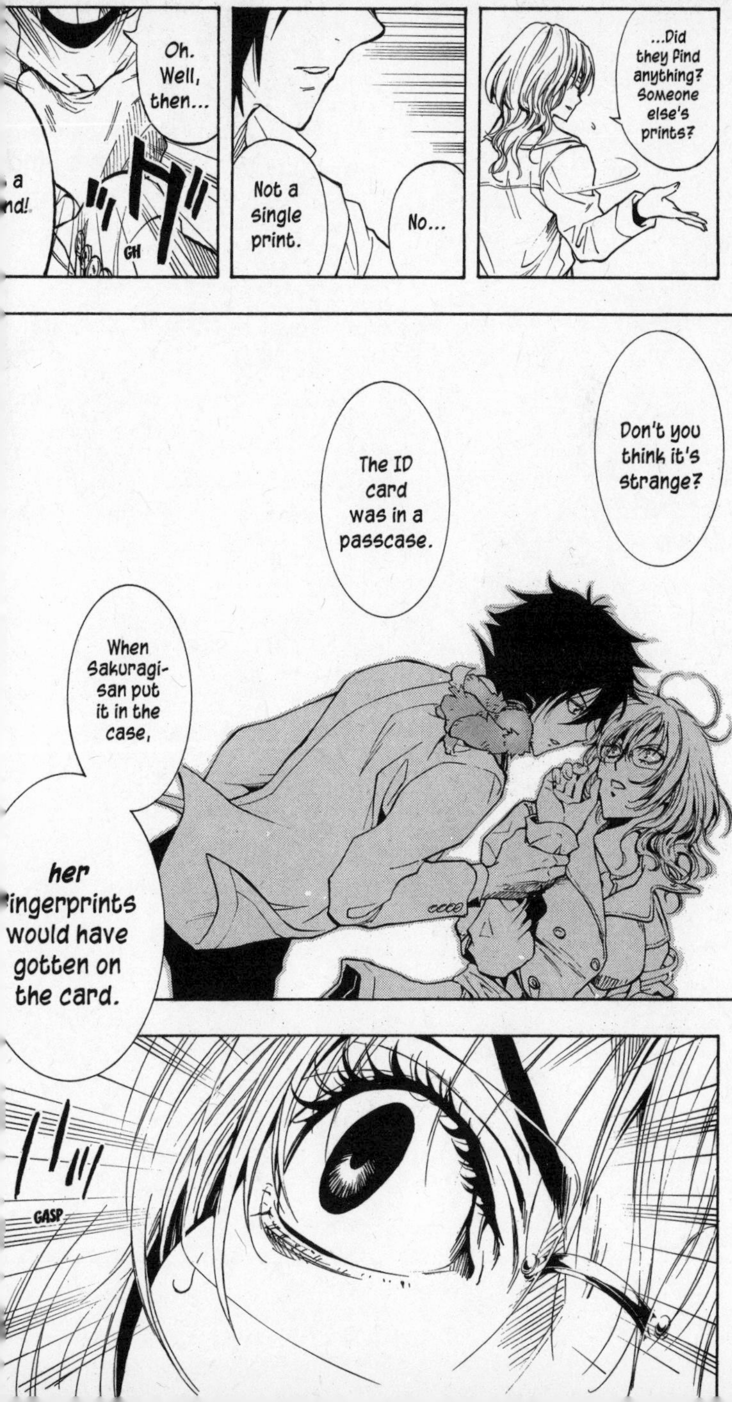

...Did they find anything? Someone else's prints?
No...
Not a single print.
Oh. Well, then...
GH
Don't you think it's strange?
The ID card was in a passcase.
When Sakuragi-san put it in the case,
her fingerprints would have gotten on the card.
GASP

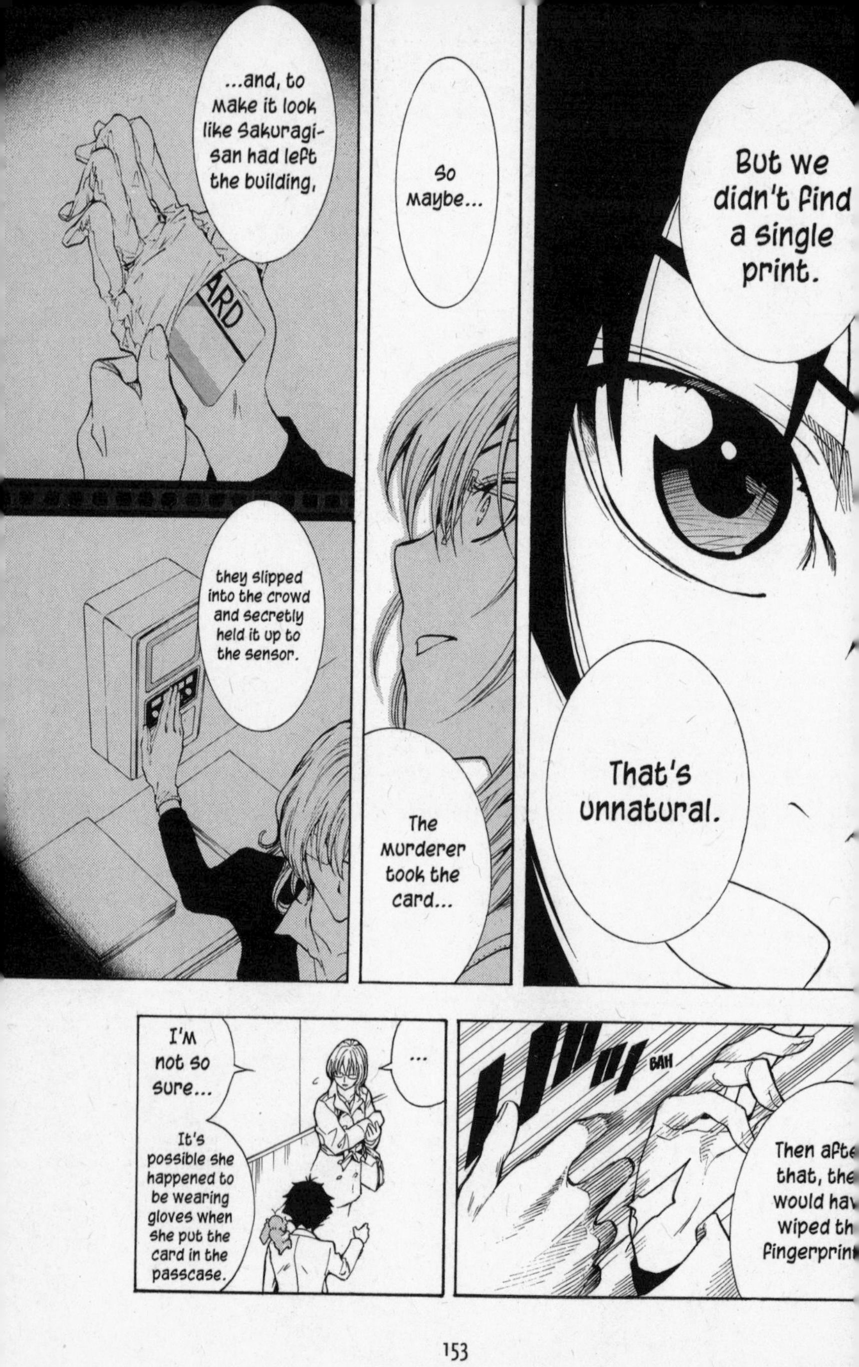
But we didn't find a single print.
That's unnatural.
So maybe...
The murderer took the card...
...and, to make it look like Sakuragi-san had left the building,
ARD
they slipped into the crowd and secretly held it up to the sensor.
BAH
Then afte that, the would hav wiped th fingerprin
...
I'm not so sure...
It's possible she happened to be wearing gloves when she put the card in the passcase.

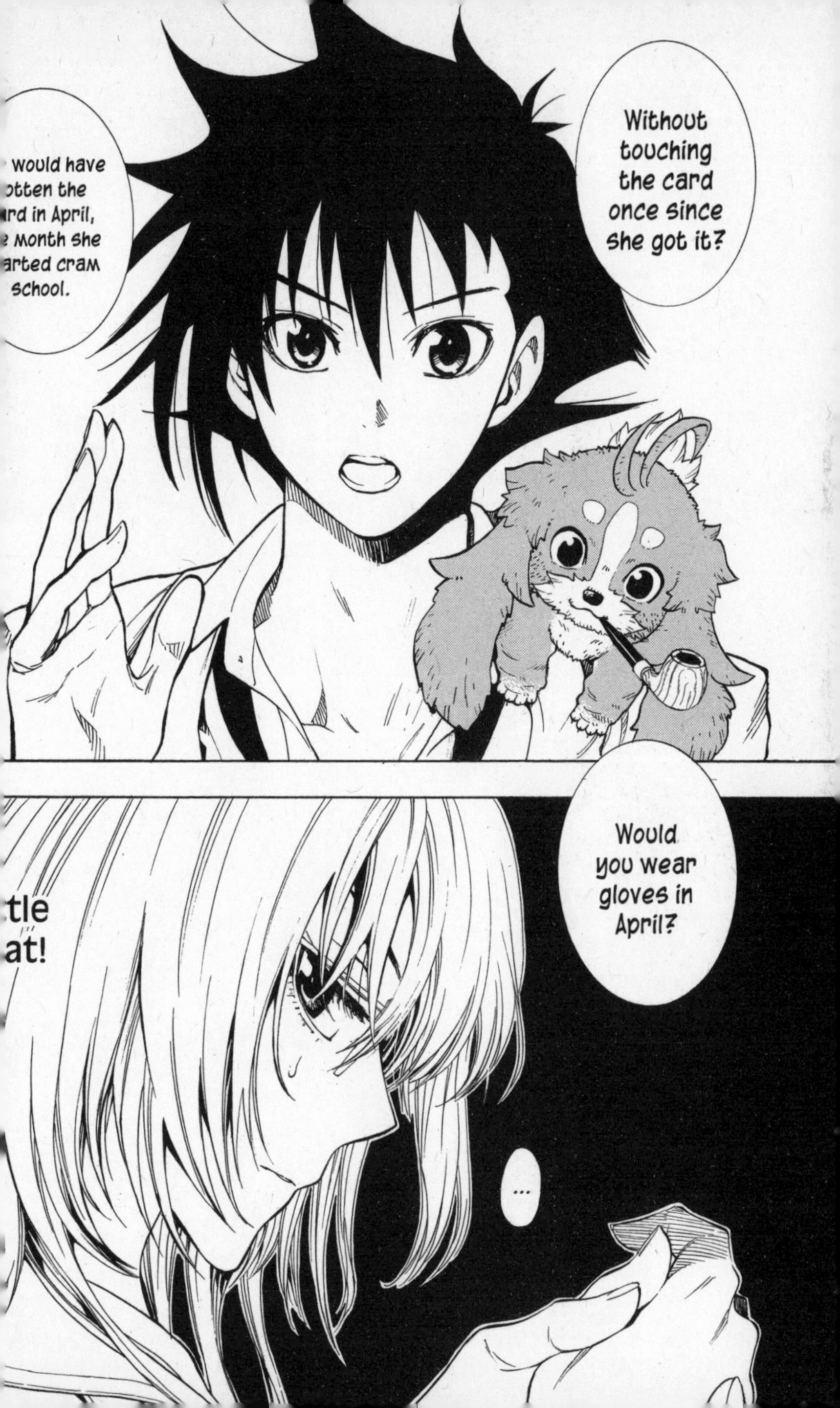
Without touching the card once since she got it?
would have otten the rd in April, e month she arted cram school.
Would you wear gloves in April?
...
tle at!

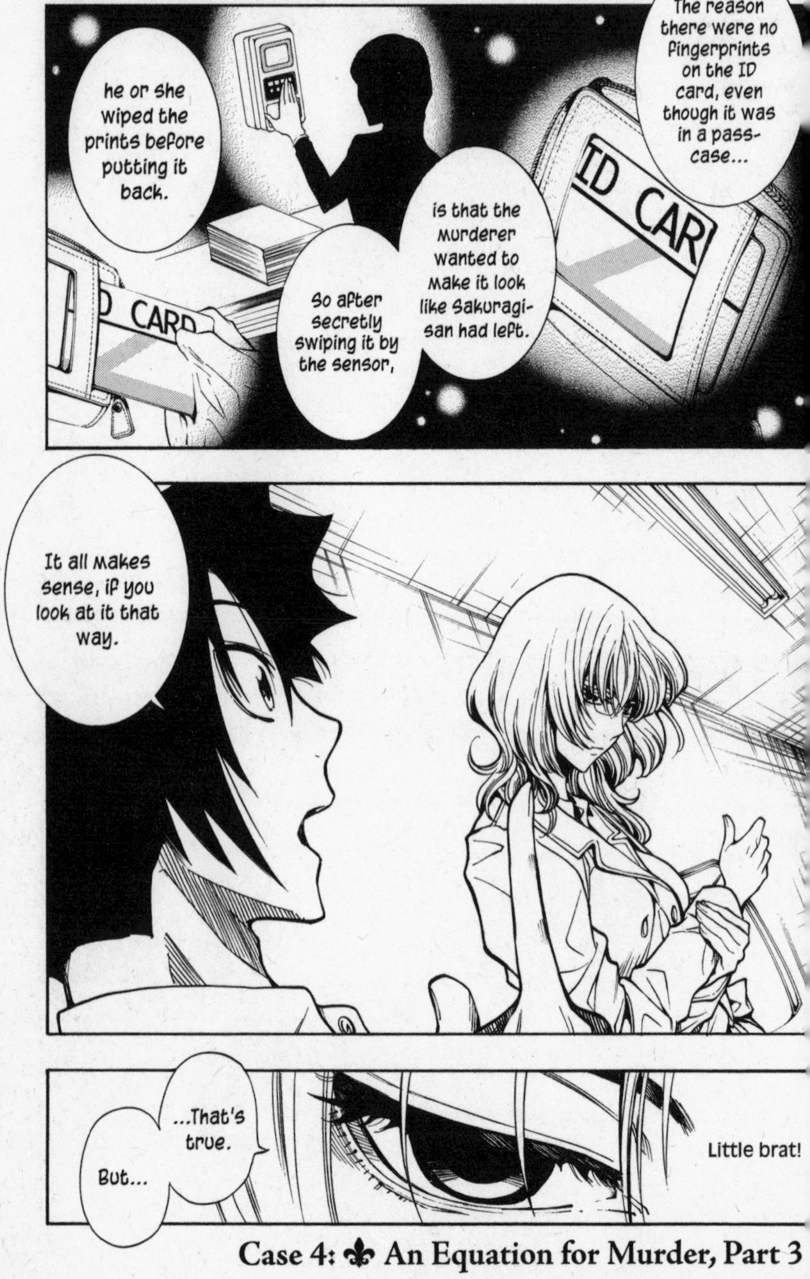
The reason there were no fingerprints on the ID card, even though it was in a pass-case...
ID CAR
is that the murderer wanted to make it look like Sakuragi-san had left.
So after secretly swiping it by the sensor,
D CARD
he or she wiped the prints before putting it back.
It all makes sense, if you look at it that way.
Little brat!
...That's true.
But...

Case 4: ⚜ An Equation for Murder, Part 3

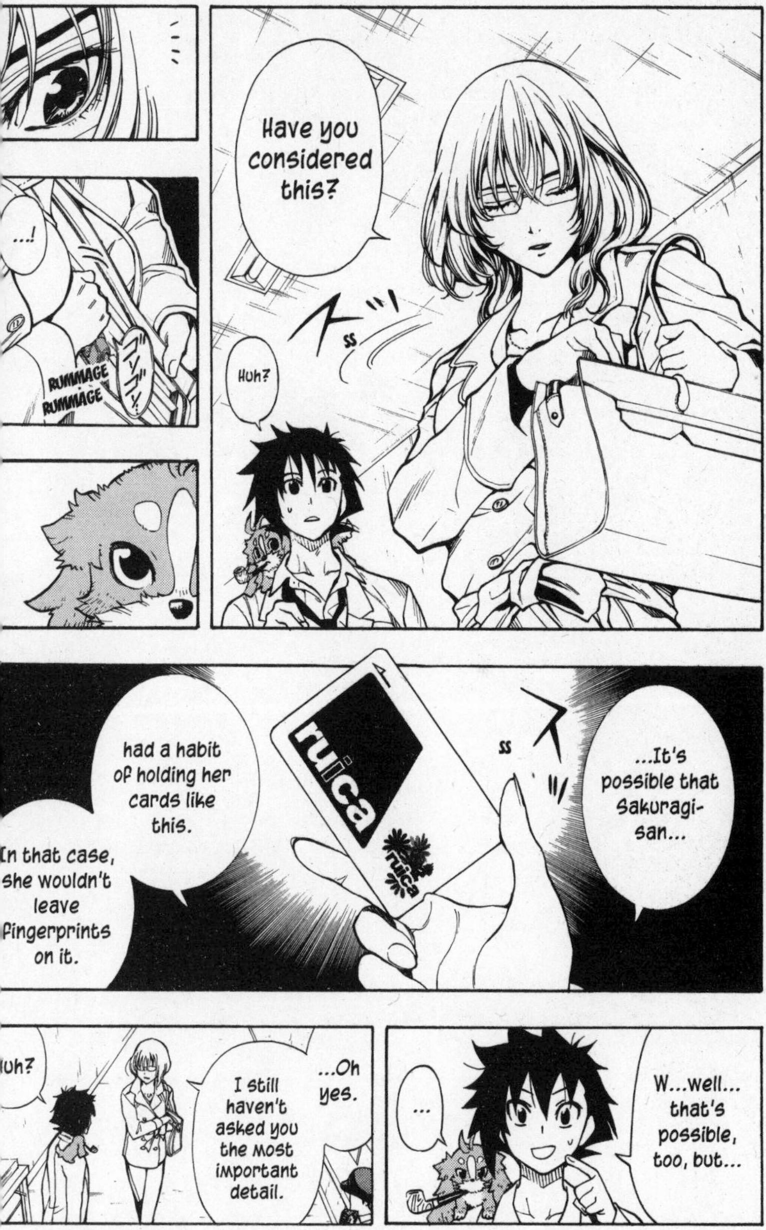
Have you considered this?
SS
Huh?
...!
RUMMAGE RUMMAGE
...It's possible that Sakuragi-san...
SS
had a habit of holding her cards like this.
ruica
In that case, she wouldn't leave fingerprints on it.
W...well... that's possible, too, but...
...
...Oh yes.
I still haven't asked you the most important detail.
uh?

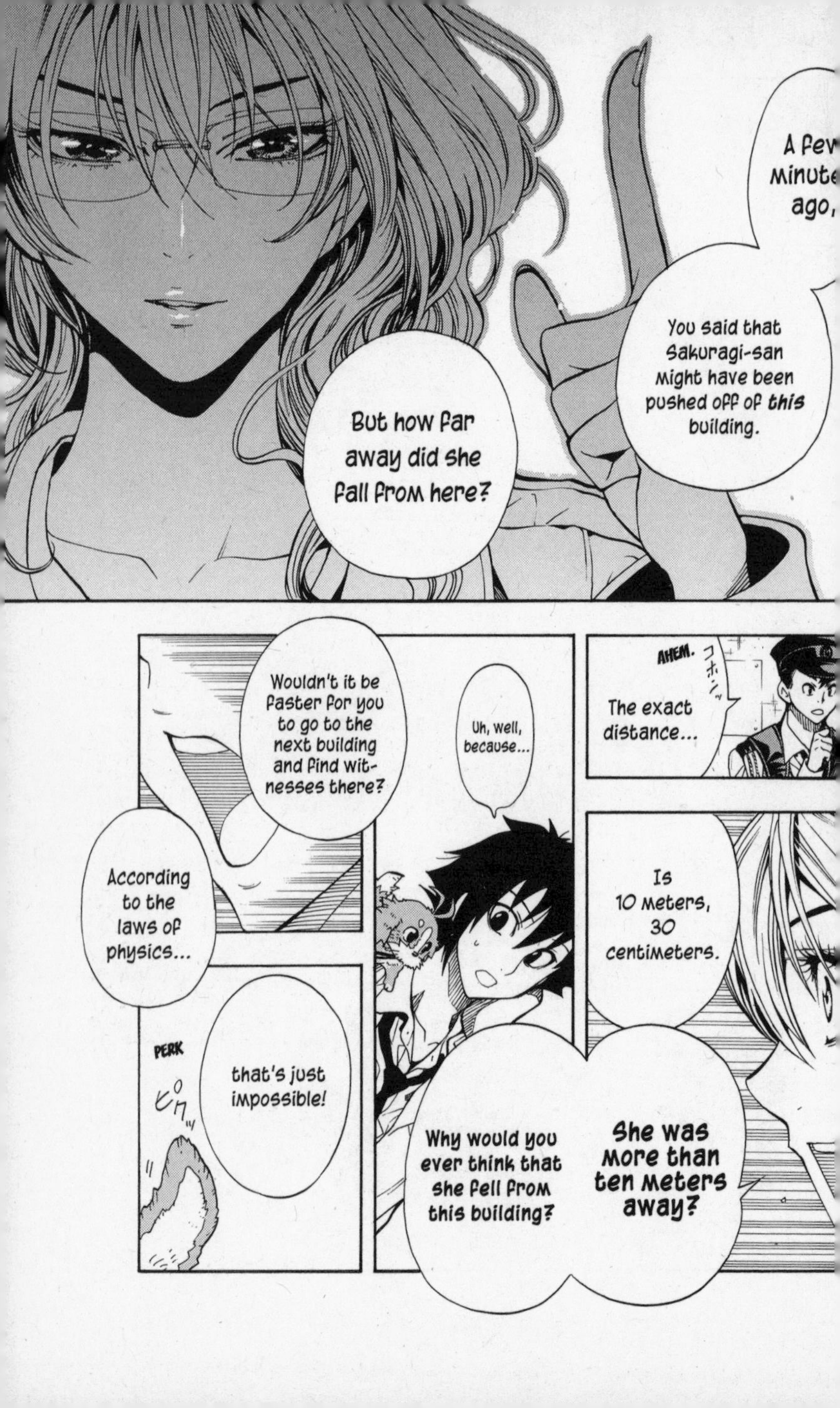
A fe
minut
ago,
You said that Sakuragi-san might have been pushed off of *this* building.
But how far away did she fall from here?
AHEM.
コホン
The exact distance...
Is 10 meters, 30 centimeters.
She was more than ten meters away?
Why would you ever think that she fell from this building?
Uh, well, because...
Wouldn't it be faster for you to go to the next building and find wit-nesses there?
According to the laws of physics...
PERK
ピクッ
that's just impossible!

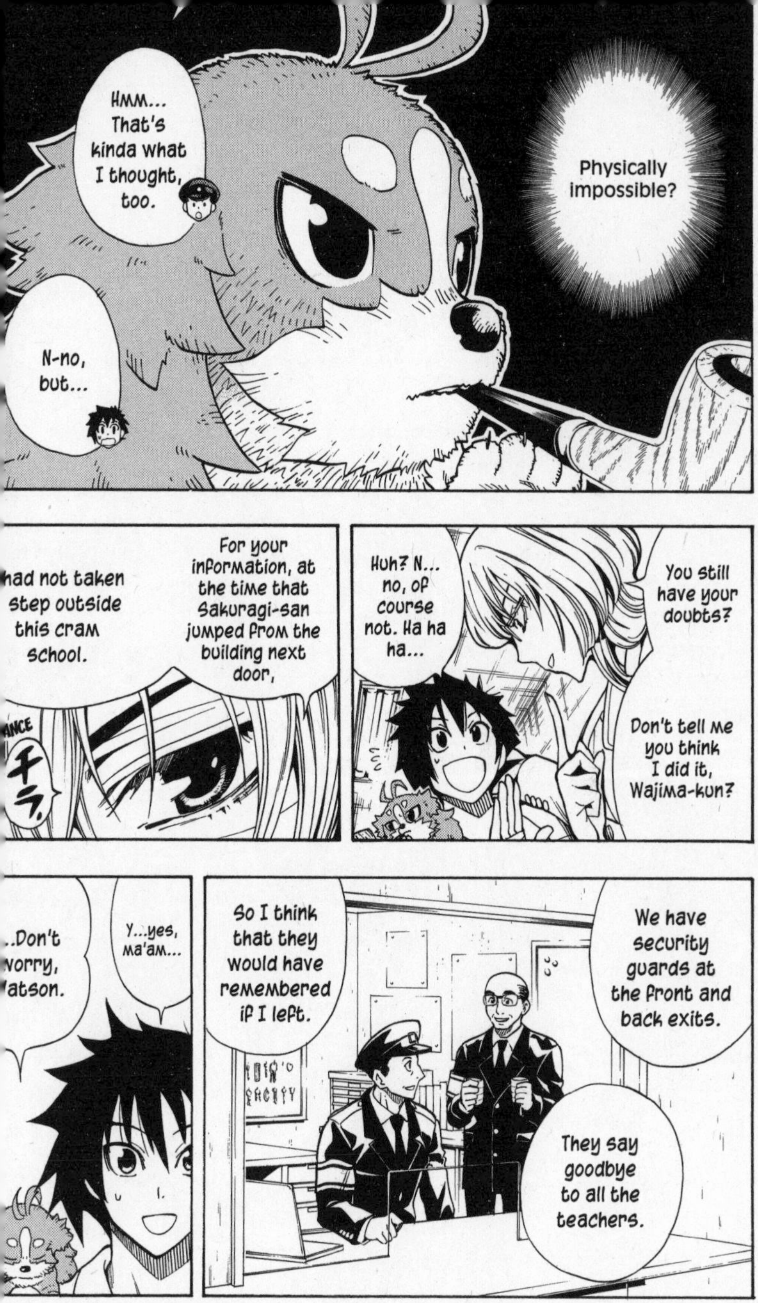
Physically impossible?
Hmm... That's kinda what I thought, too.
N-no, but...
You still have your doubts?
Huh? N... no, of course not. Ha ha ha...
Don't tell me you think I did it, Wajima-kun?
For your information, at the time that Sakuragi-san jumped from the building next door,
had not taken step outside this cram school.
ANCE
チラ
We have security guards at the front and back exits.
They say goodbye to all the teachers.
So I think that they would have remembered if I left.
Y...yes, ma'am...
..Don't worry, atson.

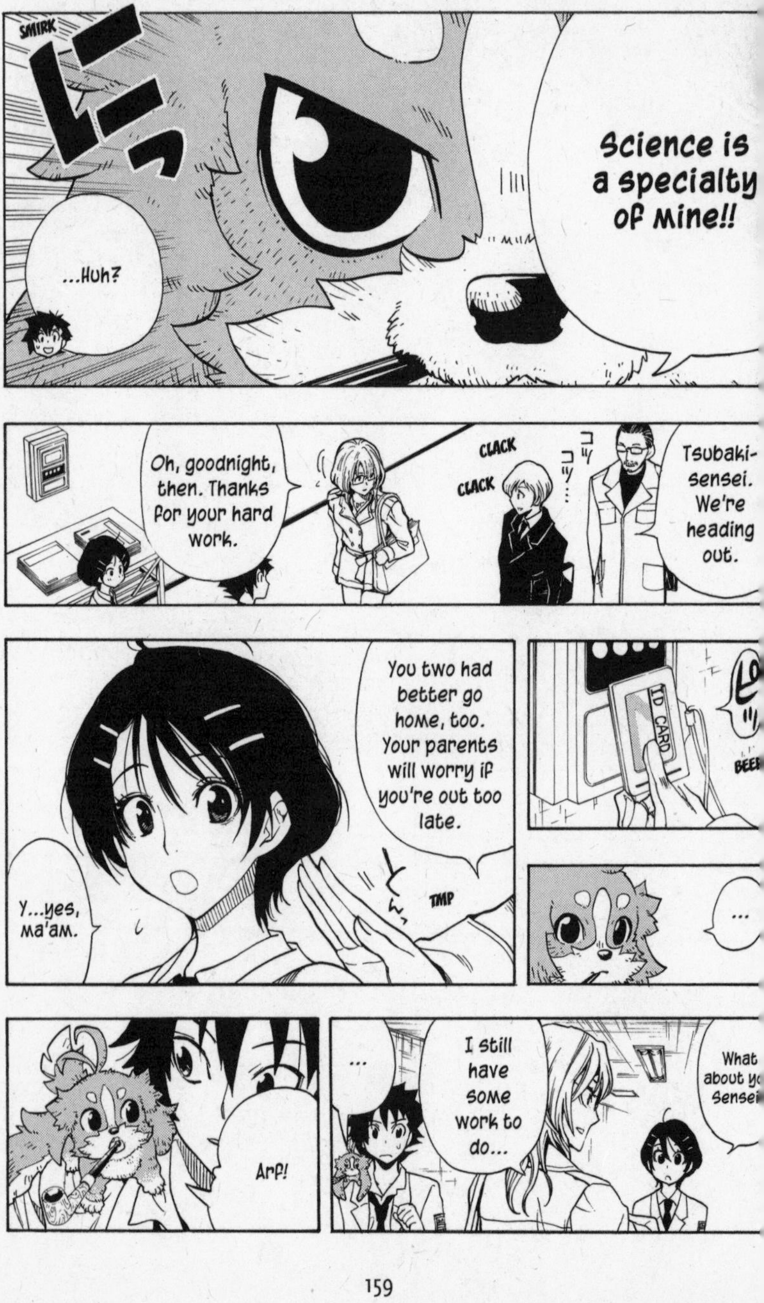
Science is a specialty of mine!!
SMIRK
...Huh?
Tsubaki-sensei. We're heading out.
CLACK
CLACK
Oh, goodnight, then. Thanks for your hard work.
BEE
ID CARD
...
You two had better go home, too. Your parents will worry if you're out too late.
TMP
Y...yes, ma'am.
What about yo
Sensei
I still have some work to do...
...
Arf!

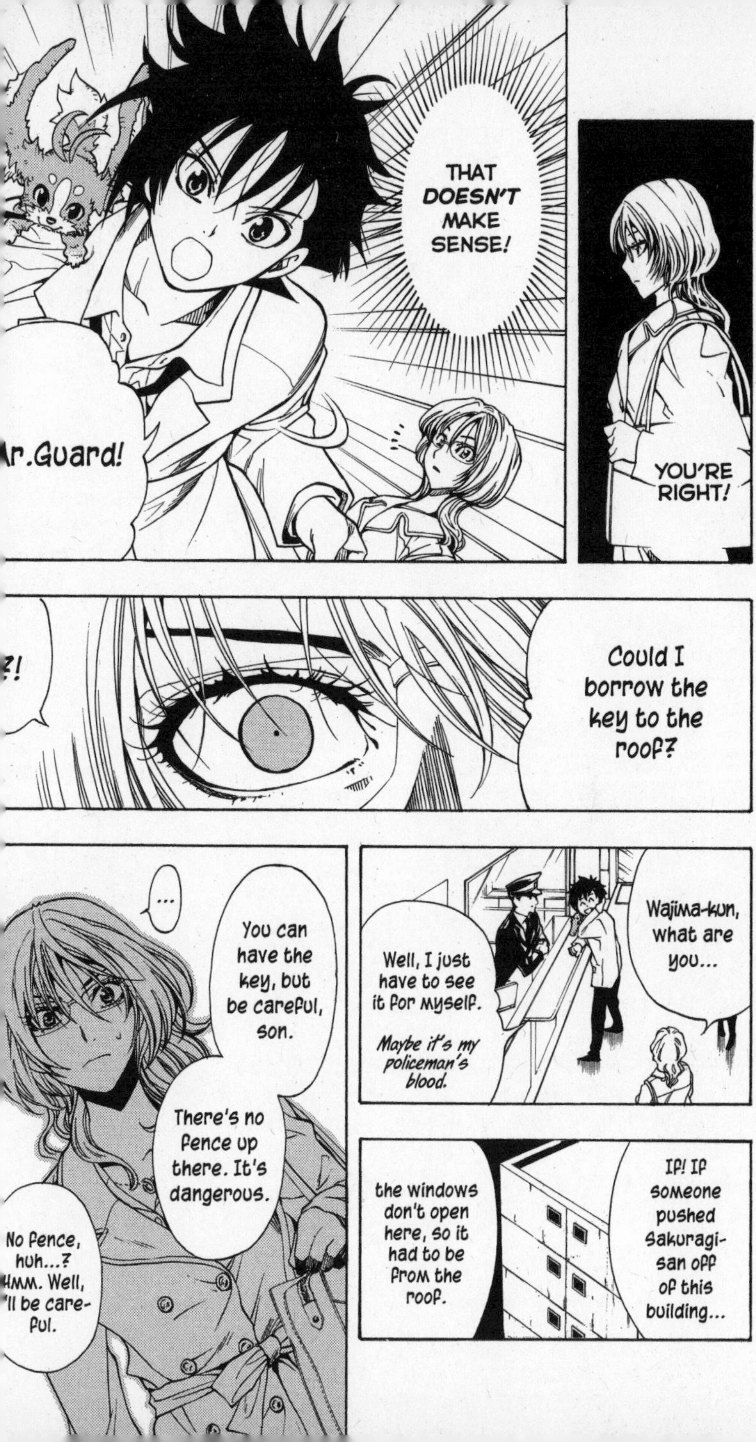
YOU'RE RIGHT!
THAT DOESN'T MAKE SENSE!
r.Guard!
Could I borrow the key to the roof?
?!
Wajima-kun, what are you...
Well, I just have to see it for myself.
Maybe it's my policeman's blood.
If! If someone pushed Sakuragi-san off of this building...
the windows don't open here, so it had to be from the roof.
...
You can have the key, but be careful, son.
There's no fence up there. It's dangerous.
No fence, huh...? HMM. Well, 'll be care-ful.

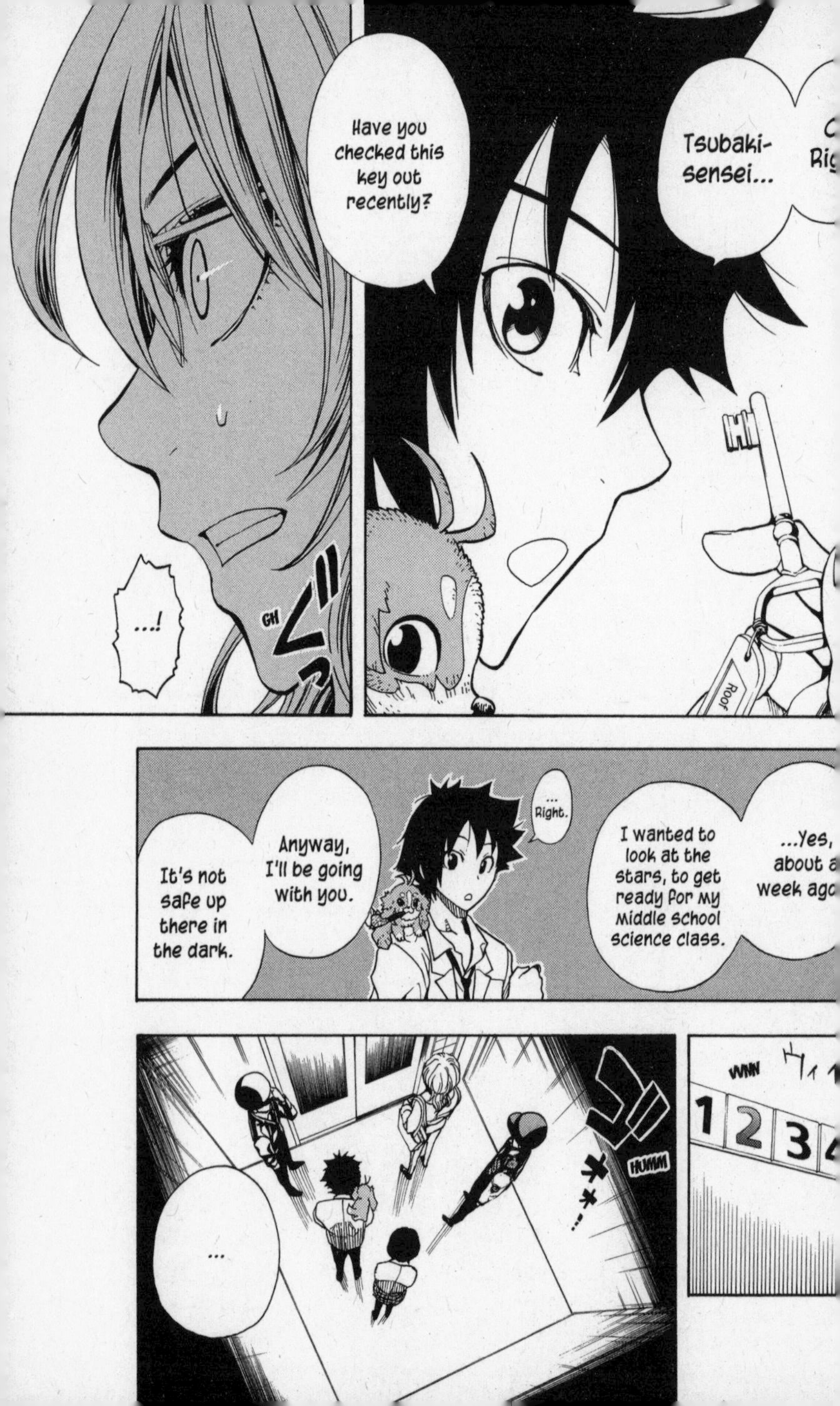
Tsubaki-sensei...
Have you checked this key out recently?
Roof
GH
...!
...Yes, about a week ago
I wanted to look at the stars, to get ready for my middle school science class.
...Right.
Anyway, I'll be going with you.
It's not safe up there in the dark.
WNN
1 2 3 4
HUMM
...

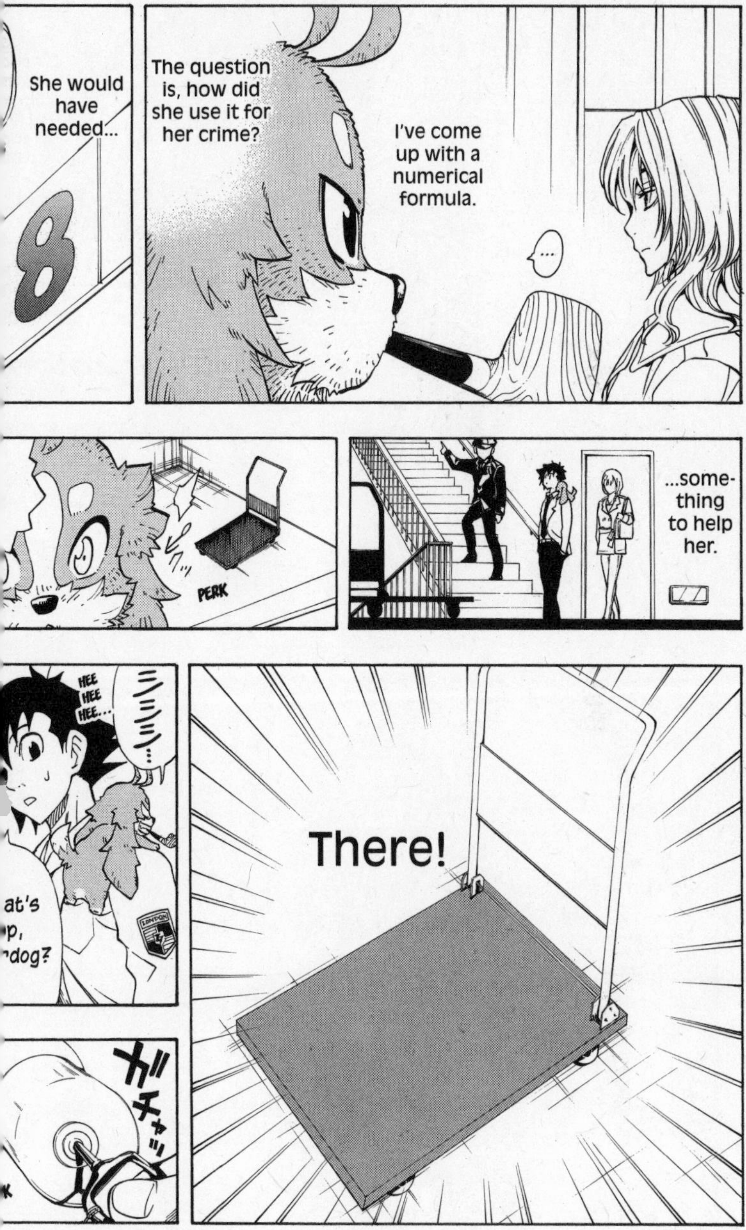
I've come up with a numerical formula.
...
The question is, how did she use it for her crime?
She would have needed...
...some-thing to help her.
PERK
There!
HEE HEE HEE...
ミミミ...
ガチャッ

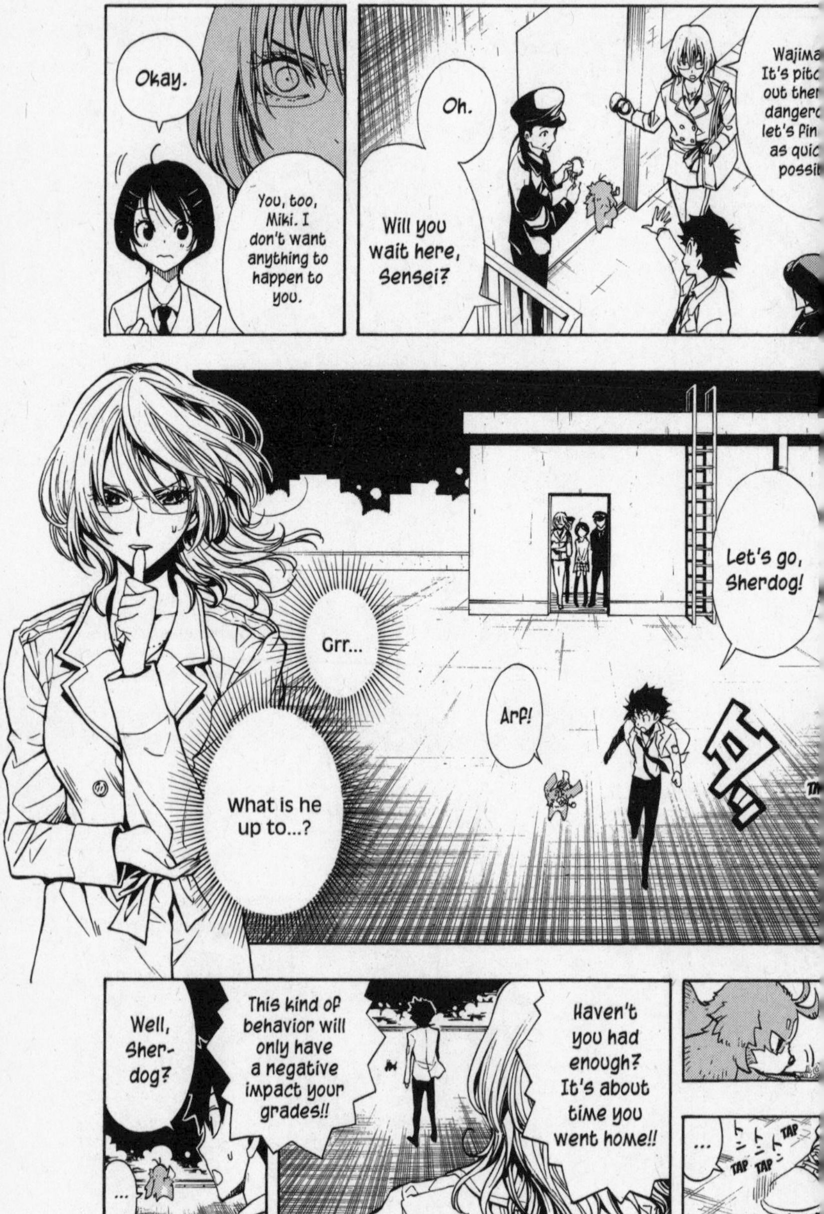
Wajima
It's pitc
out ther
dangerc
let's fin
as quic
possil
Oh.
Will you wait here, Sensei?
You, too, Miki. I don't want anything to happen to you.
Okay.
Let's go, Sherdog!
Arf!
Grr...
What is he up to...?
...
TAP TAP TAP
Haven't you had enough? It's about time you went home!!
This kind of behavior will only have a negative impact your grades!!
Well, Sher-dog?
...

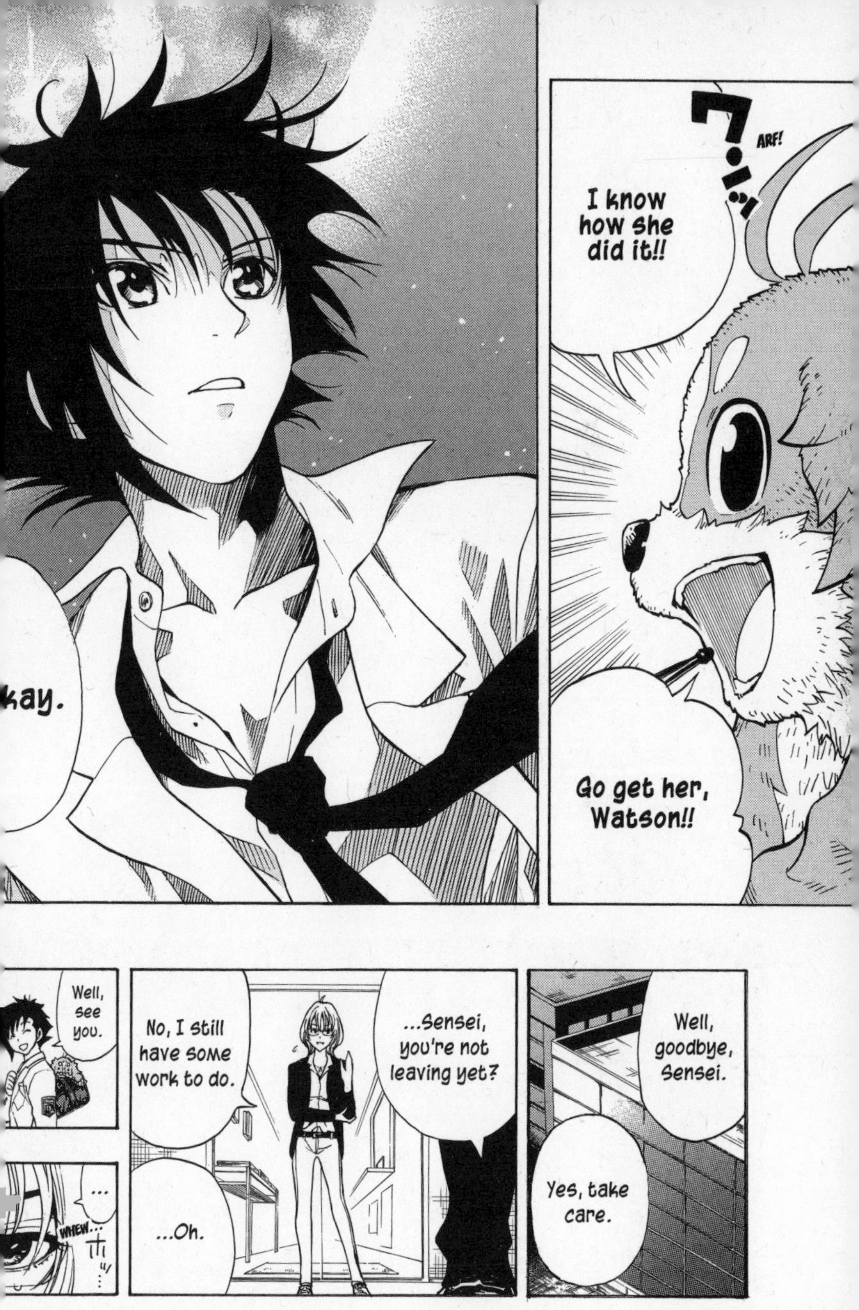

I know how she did it!!
ARF!
Go get her, Watson!!
kay.
Well, goodbye, Sensei.
Yes, take care.
...Sensei, you're not leaving yet?
No, I still have some work to do.
...Oh.
Well, see you.
...
WHEW...

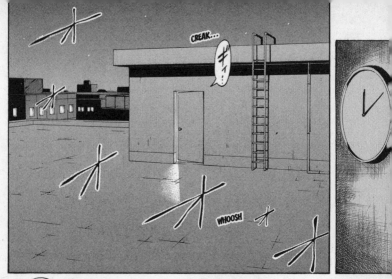

CREAK...

WHOOSH

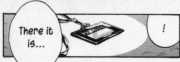

There it
is...

!

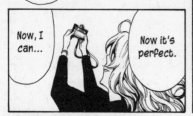

Now, I
can...

Now it's
perfect.

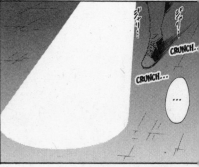

CRUNCH...

CRUNCH...

...

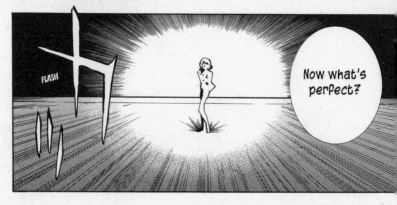

FLASH

Now what's
perfect?

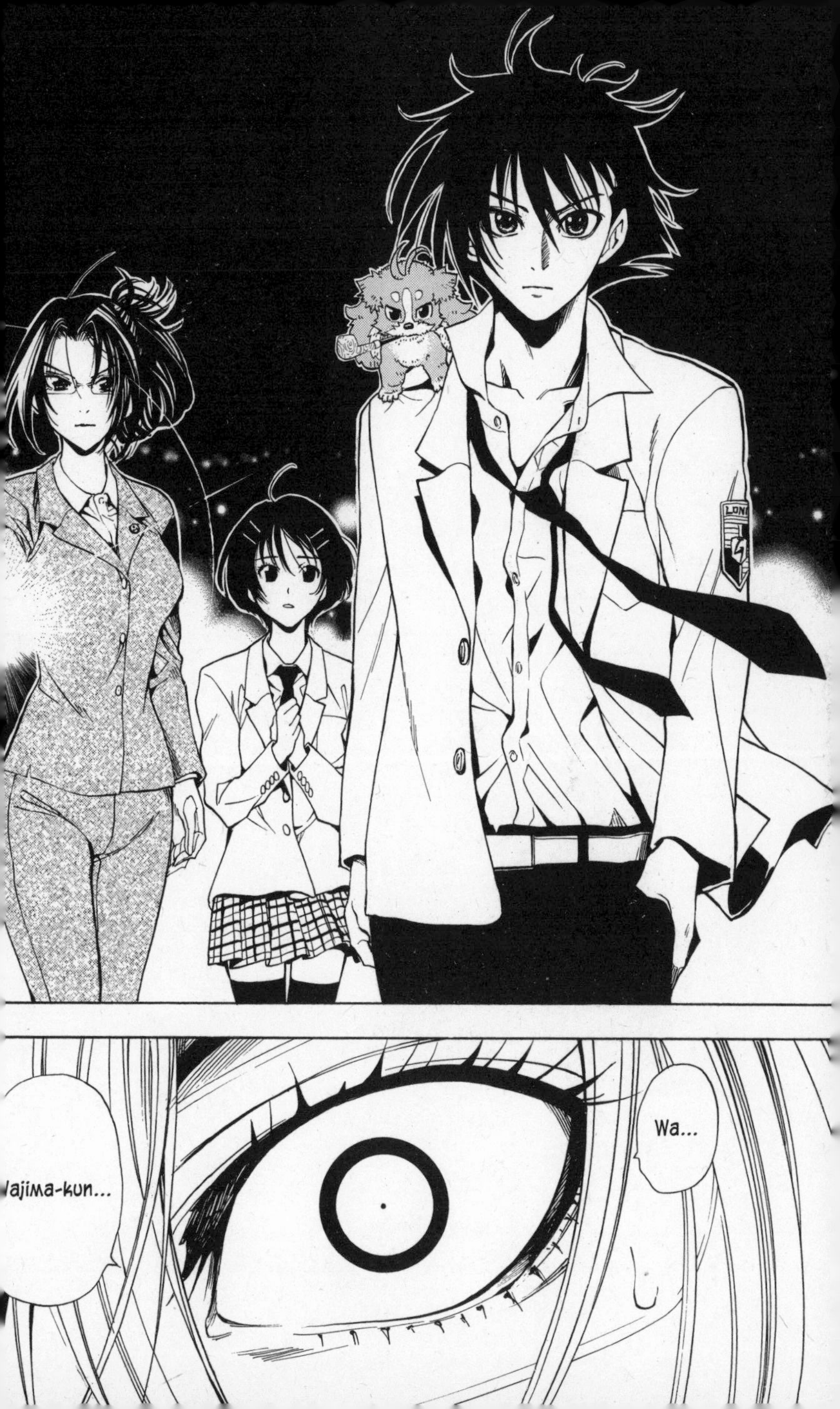
Wa...
ajima-kun...

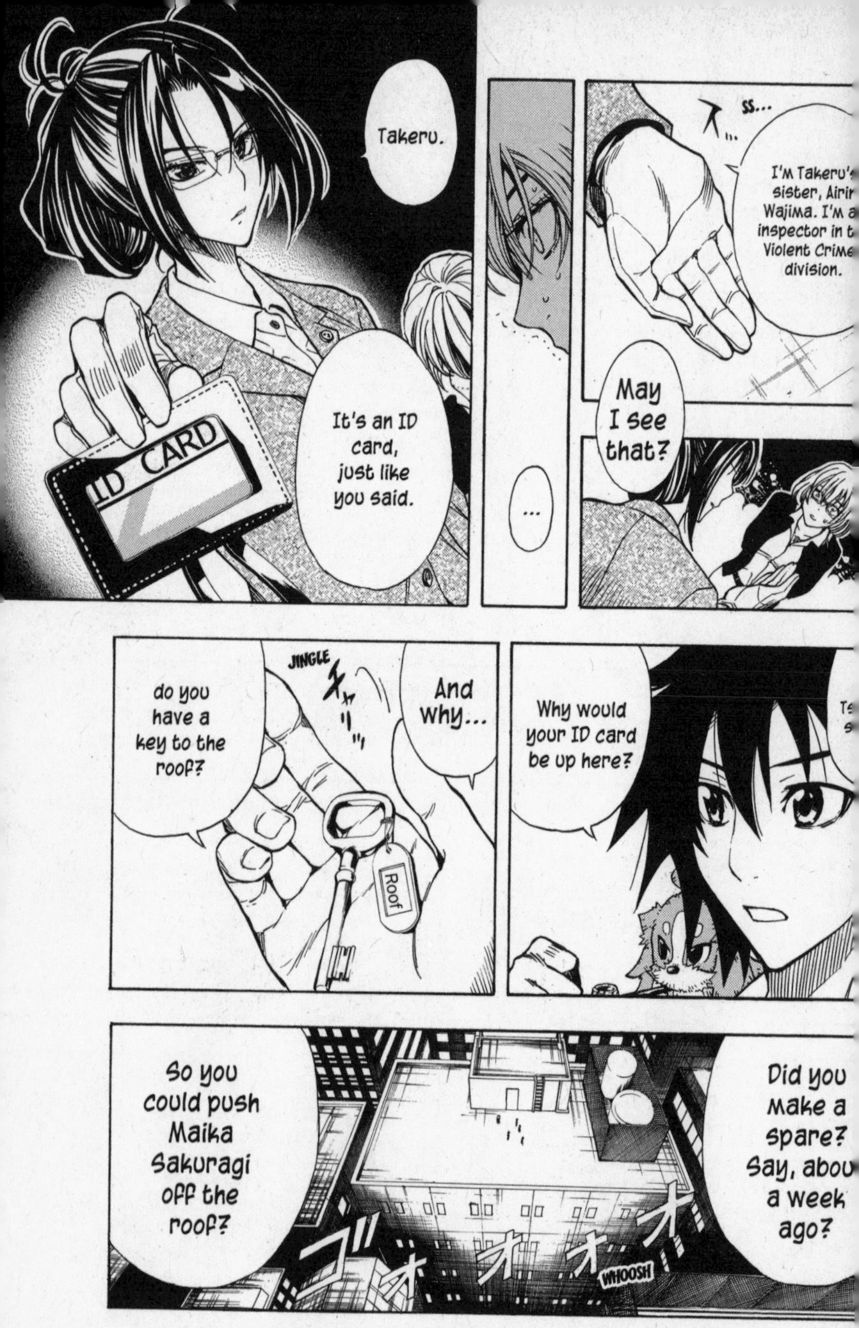
SS...
I'm Takeru's sister, Airi Wajima. I'm a inspector in t Violent Crime division.
May I see that?
...
Takeru.
ID CARD
It's an ID card, just like you said.
Why would your ID card be up here?
And why...
JINGLE
do you have a key to the roof?
Roof
Did you make a spare? Say, abou a week ago?
So you could push Maika Sakuragi off the roof?
WHOOSH

But how?
Sakuragi-san fell more than ten meters away.
It's possible.
...
We learned about it in class earlier...
Horizontal trajectories.
INCE
!
This is an eight-story building.
So if each floor is 3.5 meters high,
then the whole building would by 3.5m times 8. That's 28 meters.
28m
If we make Sakuragi-san's body mass M,
Note: The weight of M has no bearing on its downward velocity.
Vo
M
28m
10m
ve need
ermine
initial
zontal
ocity
ld be
ssary
ove M
eters
ontally
e it hits
round.

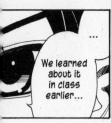

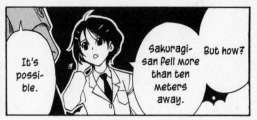

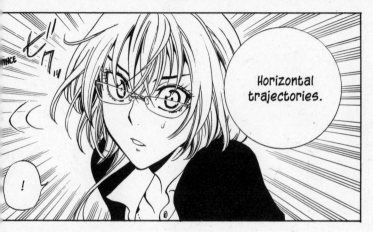

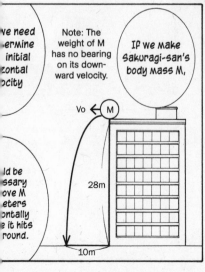

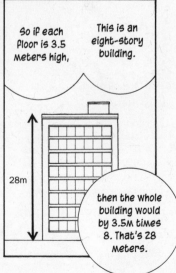

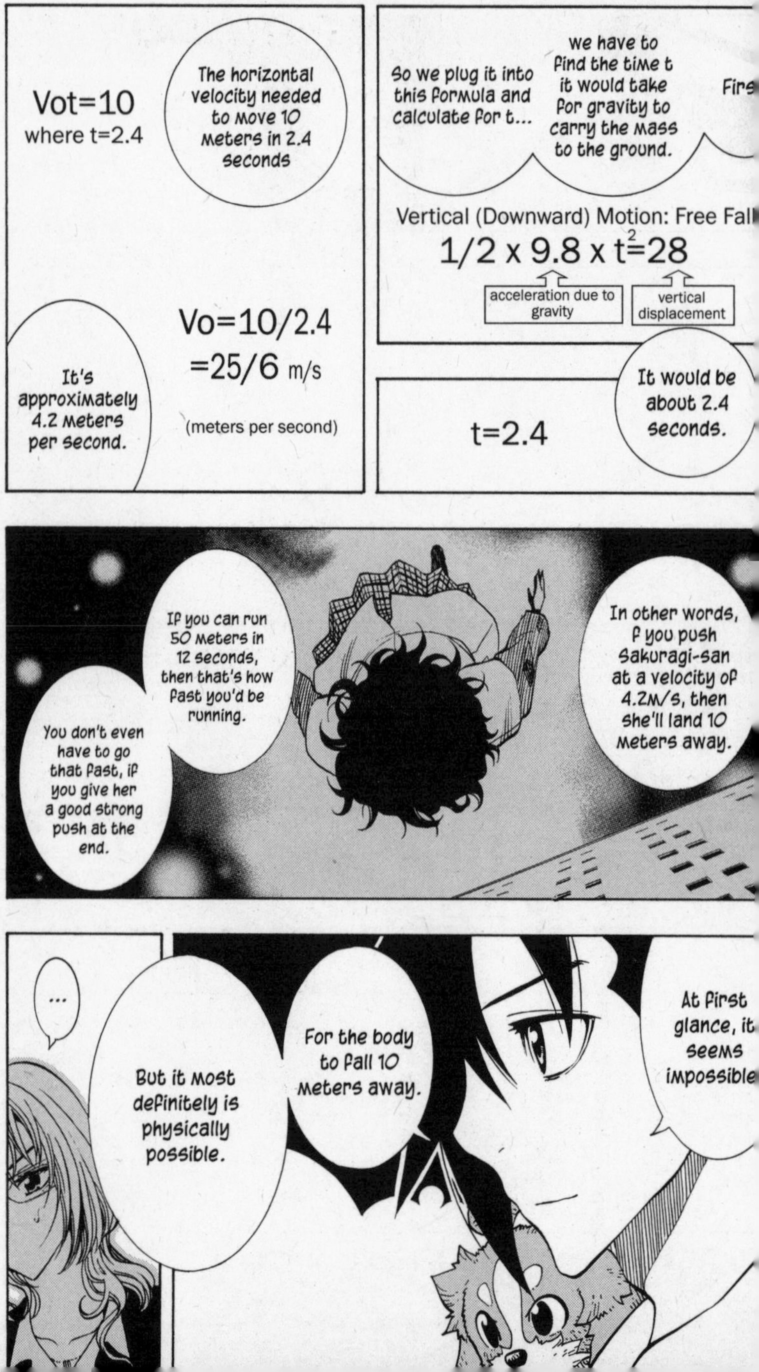
Firs
we have to find the time t it would take for gravity to carry the mass to the ground.
So we plug it into this formula and calculate for t...
Vertical (Downward) Motion: Free Fall
1/2 x 9.8 x t^2=28
acceleration due to gravity
vertical displacement
It would be about 2.4 seconds.
t=2.4
The horizontal velocity needed to move 10 meters in 2.4 seconds
Vot=10
where t=2.4
Vo=10/2.4
=25/6 m/s
(meters per second)
It's approximately 4.2 meters per second.
In other words, f you push Sakuragi-san at a velocity of 4.2m/s, then she'll land 10 meters away.
If you can run 50 meters in 12 seconds, then that's how fast you'd be running.
You don't even have to go that fast, if you give her a good strong push at the end.
At first glance, it seems impossible
For the body to fall 10 meters away.
But it most definitely is physically possible.
...

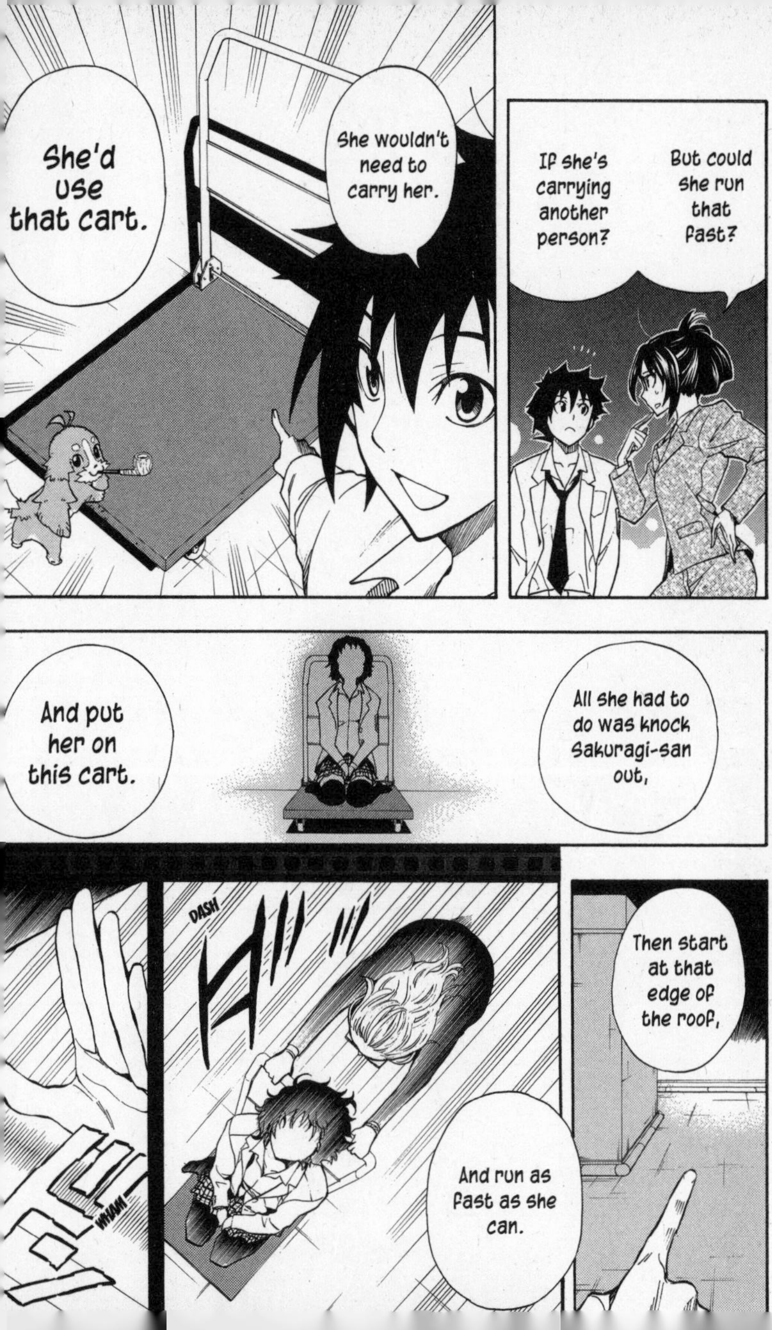
But could she run that fast?
If she's carrying another person?
She wouldn't need to carry her.
She'd use that cart.
All she had to do was knock Sakuragi-san out,
And put her on this cart.
Then start at that edge of the roof,
And run as fast as she can.
DASH
WHAM

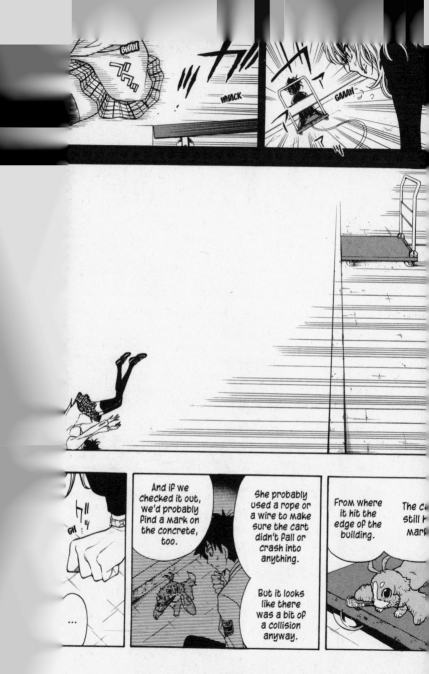

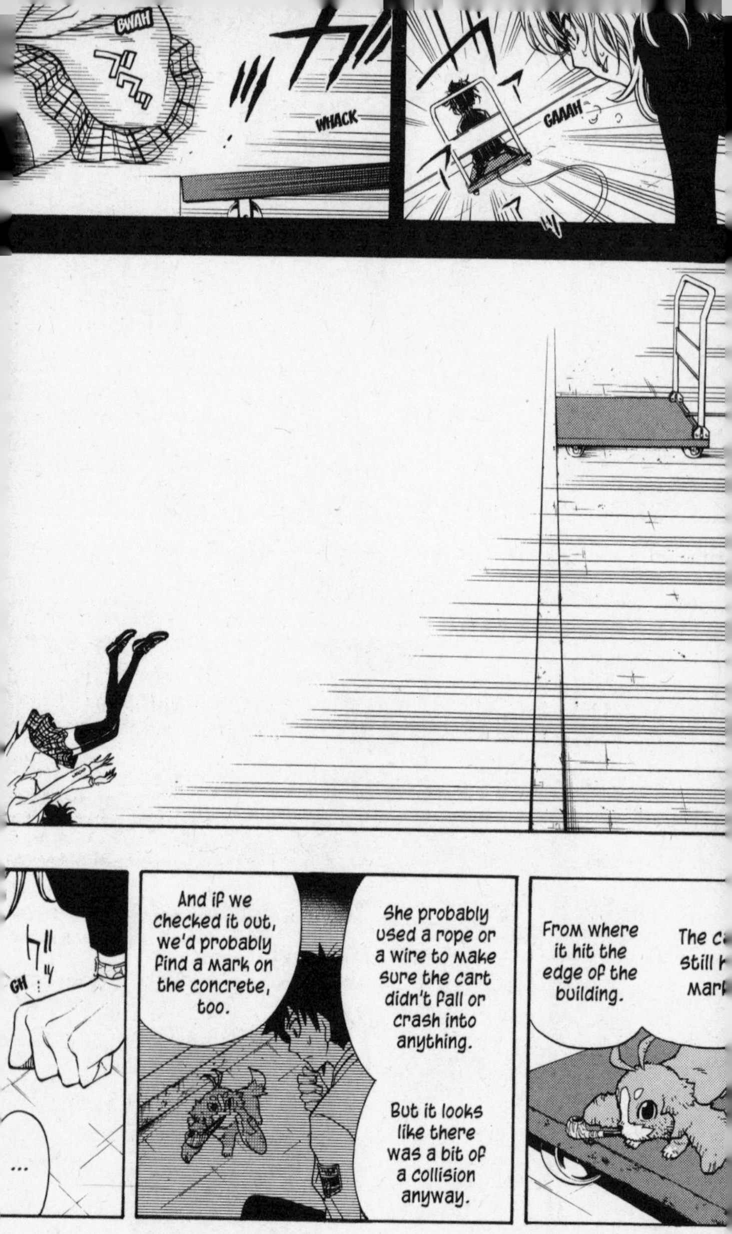
GAAAH
WHACK
BWAH
The c
still h
Mar
From where it hit the edge of the building.
She probably used a rope or a wire to make sure the cart didn't fall or crash into anything.
But it looks like there was a bit of a collision anyway.
And if we checked it out, we'd probably find a mark on the concrete, too.
GH
...

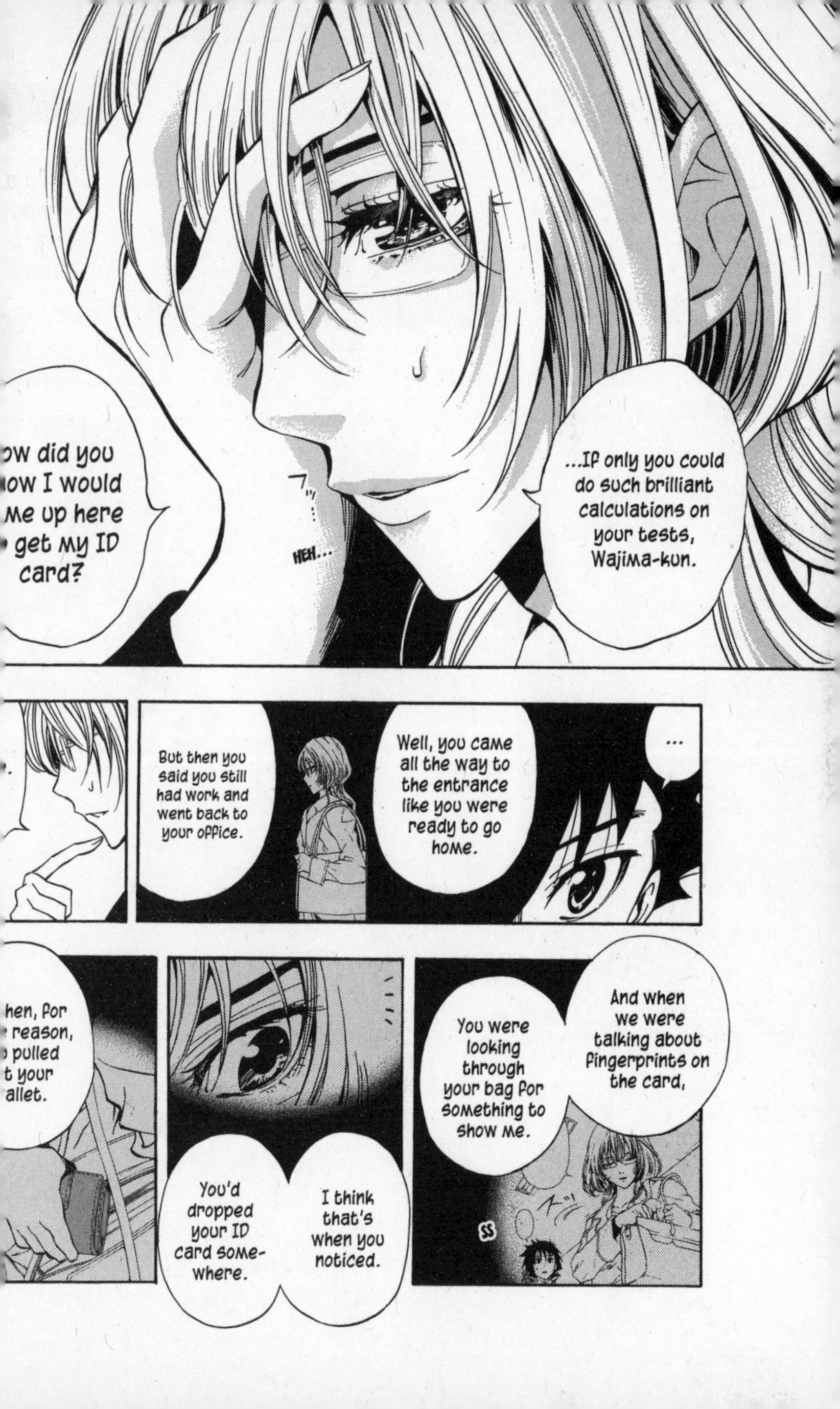
...If only you could do such brilliant calculations on your tests, Wajima-kun.
HEH...
ow did you
ow I would
me up here
get my ID
card?
...
Well, you came all the way to the entrance like you were ready to go home.
But then you said you still had work and went back to your office.
And when we were talking about fingerprints on the card,
You were looking through your bag for something to show me.
SS
I think that's when you noticed.
You'd dropped your ID card some-where.
hen, for
reason,
pulled
t your
allet.

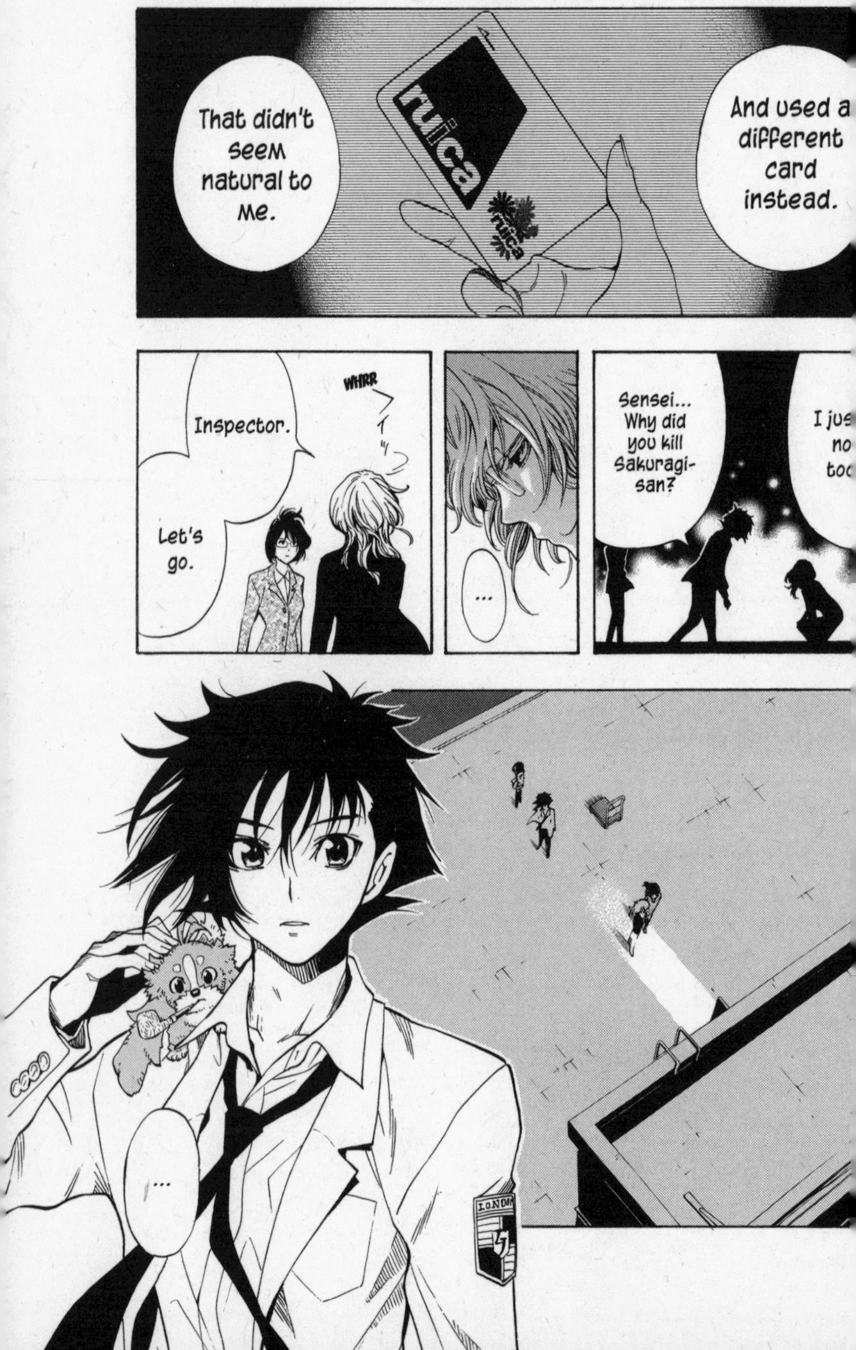
And used a different card instead.
ruica
That didn't seem natural to me.
Sensei... Why did you kill Sakuragi-san?
...
WHRR
Inspector.
Let's go.
...

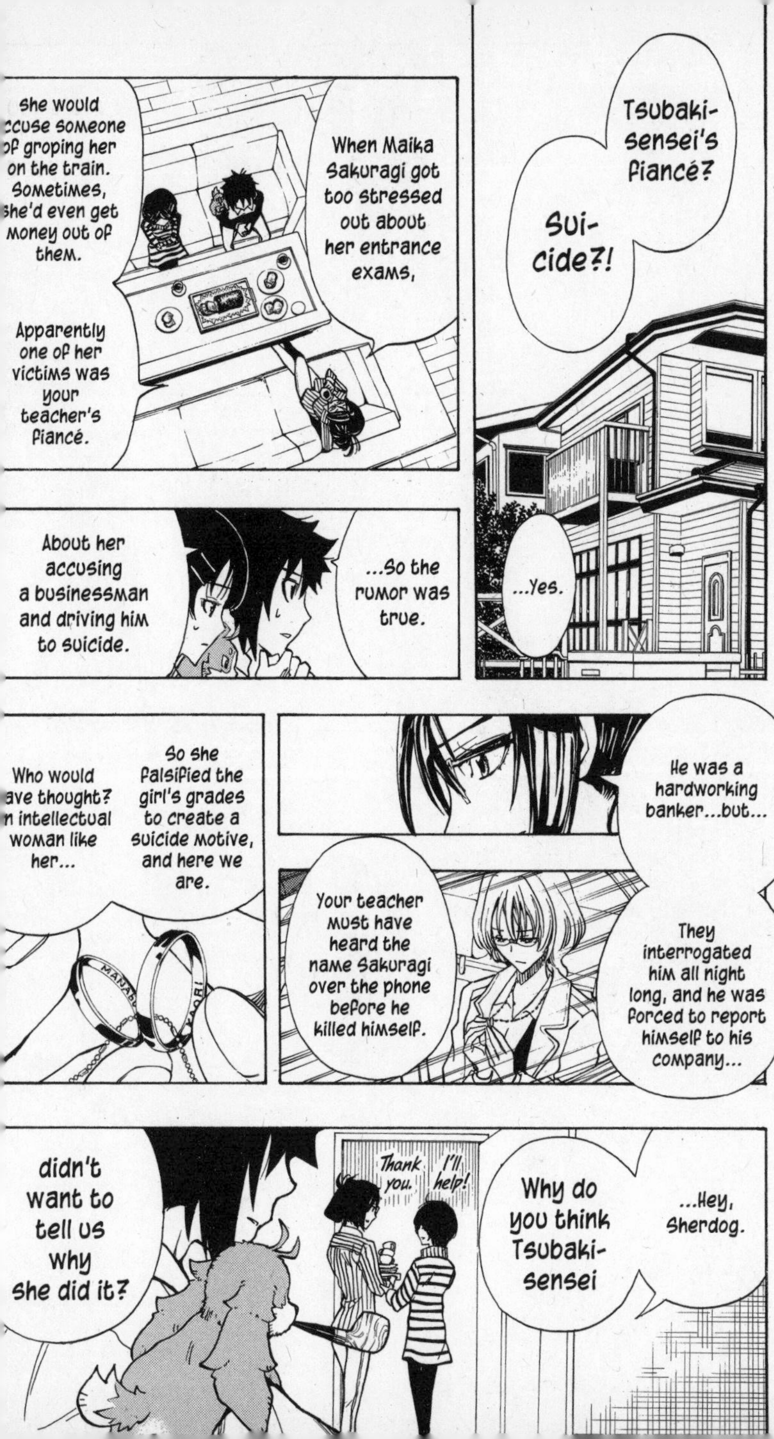
Tsubaki-sensei's fiancé?
Sui-cide?!
...Yes.
When Maika Sakuragi got too stressed out about her entrance exams,
she would ccuse someone of groping her on the train. Sometimes, she'd even get money out of them.
Apparently one of her victims was your teacher's fiancé.
...So the rumor was true.
About her accusing a businessman and driving him to suicide.
He was a hardworking banker...but...
They interrogated him all night long, and he was forced to report himself to his company...
Your teacher must have heard the name Sakuragi over the phone before he killed himself.
So she falsified the girl's grades to create a suicide motive, and here we are.
Who would ave thought? n intellectual woman like her...
...Hey, Sherdog.
Why do you think Tsubaki-sensei
I'll help!
Thank you.
didn't want to tell us why she did it?

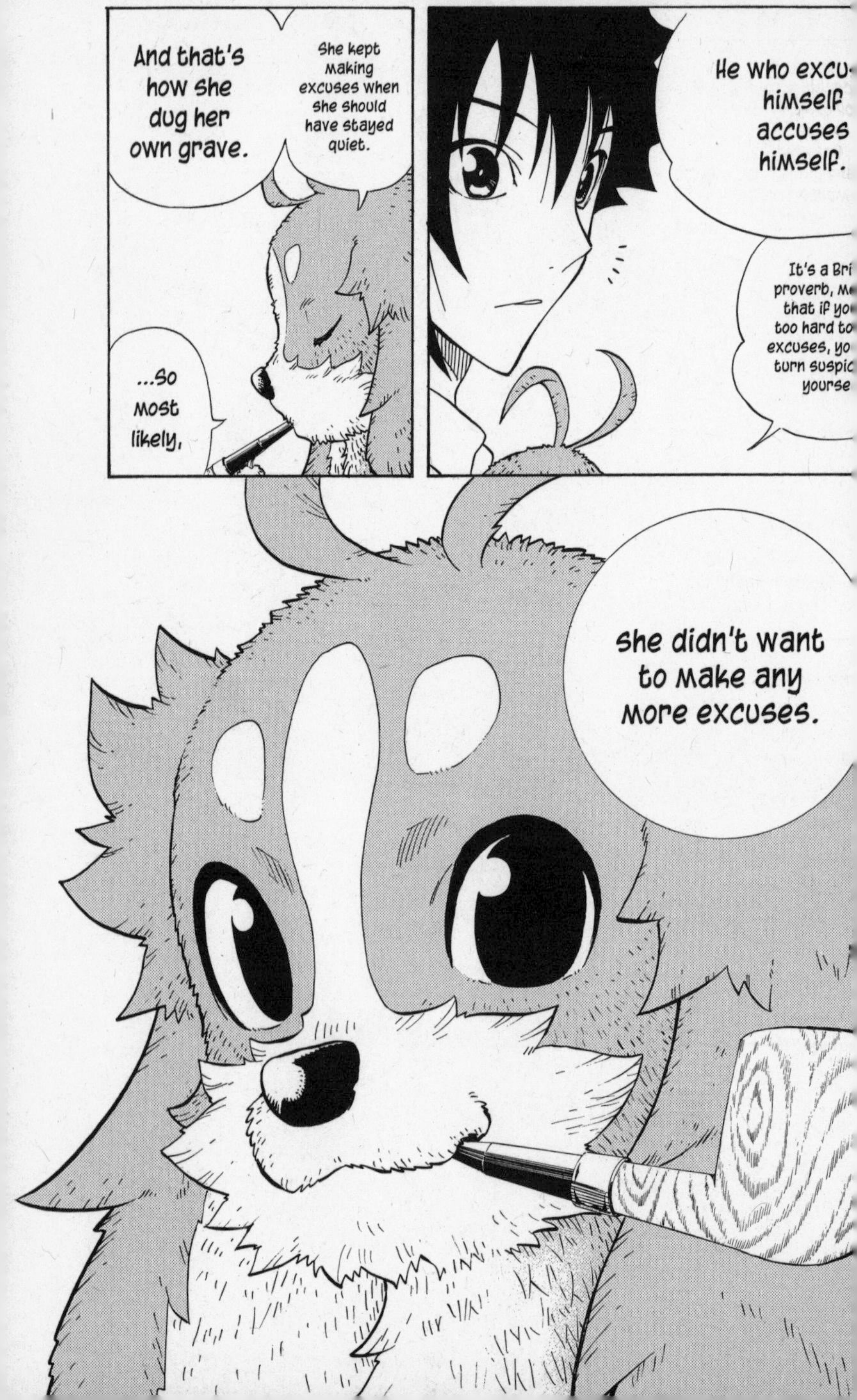

He who excu himself accuses himself.
It's a Bri proverb, M that if yo too hard to excuses, yo turn suspic yourse
She kept making excuses when she should have stayed quiet.
And that's how she dug her own grave.
...So most likely,
she didn't want to make any more excuses.

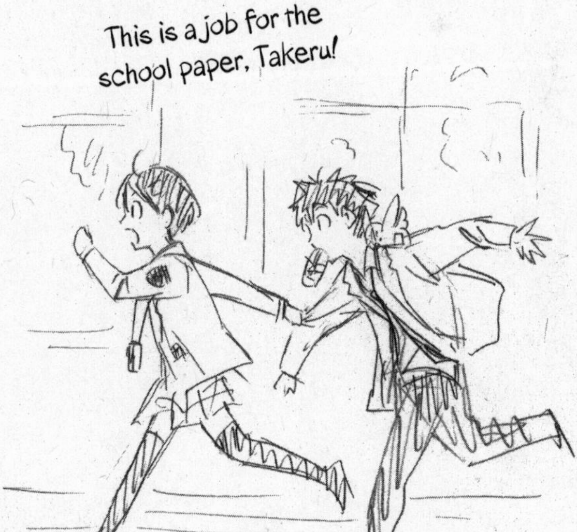
This is a job for the school paper, Takeru!

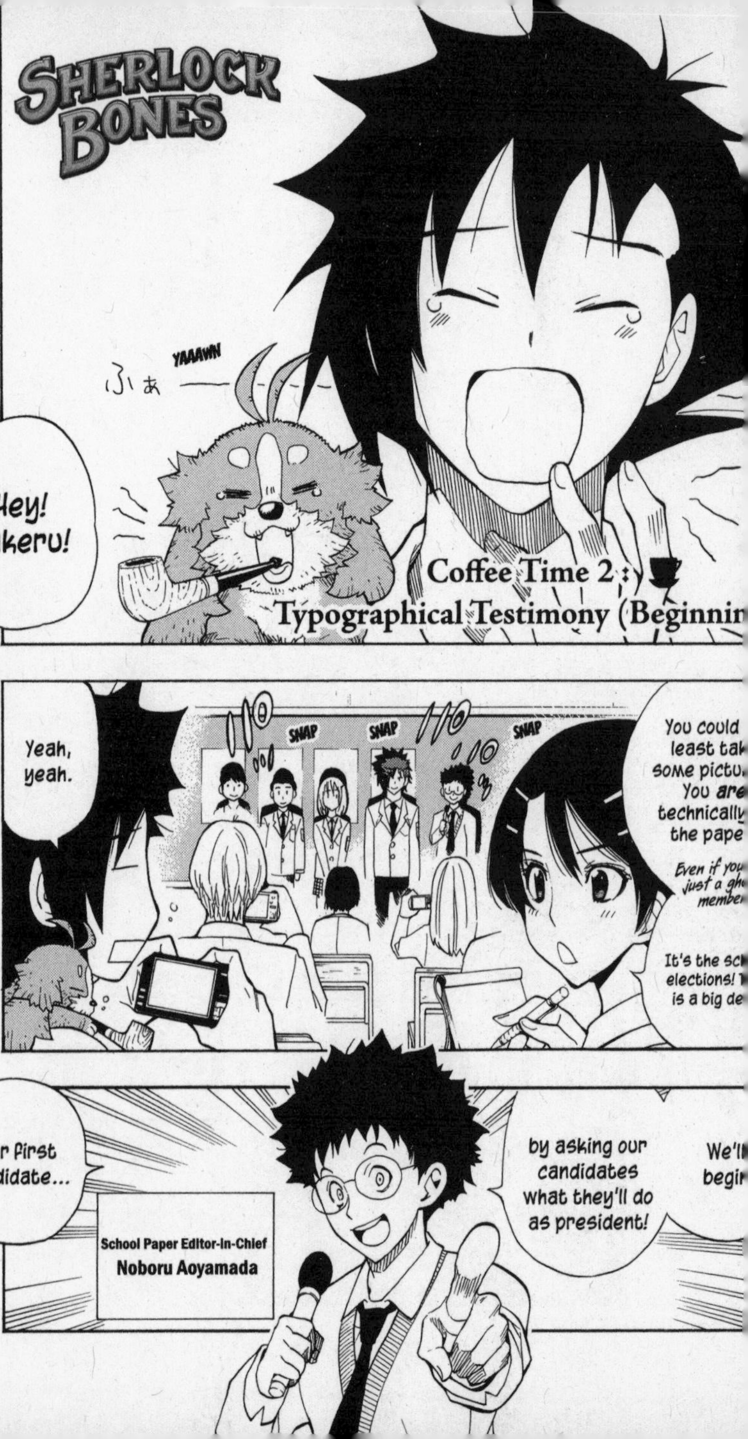

Sherlock Bones
YAAAWN
ふぁ—
Hey! Takeru!
Coffee Time 2 : Typographical Testimony (Beginnin
You could least tak some pictu. You are technically the pape
Even if you just a gh member
It's the sc elections! is a big de
SNAP
SNAP
SNAP
Yeah, yeah.
We'l begi
by asking our candidates what they'll do as president!
Our first candidate...
School Paper Editor-in-Chief
Noboru Aoyamada

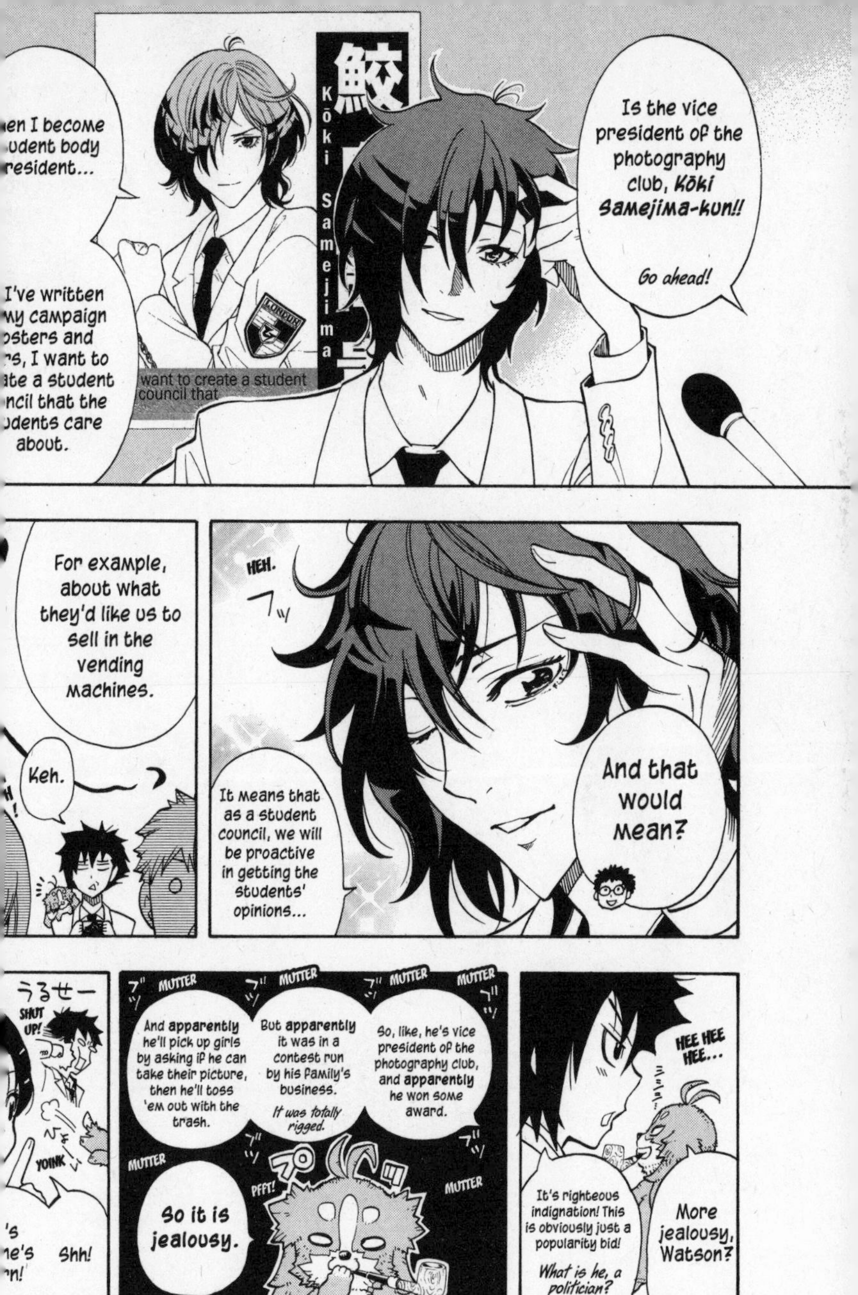
Is the vice president of the photography club, Kōki Samejima-kun!!
Go ahead!
鮫
Kōki Samejima
...en I become ...udent body ...resident...
I've written ...my campaign ...osters and ...rs, I want to ...ate a student ...ncil that the ...udents care about.
want to create a student council that
HEH.
フッ
And that would mean?
It means that as a student council, we will be proactive in getting the students' opinions...
For example, about what they'd like us to sell in the vending machines.
Keh.
HEE HEE HEE...
More jealousy, Watson?
It's righteous indignation! This is obviously just a popularity bid!
What is he, a politician?
MUTTER
MUTTER
So, like, he's vice president of the photography club, and apparently he won some award.
MUTTER
But apparently it was in a contest run by his family's business.
It was totally rigged.
MUTTER
And apparently he'll pick up girls by asking if he can take their picture, then he'll toss 'em out with the trash.
MUTTER
MUTTER
So it is jealousy.
PFFT!
プ
うるせー
SHUT UP!
YOINK
Shh!

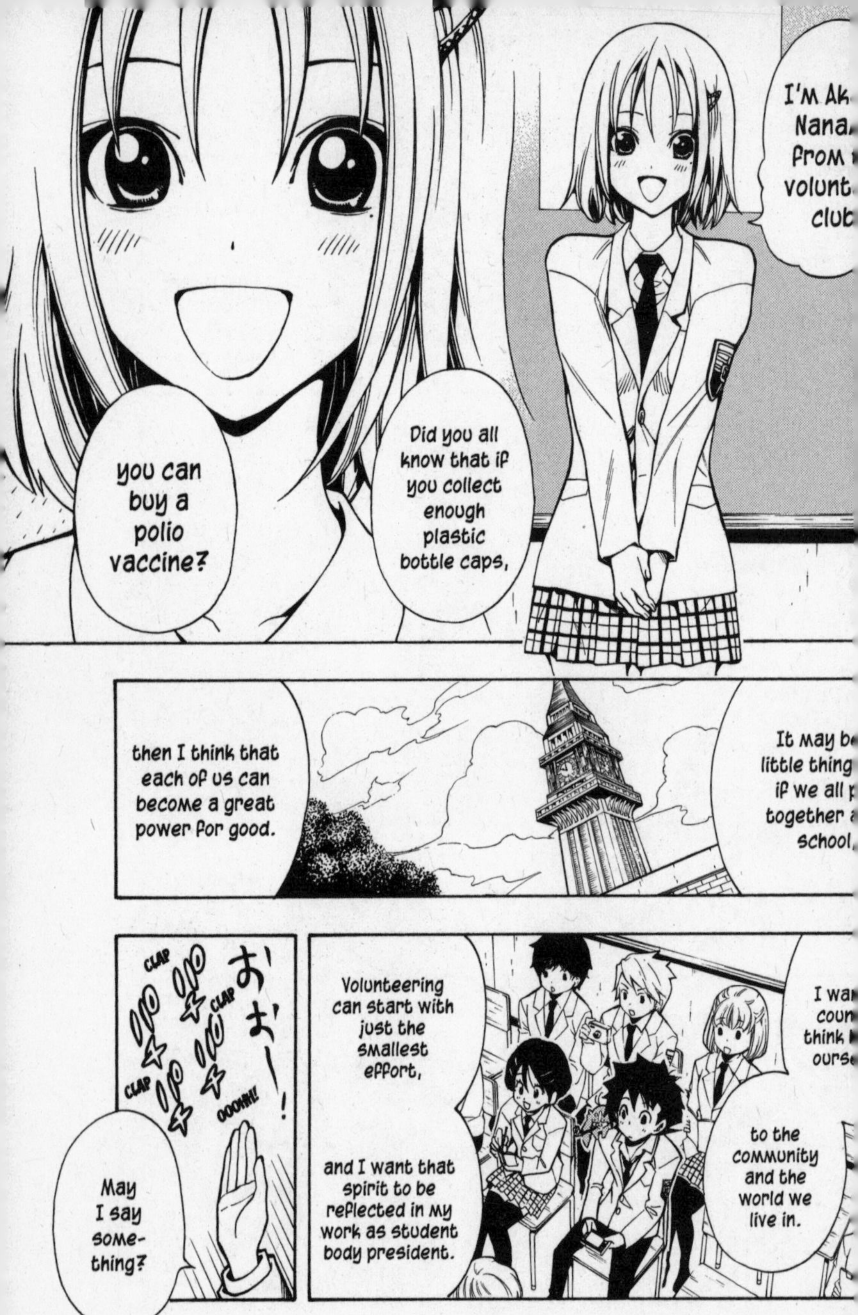
I'M Ak Nana, from volunt club
Did you all know that if you collect enough plastic bottle caps,
you can buy a polio vaccine?
It may b little thing if we all p together a school,
then I think that each of us can become a great power for good.
I wa coun think ourse
to the community and the world we live in.
Volunteering can start with just the smallest effort,
and I want that spirit to be reflected in my work as student body president.
CLAP
CLAP
CLAP
おお～!
OOOHH!
May I say some-thing?

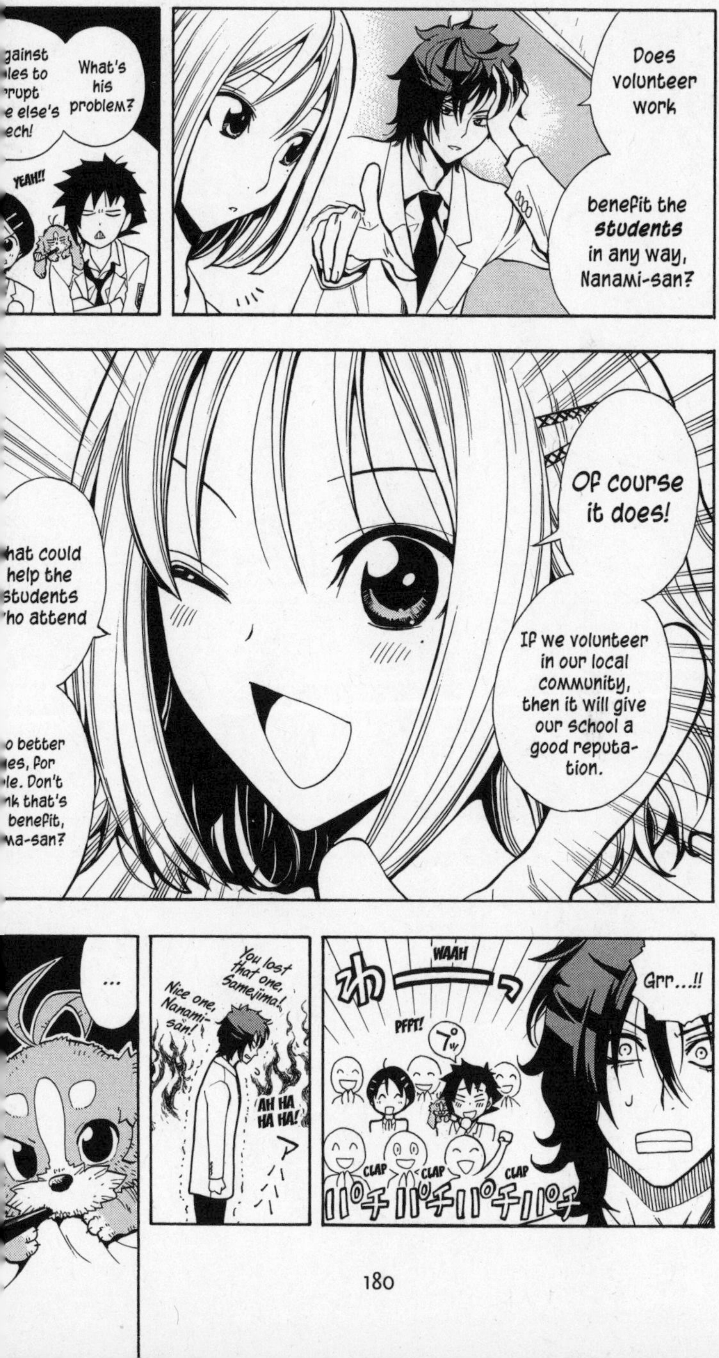

Does volunteer work
benefit the students in any way, Nanami-san?
gainst
les to
rrupt
e else's
ech!
What's his problem?
YEAH!!
Of course it does!
If we volunteer in our local community, then it will give our school a good reputation.
hat could help the students ho attend
o better
es, for
le. Don't
nk that's
benefit,
ma-san?
わーっ
WAAH
Grr...!!
PFFT!
プッ
CLAP
CLAP
CLAP
パチパチパチパチ
You lost that one, Samejima!
Nice one, Nanami-san!
AH HA HA HA!
...

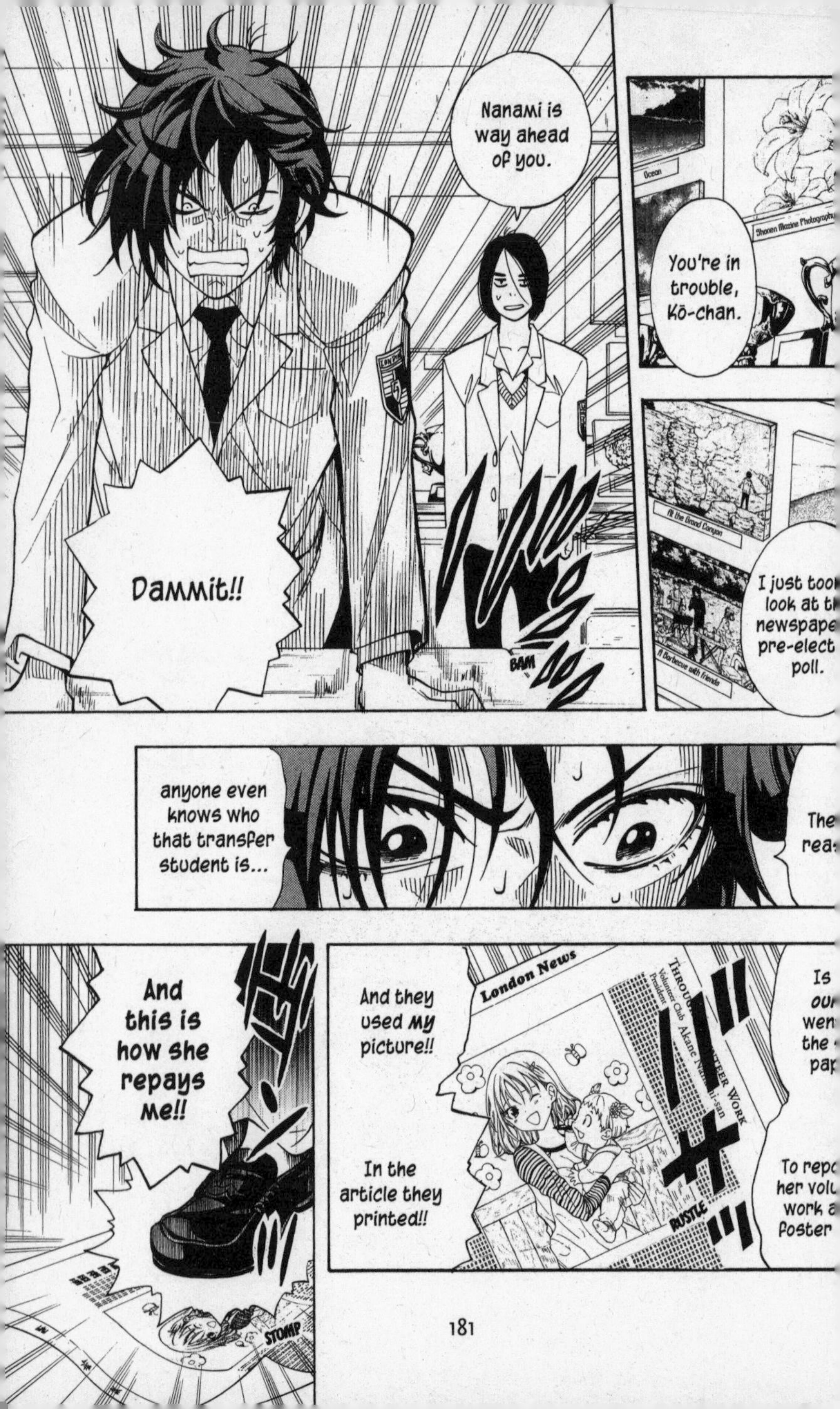
Shonen Mazine Photograph
Ocean
You're in trouble, Kō-chan.
At the Grand Canyon
A Barbecue with friends
I just took look at th newspape pre-elect poll.
Nanami is way ahead of you.
Dammit!!
BAM
The rea
anyone even knows who that transfer student is...
Is our wen the pap
To repo her volu work a foster
London News
Volunteer Club President Akane N i-san
And they used my picture!!
In the article they printed!!
RUSTLE
And this is how she repays me!!
STOMP

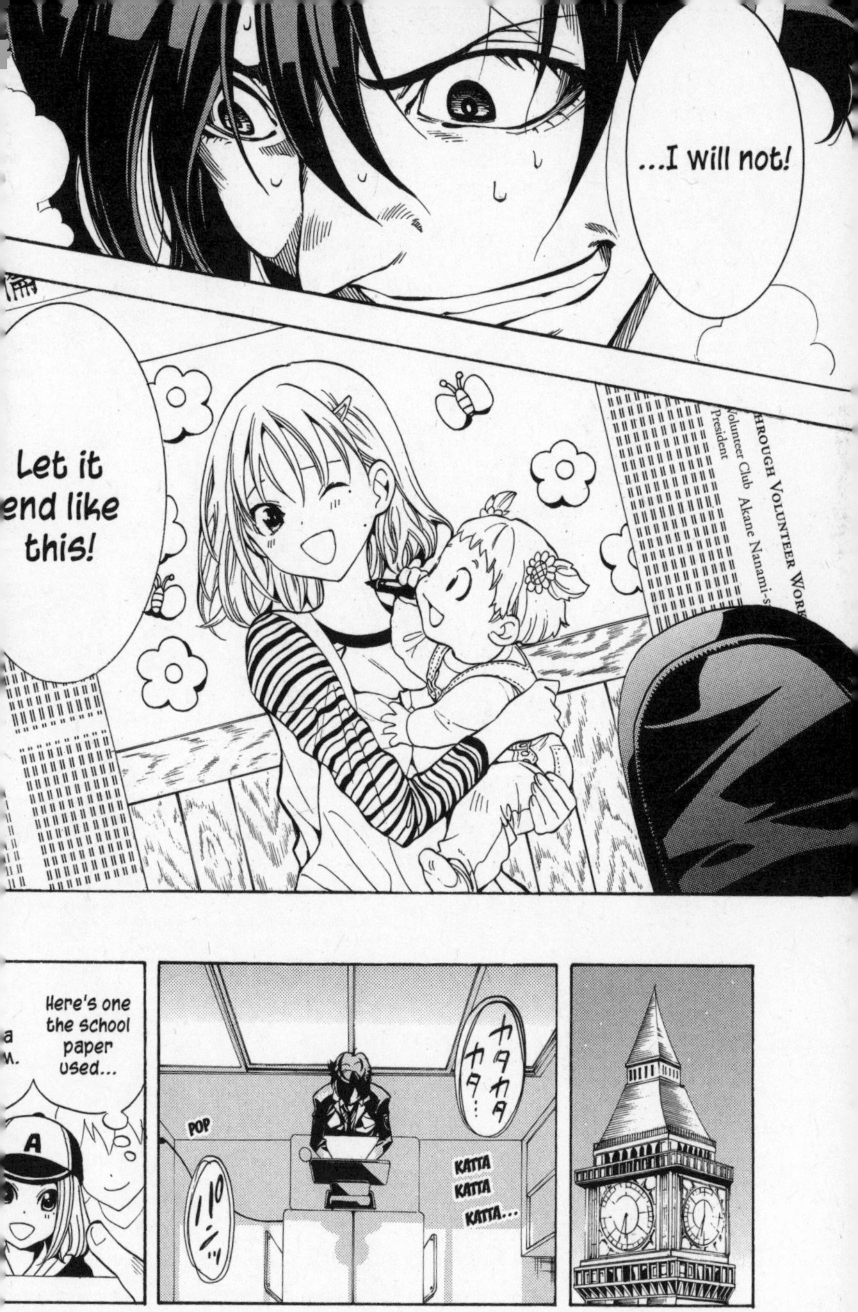

...I will not!
Let it end like this!
HROUGH VOLUNTEER WORK
Volunteer Club Akane Nanami-s
President
カタカタ
カタ…
KATTA
KATTA
KATTA...
POP
Here's one the school paper used...

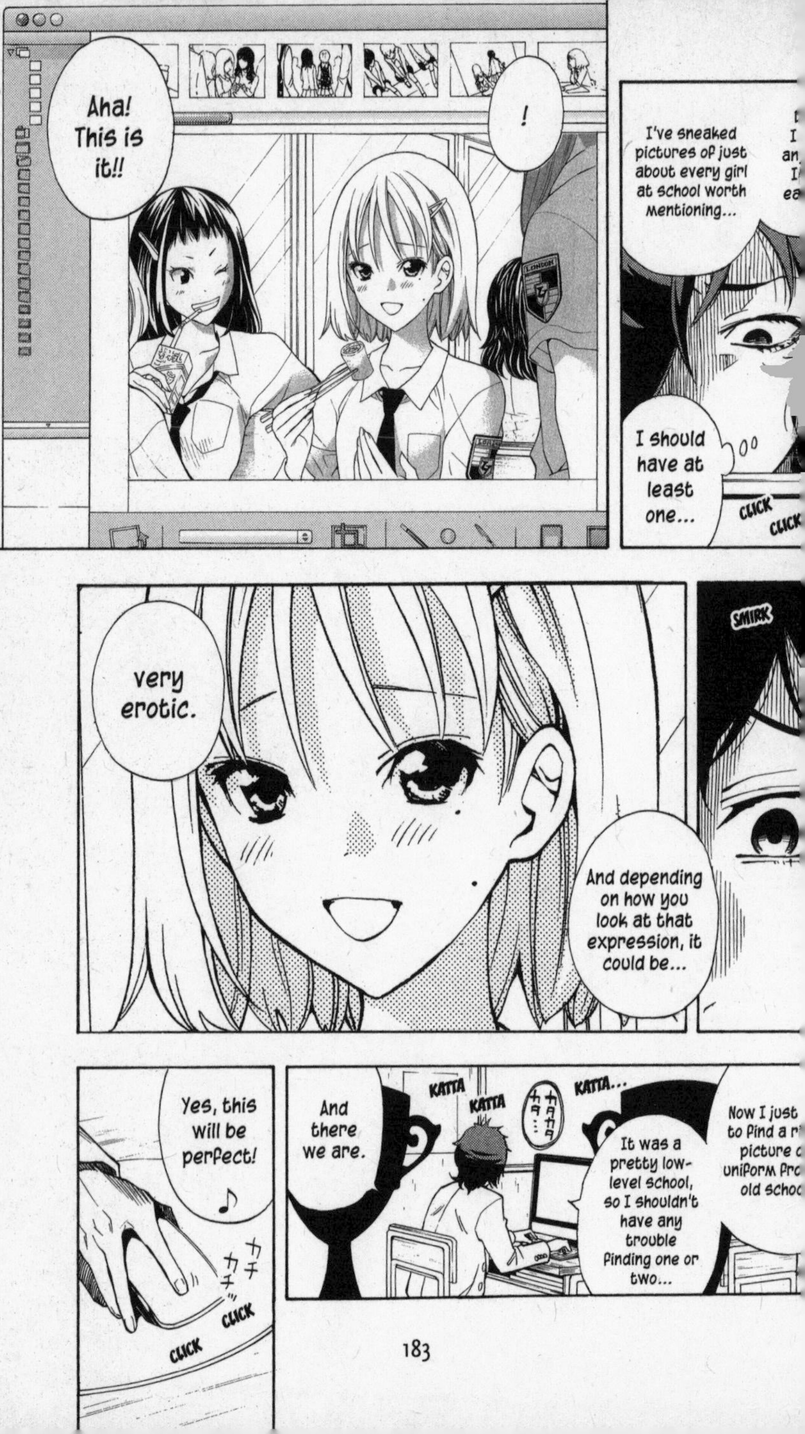

I've sneaked pictures of just about every girl at school worth mentioning...
I should have at least one...
CLICK
CLICK
!
Aha! This is it!!
SMIRK
And depending on how you look at that expression, it could be...
very erotic.
Now I just
KATTA...
It was a pretty low-level school, so I shouldn't have any trouble finding one or two...
カタカタ
KATTA
KATTA
And there we are.
Yes, this will be perfect!
♪
カチ
カチッ
CLICK
CLICK

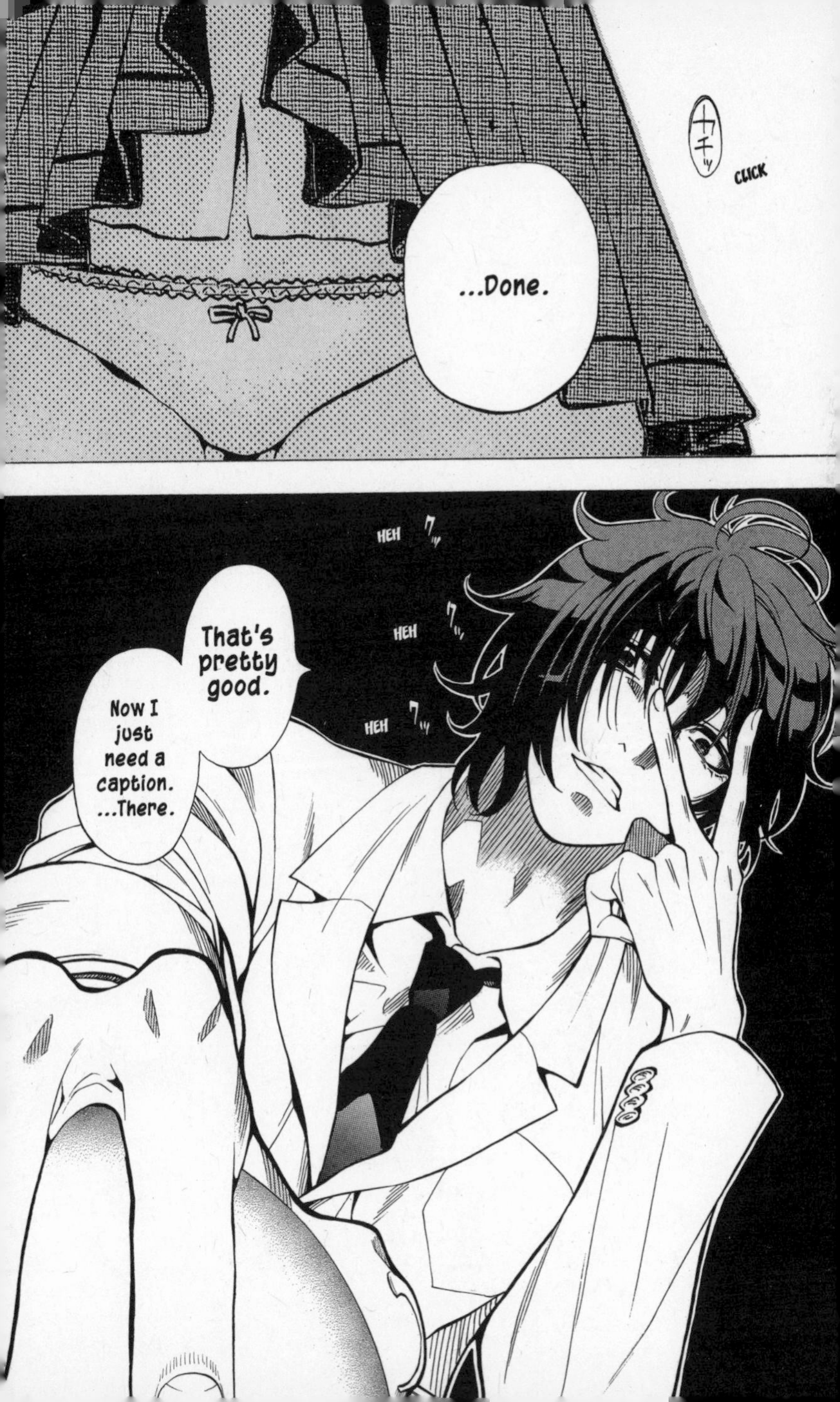
カチッ
CLICK
...Done.
HEH クッ
HEH クッ
HEH クッ
That's pretty good.
Now I just need a caption. ...There.

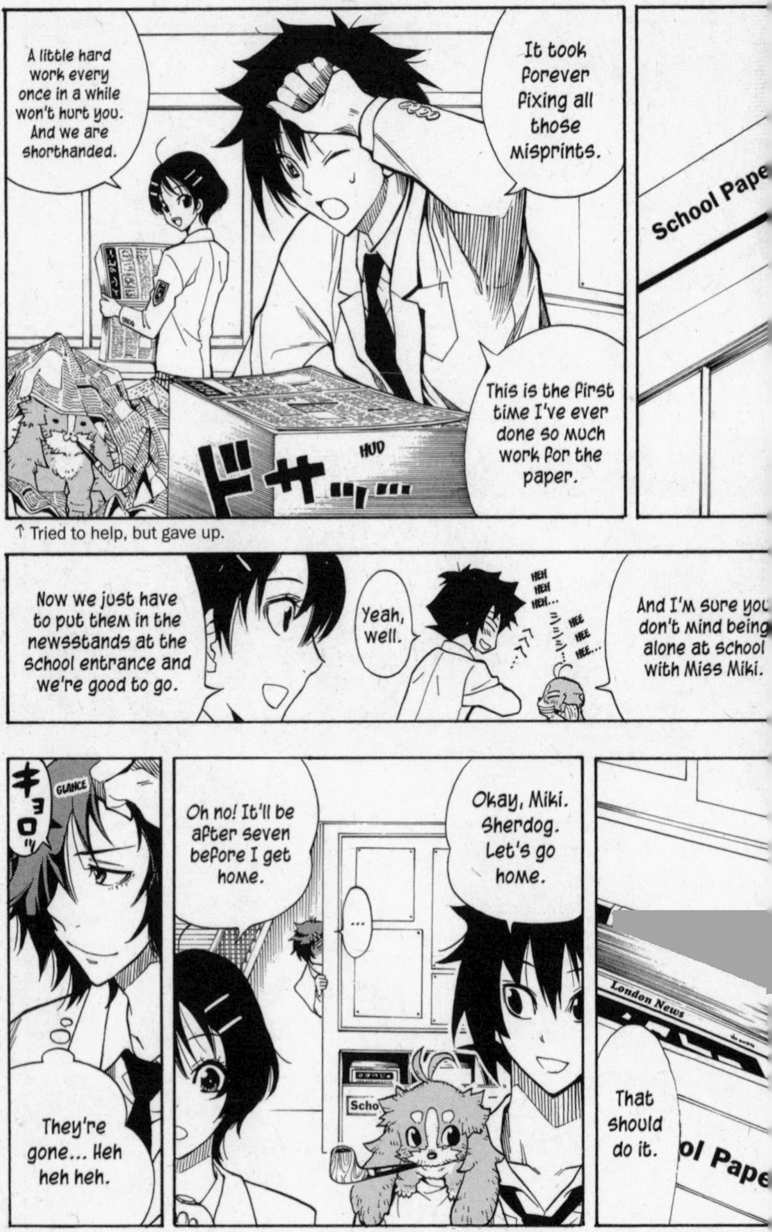
School Pape
It took forever fixing all those misprints.
This is the first time I've ever done so much work for the paper.
A little hard work every once in a while won't hurt you. And we are shorthanded.
HUD
↑ Tried to help, but gave up.
And I'm sure you don't mind being alone at school with Miss Miki.
HEH HEH HEH...
HEE HEE HEE...
Yeah, well.
Now we just have to put them in the newsstands at the school entrance and we're good to go.
London News
That should do it.
ol Pape
Okay, Miki. Sherdog. Let's go home.
Oh no! It'll be after seven before I get home.
...
Scho
GLANCE
They're gone... Heh heh heh.

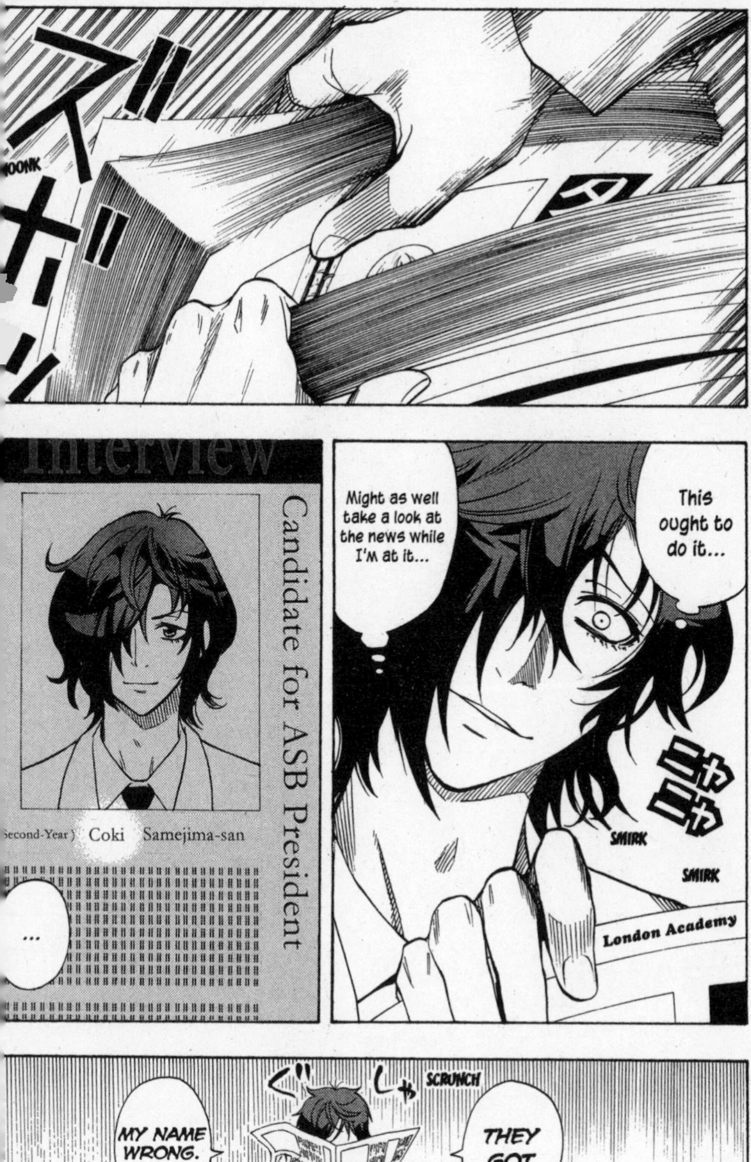
This ought to do it...
Might as well take a look at the news while I'm at it...
ニヤニヤ
SMIRK
SMIRK
London Academy
Interview
Candidate for ASB President
Second-Year) Coki Samejima-san
...
ぐしゃ
SCRUNCH
THEY GOT
MY NAME WRONG.

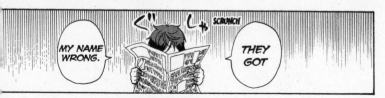

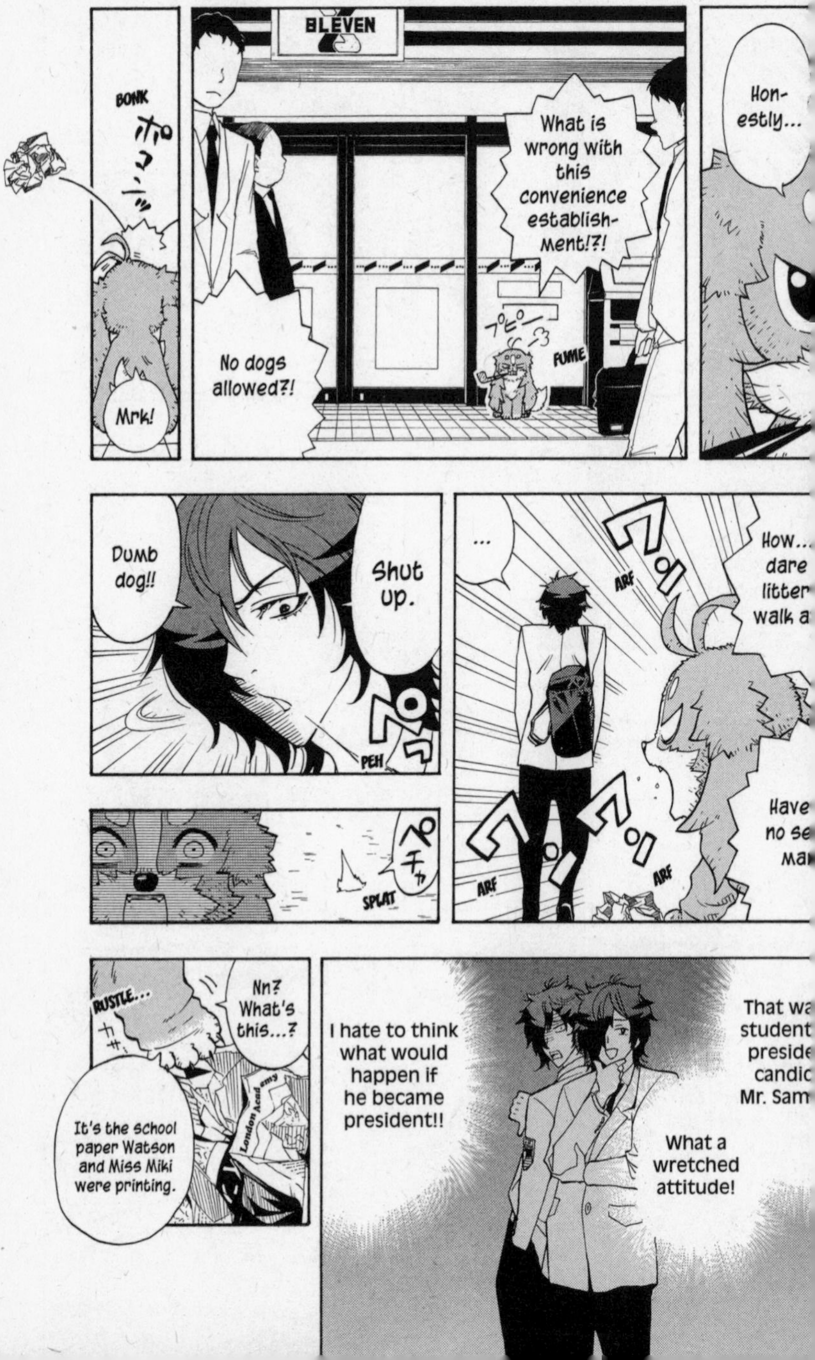

Hon-
estly...
BLEVEN
What is wrong with this convenience establish-ment!?!
No dogs allowed?!
FUME
BONK
Mrk!
How...
dare
litter
walk a
...
ARF
Have
no se
ma
ARF
ARF
Shut up.
Dumb dog!!
PEH
SPLAT
That wa
student
preside
candic
Mr. Sam
I hate to think what would happen if he became president!!
What a wretched attitude!
Nn? What's this...?
RUSTLE...
It's the school paper Watson and Miss Miki were printing.
London Academy

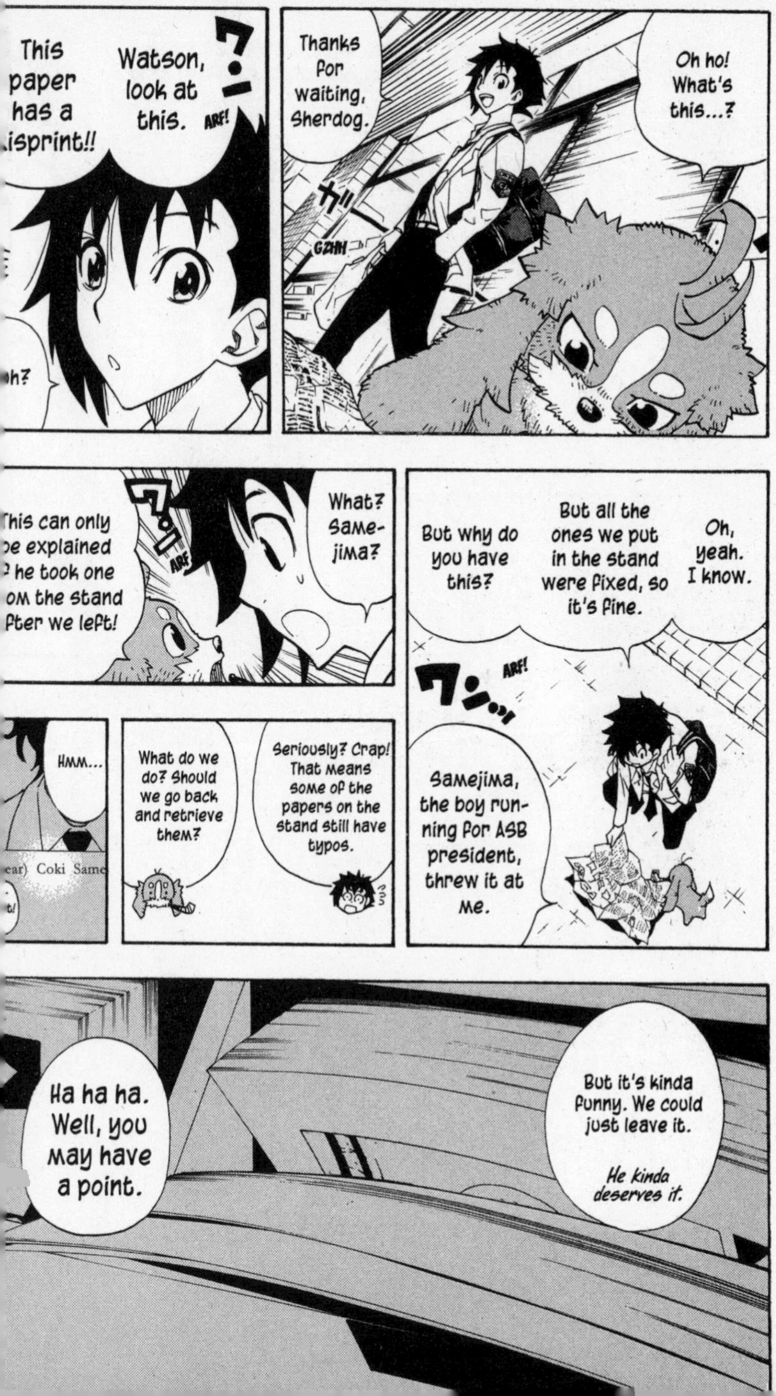

Oh ho! What's this...?
Thanks for waiting, Sherdog.
GZHH
ARF!
Watson, look at this.
This paper has a isprint!!
h?
Oh, yeah. I know.
But all the ones we put in the stand were fixed, so it's fine.
But why do you have this?
What? Same-jima?
ARF
This can only e explained he took one om the stand fter we left!
ARF!
Samejima, the boy run-ning for ASB president, threw it at me.
Seriously? Crap! That means some of the papers on the stand still have typos.
What do we do? Should we go back and retrieve them?
HMM...
ear) Coki Same
But it's kinda funny. We could just leave it.
He kinda deserves it.
Ha ha ha. Well, you may have a point.

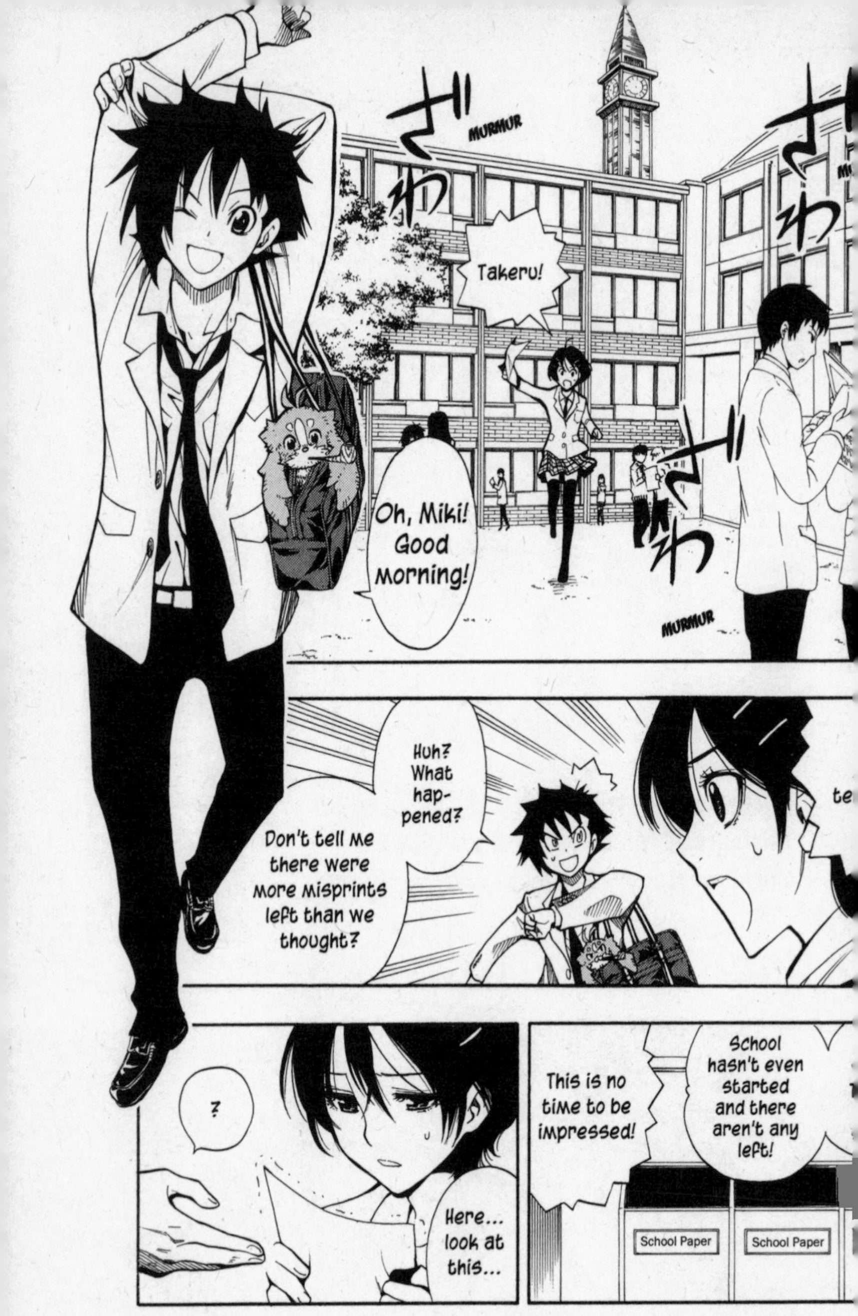

ざわ
ざわ
MURMUR
Takeru!
ざわ
MURMUR
Oh, Miki! Good Morning!
Huh? What hap-pened?
Don't tell me there were more misprints left than we thought?
School hasn't even started and there aren't any left!
This is no time to be impressed!
School Paper
School Paper
?
Here... look at this...

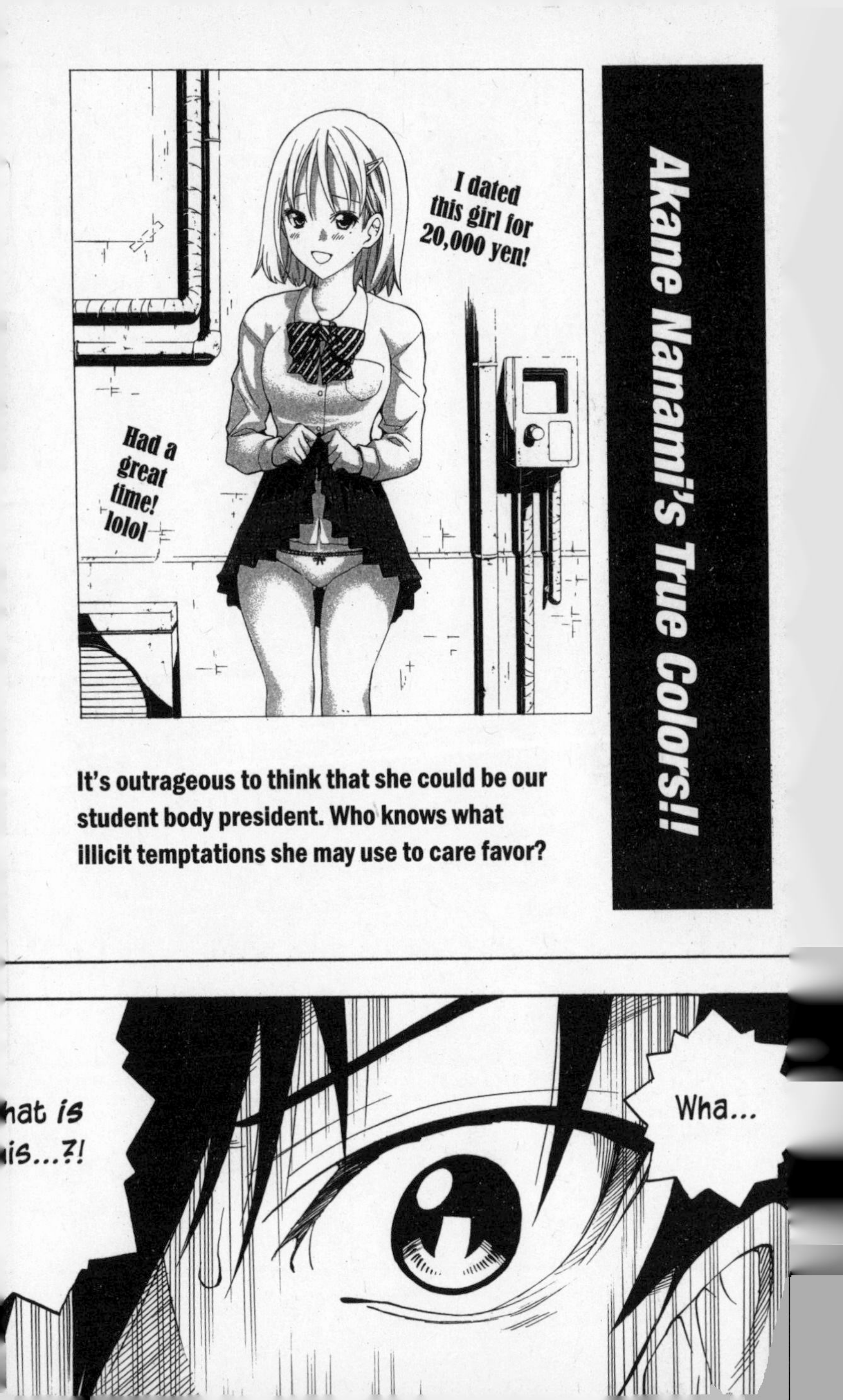
Akane Nanami's True Colors!!
I dated this girl for 20,000 yen!
Had a great time! lolol
It's outrageous to think that she could be our student body president. Who knows what illicit temptations she may use to care favor?
Wha...
hat *is*
is...?!

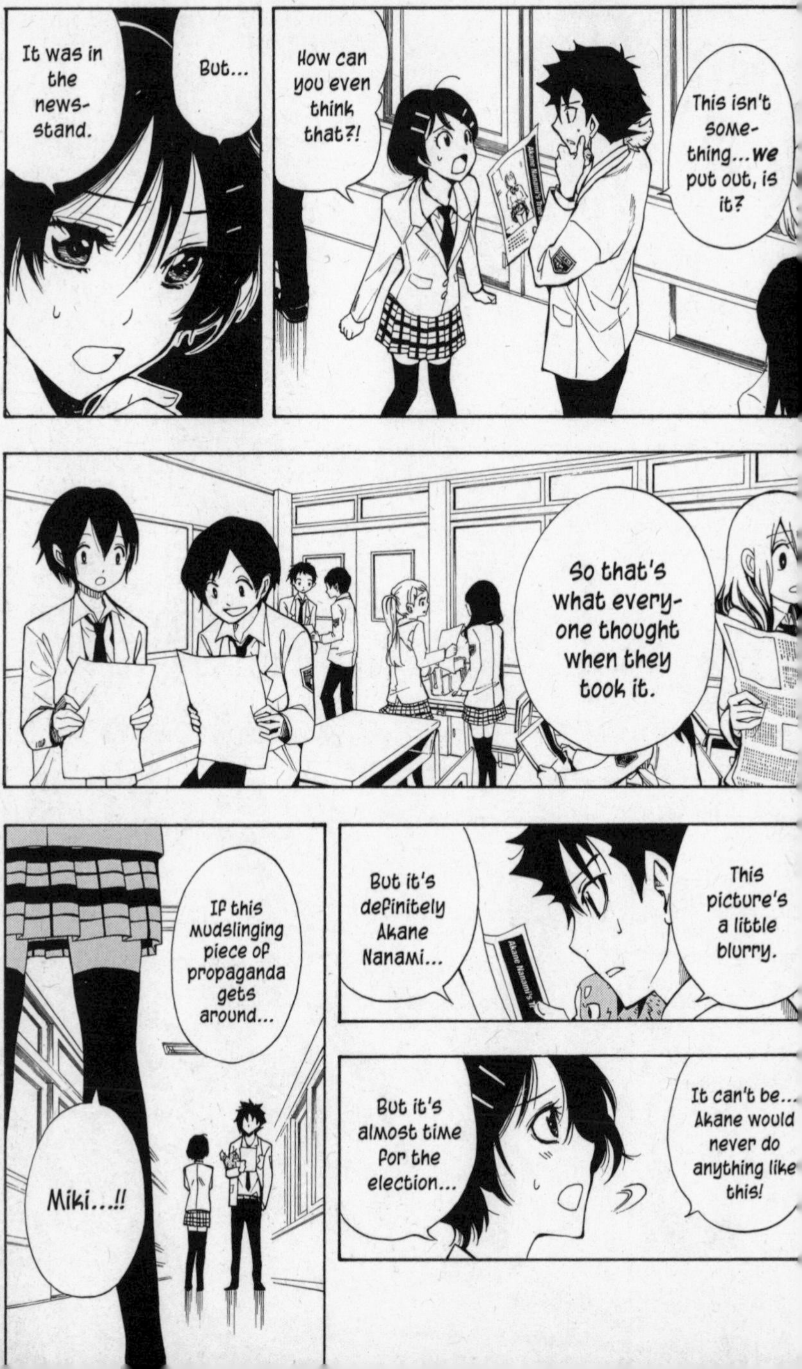
This isn't something...we put out, is it?
How can you even think that?!
But...
It was in the newsstand.
So that's what everyone thought when they took it.
This picture's a little blurry.
But it's definitely Akane Nanami...
It can't be... Akane would never do anything like this!
But it's almost time for the election...
If this mudslinging piece of propaganda gets around...
Miki...!!

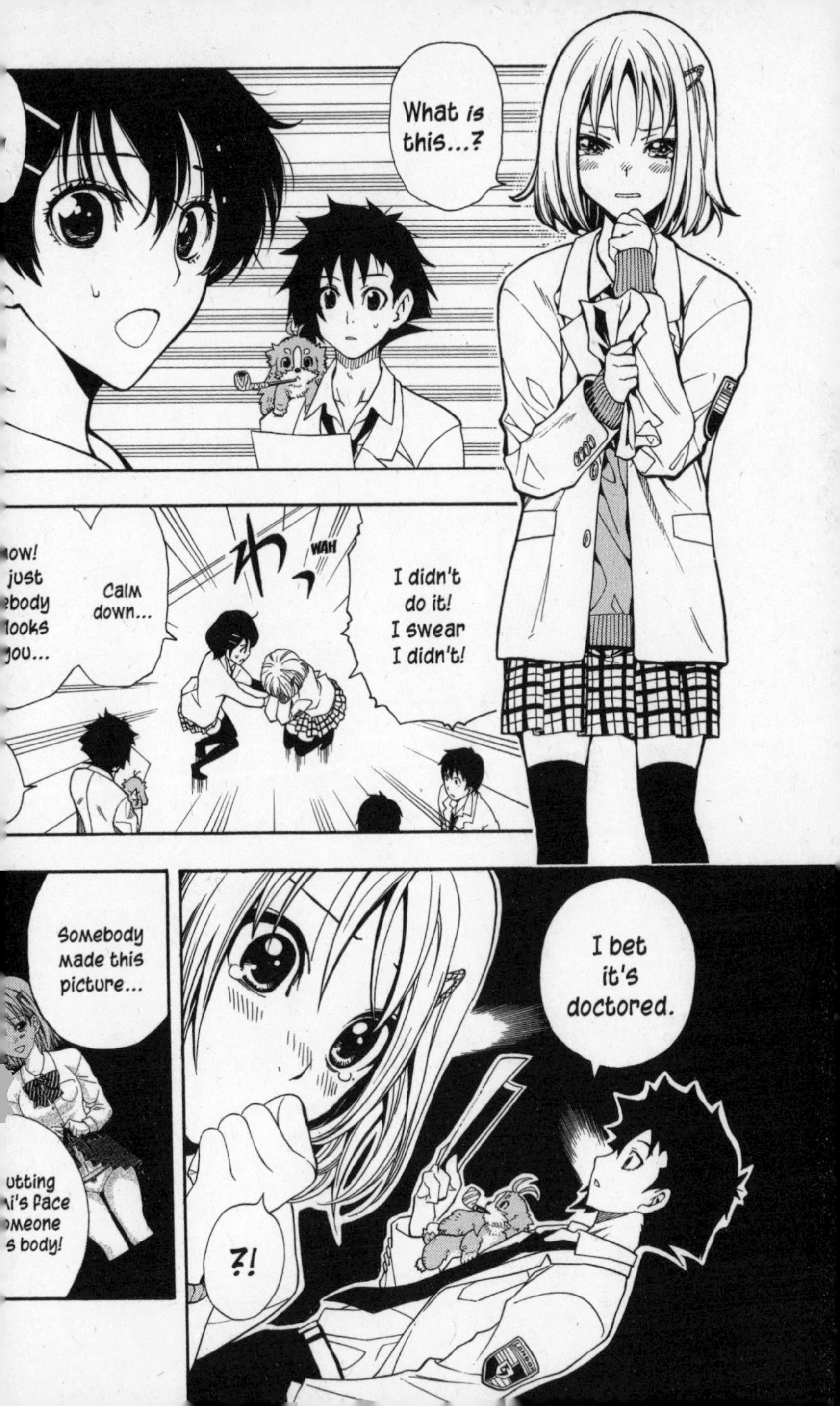
What is this...?
I didn't do it! I swear I didn't!
WAH
Calm down...
ow! just ebody looks you...
I bet it's doctored.
?!
Somebody made this picture...
utting i's face omeone s body!

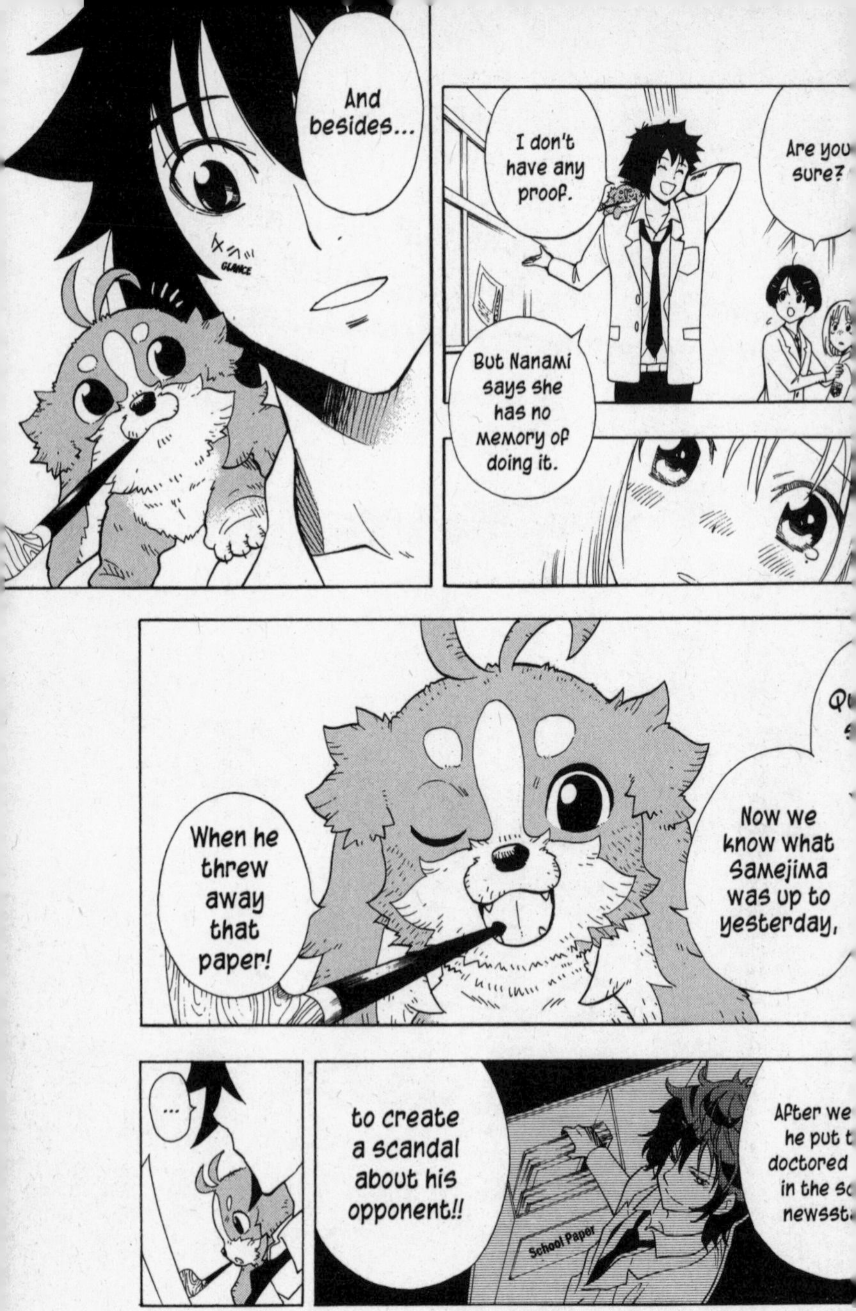
Are you sure?
I don't have any proof.
But Nanami says she has no memory of doing it.
And besides...
GLANCE
Now we know what Samejima was up to yesterday,
When he threw away that paper!
After we
he put t
doctored
in the sc
newsst
to create a scandal about his opponent!!
School Paper
...

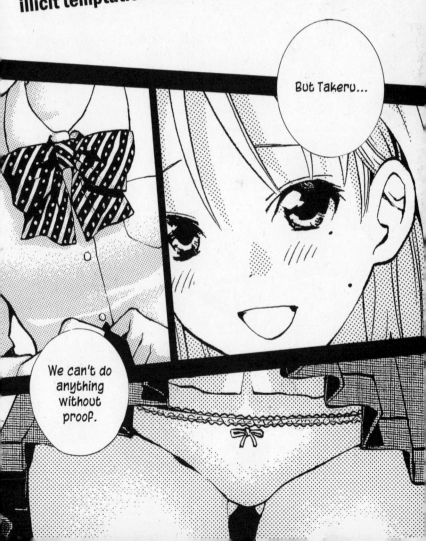
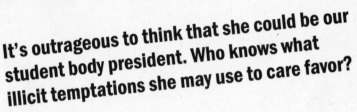

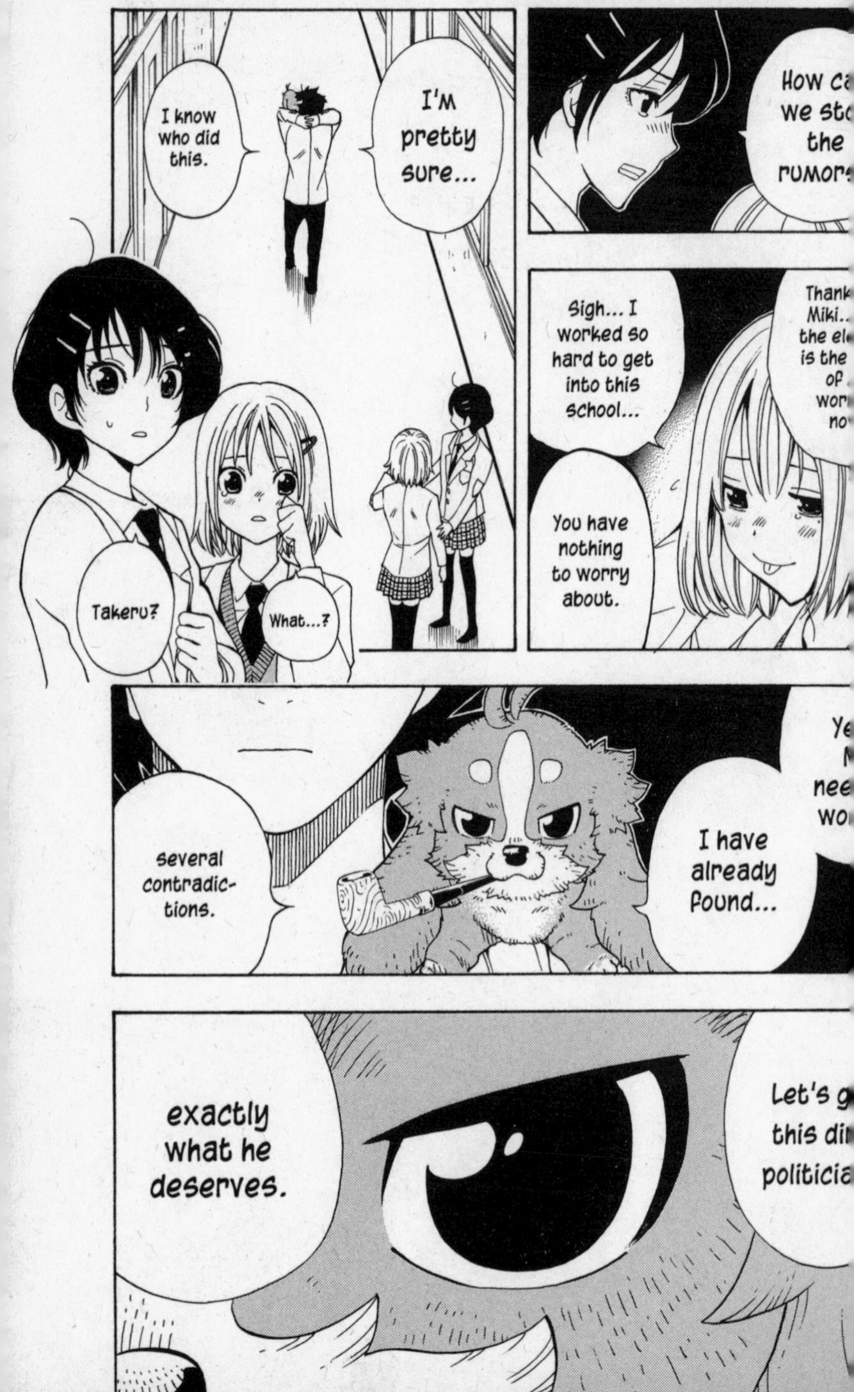

How ca we st the rumors
Thank Miki.. the el is the of wor no
Sigh... I worked so hard to get into this school...
You have nothing to worry about.
I'm pretty sure...
I know who did this.
What...?
Takeru?
Ye M nee wo
I have already found...
several contradic-tions.
Let's g this di politicia
exactly what he deserves.

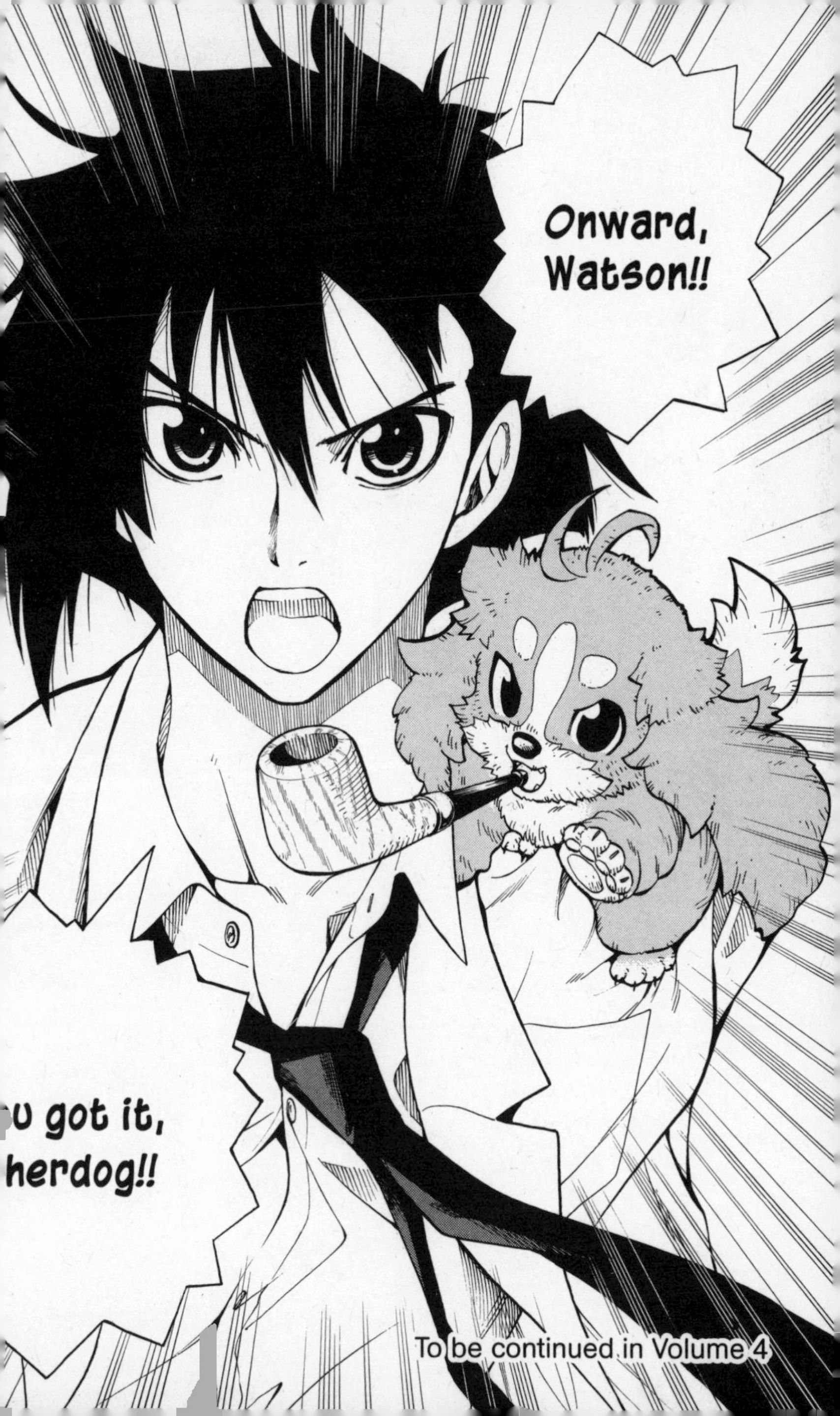
Onward, Watson!!
u got it, herdog!!
To be continued in Volume 4

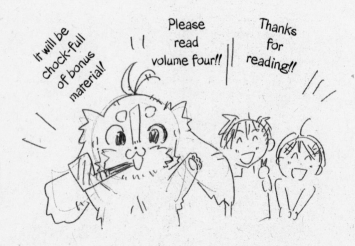

Thanks for reading!!
Please read volume four!!
It will be chock-full of bonus material!

And you'll see Sherdog's rival...maybe!!

Sherlock Bones

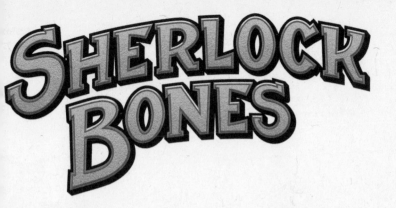

Will Samejima get away with his treachery or will Sherdog expose his cruel crime against Nanami? Find out in volume 4, coming soon. For now, enjoy this preview of Sherlock Bones 4!

Coffee Time 2 : Typographical Testimony (Conclusion

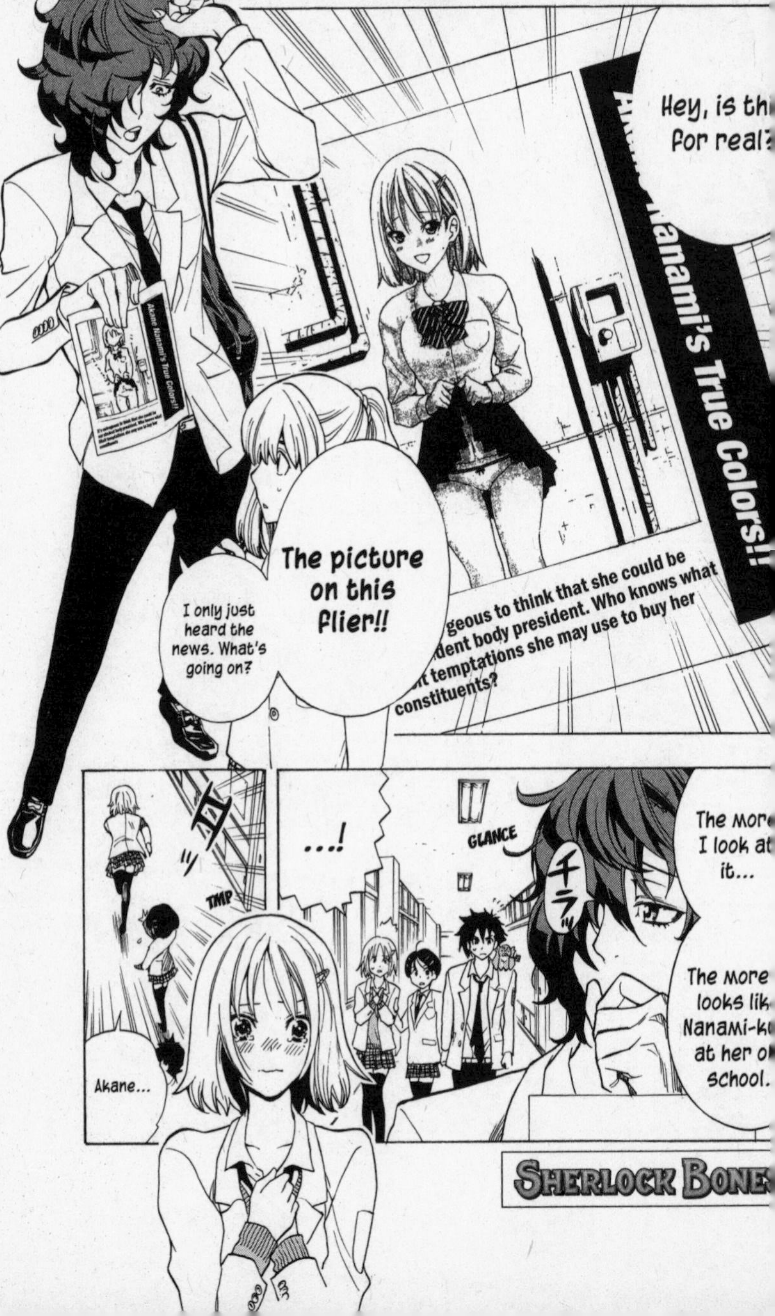
Hey, is thi
for real?
Nanami's True Colors!!
geous to think that she could be
dent body president. Who knows what
t temptations she may use to buy her
constituents?
The picture on this flier!!
I only just heard the news. What's going on?
チラッ
The more I look at it...
The more looks lik Nanami-k at her o school.
GLANCE
...!
TMP
Akane...
SHERLOCK BONES

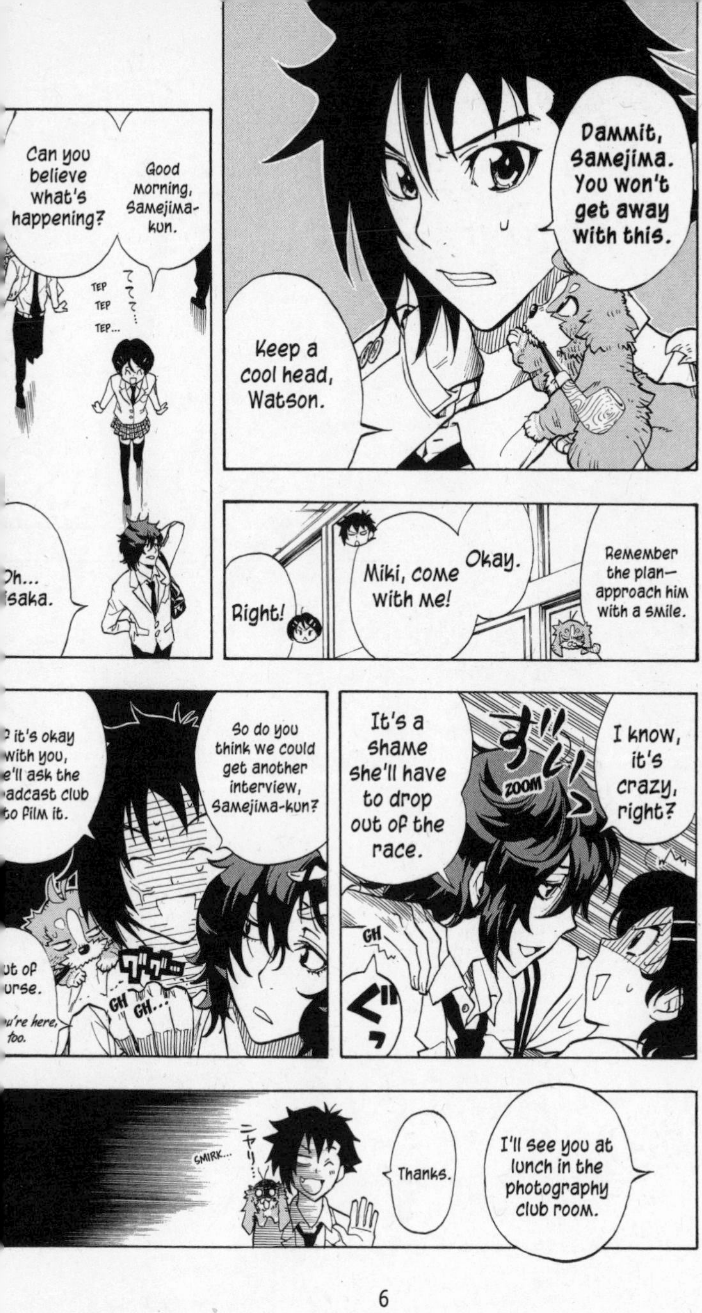
Dammit, Samejima. You won't get away with this.
Keep a cool head, Watson.
Remember the plan—approach him with a smile.
Okay.
Miki, come with me!
Right!
Good morning, Samejima-kun.
Can you believe what's happening?
TEP TEP TEP...
isaka.
I know, it's crazy, right?
ZOOM
It's a shame she'll have to drop out of the race.
GH
So do you think we could get another interview, Samejima-kun?
it's okay with you, e'll ask the adcast club to film it.
GH GH...
ut of urse.
u're here, too.
I'll see you at lunch in the photography club room.
Thanks.
SMIRK...

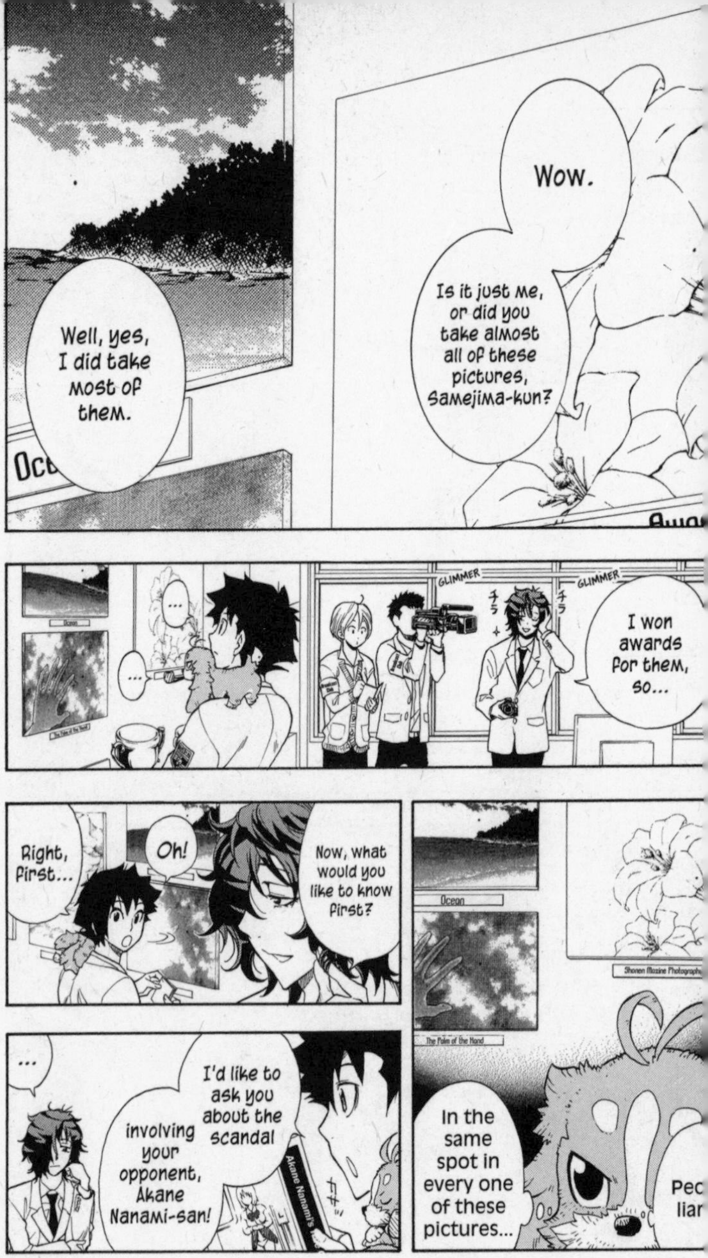
Wow.
Is it just me, or did you take almost all of these pictures, Samejima-kun?
Well, yes, I did take most of them.
I won awards for them, so...
GLIMMER
GLIMMER
チラ
チラ
...
...
Ocean
The Palm of the Hand
Ocean
Shonen Mazine Photograph
The Palm of the Hand
Now, what would you like to know first?
Oh!
Right, first...
Pec liar
In the same spot in every one of these pictures...
I'd like to ask you about the scandal involving your opponent, Akane Nanami-san!
Akane Nanami's
...

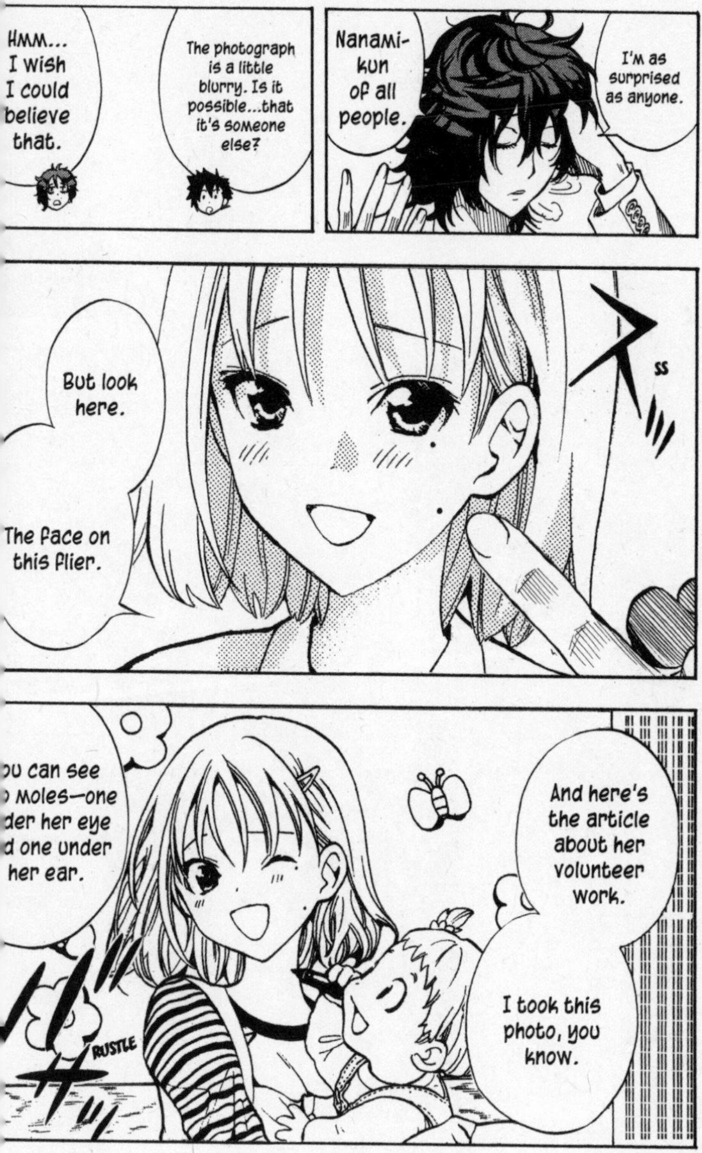
I'm as surprised as anyone.
Nanami-kun of all people.
The photograph is a little blurry. Is it possible...that it's someone else?
HMM... I wish I could believe that.
SS
But look here.
The face on this flier.
And here's the article about her volunteer work.
I took this photo, you know.
ou can see o moles—one der her eye d one under her ear.
RUSTLE

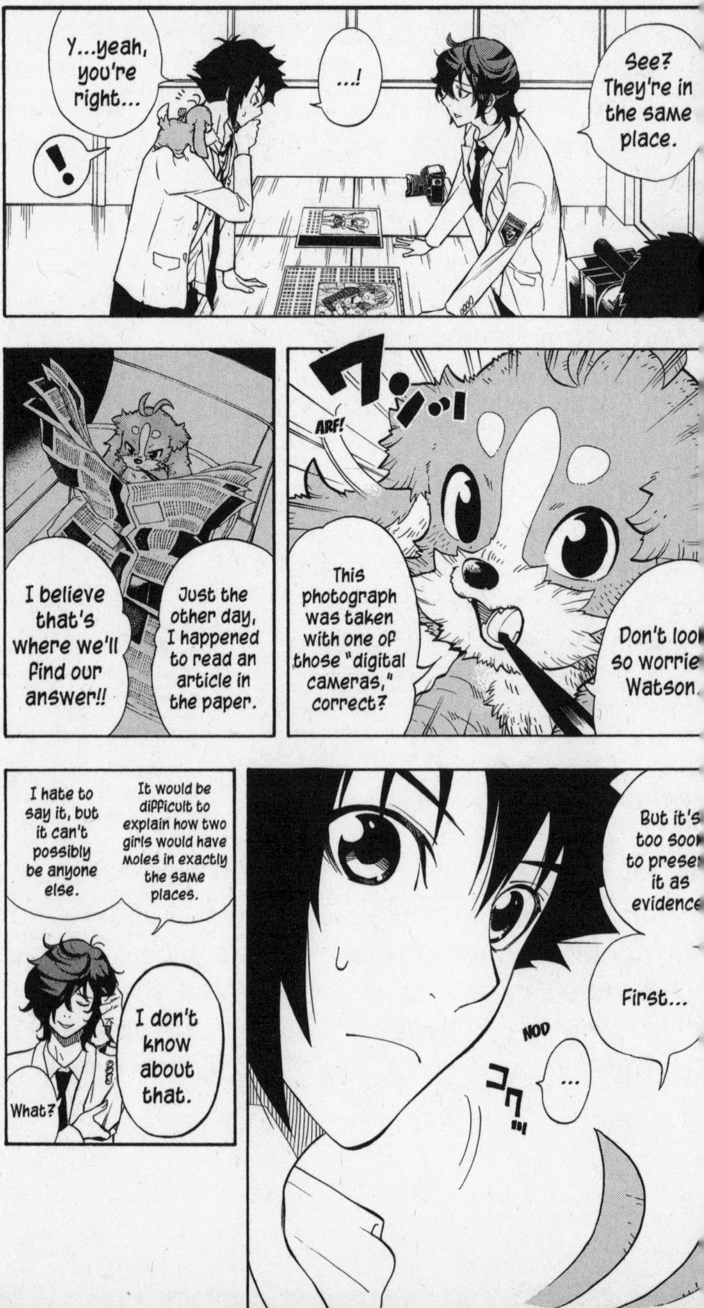
See? They're in the same place.
...!
Y...yeah, you're right...
!
ARF!
Don't loo so worrie Watson.
This photograph was taken with one of those "digital cameras," correct?
Just the other day, I happened to read an article in the paper.
I believe that's where we'll find our answer!!
But it's too soo to prese it as evidence
First...
NOD
...
It would be difficult to explain how two girls would have moles in exactly the same places.
I hate to say it, but it can't possibly be anyone else.
I don't know about that.
What?

herlock Bones 3 Translation Notes

ıpanese is a tricky language for most Westerners, ıd translation is often more art than science. For your lification and reading pleasure, here are notes on some the places where we could have gone in a different rection with our translation of the work, or where a ıpanese cultural reference is used.

ats and hot drinks, page 11

Japan, they have a word for ›ople who don't like hot drinks— ›kojita, meaning "cat tongue." ıe term came from the debatable ea that cats don't like hot food. ıe irony here, of course, is that olmes is a dog. What he really ıid in Japanese is more closely ınslated to, "So cats aren't the ıly ones with cat tongues."

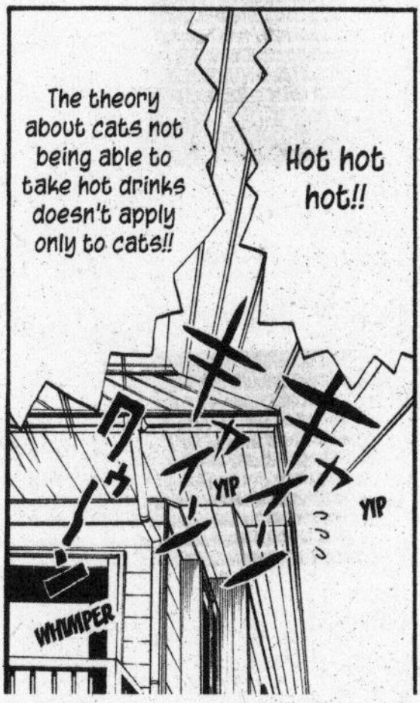
Hot hot hot!!
The theory about cats not being able to take hot drinks doesn't apply only to cats!!
YIP
YIP
WHIMPER

onko Mino, page 14

ıe character on the TV is a female(?) interpretation of e famous television personality Monta Mino. He hosted variety of TV shows, including news shows, animal ıows, quiz shows, and even the advice show Omoikkiri /! (roughly "TV Full Blast!"), which is the show be ırodied here as Kusso Omoroi TV! (Damn Funny TV!).

Hanabusa-pro, page 27

"Pro" is one of the more modern Japanese honorifics, and as you can probably guess, it's not originally Japanese. It comes from the English word "professional," and is used as a term of respect for professional athletes.

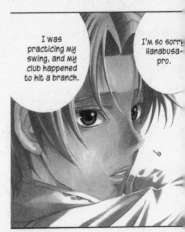

I was practicing my swing, and my club happened to hit a branch.

I'm so sorry Hanabusa-pro.

Even Kōbō could miss a brush stroke, page 45

Kōbō, also known as Kūkai, is the founder of the "True Word" school of Buddhism, but, more relevantly, he was also a renowned calligrapher. So this proverb, mentione by Takeru's father, is used to remind us that no matter how experienced and well-trained someone is, they can still make a mistake, and it's no reflection of their level o skill.

ANIMAL LAND

BY MAKOTO RAIKU

a world of animals, where
e strong eat the weak,
onoko the tanuki stumbles
ross a strange creature the
es of which has never been
en before–a human baby!
hile the newborn has no
ws or teeth to protect itself,
does have the special ability
speak to and understand all
ferent animals. Can the gift
speech between species
ange the balance of power
a land where the weak must
vays fear the strong?

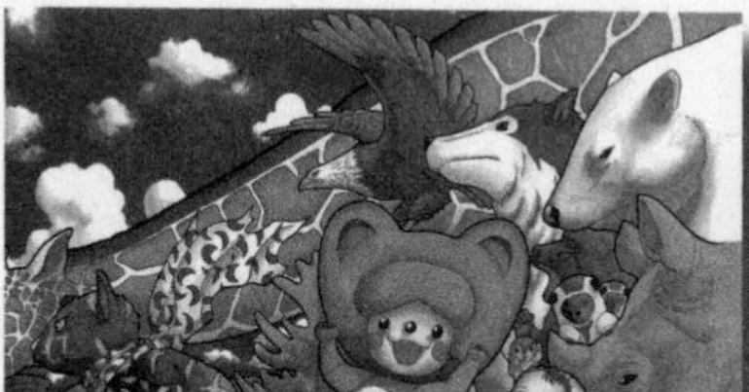

ANIMAL LAND 1
MAKOTO RAIKU

Ages 13+

KC KODANSHA COMICS

VISIT KODANSHACOMICS.COM TO:

- View release date calendars for upcoming volumes
- Find out the latest about upcoming Kodansha Comics series

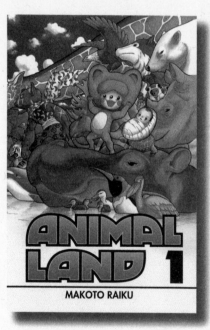

Sherlock Bones volume 3 is a work of fiction. Names, characters, places, and incidents are the products of the author's imagination or are used fictitiously. Any resemblance to actual events, locales, or persons, living or dead, is entirely coincidental.

A Kodansha Comics Trade Paperback Original.

Published in the United States by Kodansha Comics,
an imprint of Kodansha USA Publishing, LLC, New York.

Publication rights for this English edition arranged through Kodansha Ltd., Tokyo.

First published in Japan in 2012 by Kodansha Ltd., Tokyo, as *Tanteiken Sherdock* volume 3.

ISBN 978-1-61262-446-4

Printed in the United States of America.

www.kodanshacomics.com

9 8 7 6 5 4 3 2 1

Translator: Alethea Nibley and Athena Nibley
Lettering: Kiyoko Shiromasa

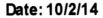

TO[STOP!]

You are going the wrong way!

Manga is a completely different
type of reading experience.

To start at the beginning, go to the end!

That's right! Authentic manga is read the traditional Japanese
way—from right to left, exactly the opposite of how American
books are read. It's easy to follow: Just go to the other end
of the book, and read each page—and each panel—from right
side to left side, starting at the top right. Now you're experi-
encing manga as it was meant to be.